THE FLETCHER JONES FOUNDATION
HUMANITIES IMPRINT

The Fletcher Jones Foundation has endowed this imprint to foster innovative and enduring scholarship in the humanities.

The publisher and the University of California Press Foundation gratefully acknowledge the generous support of the Fletcher Jones Foundation Imprint in Humanities.

Transnational Cinema Solidarity

CINEMA CULTURES IN CONTACT

Richard Abel, Giorgio Bertellini, and Matthew Solomon, Series Editors

1. *The Divo and the Duce: Promoting Film Stardom and Political Leadership in 1920s America*, by Giorgio Bertellini
2. *Relaying Cinema in Midcentury Iran: Material Cultures in Transit*, by Kaveh Askari
3. *Sirens of Modernity: World Cinema via Bombay*, by Samhita Sunya
4. *World Socialist Cinema: Alliances, Affinities, and Solidarities in the Global Cold War*, by Masha Salazkina
5. *Transnational Trailblazers of Early Cinema: Sarah Bernhardt, Gabrielle Réjane, Mistinguett*, by Victoria Duckett
6. *Transatlantic Cinephilia: Film Culture between Latin America and France, 1945–1965*, by Rielle Navitski
7. *Transnational Cinema Solidarity: Chilean Exile Film and Video after 1973*, by José Miguel Palacios

Transnational Cinema Solidarity

Chilean Exile Film and Video after 1973

José Miguel Palacios

UNIVERSITY OF CALIFORNIA PRESS

University of California Press
Oakland, California

© 2025 by José Miguel Palacios

All rights reserved.

Library of Congress Cataloging-in-Publication Data

Names: Palacios, José Miguel, author.
Title: Transnational cinema solidarity : Chilean exile film and video after 1973 / José Miguel Palacios.
Description: Oakland : University of California Press, 2025. | Series: Cinema cultures in contact ; vol 7 | Includes bibliographical references and index.
Identifiers: LCCN 2024039543 (print) | LCCN 2024039544 (ebook) | ISBN 9780520410237 (cloth) | ISBN 9780520402409 (paperback) | ISBN 9780520402416 (ebook)
Subjects: LCSH: Motion pictures—Chile—History. | Expatriate motion picture producers and directors—Chile. | Experimental films—Chile—History. | LCGFT: Film criticism.
Classification: LCC PN1993.5.C3 P35 2025 (print) | LCC PN1993.5.C3 (ebook) | DDC 791.430983—dc23/eng/20240913
LC record available at https://lccn.loc.gov/2024039543
LC ebook record available at https://lccn.loc.gov/2024039544

GPSR Authorized Representative:
Easy Access System Europe,
Mustamäe tee 50, 10621 Tallinn, Estonia,
gpsr.requests@easproject.com

34 33 32 31 30 29 28 27 26 25
10 9 8 7 6 5 4 3 2 1

Contents

Note on Translations, Titles, and Dates — vii
Preface, or Letters from the Archive — ix
Acknowledgments — xxv
Abbreviations — xxix

Introduction — 1

PART I. CINE-GEOGRAPHIES OF EXILE

1. Exile Travels and Transnational Film History — 27
2. The Production of Solidarity: Genre, Geopolitics, Internationalism — 53
3. A Film Festival Road Map — 80

PART II. THE POLITICS OF EXILE CINEMA

4. Cinemas of Resistance, Cinemas of Exile — 105
5. Subjectivity and the Unfinished Diary — 127

PART III. THE RETURN AND THE ARCHIVE

6. A Plurality of Cinematic Homecomings 153

7. Archival Returns and Digital Futures 180

Epilogue: Exile, Solidarity, and World Cinema Otherwise 205

Notes 211
Index of Filmmakers 265
General Index 269

Note on Translations, Titles, and Dates

Unless otherwise stated in the notes, all translations from written sources in Spanish and French are mine.

For first mentions of a Chilean exile film or video, I use titles in the original production language followed in parentheses by their official English translation in roman type, together with the country and year of production, as in the following example: *Gentille Alouette* (The Colonel's Star, Sergio Castilla, France, 1985). For readability, all following mentions throughout the same chapter use the English title in italic. When there is no record of distribution or festival screenings in English-speaking territories, an unofficial translation is provided in italic: *Lamento de una rima* (*Lament of a Rime*, Leo Mendoza, Netherlands, 1977).

Dating Chilean exile films is tricky business. Readers may notice that some of the dates I offer in the book do not match previously published filmographies and online databases. Sometimes it is because these catalogs contain errors, sometimes it is because they are inconsistent: they date a few films by their production year and others by their year of exhibition. I have opted here for dating the year of production, because theatrical distribution dates vary from country to country (an issue for exilic and transnational films that don't always have a single country of "origin"). In addition, when films weren't distributed in theaters, the first exhibition date might correspond to a festival screening, a solidarity soirée or community event, or a television broadcast, or there might be no record of a public showing at all. Given the possible disparities, dating films by year of production seemed more reasonable.

But that does not solve all the problems. Several Chilean exile films are the result of an interrupted production history due to the September 1973 coup and the forced displacement of their makers. Shooting may have started (and in some cases finished) before the coup, but the film was edited and completed years later in exile. Whenever that is the case, I indicate the film's double date of production because both dates are fundamental for understanding its exilic nature, as in the following example: *Queridos compañeros* (Dear Comrades, Pablo de la Barra, Chile/Venezuela, 1973/1978). I use production/copyright dates inscribed into the credits of the films themselves whenever possible. In the example above, *Dear Comrades* is dated 1977 in some catalogs, but the film itself begins with a title card that reads "Caracas, 1978"; therefore 1977 is incorrect. If a production/copyright date is unavailable on the film itself, I contrast information found in different archival materials, contracts, press kits, distributors' and festivals' catalogs, and so on. In cases where the production date differs greatly from the date of release or first public screening/broadcast, it is noted in square brackets: *De grands événements et des gens ordinaires* (Of Great Events and Ordinary People, Raúl Ruiz, France, 1978 [1983]). And whenever I have found it necessary to clarify competing dates of production/release according to different sources, additional information is provided in a note.

Preface, or Letters from the Archive

Eduardo Durán, a seventy-year-old Chilean exile living in the Netherlands for decades, is attending the International Film Festival Rotterdam (IFFR). IFFR 2024 has programmed a special focus titled "Chile in the Heart" to mark the fiftieth anniversary of the September 1973 military coup that overthrew the socialist government of Salvador Allende and unleashed a seventeen-year dictatorship led by Augusto Pinochet.[1] The Rotterdam program is the largest and most comprehensive retrospective of Chilean exile films to be screened at any festival, and therefore Durán and his wife show up at as many programs as they can. After one of the screenings, they wait a few seconds before approaching curator Olaf Möller, who has introduced the film. Durán mumbles and shyly mentions some of his connections to Chilean exile cinema. Möller listens with excitement when Eduardo says that he is the brother of Jorge Durán—an exile in Brazil who directed films like *A Cor de seu Destino* (The Color of Destiny, 1986) and wrote several screenplays for other directors, including the famous *Pixote* (Héctor Babenco, 1980). After some hesitation, Eduardo Durán finally says: "I'm also one of the producers of *Queridos compañeros*." Möller is ecstatic, as *Queridos compañeros* (Dear Comrades, Pablo de la Barra, Chile/Venezuela, 1973/1978) is one of the gems of the program. The festival's curator invites Durán to introduce the screening, scheduled for the next day. And so it is that, in late January 2024, Eduardo Durán stands in front of an audience in Rotterdam to talk about a film he produced fifty-one years earlier, a film that took multiple years, exile journeys, and iterations to come together, and that he is about to watch for the very first time.

. . .

Producer Eduardo Durán, assistant director Jorge Durán, director Pablo de la Barra, and the rest of the crew are traveling between the city of Concepción and the capital Santiago. It is June 1973, a moment of political and economic turmoil in Chile as the socialist government of Salvador Allende and his coalition Unidad Popular (UP; Popular Unity) face brutal opposition from the nation's right-wing sectors and the economic blockade led by the Nixon administration in the United States. The team is working on *Dear Comrades*, a fictional film about the nature of militancy and the limitations of traditional leftist political practices. Finding inspiration in one of de la Barra's brothers, *Dear Comrades* tells the story of Vicente and José, two members of an unnamed party modeled after the Movimiento de Izquierda Revolucionaria (MIR; Revolutionary Left Movement). Together, they seek a radicalization of leftist strategies through actions such as expropriations and land takeovers. Like many MIR militants, Vicente is a college student who belongs to the social elite of the country and betrays his upper-class background by joining a Far Left underground political movement; José, in turn, is the brother of one of the maids in Vicente's big family house and has spent months organizing shantytown dwellers in the outskirts of Concepción. The film also presents a love story between Vicente and Ana, a romance challenged by their different approaches to the revolutionary process in a subplot mostly told through flashbacks. The filmmakers conceive *Dear Comrades* as an action-packed political drama à la Costa-Gavras—a fast-paced narrative that follows the main characters as they plan an assault on a bank.[2]

With funding from friends de la Barra has met while studying in the United States, the film is shot on a 35mm Arriflex III and Fuji color stock—"a luxury" for most Chilean directors at the time, especially given the restrictions arising from the blockade.[3] The shoot takes place between late June—its start coinciding with the failed military coup attempt known as Tanquetazo or Tancazo (Tank Putsch)—and the first weeks of September, two months that accentuate the crisis leading up to the military coup. But the action is set in 1967, during the presidency of Christian Democrat Eduardo Frei Montalva and just a couple of years after the founding of the MIR. This anachronism means that the story takes place during a time, the late 1960s, in which the fractures within

FIGURE 1. Still showing characters José and Vicente, in *Queridos compañeros* (*Dear Comrades*, Pablo de la Barra, Chile/Venezuela, 1973/1978). Courtesy of Álvaro de la Barra.

the Chilean Left were beginning, whereas its date of production coincides with a more acute moment of this fissure between institutional democracy and insurrectionist strategies. On the one hand is a channeling of revolutionary energies through traditional leftist parties and within the established margins of bourgeois democracy (exemplified in real life by Allende and in the film by the character of Ana); on the other are Far Left vanguard and semiclandestine parties like the MIR, which have been inspired by guerrilla movements and favor direct political and paramilitary action (exemplified by Vicente and José).

This, at least, is how Pablo de la Barra and his crew have been thinking of *Dear Comrades* while shooting it. The coup, however, changes the nature and purpose of the film, as well as its temporal dimensions.

The last day of shooting has been scheduled for September 11, 1973—the day of the coup against Allende led by Pinochet. For obvious reasons, filming does not happen. Leonardo de la Barra, the assistant cameraman and the director's brother, grabs a 16mm Éclair and goes out to the streets to capture the events of the day: the tanks in downtown Santiago, people running, the presidential palace in flames.[4] After the coup, Pablo and Leonardo de la Barra, like many other filmmakers, are detained. Leonardo spends weeks in the detention and torture centers Londres 38 and Villa Grimaldi.[5] The secret police—Dirección de Inteligencia Nacional (DINA); National Intelligence Directorate—harass

Pablo, Leonardo, and their relatives because the real target is the third brother, Alejandro de la Barra, a political scientist, an important MIR militant, and the inspiration for *Dear Comrades*' fictional character Vicente. While Pablo and Leonardo are detained, members of the military raid their production house and destroy all the original sound elements of the film.[6] The optical negatives are in the labs of the state studio Chilefilms, which is also raided after the coup. But members of the crew are able to rescue the negatives before the raid and hide them in a series of clandestine movements involving the Spanish and German embassies.[7] After his release from prison, Pablo de la Barra receives support from the French embassy and goes into exile in Paris.[8] While in France's capital, like several others beginning their journeys of displacement, he plays a small role in Raúl Ruiz's *Diálogo de exiliados* (Dialogue of Exiles, 1974).[9] His brother Leonardo will remain in Chile for another year and leave for Brussels in September 1975.

Alejandro de la Barra's fate is different. Only one year after the coup, the dictatorship succeeds in wiping out the MIR's key figures, including its founder and leader Miguel Enríquez, in October 1974. Two months later, DINA agents find Alejandro and his wife Ana María Puga—also a MIR militant—as they are driving one afternoon to pick up their child Álvaro from the nursery in the quiet and well-off neighborhood of Providencia. Close to their destination, the agents shoot at them. Alejandro and Ana María die immediately, and the secret police take their bodies to the Villa Grimaldi detention center.[10]

The child Álvaro, just over one year old, now becomes a target. DINA agents want to use him as bait to capture more MIR militants. Leonardo and other family members protect Álvaro and move him from one home to another, until they finally send him to France with his uncle—the director of *Dear Comrades*, Pablo de la Barra. Pablo has not forgotten his film, but the drama he and his family have been suffering has made it impossible to concentrate on its completion. After hearing the news of Alejandro's execution, Pablo's father—Pedro de la Barra, one of Chile's most renowned theater directors and now an exile in Caracas, Venezuela—suffers a heart attack from which he will not recover. Soon afterward, Pablo separates from his wife and leaves Paris with his nephew, now stepson, Álvaro. The director continues his exile in Caracas, taking care of his father Pedro, who dies in 1977 due to complications from the heart attack.

Pablo de la Barra resumes his career and his unfinished film after the death of his father. Venezuela is a South American hub in the global solidarity movement with Chile, offering asylum for thousands of exiles. The daughters of Social-Democrat president Carlos Andrés Pérez have been instrumental in securing the shipping of the negatives to Caracas.[11] In 1977 the director rewrites the story with Argentinean screenwriter Jorge Goldemberg, another exile in Venezuela who later gains notoriety with the screenplays he writes for Argentine director María Luisa Bemberg: *Miss Mary* (1986) and *De eso no se habla* (I Don't Want to Talk about It, 1993). But there is still the issue of the lack of all sound materials and lists of dialogues, as most of them are improvised. An arduous process of dubbing and producing the soundtrack begins, with the help of two individuals: a Paraguayan deaf-mute woman who lip-reads and transcribes all the dialogue, and an architect, a friend of de la Barra, who builds a small and artisanal automated dialogue replacement studio room.[12]

This is now a different film. *Dear Comrades* needs to be reformulated, since the experience of militancy it narrates has lost its meaning after the death of the political project that inspired it. The title, *Dear Comrades*, works as a form of mourning, an elegy one can turn to in moments of grief. In exile's epistolary tradition, the title functions most prominently as a letter. It is a message to be sent out to the world, and the message says: "We are alive, and we are still making films."

Dear Comrades now begins with a long establishing shot that pans across Caracas, accompanied by the narrator's voice-over. Though voiced by actor Marcelo Romo, who plays Vicente, the narrator assumes the consciousness of the author and makes the "letter-film" structure evident for viewers, directly addressing them.[13] After situating the date and time (Caracas, 1978) and describing the prevailing mood as one of "pleasant melancholy," the narrator explains that members of the Venezuelan film world offered their support, and now *Dear Comrades* is finally completed. Giuliano Ferrioli, the film's editor, appears on screen and loads the print on an editing table. The voice-over details some of the difficulties that have interrupted the production process before proceeding to invite viewers to watch a film that will hopefully be "useful" in the critical analysis of the recent past.

The five years between the film's shooting and its completion, together with everything that happened in between—the coup and the beginning of the dictatorship, exile in France and Venezuela, and the brutal assassination and persecution of family members—create an inevitable distance between the film's original fast-paced roots and its now calm voice-over narration. *Dear Comrades* thus separates the strategies of direct political action performed by its fictional characters from the reflexive techniques of the filmmaker in exile.[14] This gap—an unsurmountable rift—is the defining structural quality of the film. Over and over again, *Dear Comrades* pauses its action to comment on the images shown on the screen.

One of these moments of pause and commentary occurs toward the end, in a documentary sequence shown in black and white through the small monitors of the editing table. On one of the first days of shooting, in late June 1973, the failed military coup attempt known as Tanquetazo or Tancazo (Tank Putsch) takes place. A colonel of the army leads the mutiny but faces the resistance of the military forces that remain loyal to the constitution and to Allende's government. De la Barra and his crew decide to suspend their regular shooting plan, but they keep filming and documenting the events of the day. They capture the tanks and the military in downtown Santiago and the thousands of people who have taken to the streets to demonstrate once the coup attempt has been suffocated. They shoot the main actors Marcelo Romo and Hugo Medina joining the protests and chanting as they march, in agit-prop moments that captivate precisely because of their oscillation—or indefinite status—between documentary and fiction. Toward the end of the sequence, the film and the narrator pause on a striking image of the leaders who have defeated the army's revolting troups: Minister of Defense José Tohá, Commander in Chief of the Army Carlos Prats, and General Augusto Pinochet, then in charge of the security of the presidential palace. Pinochet wears a combat helmet, holds a submachine gun in his hand, and walks next to two men whom his future dictatorship will soon kill. The film and the narrator do not need to say it explicitly, but they dwell on this bit of film to show viewers the unmistakable image of coward treason. The conspiracy of the coup that will take place months afterward is already underway. De la Barra concludes the sequence by affirming via voice-over that the crew's decision to keep filming that day shows not only their commitment to the socialist government but their unawareness and downplaying of the menacing threat to come.

The ending proceeds right after this moment, with the fast-paced editing of the protagonists' successful assault on the bank. The moment is resolved quickly, as if the film doesn't know what to do after it has given viewers the image of a still loyal Pinochet.[15] The general's presence—together with the filmmaker's remorse for his and his crew's minimizing of the upcoming danger—haunts the action of the militants and lingers in the minds of viewers during the closing sequence that follows. *Dear Comrades* ends as it started: a man takes the film out of the editing table and the voice-over tells us that the original ending—in which Vicente and Ana would have reunited in a large demonstration celebrating Allende's electoral victory in 1970—couldn't be filmed, and that it makes no sense to film it now since those characters "are dead." At last, the film presents a new pan across Caracas, with the voice-over claiming: "Volveremos, venceremos" (We shall return, we shall overcome).

The film's lack of narrative closure—and its timid promise of an uncertain future—speaks to the open-ended nature of the exile condition. The sign of the unfinished is built into the structure of *Dear Comrades* due to the halt in its production following the coup and to its lack of a resolute narrative conclusion. But the film's unfinishedness extends beyond these two aspects. The story of the vicissitudes of its making does not end in 1978—the year of its successful premiere at the Internationales Forum des Jungen Films (International Forum of Young Cinema) section of the Berlinale.

Forty years after the release of *Dear Comrades*, Pablo de la Barra's nephew and stepson, Álvaro, makes a first-person documentary about his own experience as an exile child—*Venían a buscarme* (They Were Coming to Get Me, Álvaro de la Barra, Chile, 2016). The title refers to the assassination of his parents, who were murdered by Pinochet's secret police when on their way to pick him up at the nursery. In the tradition of several Chilean and Latin American films made by the "generation of postmemory," *They Were Coming to Get Me* offers a painful account of a filmmaker in search of his own identity.[16] In the triple role of autobiographer, family historian, and detective, Álvaro de la Barra gathers the clues and bits of information that explain his life: someone persecuted by the secret police and forced to go into exile when only a baby; someone who grew up in displacement and nomadic movement between France, Venezuela, and Chile; someone who knew who his parents were, but who only acquired their last name over thirty years after his birth; someone who became a filmmaker after living a big part of his life with his uncle-father, also a film director. And like several other documentaries made by the children of the exile experience, *They Were Coming to Get Me* delves into the family archive and incorporates letters, documents, photographs, videotapes, and home movies as a way to examine the material texture of the past and its affective dimensions.[17] Particularly moving are the "video-letters" recorded by both Pablo and Álvaro de la Barra in Caracas in the early 1980s and meant to be sent abroad to the various members of the family to share with them special gatherings like birthdays or simply everyday moments of play and relaxation. In addition to these video-letters, the interviews—or "encounters," as Álvaro de la Barra prefers to call them—staged with his uncle-father show the extent to which the violence exerted over the family has impacted them both.[18] The nephew has grown up with the feeling that talking out loud about his identity and his family history is taboo, and the uncle-father has fed this unspoken prohibition with his own fears of being someone who was threatened and persecuted, someone whose closest family members were murdered. These dialogues show how the coup and the violence that followed have altered Pablo de la Barra's sense of self, and they provide a stark counterpoint to the "pleasant melancholy" of the voice-over that closes *Dear Comrades* with the promise of return and political victory.

Footage from Pablo de la Barra's film occupies a prominent place in *They Were Coming to Get Me*—a gesture of homage all the more relevant since *Dear Comrades* is still only known to a reduced circle of specialized audiences both in Chile and abroad. Early in the documentary, Álvaro and Pablo sit in the latter's living room and start watching *Dear Comrades* on the television. While the opening credits appear, Álvaro's voice-over recounts how he grew up in Caracas watching Pablo finish this movie; then, while showing one of the flashbacks of the love story between Vicente and Ana, his voice-over explains how *Dear Comrades* has shaped the way he imagines his parents—as protagonists of a love story between revolutionary militants. Freezing one frame, Álvaro's voice stresses that his uncle-father's film has given him something he didn't have in the family archive—a picture of his parents *together*. Later, the film proceeds to include the entire documentary sequence of the failed coup attempt of June 1973 captured in *Dear Comrades*, including the original voice-over and the last shot with Pinochet appearing as a general safeguarding democracy and still loyal to the UP government.

Leaving the sequence entirely unedited reinforces Álvaro de la Barra's purpose of archival "revelation," the same need to show these images of treason and cowardice that made Pablo de la Barra include them in his film forty years earlier.[19] But there's more. After going back to an interviewee, who insists on how the failed coup made evident the military conspiracy underway, *They Were Coming to Get Me* segues into its most decisive archival discovery: the 16mm footage that Álvaro's other uncle, Leonardo de la Barra, captured on the day of the September 11 coup.

These images have not been seen before—not publicly projected, not included in another film. The day of the coup is visually tied to the famous shots of the bombardment of La Moneda, the presidential palace, captured by the cameramen working for East German duo Walter

Heynowski and Gerhard Scheumann. This filmic record, together with Pedro Chakel's brief shot of the Hawker Hunter jets about to bombard the palace, is famously immortalized in the first two parts of *The Battle of Chile* (Patricio Guzmán, 1975 and 1976) and has been included in most Chilean exile films and virtually almost every film about Chile's political history.[20] Leonardo de la Barra's raw footage is altogether different and offers a counterpoint to the spectacular violence of the bombardment, providing a broader look at the events of the day. The black-and-white sequence shown in *They Were Coming to Get Me* is about four minutes long and includes people running away from the chaos in downtown Santiago, a dead body lying in the street, the tanks assaulting the city, smoke in the air, and alternative viewpoints of La Moneda in flames.

The fact that these two sequences—Pablo de la Barra's footage of the failed coup attempt of June 1973 from *Dear Comrades* and Leonardo de la Barra's unseen footage of the September 11 coup— are left intact in Álvaro de la Barra's *They Were Coming to Get Me* highlights the similarity between the events and their imaged representation: the dress rehearsal of the coup and the real one. But the inclusion of these sequences evidences something even more relevant: that these three filmic materials share both the familial bonds of their makers and another form of common lineage: the kindred alliances of the moving images shaped by exile. *They Were Coming to Get Me* provides the narrative structure for the appearance of the cinematic kinship of exile. The story of this kinship—or, if you will, the expanded history of *Dear Comrades*—is the story of Chilean exile film and video as narrated in this book, moving between nations and across historical times. The afterlives of *Dear Comrades* do not end in 2016 with the release of *They Were Coming to Get Me*. There is yet more filmic material, and yet another angle to the telling of this story.

. . .

I don't remember when I first watched *Dear Comrades*. It could have been in 2008, when Chile's Cineteca Nacional obtained a print from Cinemateca Nacional de Venezuela and screened it for the first time. It was three or four years after I graduated from college, where I had received a hands-on and production-oriented film degree. I was struggling with precarious jobs in the local film and media industry and gaining a second, self-taught education in film studies via the public library and the screening room of the national film archive, both in downtown

Santiago. By 2008 I was also into a decade-long process of political education and awakening. I watched films, read books and magazines, and talked to people who showed me the real history of my country, one very different to the tales I heard growing up in a conservative background with Pinochet supporters at home and at school. The discrepancy between my upbringing and my own beliefs and leftist sympathies only fueled my desire to learn everything I could about Chile's political history, as I wanted to better understand the "battleground" of memory that dominated the cultural debates in years that were marked by Pinochet's detention in London in 1998 and by the thirtieth anniversary of the coup in 2003.[21] Like many in my generation, I sought a deep engagement with history and memory as a moral duty. Viewing *Dear Comrades* was part of this interest in both cinema and politics, but my immediate captivation with the film responded to something much more mundane: its first sequence took place in Concepción. I don't think I had ever seen an image of my hometown on the big screen. Recognizing the streets produced a strange feeling of joy and nostalgia for a time and place I had not witnessed, and it forged a bond, however minimal, between me and the film.

Soon afterward I went to New York to pursue graduate studies and began to research and write about the Latin American film manifestos and the radical cinemas of the 1960s and 1970s. When I decided to do my dissertation on Chilean exile films, I returned to *Dear Comrades* and attempted to write about the intricacies of its multilayered political temporality (a film set in 1967, shot in 1973, and completed in exile in 1978). What I wrote did not make it to the dissertation. Back then I was fascinated by the resonances and aftershocks of the 1973 coup as an *event*; it was as if the film contained all the folds of historical time. The writing was too "theoretical" in the worst possible sense of the word: wordy, abstract, and so removed from the contingencies of history that it barely had any meaning. I put it aside. Plus, *Dear Comrades* was just one film. More than two hundred films had been made by Chilean exile directors in virtually every corner of the world, and my goal was to provide as broad an overview as possible. As I researched, I became more interested in the larger historical questions. I wanted to know what conditions had made possible the existence and survival of Chilean exile cinema, the spaces through which it had circulated, the political functions it had played then and now. And when I was completing and defending the dissertation, I became more interested in archival questions: What could a material history of film prints tell us about exile cinema?

This was a question I could only hint at. Like all the others who had gone before me, when researching the topic I encountered several difficulties: there were too many films, languages, archives, and territories. Documents and filmic materials were "in exile," scattered all over the world. I completed the project with the research I had been able to carry out in Canada, Chile, Mexico, and the United States. After a year of teaching as an adjunct in Chilean universities, I was awarded a postdoctoral grant that enabled me to investigate the archival locations and conditions of Chilean exile prints. This three-year project (2018–2020), and the funding that came with it, was fundamental for the reformulation of my research into what is now this book. For the first time I had the funds to travel and spend enough time in all the relevant archives in France, Germany, Spain, and Sweden.

The archival landscape had changed in the last decade, too. Throughout the project, I benefited from the trend to have catalogs and holdings of museums and film archives fully accessible online. Sometime in 2019, I was browsing through the database of the EYE Filmmuseum in Amsterdam. A title caught my eye: *Chili Documentaire*, a 16mm print attributed to Pablo de la Barra, the director of *Dear Comrades*. There was no other information in the catalog. I had a research trip planned for the following year coinciding with the Orphan Film Symposium in Amsterdam, but the COVID-19 pandemic broke out, and everything was canceled. I finished the project without the last in-person research trips I had originally scheduled, and later took an assistant professor job in the United States and moved to Long Beach, California. The Amsterdam title was still in my mind, though, so when the 7th EYE International Conference on Global Audiovisual Archiving accepted my paper proposal, I knew I would have a chance to look at this print—alongside other filmic materials I had inquired about.

When the EYE curator loaded the *Chili Documentaire* print on the viewing table, I realized it was not a documentary. It was a ten-minute reel of unedited footage of the day of the coup. There were images I had not seen before. The streets, the camera angles, the tanks and ambulances, the people running—they all bore a resemblance to the other existing raw footage of the coup, but they were definitely different images. And they were in color. Midway through the reel, I recognized some shots I thought I had seen before. A few weeks later I rewatched *They Were Coming to Get Me* and confirmed my suspicion—the black-and-white segment from Leonardo de la Barra's four-minute footage matched the EYE print. In fact, what I saw in Amsterdam in May 2022 was the

FIGURE 2. Shot captured by Leonardo de la Barra on September 11, 1973. 2K scan from a 16mm reel kept at the EYE Filmmuseum in Amsterdam. Courtesy of EYE and Leonardo de la Barra.

full version of the images Leonardo had captured with his 16mm Éclair camera on September 11, 1973, the day of the coup and the interrupted last day of the shooting of Pablo de la Barra's *Dear Comrades*. Recognizing the historical importance of this filmic material, I did what I had done recently with other prints located in Sweden: I arranged for a collaboration agreement between EYE and Cineteca Nacional de Chile. A gorgeous 2K scan of Leonardo de la Barra's footage is now also part of Chile's national film archive, which will make it available to local audiences.

This archival finding also allowed me to reconsider the career of someone who had played a small role in the historiography of Chilean exile cinema, a minor position my own research had not bothered to question.

Leonardo de la Barra had lived most of his exile in Belgium, directing independent short films like *Éramos una vez* (*Once We Were*, 1979) and *El tren en la ventana* (*The Train in the Window*, 1981), and working as a cameraman and director of photography on some of his fellow exile filmmakers' projects, like Valeria Sarmiento's *Gens de nulle* part... *Gens de toutes parts* (People from Nowhere... People from Everywhere, Belgium, 1979) and *Wenn wir zusammen lebten*... (If We Lived Together..., Antonio Skármeta, West Germany, 1983). After the regaining of democracy in 1990, like many other exiles he began to live his life moving between Belgium and Chile, though he never returned permanently. In the context of the fiftieth anniversary of the military coup in September 2023, however, Leonardo de la Barra embarked on his own personal journey of return. The anniversary of the coup enabled his final relocation to Chile and the long-awaited opening of his "memory box."[22] His previous hesitancy was similar to that of other victims of the dictatorship's terror and state violence: having spent time in torture centers and having had one of his brothers executed, silence and a self-imposed refusal to speak about these issues were a mark of the trauma. But the commemorative nature of the fiftieth anniversary was a powerful marker of time and distance. He wrote and published a short book about his weeks as a detainee, *En los repliegues del silencio* (*In the Folds of Silence*, Ocho Libros, 2023). The publication falls somewhere in between a play, a screenplay for a short film, a shooting script (with some annotations for cinematography and directing), and an illustrated book. With that hybrid form, Leonardo de la Barra gives voice to the inner thoughts of the detainees, who claim, in a direct echo of his real-life story with his brother Alejandro: "The only thing we cannot do is say where our brother and his family live."[23] In the last "sequence," before the final fade out, the narrator says, "It took me fifty years to try to express the indescribable and leave a trace of what can't be forgotten: the experience of cruelty, the absolute fear that remained forever inscribed in me, my family, and my children."[24]

In 2023, the year of his return to Chile, Leonardo de la Barra participated in Q&A sessions after public screenings of *Dear Comrades*, did interviews about his book, and donated copies of his September 11 raw footage to both Cineteca Nacional de Chile and Museo de la Memoria y los Derechos Humanos (MMDH; Museum of Memory and Human Rights). He also donated an artifact to the latter: the 16mm Éclair camera with which he captured the events on the day of the coup.

...

I begin *Transnational Cinema Solidarity* with this constellation of filmic materials because their common lineage points to several key issues explored in this book. First, the expanded tale of the making of *Dear Comrades* serves as a reminder that to be a filmmaker in times of political urgency and in defiance of military dictatorship means putting one's life in real danger. The separation between the realms of the personal and the professional are blurry, perhaps meaningless. This is a history of cinematic resistance, an alternative way of understanding the history of world cinema by centering radical film cultures and the stories of those who risked their lives by using cinema as an instrument against oppression.

Second, *Dear Comrades* is just one in a list of films that were shot in Chile toward the end of the UP government and finished later in exile—usually after a long process through which exile directors reunited with their filmic materials, thanks to numerous solidarity actions of people and institutions across nations. These transnational movements, made possible by networks of cinema solidarity, lie at the heart of this book. They are its main object of study as well as its inspiration.

Third, the book follows the exile routes of numerous people. The list includes what are probably the most well-known Chilean exile filmmakers—Patricio Guzmán, Miguel Littin, and Raúl Ruiz—but deliberately goes beyond them. This is why I begin with the stories of the de la Barra family, and this is why throughout the chapters that follow I concentrate on the work of female filmmakers like Marilú Mallet, Valeria Sarmiento, and Angelina Vázquez, alongside several other figures whose names have been neglected in histories of Latin American cinema (or Third Cinema, radical screen cultures, and exile cinemas more generally). The transnational history I pursue here also follows the exile routes implied by the work of institutions like film festivals, or those of the peculiar Cinemateca Chilena en el Exilio—a transnational and exilic film archive, research center, and production and distribution company.

Fourth, *Transnational Cinema Solidarity* follows the exile routes of film prints themselves. Tracing the material lives of exile prints and videotapes is inherent to the kind of history told here—attentive to the multiple silences and gaps in the archives and museums that store Chilean exile films. This is especially relevant when such prints open questions rather than provide definitive answers. For instance, it is still not clear how the 16mm reel of Leonardo de la Barra's September 11 footage ended up in the EYE Filmmuseum and why it is different from the one he kept all those years in Belgium. Apparently, to get it out of Chile, Leonardo's brother Pablo gave the film reel to a Dutch citizen, which might explain why the can was attributed to him and not to Leonardo.[25] The fact that the reel was labeled in French suggests that its presence in Amsterdam responds to the complexities of the exile movements followed by the de la Barra family when escaping from the dictatorship.

At last, in this book I argue that the exile experience and Chilean exile cinema are open and unfinished processes that cannot be reduced to the 1970s and 1980s—the decades that coincide with the military dictatorship and the displacement of Chilean filmmakers. This sense of incompletion can be easily perceived through this preface and the cinematic kinship formed by Pablo de la Barra's 1973/1978 fiction film, Leonardo de la Barra's raw footage of the day of the coup (both his abridged black-and-white print and the full one-reel color print held in the vaults of the EYE Filmmuseum), and Álvaro de la Barra's 2016 documentary *They Were Coming to Get Me*. It can also be seen in the story of Eduardo Durán, who reconnected with his own role in *Dear Comrades* after its Rotterdam screening in January 2024. As I write these lines, a digital restoration based on a different 35mm print of *Dear Comrades* and a documentary about the film's material history and survival are currently being produced.

All these facts show a basic premise of this book at work: the transnational history of Chilean exile cinema is a living one, still in the making.

Acknowledgments

This book has been in the making for over ten years. There are probably more people and institutions to thank than I can remember, but here's my best attempt.

I begin with my teachers and mentors. At New York University, Jung-Bong Choi, Manthia Diawara, Anna McCarthy, and Robert Stam were fundamental for my intellectual formation. (And so were their respective seminars on paradigms of globalization, Black European cinema, theories of history, and Bakhtin). As my main dissertation adviser, Bob Stam deserves a special kind of gratitude. We had long conversations that always left me reassured in my efforts and energized after the gift of seeing my research through his eyes. Whatever piece of writing I sent him, Bob read it quickly and offered detailed feedback and edits. Draft after draft, his annotations made me a better writer and scholar. The same gratitude goes to Jane Gaines, who became a mentor from the very first days of my masters at Columbia University and has remained one ever since. I could say a lot about her implicit presence in this book, but let me simply thank her for teaching and showing me how to do archival thinking, and how to do film history indissociable from theoretical inquiry.

Transnational Cinema Solidarity relies on archival research conducted over the course of a decade in multiple places. I would like to thank the heads of archives, archivists, librarians, curators, and staff members who offered invaluable help and guidance in navigating their institutions. In Santiago, Chile, I extend my deepest gratitude to Mónica Villarroel, Marcelo Morales, and Pablo Insunza at Cineteca Nacional de Chile; José Manuel Rodríguez, Miguel Carrasco, and Verónica Sánchez at Museo de la Memoria y los Derechos Humanos; Bruno Cuneo and Felipe Poblete at Archivo Ruiz-Sarmiento (Instituto de Arte, Pontificia Universidad Católica de Valparaíso); Isabel Mardones at Goethe Institut Santiago; and Luis Horta at Cineteca Universidad de Chile. "In exile," I want to thank Jon Wengström and Kaija Selander at the Swedish Film Institute in Stockholm; Giovanna Fossati, Simona Monizza, and Rommy Albers at the EYE Filmmuseum in Amsterdam; Marion Boulestreau at Ciné Archives in Paris; Julienne Boudreau at Cinémathèque québécoise in Montreal; Nahún Calleros Carriles at Filmoteca UNAM in Mexico City; Kelly R. Haydon at NYU's Tamiment Library in New York; Hiltrud Schulz and Sky Arndt-Briggs at DEFA Film Library (University of Massachusetts Amherst); Jason Sanders at BAMPFA in Berkeley; and Markus Ruff at Arsenal, Mirko Wiermann and Sabine Söhner at DEFA, Kerstin Lommatzsch at PROGRESS, Adelheid Heftberger at Bundesarchiv-Filmarchiv, and Lisa Roth, Anke Hahn, and Anke Vetter at Deutsche Kinemathek (all in Berlin). Additionally, I thank a series of anonymous staff members from the following institutions: Cineteca Nacional México; Filmoteca Española in Madrid; Biblioteca Iberoamericana in Berlin; the Getty Research Institute in Los Angeles; Library and Archives Canada in Ottawa; University of Toronto Libraries and Toronto Metropolitan University Libraries in Toronto; and Cinémathèque française, INA, and IMEC in Paris.

Conversations and interviews with filmmakers were also crucial for this project. My thanks to Leonardo Céspedes, Pedro Chaskel, Álvaro de la Barra, Leonardo de la Barra, Franci Duran, Luis García, Leopoldo Gutiérrez, Patricio Henríquez, Miguel Littin, Orlando Lübbert, and Leutén Rojas. Marilú Mallet and Angelina Vázquez deserve uniquely special thanks, for opening their personal files and documents and for a sustained dialogue that proved to be an endless source of knowledge and inspiration. A big thank you to Angelina Vázquez and Pablo Perelman for authorizing the image for the cover.

Elizabeth Ramírez-Soto's work on memory and postdictatorship documentary, exile cinema, and women filmmakers forcefully shaped my own. For years we talked and discussed, did research together, shared archival findings, cowrote articles and coprogrammed events, and read and commented on each other's writing. I cannot thank her enough for the influence she has had on this book.

For the brief sense of being part of a community in the making, for the (also brief) feeling of youth, for believing we had something to say that others could not, I thank Claudia Bossay, Jorge Iturriaga, María Paz Peirano, Iván Pinto, Elizabeth Ramírez-Soto, and Ximena Vergara— aka *los jóvenes investigadores*. Perhaps a WhatsApp group was all we ever were; still, at some point it meant a lot. My gratitude and appreciation go to Iván for being a cultural agitator when we needed one the most. Other colleagues and friends have left their mark on this book in one way or another: César Barros, Janet Ceja Alcalá, Ángeles Donoso, Catalina Donoso Pinto, Miguel Errazu, Julio Sebastián Figueroa, Marc Francis, Leo Goldsmith, Jessica Gordon-Burroughs (thanks for your comments on chapter 7!), Joshua Malitsky, Paola Margulis, Chris Moore, Mariano Mestman, Asli Özgen, Floris Paalman, Alejandro Pedregal, Fernando Pérez Villalón, Julio Ramos, Ana María Risco, Claudia Sandberg, Sukhdev Sandhu, Joshua Sperling, Juana Suárez, Jamie H. Trnka, and David Wood. Elena Razlogova and Isabel Mardones generously shared documents that saved me important archival trips. Kartik Nair provided excellent suggestions after reading the book's proposal before I sent it out to the press. Beth Tsai read selected chapters and provided great notes on the book's title and list of images—for that and all the love and support throughout the last stages, *gracias*! Susan Lord's encouraging words were a true gift. Masha Salazkina read the whole manuscript in a matter of days and gave invaluable feedback. My deepest gratitude to her for offering a scholarly model of generosity at a key moment in this book's life.

An earlier version of chapter 7 was previously published as "Exile, Archives, and Transnational Film History: The Returns of Chilean Exile Cinema," *The Moving Image* 22, no. 2 (Fall 2022). I thank editor Devin Orgeron and the University of Minnesota Press for permission to reproduce an expanded version here. Small parts of chapters 5 and 6 appeared previously and in modified form as "Chilean Exile Cinema and Its Homecoming Documentaries," in *Cinematic Homecomings: Exile and Return in Transnational Cinema*, ed. Rebecca Prime (New York: Bloomsbury, 2015). I thank Bloomsbury Academic for permission to reproduce these excerpts here, and Rebecca Prime for advice and encouragement in the last stages of writing this book.

Chile's National Research Council CONICYT—now ANID—awarded me a postdoctoral grant thanks to which I accomplished a great part of the archival research for this book during the years 2018–20 (Fondecyt no. 3180208, "Imagen, archivo, memoria: Los retornos del cine chileno del exilio"). Without their generous funding, extensive international travel would have been impossible. The College of the Arts at California State University Long Beach awarded me a Faculty Small Grant for the year 2023–24 that helped cover part of the costs during the last stages of writing and editing this book. At CSULB I want to thank all my students and colleagues in the Department of Cinematic Arts, especially Seung-hoon Jeong and Matt Montoya, for reading the introduction and the preface.

For a book that talks so much about exile, a few final notes on *home*. I am happy this book has found a home at the University of California Press, and in the series Cinema Cultures in Contact. My thanks to acquisition editor Raina Polivka; to series editors Richard Abel, Giorgio Bertellini, and Matthew Solomon for believing in the project from the beginning; to editorial assistant Sam Warren for all the guidance during the last stages of production; to copy editor Sharon Langworthy for catching all my silly mistakes; to project manager Jon Dertien and indexer Sarah Osment; and to the peer reviewers, whose comments helped improve the book. I also thank author Samhita Sunya for sharing her experience publishing in this series and encouraging me to do the same.

Dearest friends have been my home, too: Claudia Bossay, Carl Fischer, Linnéa Hussein, Constanza Vergara, and Jaap Verheul. They have all played a huge role both in my personal life and in my trajectory as a scholar. I met Carl Fischer at a conference in Santiago in 2012 when I desperately asked someone in the audience for an adapter to hook up my computer to the screen. Ever since, Carl has been more than an outstanding friend—a reader, mentor, colleague, and confidant.

To my mom, Ruth, and my sister, Isabel, a big thanks simply for being there, at home, always. To my sister's dog Roma: thanks for all the love and for distracting me whenever I wanted to sit in front of the computer to write.

At last, Zuzana M. Pick welcomed me into her and Leutén Rojas's home when I visited Ottawa one day in January 2014 during a cold Canadian winter. Thirty years earlier, she wrote several articles and book chapters about Chilean exile cinema in the most rigorous and intelligent possible way. Her writing is inescapable for anyone working on Latin American film and exile cinema. For me, her research has meant so much more. This is not the book she would have written on the topic, but at least I hope it's one that does justice to her immense work. I dedicate the book to you, Zuzana, and in memory of Leutén.

Abbreviations

APTA	Asociación de Profesionales y Técnicos del Cine (Association of Film Professionals and Technicians)
BAMPFA	Berkeley Art Museum and Pacific Film Archive
BBC	British Broadcasting Corporation
CAFOD	Catholic Agency for Overseas Development
CONFER	Conferencia de Religiosos de Nicaragua (Nicaragua National Conference of Religious)
DEC	Development Education Center
DEFA	Deutsche Film-Aktiengesellschaft (East German Film Studio)
DINA	Dirección de Inteligencia Nacional (National Intelligence Directorate)
FASIC	Fundación de Ayuda Social de las Iglesias Cristianas (Social Assistance Foundation of the Christian Churches)
FIAF	Fédération internationale des archives du film (International Federation of Film Archives)
FIDOCS	Festival Internacional de Documentales de Santiago (Santiago International Documentary Film Festival)
FIPRESCI	Fédération Internationale de la Presse Cinématographique (International Federation of Film Critics)

FPMR	Frente Patriótico Manuel Rodríguez (Manuel Rodríguez Patriotic Front)
FRELIMO	Frente de Libertação de Moçambique (Mozambican Liberation Front)
FSLN	Frente Sandinista de Liberación Nacional (Sandinista National Liberation Front)
FTQ	Fédération des travailleurs du Québec (Federation of Workers of Quebec)
GDR	German Democratic Republic (East Germany)
GFR	German Federal Republic (West Germany)
GREC	Groupe de Recherches et d'Essais Cinématographiques (Group of Investigations and Cinematic Essays)
ICAIC	Instituto Cubano del Arte e Industria Cinematográficos (Cuban Institute of Cinematic Arts and Industries)
IFFR	International Film Festival Rotterdam
IMEC	Institut Mémoires de l'édition contemporaine (Institute for Contemporary Publishing Archives)
INA	Institut national de l'audiovisuel (National Audiovisual Institute)
INCINE	Instituto Nicaragüense de Cine (Nicaraguan Film Institute)
INPRHU	Instituto de Promoción Humana (Nicaraguan Institute of Human Promotion)
IOM/OIM	International Organization for Migration / Organisation internationale pour les migrations
MECLA	Mercado del Nuevo Cine Latinoamericano (Market of the New Latin American Cinema)
MIR	Movimiento de Izquierda Revolucionaria (Revolutionary Left Movement)
MIRSA	Museo Internacional de la Resistencia Salvador Allende (International Museum of Resistance Salvador Allende)
MMDH	Museo de la Memoria y los Derechos Humanos (Museum of Memory and Human Rights)
MSSA	Museo de la Solidaridad Salvador Allende (Museum of Solidarity Salvador Allende)
NFB/ONF	National Film Board of Canada/Office national du film du Canada
NLAC	New Latin American Cinema

PFA	Pacific Film Archive
PIDEE	Protección de la Infancia Dañada por los Estados de Emergencia (Protection of Youth Damaged by States of Emergency)
RAI	Radiotelevisione italiana (Italian National Broadcasting Company)
RTVE	Radio Televisión Española (Spanish Public Television and Radio)
SFI	Svenska Filminstitutet (Swedish Film Institute)
SML	Servicio Médico Legal (Medical Legal Institute)
SVT	Sveriges Television (Swedish Public Television)
UCAL	Unión de Cinematecas de América Latina (Union of Latin American Cinematheques)
UN	United Nations
UNESCO	United Nations Educational, Scientific and Cultural Organization
UNHCR	United Nations High Commissioner for Refugees
UP	Unidad Popular (Popular Unity)
USSR	Union of Soviet Socialist Republics
VGIK	Vserossiyskiy gosudarstvyennyy institut kinematografii imyeni (Gerasimov Institute of Cinematography)
WUS	World University Service
YLE	Yleisradio (Finnish Broadcasting Company)
ZDF	Zweites Deutsches Fernsehen (Second German Television)

Introduction

This book tells the story of Chilean exile film and video, from their global emergence out of networks of solidarity in the 1970s to their ongoing return to Chilean archives in the last decade. The pages that follow, however, are not simply about Chilean exile cinema. By this I mean that the book does something more than concentrate on this vast diasporic corpus: more than two hundred works made by exiled filmmakers throughout the world, primarily though not exclusively between 1973 and 1990, the period coinciding with the military dictatorship. I argue here for a historical understanding of transnational cinema solidarity as a widespread geography of political and artistic friendships that shape film production and circulation. *Transnational Cinema Solidarity* thinks of Chilean exile cinema less as a fixed group of films restricted to the spaces of exile and to the years of the dictatorship and more as an open and ongoing experience defined by transnational exchanges. Chilean exile cinema travels among nations; moves across circuits of film production and exhibition; and traverses different historical times, from its early development in the ideological framework of the Cold War to its material and symbolic presence in the archives and memory battlegrounds of contemporary Chile. While this narrative arc echoes the journey of exile and return, the interactions examined in this book imply routes and off-ramps that do not necessarily lead back home. To write a transnational history of Chilean exile film and video is therefore to call into question the categories of national and exile cinemas, as well as to reimagine the territorial and political boundaries of our cinematic world map. Solidarity and the movements of exile cinema call for a politicized remaking of world cinema.

As several proponents of the transnational and world cinema "turns" in film studies have made clear, this is not simply a history that does away with the concept of the national, nor is it one that functions as an aggregate of distinct national film histories. It is not a history in which the world means little more than the West's "Rest," either.[1] The kind of transnational and world cinema history that this book develops is inspired by Ella Shohat's and Robert Stam's early call to decolonize the discipline and "unthink" its Eurocentrism, by Masha Salazkina's "systemic and relational" understanding of the expanded geographies that make up world cinema histories, and by Nataša Ďurovičová's defense of transnationalism as a spatial lens through which to map how cinema *moves* through borders of various kinds.[2] Building from their work, I am proposing here an alternative to the geopolitical arrangement of world cinema as we know it. The "world" that this book brings into view is shaped by solidarity and by the travels of forced political displacement, and the "cinema" it invokes refers to a wide range of actors beyond the figure of the director: production companies, festivals, exile communities, embassies, universities, political organizations, and the life of film prints themselves as material and archival artifacts.

THE BATTLE MOVES

A detained film director sits in the stands of a sports stadium, surrounded by other political prisoners. It's September 1973 in Santiago, Chile, shortly after the coup that toppled the government of Salvador Allende. The "Chilean way" to socialism, the experiment that seduced the political imagination of the Left on a global scale, is now over. The images of the bombardment of the house of government are already being broadcast on television channels all over the world. The military junta that gains control of the country quickly installs a regime of terror. Dead bodies pile up on the streets. Concentration camps and illegal prisons are set up throughout the country. Led by Augusto Pinochet, the junta applies an internal enemy doctrine based on total annihilation of political dissent. While not all filmmakers are militants of the leftist parties that form the Unidad Popular (UP; Popular Unity) coalition, most have been involved in a range of documentaries and fictions that show in one way or another their commitment to Allende's project. The junta thinks of them as part of the "Marxist cancer" that must be wiped out of the country.

Military officials raid Chilefilms, the state-owned production company, and the rumors of soldiers destroying prints and negatives spread across the filmmaking community like the fire that burns their films.[3] So does the news of numerous colleagues in prison. The one held captive in the National Stadium is no other than Patricio Guzmán, who sits in the largest detention center established in the wake of the coup. Together with a collective, he has been filming history in the making, shooting the daily demonstrations, assemblies, strikes, meetings, governmental ceremonies, speeches, and street confrontations that took place prior to the coup. As the secret police interrogate Guzmán in the stadium and threaten him with execution, another plot concerning his film, one that resembles more of a thriller, is taking place.[4] Several courageous institutions and people perform small actions that end up saving what will later become a landmark political documentary.[5] Guzmán's uncle hides the reels. Together with Swedish citizen Lilian Indseth, who was at that time married to Chilean film director Sergio Castilla, and other members of the crew like Federico Elton and Bernardo Menz, they bring the bits of film to Harald Edelstam, the Swedish ambassador. Edelman, sometimes referred to as Chile's Schindler for his role in securing asylum for hundreds of exiles, breaks the embassy's rules and includes the negatives and original sound elements in a diplomatic pouch. The materials move hidden in trunks, and in the end they sail for Sweden in a ship called *Rio de Janeiro*. Soon after his release from prison, Guzmán travels to Stockholm. He is at the port with Elton the moment the ship arrives at the docks. Days later they meet with the director of the Swedish Film Institute, who takes them to the room where the materials were being kept.[6] If the safeguarding of these reels—enabled by the efforts of family members, friends, diplomats, and film archives—is relevant to the future of the film, so is the intervention of the Instituto Cubano del Arte e Industria Cinematográficos (ICAIC; Cuban Institute of Cinematic Arts and Industries). Although reunited with the filmic materials in Sweden, Guzmán considers living his exile in Spain, as he attended Madrid's Escuela Oficial de Cinematografía in the late 1960s. But ICAIC offers the filmmaker the time and space to use its labs and editing equipment to work on his new documentary for years, and so he goes to Havana. The filmic materials arrive in Cuba via France. The Cuban institute brings to the island other crew members, Elton and José Pino, plus a new figure, editor Pedro Chaskel. ICAIC also provides the team with notable advisers: critics and filmmakers Julio García Espinosa and Tomás Gutiérrez Alea and Marxist theorist Marta Harnecker. They debate cinema and ideology with the filmmakers, creating an atmosphere of critical reflection that is instrumental for the labor of political analysis performed by the resulting film.

The Battle of Chile—made by Patricio Guzmán and Equipo Tercer Año, shot in Chile between 1972 and 1973, edited and completed in Cuba, and released in three parts in 1975, 1976, and 1979—was immediately celebrated. The film was a success everywhere it played: in Parisian theaters; in repertory houses in New York; in festivals in Leipzig and Pesaro; in special programs in London, Mexico, and Madrid; and in film clubs, unions, and universities in different corners of the world. At the Pacific Film Archive in Berkeley, it "gripped the entire audience," and with only three screenings it became "the most popular film of any kind" shown in 1977.[7] A decade later, at the height of the dictatorship, the film would slowly begin to find its way back to Chile through other filmmakers, who brought home bootlegged copies by hand.[8] Then another decade later, with Chile under democratic rule, Patricio Guzmán himself would bring the film home and make a new one out of this journey of return. In *Chile, Obstinate Memory* (1997), he examined the traces of the past in the images of *The Battle of Chile*, screened the trilogy to different audiences, particularly high school and university students, and documented their reactions. Both *The Battle of Chile* and *Chile, Obstinate Memory* were screened in a grand homecoming of sorts, during the first edition of the documentary film festival Guzmán created, which took place at the Goethe Institute Santiago in 1997: Festival Internacional de Documentales de Santiago (FIDOCS; Santiago International Documentary Film Festival).[9] In September 2021, over two decades after this screening and almost fifty years after its making, *The Battle of Chile* had its premiere on national television, aired by the private station La Red. And in September 2023, in the context of the commemorations of the fiftieth anniversary of the coup, a digital restoration of the trilogy was released to wide acclaim in cities like New York, Paris, and Santiago.

This is just a small part of the journey of what is probably the most famous Chilean exile film. The anecdotes of the shooting, editing, distributing, and exhibiting of Guzmán's trilogy could fill up the pages of a whole book, but that is not what this one is about.[10] The implications of the story I have just told—how an exile cinema moves across several nations, cultural contexts, modes of production and circulation, exhibition settings, and historical periods—constitute the heart of *Transnational Cinema Solidarity*. The example of *The Battle of Chile* evidences

Introduction | 5

FIGURE 3. Tricontinental Film Center's promotional materials for parts 1 and 2 of *La batalla de Chile* (*The Battle of Chile*, Patricio Guzmán, 1975, 1976). Courtesy of University of California, Berkeley—Berkeley Art Museum/Pacific Film Archive Film Library.

my interest in how film reels were smuggled out of Chile after the military coup and traveled through embassies and consulates, but the book lingers on other facets related to this example. It emphasizes the many movements through which networks of solidarity are formed and exercised: how the specific routes followed by exile directors shape their careers and films, how different ideas of exile and political cinema travel across film festivals and other gatherings, and how the transits of film prints provide new meanings to the notions of homecoming and return. With its focus on journeys of various kinds, the book expands the geopolitical coordinates of film studies and the discipline's understanding of exile, world, transnational, and solidarity cinemas.

EXILE, WORLD, TRANSNATIONAL, SOLIDARITY

Exile. There are many related terms in film studies—*intercultural, multicultural, accented, minor cinemas*—and in critical theory—*diaspora, migrancy, errantry, nomadism.*[11] But as a specific kind of forced displacement, exile is no metaphor, no word to be easily interchanged with the plurality of terms that form the "semantic domain and vocabulary of transnationalism."[12] I speak here of exile and exile cinema simply because they are the appropriate historical concepts. Chilean exile cinema is the product of a historical context shaped by the military dictatorships of the Southern Cone and the ensuing exile of hundreds of thousands of Latin Americans; by the Cold War in its global, continental, and local dimensions; by discourses of Third Worldism and internationalist solidarity; and by emerging frameworks of human rights and memory.

For Hamid Naficy, exile filmmakers oscillate between homeland and foster nation in a permanent state of in-betweenness, a dislocated position inscribed into the films' form. Naficy summarizes these cinematic dislocations as the "interstitiality" of exile and accented cinemas.[13] Bearing the "accent" or mark of their displacement, exile films function as an allegory for the experience of their makers: always in between cultures and in between cinematic production practices.[14] While indebted to Naficy's groundbreaking work, this book departs from his approach in that my emphasis is not on theorizing a particular "accented style."[15] Rather, I am more interested in tracing a transnational history of cinematic exchanges shaped by exile and solidarity. The book follows cultural exchanges alongside the close reading of cinematic texts—an analysis that shows how transnational interactions find resonances, divergences, and points of contact with actual aesthetic practices. This analysis demonstrates that the interlaced travels and sites of encounters that give life to Chilean exile cinema are irreducible to the dialectic of exile and homeland. As much as Chile—the homeland—may act as a centripetal force that exerts its power across different types of filmic, historical, cultural, and political interactions, Chilean exile cinema expands into other territories, topics, and cultural affiliations that are not always related to Chile. Chilean exile cinema thus works as an emblematic case study to redefine the geographies of world cinema.

World/transnational. Notions of world cinema continue to be attached to a center-periphery model in which clearly demarcated areas of the world such as Latin America, Asia, or Africa are posited as signifiers of otherness and difference—alternatives that enrich and diversify the global market of "art cinema" in which films made in Europe remain the norm.[16] I join recent scholarship in the critique of this "too easy" task of "territorializing" cinema, calling instead for new means for the tracking of world cinema's movements against their usual national and political barriers.[17] Along similar lines, transnational cinema designates a theoretical lens to think about forms of mobility and "cultural interconnectedness" that defy the borders of the nation-state.[18] In its simplest coinage, *transnational* functions as an adjective that describes how films are made and seen, sometimes meaning little more than international coproductions or diasporic audiences.[19] Multinational funding, stories about journeys of displacement, a critique of the national space as the privileged site for the production of social identities and subjectivities, and multilinguality are all features of both transnationalism and exilic cinemas. For this reason, exile cinema is sometimes discussed as one modality of transnational film and media, or as one theoretical approach within the broader transnational and world cinema turns in film studies.[20]

World and transnational cinema are regarded as responses to an "acceleration" in the process of globalization since the mid-1970s.[21] As a result, most scholarship under these labels concentrates on industry issues of financing, coproducing, distributing, and viewing films in a globalized twenty-first-century world that has altered the nation-centric rules that governed film markets in the past. Salazkina even claimed that work published under the categories of transnational and global film and media were not generally concerned with "history or with questions of historiography."[22] There are notable exceptions, though, including in the literature that addresses forms of transnationalism that predate globalization in Latin American cinema.[23] Ana M. López, for example, traced the histories of traveling filmmakers in the region, analyzed the intraregional and pancontinental dialogues at work in early cinema and in the New Latin American Cinema (NLAC) of the 1960s, and discussed transnational modes of financial and cultural exchange in the first half of the twentieth century.[24] But even when scholars turn their attention to these earlier moments in film history, such as the periods associated with classical cinemas or the various industrial projects in Latin America during the 1930s and 1940s, the emphasis is still mostly placed on market logics of "commodity circulation and industrial exchange" or on the cross-national journeys of stars and directors working in vernacular modes of studio filmmaking.[25] As such, the world and transnational frameworks, at least in their dominant scholarly forms, tend to leave aside radical film cultures that cannot be readily aligned with the commercial markets of the global art cinema or with those of global Hollywood.

A critical appraisal of solidarity allows this book to offer an alternative model or "method" for doing transnational film history.[26] I move away from the scholarly emphasis on economic and industrial forces and concentrate instead on historicizing a dynamic of exilic travels that are marked by political friendships and a series of formal and informal networks—a shifting geography of transnational cinema solidarity that the book sets in motion.

Though solidarity remains "relatively understudied," the notion has seen a critical resurgence in recent years due to the emergence of new waves of social movements that have garnered solidarity actions around the world.[27] Examples include the demonstrations in solidarity with Black people in the United States protesting police brutality after the murder of George Floyd in 2020 and the massive solidarity protests against Israel's latest war on Palestinians in late 2023. Some of these forms of organizing are predicated on practices of transnational solidarity; that is, they establish part of their political project and horizon based on a shared practice of resistance. In the imagination of this resistance, cultural and creative practices in the arts—and networks of artistic solidarity broadly speaking—have been crucial.[28] They have provided a lens for understanding how solidarity works; how it is "conceived, imagined, and radically enacted"; and how it mobilizes political sensibilities and constructs a sense of community across borders.[29] Given the central role that images of different kinds play in this political mobilization, solidarity has garnered the attention of art historians and scholars of visual culture.[30] In film and media, however, solidarity is only beginning to be theorized and historicized.[31] Recent publications by Rossen Djagalov and Masha Salazkina demonstrate what this strand of research can offer by privileging "entangled" histories of internationalist solidarities and transnational encounters between the Second and Third Worlds.[32]

Building from their work, this book thinks about what solidarity might mean and do for film studies as a discipline. What would our film history look like if we set a geography of networked solidarities into motion, if we studied its transits across continents and decades? In their introduction to *Transnational Solidarities*, Zeina Maasri, Cathy Bergin, and Francesca Burke argue that the point of studying solidarity is not merely to add neglected stories to the radical history of the 1960s and 1970s and expand its geographical map; these overlooked histories of solidarity tell us something different about the political imagination of revolutionary movements.[33] Similarly, I argue that a history of cinema solidarity not only expands the geography of world cinema but altogether redefines it, in that it imagines a different global articulation of film history based on political friendships and struggles of cinematic resistance. This is transnational cinema solidarity "as worldmaking"—a vision of the world based on the political potential of cinema in response to oppression and based on the erasure of the borders that separate Arab, African, Asian, European, Latin American, Middle Eastern, and North American cinemas.[34]

TRANSNATIONAL CINEMA SOLIDARITY

With transnational cinema solidarity I name simultaneously a concept, a set of practices, and a mode of political subjectivity. As a concept, solidarity determines the cultural and political function played by exiles on the geopolitical map of the 1970s.[35] This conceptual function is shaped by the Cold War but also exceeds its logic of polar divisions, including a wider range of Third Worldist alliances. Together with resistance, solidarity is *the* keyword in the political vocabulary of the Chilean diaspora, based on the need to agglutinate individuals, groups, and nation-states in the struggle against Pinochet's regime.[36] As practice, solidarity names a range of actions in support of the Chilean people and filmmakers (and Latin American and Third World peoples and filmmakers more generally). In their host countries, exiles encountered the solidarity of peers and strangers. It was a form of transnational solidarity that had emerged spontaneously as an expression of support to a nation going through a unique revolutionary process, but that had been multiplied and transformed after 1973 into a huge worldwide solidarity movement, now in support of a people resisting a military dictatorship.[37] "The plight of Chile," as has been documented by numerous studies, "became one of the main post-war *causes célèbres* for activism by innumerable citizens and a broad range of human rights and solidarity organizations across the globe."[38] Solidarity was thus visible in economic boycotts, in street protests, and in the creation of "anti-Fascist," "Chile," or "solidarity" committees—organizations formed by local members of the host society together with the Chilean exile community.[39] They raised funds, demonstrated, and engaged in group fasts, among other actions to give visibility to the crimes of the dictatorship. These associations grew rapidly in every city in which a significant number of exiles resided. Therefore, for exiles, and for exile filmmakers, solidarity provided them with a new range of strategies with which to act in the public sphere.[40]

This spirit of solidarity is also the political impulse behind a cluster of actions and tasks realized by diverse people and institutions: to organize public campaigns to get filmmakers out of detention and torture centers, to find refuge for filmmakers, to store footage in embassies and send film materials to various destinations via diplomatic services, to

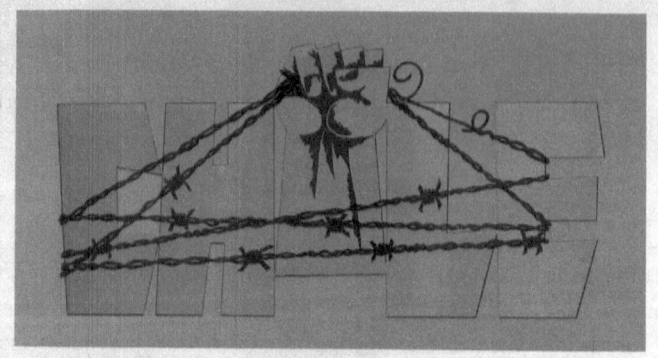

FIGURE 4. Poster for a public forum and solidarity demonstration in Tegucigalpa, Honduras, 1974. Fondo Jorge Acuña, colección Museo de la Memoria y los Derechos Humanos. Courtesy of MMDH.

FIGURE 5. Poster for a solidarity demonstration in London, 1974. Fondo Jorge Acuña, colección Museo de la Memoria y los Derechos Humanos. Courtesy of MMDH.

FIGURE 6. "Chile: Ten Years of Struggle." Postcard from the Salvador Allende Committee in Copenhagen, issued for the tenth anniversary of the coup in 1983. Fondo Miguel Lawner, colección Museo de la Memoria y los Derechos Humanos. Courtesy of MMDH.

locate homes and jobs for exile directors, to integrate them into their respective film industries, to look for funding to complete the films Chilean exiles had been working on prior to the coup, to exhibit films in cultural events and film festivals, and more recently, to secure institutional agreements for the repatriation and return of exile films to Chilean archives and museums. As I illustrate in the following chapters of this book, the production and reception history of many exile films is often the result of concrete actions performed by these transnational networks of cinema solidarity.

As a mode of political subjectivity, solidarity is a way of being moved by the events shaping the world, together with the desire to act within and to transform the world. This desire—both an ethos and a political affect—can be traced back to the history of internationalist movements, frequently attached to the association of communist and socialist parties and militias in the late nineteenth century, to the brigades in support of the Republic in the Spanish Civil War in the 1930s, and to the anticolonial movements of liberation in the 1960s and 1970s.[41] Solidarity in this regard is unthinkable without an invocation of internationalism. Writing about the history of political cinema, Nicole Brenez has said that internationalism is seen in "filmmakers who are trying to help, through images, people other than their own."[42] This is the same principle behind most notions of solidarity.[43] Both solidarity and internationalism imply an affective dimension: an "emotional apparatus" that "enables our metaphoric identification with the other."[44] One must not be naïve here: this book shows that the affective dimensions of solidarity often mask the uneven power relations shaping transnational cultural interactions. Solidarity is the name for a concept and a social practice onto which a series of different (sometimes divergent) political goals and strategies are projected. The negotiation between these inevitably takes place in an arena marked more by asymmetry than by equality.

The conflation of all these elements is what I call *transnational cinema solidarity*. The book therefore thinks of the concept in as capacious a form as possible. It is used as a genre—as in internationalist films that seek to mobilize viewers in support of the Chilean people—and as the overarching name for a series of political tasks and actions, like boycotts, raising funds, or organizing cultural events. The concept also illustrates the transnational networks—political, cultural, artistic, personal—that enable the emergence and development of Chilean exile cinema. Finally, transnational cinema solidarity indicates an "affective state" that speaks to a particular kind of political subjectivity.[45]

Bringing political subjectivity into the equation suggests an intimate link between transnationalism and solidarity. The historical moment of the Cold War sees the emergence of Third Worldism and tricontinentalism. Based on shared experiences of subjection to colonial and imperial power, these discourses imagine a new political subject that surpasses the boundaries of the nation-state. Solidarity is at the core of this political subject. In the words of Anne Garland Mahler, solidarity calls for a "community of feeling" that "transcends national and regional geography and whose affinities are not based on location, language, or blood."[46] Internationalist solidarity was the concept used at the time, and throughout this book I reserve it for those cinematic cross-national exchanges that are more explicitly inflected by the political lexicon of the Cold War and by Cuba's model of "exporting revolution" and solidarity on a global scale.[47] More generally, I prefer to speak of transnational solidarity as it points to a diverse range of cultural exchanges that defy national borders and that cannot be restricted solely to the Cold War era or to its political vocabulary.

Transnational Cinema Solidarity demonstrates that the "communities of feeling" Mahler speaks of follow specific routes of circulation and networks that mediate them. Rather than relying on exile as a metaphor for an age marked by displacement or on the transnational as an abstract image for a globalized world traversed by unspecified movements, I am driven by a strand of "critical transnationalism" that pays attention to "concrete-specific" flows of exchange.[48] This is why the book insists on historicizing the transnational journeys of exilic institutions, filmmakers, and their films. Before moving forward, a modicum of historical context is thus necessary.

FROM REVOLUTION TO EXILE

On the night of September 4, 1970, the Chilean people went to the streets to celebrate Salvador Allende, who had just become the first Marxist in the country's history to be democratically elected as president. Chile quickly captured the attention of artists, intellectuals, and politicians throughout the world because the new socialist government had a resolute vision. Known as the Vía Chilena, or Chilean Way, Allende's proposal was an unprecedented "democratic revolution" to achieve socialism: a peaceful process of change within the boundaries of bourgeois, constitutional democracy.[49]

Allende took office with an ambitious program of social transformations that included the nationalization of major industries and the redistribution of land to peasants. The experience triggered immediate resistance from the country's reactionary forces—the upper classes, transnational corporations, conservative guilds and professional associations, right-wing media—and from the US government, which helped fund the military coup that eventually toppled Allende on September 11, 1973.[50] The Chilean Way had to deal with internal opposition, too. The UP—a coalition of several parties supporting Allende—was the result of two contradictory positions within the Chilean Left. One tendency thought that the adequate path toward socialism had to be developed within existing legal and institutional structures. The other sought to intensify strategies of direct democracy and "popular power," with the ultimate goal of destroying the constitutional order—thereby making room for the advent of true socialism.[51]

The political fragmentation of the Left at the time found its equivalent in the variety of cinematic responses to the social process experienced right before and under the UP government. The NLAC had emerged out of the legacy of neorealism, and the aesthetic rebellion derived from the new waves, together with anti-imperialist and anti-colonial sentiments. The 1967 and 1969 festivals of the NLAC, which took place in Viña del Mar, Chile, were crucial instances for the continental projection of the movement. In Chile, the most acclaimed feature-length fictions were exhibited at the second festival: *Tres tristes tigres* (Three Sad Tigers, Raúl Ruiz, 1968), *Caliche Sangriento* (Bloody Nitrate, Helvio Soto, 1968), *Valparaíso, mi amor* (Valparaíso, my love, Aldo Francia, 1969) and *El chacal de Nahueltoro* (The Jackal of Nahueltoro, Miguel Littin, 1969). These films established the parameters of the New Chilean Cinema and proposed more socially and politically engaged forms of filmmaking. But the history of Chilean cinema in the late 1960s is a complex one, irreducible to the aforementioned canon. There were plenty of other directors; feature-length fiction films that attempted stories and aesthetic treatments that deviated from the modes of *cinéma engagé*; and a robust production of documentary short films, especially through university centers such Centro de Cine Experimental at the state university Universidad de Chile, one of the main hubs of Chilean film culture at the time.[52]

Soon before Allende's election, in 1970, filmmakers wrote a manifesto in which they claimed: "Before filmmakers, we are men engaged within the political and social phenomenon of our people and with its great task:

the construction of socialism."⁵³ The influence that this text, authored by Littin and signed by most Chilean directors, may have had on the films produced after its publication has been disputed; nonetheless, the manifesto still functions as a significant document of filmmakers' revolutionary aspirations.⁵⁴ After taking office, President Allende appointed Littin as head of the state-owned studio Chilefilms, for which Littin envisioned an ambitious program of "education of the masses" through a series of film workshops. Who gets to be a filmmaker in revolutionary times was a highly debated question for the NLAC directors. Beyond the idea of making films *with*—and not necessarily *for*—the people, the utopia of the workers, peasants, and ordinary citizens of the nation as filmmakers was a central aspect favored by Littin with the workshops he promoted while presiding over Chilefilms. The emphasis on popular education resulted in a total lack of films fully produced by the studio. Ten months after his appointment and amid a financial crisis, Littin was forced to resign.

The films produced during the three years of the UP were heterogeneous in their range of aesthetic and narrative choices. They were mostly made by artists and production companies outside of Chilefilms and were often critical of the historical process the country was experiencing.⁵⁵ This cinema, far from being monolithic, reveals the political complexity of the Allende years. Since most filmmakers were members either of the Communist Party, the Socialist Party, or the MIR (Movimiento de Izquierda Revolucionaria; Revolutionary Left Movement), internal partisan debates inevitably permeated their cinematic practice. The UP government did not develop any homogeneous or unified film program for imagining, capturing, allegorizing, or thinking with and through the social changes that were taking place in Allende's Chile. The discussions grew more acute in the months preceding the coup, insofar as the radicalization of the social and political landscape called for an equally radicalized or revolutionary cinema. What united Chilean filmmakers was their desire to intervene in the political sphere; however, the question of what made cinema "revolutionary" or "political" was up for debate. As chapters 3 and 4 show, filmmakers continued these debates once in exile, almost without pause. They engaged in sustained reflection about their recent role during the UP years and about their new role as filmmakers in exile, sometimes with conflicting views that expressed themselves in the form of harsh criticism and "bitter polemics."⁵⁶

After the coup, the dictatorship embarked on a project of systematically destroying the cultural apparatus of the state, which meant dismantling museums and cinematheques, intervening in universities, shutting down presses, closing educational programs of various kinds, and persecuting artists and cultural workers. For the military, the activist stance that filmmakers had developed during Allende's government made them enemies of the nation. The junta imprisoned, tortured, executed, disappeared, and forced into exile thousands of Allende's supporters, including filmmakers.

Pinochet's military junta was of course not unique in the Southern Cone. Brazil had experienced its own coup in 1964 and went through a dictatorship that lasted two decades, until 1985. In 1964 Bolivia saw a succession of coups and short military governments, leading to Hugo Banzer's dictatorship—a much more repressive regime that lasted from 1971 until 1978. Uruguay faced a coup in 1973, a few months before Chile, and went through a twelve-year dictatorship. And in 1976 a new coup initiated a brutal military dictatorship in Argentina. All these authoritarian regimes engaged in the same practices of political annihilation—torturing, executing, and exiling leftist militants and supporters—a fate that was shared by many politically committed film directors from all countries. Some of them became exiles twice displaced. For example, several Brazilian directors had been exiles in Chile during the UP government and after the September 1973 coup had to relocate somewhere else.[57]

While official data on Chilean exiles is disputed, the literature agrees on the figure of two hundred thousand exiles as the most reliable.[58] Exile meant radical transformations in the lives of Chileans. According to Ana Vásquez and Ana María Araujo, exiles mourned the political project that was defeated by the coup, while dealing with the trauma of torture and political violence. They felt guilty for having survived while many of their friends and comrades had not. They went through a long process of adjustment to a new setting, with ambivalent feelings toward their foster nations and their symbols. They struggled with learning a new language while their kids learned much faster at school. They took refuge in activism and fostered the creation of exile communities: sports and social clubs, research centers, and artists groups. In new work and social environments, they redefined their preconceptions of race, class, and gender. They divorced and remarried. They found new jobs or new careers. And when they had settled into their new lives, they debated whether to return or not once the dictatorship was over. Those who were more involved in political activities did; a significant number of Chilean exiles did not.[59]

Exile was a watershed experience for the arts as well. Countless novelists, poets, theater directors, performers, visual artists, and filmmakers sought to leave the country and resume their lives abroad. For filmmakers, exile was practically the only alternative, since the imprisonment of Guzmán and many other directors was highly effective in instilling fear. The seriousness of the danger was evidenced later by the detention of Jorge Müller, the cinematographer of *The Battle of Chile*, and his partner Carmen Bueno, a prolific actress who played many roles in the films of the early 1970s, including a prophetic scene in *La tierra prometida* (The Promised Land, Miguel Littin, 1973), in which her character is seen naked and covered in blood after a violent attack by the military with their sabers. Müller and Bueno were kidnapped after the premiere of the first and one of the few features produced and released in Chile after the coup—*A la sombra del sol* (*In the Shadow of the Sun*, Silvio Caiozzi and Pablo Perelman, 1974). Müller and Bueno were disappeared, and their remains are yet to be found.[60] Their kidnapping was a definitive blow and traumatic event for Chilean filmmakers. By the time of their detention in September 1974, only a handful of filmmakers were living in Chile. Most had already gone into exile.

DEFINING CHILEAN EXILE CINEMA

Due to the inter-American dimensions of the Cold War and the transnational articulations of the military dictatorships that swept across the continent, Chilean exile cinema was not the only diasporic film practice in Latin America. While there were Argentinean, Brazilian, Bolivian, and Uruguayan exile filmmakers, their cinemas did not configure an experience as robust as the Chilean case, both in terms of the number of exile films produced and the transnational networks of solidarity that supported them.[61] The same can be said about the critical literature and scholarship devoted to these different cases.[62] Film directors, critics, programmers, and scholars have written about different aspects of Chilean exile cinema since the late 1970s. Taken together, these contributions advance what can be called a standard narrative, which I summarize and complement in three key points below.[63]

First, writers defined "Chilean cinema in exile" as the vast cinematic corpus that was made all over the world while Chilean filmmakers were in exile and while the military dictatorship ruled in Chile (1973–90). In this book I get rid of the "in" in "Chilean cinema in exile" and prefer to speak of "Chilean exile cinema." The phrase highlights that exile is no specific place, and certainly not the sum of all territories except the one delimited by Chilean borders. In using *Chilean exile cinema* I refer to two interconnected processes: "Chilean exile"—the historical conditions and development of the Chilean diaspora after the 1973 military coup—and "exile cinema"—the particular case of a proliferation of diasporic films and videos whose bonds with Chile oscillate between transparency and opacity.[64] Sometimes this cinema ties itself to the Chilean nation, its history, and its territory through a sort of umbilical cord; sometimes this cinema only wishes to distance itself from Chile, thus exceeding the labels of "national" and "exile" cinema that scholars impose on this cultural phenomenon to understand it.[65] In short, I speak of Chilean exile cinema because the phrase alludes to a cinema both *in* and *about* exile; emphasizes the inherent instability of the condition of exile, irreducible to a single position; and produces an intertwining of "exile cinema" with the historical development of the "Chilean exile" experience.

The temporal demarcation implicit in the standard definition of Chilean exile film and video also needs to be questioned. When does an exile cinema end? What marks the "after" exile? Even when returning is possible, exile remains a ceaseless and unfinished condition.[66] To date the end of Chilean exile cinema in 1990, the year in which democracy was regained, does not account for a series of factors that oblige me to extend its temporality. Various exile directors never returned to the country after the end of the military rule; many kept on making films that deal explicitly with the condition of exile; and several filmmakers of the "second generation," the children of the diaspora, are nowadays producing films about the lasting effects of exile and return on their lives. For these reasons, Chilean exile cinema remains alive. But there is yet another reason to claim that Chilean exile cinema does not belong to the past. Since the mid-2000s, part of this corpus has begun its return to Chilean archives and museums. As the book's last chapter shows, this is an incomplete process that simultaneously points to North-South imbalances in global archival networks as well as to the political potential of an unseen cinema that is beginning to encounter its audiences in Chile and abroad.

Second, the standard narrative of Chilean exile film and video celebrates the diversity of the corpus while stressing that there is a dominant and recurring thread: the films are fundamentally concerned with the struggle against fascism in Chile. Many directors and critics thus preferred the phrase "cinema of resistance," as this notion expressed more forcefully the common political intention of their films. Film historian Jacqueline Mouesca—herself an exile in Paris—traces a thematic progression. There is an initial phase of exile films that address political issues and questions of Chilean history head on, in a rather militant and straightforward way that is aligned with the tactics of resistance against the dictatorship. This phase is followed by an opening toward multiple other themes and aesthetic approaches for dealing with the condition of exile.[67]

In a general sense this statement is not inaccurate, but I present in this book a different way to look at the politics of exile cinema and its themes. As chapters 4 and 5 make clear, insisting on the idea of a progression and an opening—a branching out from exile, revolution, and resistance toward multiple other topics—does not account for the sheer heterogeneity of the phenomenon from its very beginning. It also fails to grasp the stakes behind the debates filmmakers had regarding how to conceive of a political cinema of exile and resistance. This book situates these discussions in their appropriate historical context, emphasizing how they moved from one iteration to the other, while also presenting them as contributions to broader debates on Third Cinema and political filmmaking.

Third, the standard narrative discusses Chilean exile cinema in terms of the developments of a national cinema that was carried out abroad and characterizes this exilic output as the "most important" in Chilean film history and an "astonishing" and "exceptional" phenomenon in global film history.[68] The claims of exceptionalism can be attributed to an excess of enthusiasm on the part of European and North American critics who were committed to the political and aesthetic projects of the UP government and of the NLAC. Likewise, these critics were invested in giving visibility to the Chilean exile experience precisely as a gesture of solidarity and a radical critique of imperialism and its effects in the cultural sphere. What matters most to me here is that regardless of how well attuned or not they might have been to the nuances of the films and political contexts they analyzed, all these writings thought of this corpus as a national cinema that was developed elsewhere because the filmmakers were banished from their homeland. Scholar Zuzana M. Pick's work constitutes the exception.

A daughter of Eastern Europeans who had fled the Second World War and immigrated to Colombia, Pick was the main scholar to write about Chilean exile cinema in the 1970s and 1980s, first as a doctoral student in Paris and then as a film studies professor at Carleton University in Ottawa, Canada. In between she married Leutén Rojas, a Chilean exile filmmaker, and developed close personal and professional ties with other exile directors. In a landmark essay devoted to Chilean exile cinema and published in 1988 in *Framework*, Pick offered a more layered view. She paid simultaneous attention to aesthetics and narrative form;

to modes and conditions of film production in exile; to the place of exile in the cultural imaginary of Latin American intellectuals and artists; and to issues of ideology, nation-building, and subjectivity. She went beyond traditional understandings of exile as political banishment and acknowledged that the formation of cultural identities produced by exile challenged ideas of nation, roots, place, and political militancy. This is what she called "the subjective paradox" of exile, a condition forcing ongoing reinvention and renegotiation of the exiled filmmaker's past, present, and future.[69] In the last paragraphs of this article, Pick identified a methodological gap between the critical tools and vocabularies available at the time and the demands emerging from the study of Chilean exile cinema. New methods were required to analyze a cinema that questioned the alignments of nationality with "specific territorial boundaries." Another critical map was needed. "Only then is it possible to go beyond the situation of exile as a monolithic response to a specific political event."[70]

It could be argued that Pick's critique was solved ten years later by the terminology that emerged from the scholarly literature devoted to exilic, accented, diasporic, multicultural, transnational, and world cinemas. This body of work has been precisely concerned with the gaps and cinematic nonalignments between nationhood, belonging, and identity that Pick identified. In this regard, her work foreshadows that of Naficy and many others, and it deserves wider recognition as a foundational contribution to the critical literature on transnational cinema.[71] But Pick's need for a new critical map is still here with us, two decades into the transnational and world cinema turns in film studies.

This book traces such a map in the forms of transnational interactions that configure a politicized remaking of world cinema. *Transnational Cinema Solidarity* proposes an alternative global film map, one in which no specific place is properly a center and distant localities, which would normally be conceived of as "marginal," work together to form poles of articulation that bypass national, linguistic, cultural, and political barriers.

STRUCTURE OF THE BOOK

In its narrative arc, *Transnational Cinema Solidarity* echoes an exilic journey, beginning with departure into exile and closing with the recent return and repatriation of exile prints to Chilean archives. In between, the three parts of the book examine the following key issues: (1) cinegeographies of exile (the range of transnational exchanges mediating the existence of this diasporic cultural phenomenon); (2) the politics of exile cinema (the aesthetic and discursive operations in the films, the different understandings of exile and resistance, the radical interventions of feminist directors, and the turn to subjectivity and the diary film); and (3) the return and the archive (exploring the symbolic weight of narratives of homecoming and the return of exile prints to Chile, an incomplete process highlighting that the "archival worlds" of world cinema history are built on relations of power imbalance). Parts I and III privilege historical arguments, while part II engages with more detailed forms of textual analysis to account for the films's formal procedures.

Part I, "Cine-geographies of Exile," refers to the movements of Chilean exile cinema across funding structures, nations, and film circuitries of different kinds. This part draws inspiration from Kodwo Eshun and Ros Gray, who thought of the concept of *cine-geography* as a way to map the exchanges between different political, industrial, and artistic movements associated with the "militant image."[72] Designating "situated cinecultural practices in an expanded sense," a cine-geography makes thinkable the transnational connections between forms of political organization; modes of film production/distribution/exhibition; and "discursive platforms" such as gatherings, meetings, and manifestos.[73] Going from the general to the particular, each chapter in part I explores one form of cine-geography: exile as transnational cinema, networks of cinema solidarity, and film festivals.

Chapter 1 maps out a history of Chilean exile film and video from a transnational perspective. The chapter tracks the journeys followed by exile filmmakers like Raúl Ruiz, analyzes different modes of production and circulation that move between the local and the transnational, and provides an overview of Cinemateca Chilena—an archive and documentation center that had no seat and operated simultaneously in various countries. Through the work of Cinemateca Chilena I discuss "nodes" such as Montreal and Havana—places that became poles of articulation for Chilean exile cinema even as they defied traditional notions of center and periphery.

Chapter 2 expands this introduction's argument of solidarity as a key concept in the vocabulary of the diaspora, a set of practices and concrete actions in support of the Chilean people, and a mode of political subjectivity. The chapter discusses the "solidarity genre" in Chilean exile films as well as the geopolitics of cinema solidarity with the case study of Chile and the German Democratic Republic (GDR). Next, I focus on more subtle forms of solidarity with a case study of *Les Borges* (Marilú

Mallet, 1978), a documentary made for the National Film Board of Canada's Challenge for Change program, before exploring issues of labor, friendship, and collaboration in the notion of "lived solidarity" as developed by Finland-based exile filmmaker Angelina Vázquez. A short analysis of Vázquez's *Apuntes nicaragüenses* (*Sketches on Nicaragua*, 1982) segues into the last section on the internationalism of exile film projects that deal with the Nicaraguan revolution.

Chapter 3 focuses on a distinctive instance of cinema solidarity: film festivals. It begins in Caracas (1974) and ends in San Sebastián (1987), with stops in Pesaro (1974 and 1975), Tashkent (1976), Havana and Moscow (1979), and Leipzig (1983). The ubiquitous notion of solidarity overdetermined the cinematic and political discourse in all these gatherings. Drawing on the literature devoted to film festivals, the chapter argues that these events became crucial tools through which Chilean exile filmmakers navigated the fraught geopolitical space of the Cold War. Film festivals were instrumental as exhibition platforms, as places of encounter between filmmakers, and as sites for aesthetic and political discussion.

Part II, "The Politics of Exile Cinema," is devoted to some of these debates. The condition of exile raised new questions, forcing Chilean filmmakers to redefine both the "political" and "cinema" as they had known them in the heyday of the NLAC and the UP government. What kind of films should they make? How could one situate oneself as an exile filmmaker in the public sphere? Part II explores some of the main approaches to the politics of exile cinema by focusing on filmmakers' discourse (as manifested in speeches, interviews, grant proposals, and project treatments) as well as on their cinematic practice (as evidenced by the aesthetic and narrative operations in their films). The chapters of this section deal with the two fundamental concepts of these approaches: resistance and subjectivity.

Speaking in Caracas one year after the coup, director Miguel Littin defined the cinema of resistance as films that "have as a priority to forge the image of a people in struggle and with faith in victory."[74] Chapter 4 calls into question this hegemonic definition and explores the plural meanings of resistance. The chapter discusses short agitational films; the early work of Raúl Ruiz and his "cinema of inquiry"; the feminist gaze of directors like Mallet, Vázquez, and Valeria Sarmiento; and the emergence of an exilic discourse as an alternative to the rhetoric of resistance with the film *Il n'y a pas d'oubli* (*There Is No Forgetting*, Rodrigo González, Marilú Mallet, and Jorge Fajardo, 1975).

Chapter 5 pushes filmmakers' exilic discourse further. It begins with a discussion of a sentence found in the project description of a film originally titled *Les lettres*, conceived as a transatlantic and cinematic epistolary exchange between filmmakers Marilú Mallet (based in Montreal) and Valeria Sarmiento (in Paris). In this document, Mallet and Sarmiento wrote: "Two friends dialogue from a distance, and their subjectivity becomes the measure of everything."[75] The chapter focuses on the multiple implications of this sentence and relies on close textual analysis to discuss three diary films: *Journal inachevé* (Unfinished Diary, Marilú Mallet, Canada, 1982), *Fragmentos de un diario inacabado* (Fragments from an Unfinished Diary, Angelina Vázquez, Finland/Chile, 1983), and *Wenn wir zusammen lebten . . . (If We Lived Together . . .*, Antonio Skármeta, West Germany, 1983). These films reveal themselves as highly experimental pieces in which the renovation of aesthetic forms is conjugated with a new exilic discourse that moves away from the logic of resistance as struggle and now centers on the question of subjectivity. The chapter ends by considering the implications that the notion of the unfinished has both for these films and for the overall arguments of this book, moving into its last part on incomplete histories of return.

Part III, "The Return and the Archive," examines the weight of return both symbolically, within the themes and forms of exile films themselves, and materially, by looking at archival practices. The two chapters thus engage with cinematic homecomings and archival returns, for return is the concept that connects the films as a form of cultural heritage with the specific historical condition that produced them: exile.

Chapter 6 traces a brief historical account of the return faced by the Chilean diaspora from 1978 onward alongside the homecoming routes of exile filmmakers. It continues with an overview of fiction films, first-person documentaries, and alternative video practices that engage with the question of homecoming in one way or another, followed by a discussion of the 1990 Viña International Film Festival as an institutional site of homecoming and as a performative act of "re-encounter" between the Chilean filmmakers who worked in exile and those who made their films in Chile. The chapter ends by considering subsequent waves of return after the end of the dictatorship, including the trend of second-generation exile directors whose contemporary work points to the ongoing and unfinished nature of the exile experience.

There is another angle to the history of return. Most Chilean exile 16mm and 35mm prints remain in an exile of sorts, scattered across national film archives and cinematheques, television archives, film museums, and university libraries throughout the world. In the last fifteen years, however, an important part of these films has "returned" home thanks to donations by filmmakers, the programming of special retrospectives, and the signing of international cooperation agreements. Chapter 7 tells the story of this incomplete return and charts its political and theoretical implications for world cinema history. The chapter distinguishes "return" from the more common notion of film repatriation, examines the current archival condition of Chilean exile cinema as a scattered body spread across the globe, and discusses four Chilean archives and the projects they have undertaken to achieve filmic returns from exile. The final section considers how archival online websites enable spaces of virtual collection that are not tied to a single location and that might be more suited for an exile cinema with various national affiliations and cultural belongings.

An "archival impulse" thus lies at the core of this book.[76] My approach moves away from an emphasis on "the archive" as a singular noun to be theorized—in general and in abstraction— and privileges instead the concrete histories of specific archives and their policies. I place a similar kind of material attention on archival documents themselves: unpublished interviews, funding proposals, handwritten annotations, catalogs, and especially letters. The correspondence I found in various archives has enabled me to resist the standard narrative of Chilean exile filmmakers as isolated artists and instead to highlight the plurality of affective, political, and cinematic bonds they forged despite their dispersal.

These documents also account for exile filmmakers' vitality as thinkers and theorists who were preoccupied with proposing new avenues for political cinema while they were concerned with understanding the condition of exile as they were enduring it. Encountering these documents has been a privilege, in the material sense that these journeys into the transnational archive of exile, spread as it is across the world, require the luxury of time and the luxury of grants and other university funds. (Not to mention the luxury of visa waivers and the privilege of a passport that allows a relative ease in moving across borders.) This encounter has also meant a reactivation of these documents, in the sense of bringing new life to them and making them speak through a voice, my own, that has attempted both to do justice to their meanings *and* to use them for what mattered to me the most: the tracing of an expanded geography of world cinema through networks of solidarity and the travels of forced political displacement.

PART I

Cine-geographies of Exile

CHAPTER 1

Exile Travels and Transnational Film History

What is Chilean exile film and video? The phrase often refers to a cinematic corpus made in exile. The September 1973 coup toppled the socialist government of Salvador Allende and inaugurated a seventeen-year military dictatorship led by Augusto Pinochet. Fearing for their lives, most Chilean filmmakers fled the country and went into exile, where they resumed their careers during the 1970s and 1980s—the decades that coincided with the dictatorship at home. Living in displacement, Chilean filmmakers made over 230 short, medium, and feature-length fiction films, documentaries, animations, videos, and works for television in countries as varied as Cuba, Canada, Finland, France, East and West Germany, Mexico, Mozambique, Romania, Spain, Sweden, the United Kingdom, the United States, the USSR, and Venezuela.[1]

Shot on 16mm, 35mm, and different forms of magnetic tape, Chilean exile films and videos varied in genre, style, and theme, though the majority were in one way or another connected to Chile. Many constituted examples of a radical cinema that sought to agitate and move viewers toward political action—like the shorts *Chile lebt* (Chile Lives, Juan Forch and Michael Börner, GDR, 1976) and *Quisiera, quisiera tener un hijo* (I Wish, I Wish I Had a Son, Sergio Castilla, Sweden, 1974). Several films were devoted to exile itself—*Fragmentos de un diario inacabado* (Fragments from an Unfinished Diary, Angelina Vázquez, Finland/Chile, 1983)—or to questions of Chilean history and politics—*Il Pleut sur Santiago* (It's Raining on Santiago, Helvio Soto, Bulgaria/France, 1975). In

FIGURE 7. Still from *Chile lebt* (*Chile Lives*, Juan Forch and Michael Börner, GDR, 1976). © DEFA-Stiftung/Michael Börner.

some cases, filmmakers found ways to discuss exile through a larger lens, thinking about displacement and migration in the wake of a globalized world: *Les Borges* (Marilú Mallet, Canada, 1978). They created fictional stories about historical events—*Noch nad Chili* (Night over Chile, Sebastián Alarcón, USSR, 1977) or films that functioned as ciphered political allegories—*Mémoire des apparences* (Life Is a Dream, Raúl Ruiz, France, 1986). They reflected on the meanings of the nation by interrogating other shared belongings and communities, such as indigenous identities in Latin America—*Guambianos* (Wolfgang Tirado and Jackie Reiter, UK/Colombia, 1981). They centered their attention on other revolutionary projects, such as the Sandinista program in Nicaragua: *Sandino* (Miguel Littin, Spain, 1990). In many cases they purposefully tried to do away with explicit ties connecting them to Chile or to exile. They made melodramas—*Notre mariage* (Our Wedding, Valeria Sarmiento, Portugal/France, 1984)—thrillers—*La triple muerte del tercer personaje* (The Triple Death of the Third Character, Helvio Soto, Spain/Belgium, 1979)—comedies—*Gentille Alouette* (The Colonel's Star, Sergio Castilla, France, 1985)—experimental films—*Lamento de una rima* (Lament of a Rime, Leo Mendoza, Netherlands, 1977)—and feminist documentaries—*El hombre cuando es hombre* (A Man When He is a Man, Valeria Sarmiento, West Germany, 1982).[2]

Even this narrow definition, that of a filmic corpus circumscribed in spatial, temporal, and political terms, presents challenges for film history.

In the preceding summary, "Chile" alludes to the nationality of the filmmakers and to the political and historical events derived from the military coup. The signifier Chile may function as a symbolic center, but a quick glance at the list of territories immediately calls for unruly expansion: too many countries, too many languages, too many films of different kinds.

Besides a wide thematic and aesthetic range, Chilean exile cinema is the result of a variety of modes of production found by filmmakers in the different cultural and political contexts in which they worked. Some made films for state studios in socialist countries, like Deutsche Film-Aktiengesellschaft (DEFA; East German Film Studio) in the GDR (Vivienne Barry and Juan Forch) or Mosfilm in the Soviet Union (Sebastián Alarcón). Other filmmakers benefited from small programs of multicultural aid or from the support of larger national film institutes, like the National Film Board of Canada (NFB) (Marilú Mallet and Jorge Fajardo), the Svenska Filminstitutet in Sweden (Sergio Castilla), or the Instituto Nacional do Cinema in Mozambique (Rodrigo Gonçalves). Some developed big-budget international coproductions (Miguel Littin), while others realized their projects with the support of independent companies (Angelina Vázquez in Finland). In terms of distribution and exhibition, Chilean exile films were released in theaters, aired on television networks, and played regularly in film festivals around the world. But they also enjoyed a life in a range of alternative exhibition settings, including film clubs, unions, museums and galleries, public access TV, and solidarity soirées—events that mixed film screenings with music performances and political speeches. This heterogeneity led Zuzana M. Pick to claim that Chilean exile cinema did not constitute a movement in the programmatic sense of the term.[3] For how do we speak of one body of work if the corpus brings together such disparate objects?

This chapter argues that more than a filmic corpus, Chilean exile cinema names the process by which filmmakers and institutions forge relations of transnational exchange that are mediated by notions and practices of solidarity. To examine the emergence and survival of this cultural phenomenon, I propose to suspend the emphasis on the "objects" it produced: the films. I want to focus here instead on the conditions enabling the existence of Chilean exile film and video: exilic routes and networks of production and circulation. In doing so, this initial chapter offers both a brief history of this exile cinema and a general framework for examining its transnationalism, understanding the latter as a lens that emphasizes movements across various borders: territorial, cultural,

FIGURE 8. Poster for a Chilean film program in Palaiseau, France, with exile filmmaker Helvio Soto in attendance, 1976. Fondo Carlos Barthou, colección Museo de la Memoria y los Derechos Humanos. Courtesy of MMDH.

ideological, geopolitical, and financial. This "specific" mode of engagement with the transnational method, avoiding conceptual abstraction, presupposes a form of mapping that echoes spatial theories of exile.[4] Karen Elizabeth Bishop understands exile as a "cartographical condition," concerned with the drawing of lines that provide us with images of the world that are inevitably marked by "tools of exclusion."[5] The strategy of mapping also lies at the core of Kodwo Eshun's and Ros Gray's notion of "cine-geography," a concept that "makes thinkable" and visible the transnational exchanges at work in the making of revolutionary cinemas.⁶ For my purposes here, *cine-geographies of exile* refer to the plural movements of Chilean exile cinema across nations, funding structures, and film circuitries of different kinds. If maps and imaged descriptions of the world "narrate the muted history of exile," what secret history does a cine-geography of exile trace?

Chilean exile cinema is the product of a series of transnational interactions between exile filmmakers and (1) film industry agents, such as TV stations and production and distribution companies; (2) national cultural policy agents, such as national film institutes or boards, national archives, and/or museums; (3) diplomatic corps in consulates and embassies; (4) filmmakers living in Chile, who smuggled out "internal" images to be included in exile films, traveled to participate in films produced in exile, or collaborated with exile directors whenever these were able to return to Chile to shoot; (5) exile communities, via the work of what were called "solidarity committees"—associations formed by local members of the host society together with exiles; (6) journals and magazines, which interviewed directors, reviewed films, transcribed roundtable discussions, and published essays on the trajectory of Chilean exile cinema; (7) scholars, critics, and programmers, who worked to ensure the visibility and availability of this cinema; (8) film festivals, which included Chilean exile films in their competitions or programmed special retrospectives; and (9) Cinemateca Chilena, a relevant institution that functioned simultaneously as an archive, research center, and production and distribution company for Chilean exile cinema.

This list indicates the broad matrix of transnational exchanges that shape the making and viewing of Chilean exile film and video. To historicize these interactions demands first knowing the routes of exile cinema and then tracing the networks of industry, solidarity, and friendship that sustained these routes. The metaphor of the route comes in as a spatial image to reflect on exile as a historically situated experience.⁷ Exile tells a story of travel. Specific routes mediate the travels and condition the biographies of all exiles. If they can make sense of their lives, it is partly because exiles know the paths they traveled and the journey they experienced. The same must be said about their work: exile cinema moves through various channels and spaces of production, distribution, and exhibition. If routes help visualize these passages of cinematic circulation, networks allow the imagining of intersectional points between actors and organizations—as exemplified at the end of the chapter by the case of Cinemateca Chilena.⁸

ROUTES AND NETWORKS

To exit, leave, leap across a territorial frontier: exile activates by definition a centrifugal force. The imprisonment of directors like Patricio Guzmán and others like Pablo and Leonardo de la Barra was a clear sign that filmmakers' lives were in danger. They had to leave. In exile, filmmakers' official status varied depending on the embassies participating in their departure as well as the involvement (if any) of international organizations such as the United Nations High Commissioner for Refugees (UNHCR) or the International Organization for Migration (IOM). The host nation's asylum policies and/or specific refuge policies for Chileans after the coup were also key factors in determining the legal immigration status of exiles.[9] Filmmakers moved between safe-conducts, temporary visas, residence permits, and sometimes official refugee status (which in welfare states like Sweden, France, and Canada often came with social benefits). This aspect should be underscored, as any exile cinema is the result of varying degrees of passport privilege and forms of state control through visa regimes and intricate immigration rules and procedures.[10]

Several exile filmmakers relied on earlier familial or personal connections. Juan Andrés Racz, film director and militant of the MIR Party, was the son of visual artist and Columbia University professor Andre Racz.[11] After the coup, Juan Andrés Racz studied film at Columbia and worked for the radical film distributor Tricontinental Film Center. In this role, he promoted Chilean cinema, attended gatherings like the 1974 Rencontres internationales pour un nouveau cinéma in Montreal, and participated in the making of *A los pueblos del mundo* (To the Peoples of the World), produced in 1975 by the Latin American Film Project in the United States.[12]

Other exile directors turned to professional networks they had developed with foreign peers, colleagues who helped them secure a new country to live in. Antonio Skármeta had written the screenplay for *La victoria* (1973), a West German film set in Chile, directed by Peter Lilienthal and produced by the public television network Zweites Deutsches Fernsehen (ZDF; Second German Television). Director and writer became friends, and after the coup Lilienthal helped Skármeta to obtain a residence permit to live in West Berlin.[13] Sergio Castilla was married to Swedish citizen and embassy officer Lilian Indseth.[14] Castilla therefore went to Stockholm, though he would later live in Paris, Havana, and Brooklyn, depending on the projects he was working on. These constant movements were due to the precarity of what Verónica Cortínez called his "solitary nomadism," an inability to form lasting bonds with the film industries of the countries where Castilla resided.[15] Other filmmakers looked for asylum wherever they were offered it, and through the work of various embassies they ended up in cities such as Montreal, Toronto, Stockholm, Havana, and East Berlin. Miguel Littin and Orlando Lübert boarded the same flight that took them to Mexico, a key country in the solidarity movement with Chile since it had offered asylum to Allende's widow Hortensia Bussi and had arranged for several flights for exiles from Santiago to Mexico City in late 1973.[16] Some filmmakers went into exile and immediately enrolled in film or visual art schools in places like Bucharest (Luis Vera), Amsterdam (Leo Mendoza), and London (Luis Mora and José Echeverría), while other exile trajectories predated the coup. Filmmakers like Sebastián Alarcón and Cristián Valdés were already students at the Gerasimov Institute of Cinematography (Vserossiyskiy gosudarstvyennyy institut kinematografii imyeni, VGIK) in Moscow when the coup took place.[17] Knowing that returning to a country now under military rule was impossible, they stayed in the Soviet Union and never left.[18]

And then there were directors and producers who simply followed their own films. The centrifugal impulse that gave birth to Chilean exile cinema was not limited to the travels of individuals alone. Film materials—negatives, original sound elements, work prints—also left the country and moved through boxes, trunks, ships, and planes that took them across various countries until they reached their destination, reunited with their makers. As mentioned in the preface and the introduction, that is what happened to *Dear Comrades* and *The Battle of Chile*, but it was also the case for several other films, including *Die Fäuste vor der Kanone* (Fists against the Cannons, Gastón Ancelovici and Orlando Lübbert, West Germany, 1972/1974). This film arrived via Sweden in West Germany, where the two directors edited and completed the work thanks to the aid provided by the Arsenal-Institut für Film und Videokunst (Arsenal Institute for Film and Video Art), then called Friends of the German Cinematheque, and the West German embassy in Mexico. Heiner Ross, head of Arsenal and cofounder of the Berlinale's Internationales Forum des Jungen Films (International Forum of Young Cinema), arranged meetings with the Mexican ambassador and the West German police to secure the legal permanency of Lübbert and his wife in Berlin for the duration of the editing process and until the premiere of the film at Berlinale's Forum.[19] Arsenal managed to get tickets for codirector Ancelovici, who was coming from France, whereas the flights for

FIGURE 9. Promotional flyer for *Die Fäuste vor der Kanone* (Fists against the Cannons, Gastón Ancelovici and Orlando Lübbert, Chile/West Germany, 1972/1974). Courtesy of Orlando Lübbert.

Lübbert's wife were covered through the solidarity efforts of the Spanish press Editorial Aguilar in Mexico.[20] While this summary may seem like an effortless coordination between different actors, these solidarity gestures require a complex chain of communications, with unforeseen problems at each stage. In fact, Lübbert's permits were delayed, and a former Mexican ambassador in East Germany was able to produce a visa for the filmmaker's stay in the GDR. Much to the surprise of police officers from both sides of the Berlin wall, Lübbert was finally able to enter West Berlin via the East and work together with Ancelovici on their film until its successful screening at the forum.[21]

Filmmakers' departures after the coup—and the various routes they and their filmic materials followed—do not exhaust the centrifugal force in Chilean exile cinema. Later in the 1970s and throughout the 1980s, this impulse persisted in the departure of raw footage that traveled abroad to encounter exile directors who integrated the footage into their films or who created new films entirely made of these images captured in Chile. It happened mostly with the work of film collectives—groups including members living under the dictatorship in Chile and others living in exile—as can be seen in *Recado de Chile* (*Message from Chile*, 1979), centered on the activities of the Asociación de Familiares de Detenidos Desaparecidos (AFDD; Association of Relatives of the Detained Disappeared). *Recado de Chile* has been credited to Guillermo Cahn, José de la Vega, Carlos Flores del Pino, Jaime Reyes, José Román, Raquel Salinas (in Chile), and Pedro Chaskel, Fedora Robles, and Nelson Villagra (in exile in Cuba).[22] As Elizabeth Ramírez-Soto recounts, after receiving the sequences that the Chilean residents of the group had shot clandestinely, Pedro Chaskel and Fedora Robles, who also provided the voice-over commentary, edited and completed the film in Havana.[23] The title indicates that the documentary is a "message from Chile," made to be sent abroad, to be disseminated as information about and condemnation of the crimes of the junta.[24] For these images to become a film, they needed to be smuggled out of the country and follow the routes of international solidarity that took them, once again, to Cuba's ICAIC, and later to audiences in film festivals around the world. (*Recado de Chile* premiered during the first Festival of the New Latin American Cinema held in Havana in 1979, where it received an award.)[25]

The transnational travels of raw footage continued later in the 1980s with independent cameramen such as Pablo Salas, Hernán Castro, Jaime Reyes, and Raúl Cuevas, whose images, especially documentations of massive protests against the regime, were distributed not only to international news agencies and foreign television networks, but also to Chilean exile directors who required them. *Memories of an Everyday War* (Gastón Ancelovici, 1986), produced by Ancelovici and Jaime Barrios for the NFB; *En nombre de Dios* (In the Name of God, Patricio Guzmán, Spain, 1987); and *Imágenes de una dictadura* (*Images from a Dictatorship*, Patricio Henríquez, Canada, 2004) constitute three examples of this trend.[26] These documentaries and the continuous recirculation and reappearance of sequences shot in Chile in multiple exile films are evidence of the prolonged ties that were developed between exile directors and those who remained working in Chile.

As this discussion shows, exilic routes are not random or innocuous. Movements followed by individuals and their work condition the future nature of each film as much as they determine the career trajectory of each filmmaker. A case in point is Raúl Ruiz, whose transits exceed the binary exile/homeland and whose success in the world of "art cinema" results from his ability to benefit from the transnational itineraries that were offered to him.

DISLOCATION, COSMOPOLITANISM, AND RAÚL RUIZ

On the afternoon of April 29, 1990, Raúl Ruiz went up to the stage of the Pacific Film Archive (PFA) for a Q&A after the screening of his dance film *Derrière le mur* (Behind the wall, France, 1989). At some point, a baffled and rather angry spectator interrupted Ruiz and asked, "Where are you located?" He could not understand the multidirectionality of Ruiz's movements in the first few months of the year 1990, going between Cambridge in Massachusetts, New York, Santiago, Viña del mar, Paris, and Berkeley, where he was for that Q&A. (Though according to the moderator, Ruiz wanted to be elsewhere: in San Francisco's Mission district, listening to mariachis.) Ruiz's response to this spectator was all the more baffling: "I'm not located. I try to dis-locate."[27] He was making a joke and got a few laughs from the audience. But the exchange revealed a deeper truth. It pointed to his experience between 1989 and 1990: teaching at Harvard in Massachusetts; making *The Golden Boat* in New York; stopping at "home" in Paris; shooting *La telenovela errante* (The Wandering Soap Opera, Chile, 1990/2017) in Santiago; and participating in the third Viña del mar film festival, just a few months after democracy was regained in Chile. Someone who is in so many places at the same time is effectively dislocated—out of place. Most importantly, the joke spoke of an endless sense of displacement constitutive of the experience of exile, exacerbated in Ruiz's case due to his propensity to be always on the move and to form worldly affiliations that are closer to cosmopolitanism—an allegiance "to the worldwide community of human beings."[28] More than the "claims of universality" that define the cosmopolitan ideal, Ruiz's transnational travels indicate the continuous relevance of the modern Latin American literary tradition that Mariano Siskind calls *deseo de mundo* (desire for the world).[29] This desire implies the search for a "symbolic horizon" that allows an "escape" from the boundaries of the national as well as a liberation from the marginal positionality of the exile subject.[30] Cosmopolitan filmmakers like Ruiz "force their way into the realm of universality," and in doing so, they challenge the Eurocentric mindsets that reduce them to a position of difference—Chilean, Latin American, *other*.[31]

By the late 1960s Ruiz had acquired a reputation as a unique figure within the cohort of the NLAC filmmakers—he had a relentless experimental vocation mixed with an unconventional approach to politics, less direct and less militant than his peers. The Golden Leopard award—the top prize—that he received at Locarno Film Festival for *Tres tristes tigres*

(Three Sad Tigers, 1968) established his name as an auteur in the European circles of art cinema. After the coup, Ruiz made more than one hundred films in France, Portugal, Germany, the United States, the Netherlands, and Taiwan, among other places. Ruiz's work was inherently cosmopolitan, in that his transnational travels implied "forms of prestige tied to a specifically international brand of cultural capital."[32] His prolific and widely revered career can be explained, in great part, by how he benefited from institutions that favored experimental work, like Institut national de l'audiovisuel (INA; National Audiovisual Institute) and La Maison de la Culture du Havre in France—the latter being a cultural center that Ruiz directed for a few years in the late 1980s.[33] In addition, Ruiz cultivated circles of intellectual, artistic, and academic friendship with a clear aura of prestige—including philosopher Jean Baudrillard and Argentine exile directors Edgardo Cozarinsky and Hugo Santiago.

Although fundamentally associated with France and French cinema, Ruiz's exile journey began in West Germany. He had a small acting role in Lilienthal's *La victoria* and, in October 1973, the German filmmaker interceded and got him to West Berlin via Buenos Aires, Dakar, and Morocco, just as he had done for Antonio Skármeta (in fact, they were both traveling together on the same flights).[34] Ruiz's wife and editor Valeria Sarmiento joined him a month later and worked briefly at the German Film and Television Academy in Berlin.[35] Early in 1974, Ruiz got support from the broadcaster ZDF for the making of his first exile film, *Mensch verstreut und Welt verkehrt* (The Scattered Body and the World Upside Down, 1975), also known as *Utopía* (*Utopia*). In the conception of this film, the original plan was to shoot it in Peru, where Ruiz would have peasants performing and reacting to situations that configured a form of utopian socialism (a world with no family, nation, or private property). But as Yenny Cáceres has reconstructed, during a short visit to Paris in February 1974, Ruiz and Sarmiento met with Brazilian exile cinematographer Gilberto Azevedo, who convinced them to shoot the film in Paris with the help and solidarity of technicians from Unicité, the production company of the French Communist Party.[36] This decision caused immediate tensions with the ZDF commissioning editors, who requested Latin American directors who worked with them to shoot their projects in Latin America.[37] The conflicts that derived from the preproduction of *Utopia*, plus the difficulties that both Ruiz and Sarmiento were experiencing with the German language, propelled them to move to Paris and switch projects. It is only after Sarmiento completed the editing of *La expropiación* (*The Expropriation*), originally directed by Ruiz in 1971 in Chile, and after filming and premiering *Dialogue d'exilés* (Dialogues of Exiles, France, 1974), that Ruiz would return to what had been his initial exile project, *The Scattered Body and the World Upside Down*, which was shot in the end in Honduras and produced and broadcast by ZDF in 1975.[38]

The first years in France were difficult, with scarce work until Ruiz's involvement with INA and its department of audiovisual productions. INA provided the space and the resources for the flourishing of Ruiz's experimental vocation: shooting film and media projects of various length and kind, and doing so extremely fast. The friendship Ruiz developed with the critics of *Cahiers du Cinéma*—Pascal Bonitzer, Serge Toubiana, and Serge Daney—and the special issue the magazine devoted to his work in 1983 were instrumental in his recognition as an auteur and hidden gem of European cinema. The introductory text by Toubiana called Ruiz a "magician" and equated the "mini lab" and "production workshop" he developed while at INA with the early studio of Georges Méliès.[39]

Around the same time, the encounter with Portuguese producer Paulo Branco led Ruiz to a series of films and TV series shot in Portugal and co-produced with France: *Les trois couronnes du matelot* (Three Crowns of the Sailor, 1983), *La Ville des pirates* (City of Pirates, 1983), and *Les Destins de Manoel* (Manoel's Destinies, 1984).[40] An invitation from Harvard University to teach during the academic year 1989–1990 was a key step in what would turn out to be a sustained engagement with the United States.[41] In addition to teaching at Harvard, Ruiz's US journey included working with the New York experimental arts center The Kitchen on *The Golden Boat* (1990), creating gallery installations like *The Expulsion of the Moors* for Boston's Institute of Contemporary Arts, and later going to Duke University in 1994 for a series of talks that would eventually become his *Poetics of Cinema* books.[42] The connection with Duke happened via scholar Alberto Moreiras, whom Ruiz had met in Santiago in 1993 during a seminar on the topic of his ZDF film, *Utopia*.[43]

This summary constitutes a small sample of Ruiz's exile travels. What I want to stress here is that his career was not the result of the "vertigo" of his extreme productivity or to some form of artistic genius.[44] Ruiz's work is inseparable from the personal and professional networks he forged; likewise, the multiple directions his career underwent are indistinguishable from the exile routes he followed. Sometimes these routes were enabled by existing networks (it is only through the Lilienthal connection that Ruiz began his exile journey in West Berlin and with the

ZDF channel); sometimes a route enables the forging of a new network (Harvard's invitation led to a plurality of professional ties to the United States). The auteurist lens that is applied to the study of Ruiz often elides these practical and material set of conditions.[45]

If transnational and cosmopolitan pathways partly construct Ruiz as an auteur, the same can be said about his ability to adapt to disparate modes of production. As Ruiz commented during the Q&A session at Berkeley's PFA in 1989, he was used to working in three budget categories: "low-low (under US$1,000), low (under $25,000), and comfortable low (under 100,000)."[46] These categories find resonances in the experiences of other exile directors. Depending on the film industries of their respective host nations, Chilean exile filmmakers engaged in several modes of production, oscillating between local, national, regional, and transnational affiliations. While Ruiz worked in all these modes, most Chilean exile filmmakers were restricted to one or two.

MODES OF PRODUCTION BETWEEN THE LOCAL AND THE TRANSNATIONAL

Marginal. Exile filmmakers work in the marginal modality as a way of replicating the "artisanal" modes of production developed by Latin American filmmakers throughout the 1960s.[47] Marginality thus involves carrying out a whole project on their own or at best with a couple of collaborators, avoiding funding structures tied to state or municipal funds, and eschewing coproducers and distributors; in short, situating themselves outside of anything close to an industry. Exile films made in the marginal mode are often short experimental or documentary films, they lack formal channels of distribution, and they remain bound to their local and national spheres (they do not resort to transnational sources of funding, and they do not circulate beyond their national borders). Most works by Jorge Lübbert and Leonardo de la Barra in Belgium, or Luis Mora in Britain, fit in this category. The marginal mode is also common when directors have recently arrived in exile and their careers are just starting. Consider *I Remember Too* (Leutén Rojas, Canada, 1975), a short documentary about exile children that uses their drawings as a main narrative source. *I Remember Too* was Rojas's first film in exile. It was made independently, though with partial support from the Toronto collective known as Film League and the collaboration of some of its members in sound and cinematography.[48] The group belonged to the radical tradition of alternative film production and occupied a marginal position within the industry. Nevertheless, Rojas's early experience with this short led to future films with the collective about labor and migration in Toronto that he either directed—*Canadian Experience* (1979)—or produced—*Up from the Bargain Basement* (Glen Richards and Jacquelin Levitin, 1979). Without necessarily planning it, Rojas had already moved into the realm of the interstitial.

Interstitial. The great majority of Chilean exile films and videos belong to what Hamid Naficy has called the "interstitial" mode of production: a liminal space, rather than a fully marginal one.[49] If marginality means to be situated outside an industry, interstitiality must be understood as a way of operating "both within and astride the cracks of the system, benefiting from its contradictions, anomalies, and heterogeneity."[50] Chilean exile films are made in the productive in-between space opened by these cracks, which implies varying degrees of border crossings and transnational interactions. *Los ojos como mi papá* (*Eyes Like My Dad*, Cuba, 1979), about the experiences of a group of Chilean exile children in Havana, was directed by Pedro Chaskel and produced by ICAIC. Chaskel's documentary is interstitial in Naficy's sense, in that it introduces exile protagonists and crew members in the heart of the Cuban industry, at the same time that it functions within the state apparatus, directly benefiting from its institutions throughout the whole chain of production and distribution. As Catalina Donoso Pinto and I have argued elsewhere, this interstitiality at the level of production is replicated within the documentary itself, which explores an unresolved tension between the childhood subjectivity in exile and the projection of an official revolutionary subjectivity, anchored in the discursive apparatus of the state of Cuba as represented by the school.[51]

Survival and developmentalism. The married couple Raúl Ruiz and Valeria Sarmiento turned to UN agencies like the UNHCR and the United Nations Educational, Scientific and Cultural Organization (UNESCO) to produce some of their early short films in exile: *Sotelo* (Raúl Ruiz, France, 1975) and *Le mal du pays* (*Nostalgia*, Valeria Sarmiento, France, 1979).[52] *Sotelo* offers a moving portrait of an exile painter, Raúl Sotomayor, in the Parisian apartment he and his family had been living in as refugees since late 1974. *Le mal du pays* focuses on the exile children living in social housing projects in the *banlieues* of Paris. I refer to this mode as "survival" because the couple turned to these UN commissions in order to put food on the table in a moment of great financial necessity. When they made *Sotelo*, Ruiz and Sarmiento had been living in Paris for about a year, after moving from West Berlin. Ruiz had already directed *Dialogues of Exiles*, but its theatrical release was scheduled for April 1975. Sarmiento, in turn, had yet to obtain a grant from Groupe de Recherches et d'Essais Cinématographiques (GREC) to make her first exile short, *La femme au foyer* (*The Housewife*, France, 1976). Given the precarity of their situation at the time, Sarmiento herself used the term *survival* to describe their need to take on any job that came their way.[53] In fact, by the time she was commissioned to make *Le mal du pays* in 1979, Sarmiento's only exile work as director had been the short film funded by GREC. These films belong to what scholars now label "developmentalist media"—a consequence of the involvement of UN agencies and a variety of nongovernmental organizations (NGOs) in the commissioning and support of media projects that tackle issues of migration, human rights, and inequality rooted in the political framework of developmentalism.[54]

Coproductions and TV commissions. Exile filmmakers favored the coproduction model in its various forms. In some cases, coproductions took place exclusively at the level of the national and involved public television broadcasters. Angelina Vázquez made films in Finland by relying on a mode of coproduction between the independent company EPIDEM and the national TV channel Yleisradio (YLE; Finnish Broadcasting Company). Marilú Mallet in Canada benefited from a similar model with the broadcaster Radio-Québec, but often involved the production company she and Dominique Pinel had created—Les Films de l'Atalante—and a series of other cultural and public agencies at the local/regional (Quebec) and national (Canada) levels. For example, Mallet's celebrated *Journal inachevé* (Unfinished Diary, 1982) was coproduced by Radio-Québec and Les Films de l'Atalante with additional financial support from the recently created Institut québécois du cinéma plus significant national grants from Conseil des Arts du Canada.[55]

Particularly in Europe, television was a key player not only as broadcaster but as financial backer, acting as pre-buyer, producer, coproducer, and sometimes commissioner. As Elizabeth Ramírez-Soto has shown in new research about "transnational experimental television," numerous filmmakers from Latin America, Asia, and Africa—together with diasporic and refugee directors from these regions living in Europe—benefited from TV commissioning and emerging forms of cross-national exchanges during the 1970s and 1980s.[56] Agencies like INA in France and public broadcasters like ZDF in West Germany and Channel Four in the United Kingdom were at the forefront of a model that favored transnationalism and experimentation in dedicated slots or "series" that blurred the boundaries between cinema and television, and which functioned as "a rehearsal studio on the fringes of television."[57] Ruiz and Sarmiento made short, medium, and feature-length films for the series *Das kleine Fernsehspiel* (The Little Television Play) at ZDF; *South* at Channel Four; and for a variety of slots coproduced by INA and French stations like FR3 or Antenne 2, such as *Rue des Archives* (1979), *Botaniques* (1982), and *Cinéma, Cinémas* (1982–1991).[58] Chilean exile filmmakers who were outside of Europe also participated in these modes of transnational and experimental coproduction, though less frequently. Marilú Mallet directed *Chère Amérique* (Dear America, Canada, 1990), a 16mm film made for the series *Parler d'Amérique*, coproduced by Canada's NFB and France's INA, and broadcast by Radio-Québec.[59]

These examples indicate the relevance of television and coproduction for numerous exile films that favor an aesthetic and mode of production that can be called "minor," especially experimental, short documentaries, or hybrid forms between fiction and nonfiction.[60] But coproduction models that involved television and national film agencies are also present in the making of feature-length exile films that aspired to larger audiences, such as *Prisioneros desaparecidos* (Sergio Castilla, Sweden/Cuba, 1979), coproduced by the Swedish Film Institute and Cuba's ICAIC, with the support of the Swedish broadcaster STV1. Television, as Ramírez-Soto has argued, lay at the heart of the discussions many Chilean exile directors—and Latin American and Third World filmmakers—were having in the 1980s.[61] Debates about television reflect changing attitudes regarding the structure of national film and media industries as well as the nature and function of transnational articulations to produce exile cinema. Television became a site of contention for some who were used to more artisanal and alternative ways of conceiving of the industry. For others, as the previous examples show, television—and particularly coproduction with European broadcasters—became an "indispensable link" in the making of exile and Latin American films.[62]

The exilic superproduction. Chilean exile productions that relied on big budgets and internationally recognized stars and talent, and which intended to appeal to mass audiences through strategies of transnational coproduction and distribution, constituted the minority. *Il pleut sur Santiago* (It's Raining on Santiago, Helvio Soto, France/Bulgaria, 1975) was one of them, with a soundtrack by famous composer Astor Piazolla; performances by European stars like Jean-Louis Trintignant, Bibi Andersson, and Annie Girardot; and a large-scale reconstruction of the presidential palace La Moneda in Bulgaria. The first and one of the very few Chilean exile films conceived for mass appeal, *It's Raining on Santiago* enjoyed a wide theatrical release in close to fifty countries around the world.

The other exilic superproductions were mostly tied to Miguel Littin, whose name was a synonym for a recognized style of large-scale historical epic with the masses as protagonists. In exile, Littin would develop an ambitious model of transnational exchange. *Alsino y el Cóndor* (Alsino and the Condor, 1982) was the first feature-length fiction film produced by the Nicaraguan Film Institute (Instituto Nicaragüense de Cine, INCINE), and it was coproduced with Cuba's ICAIC and with additional companies from Mexico and Costa Rica.[63] *Alsino y el Cóndor*'s transnationalism was mostly continental—restricted to Latin America—though it gained worldwide visibility through a robust presence in international festivals and an Academy Award nomination for Best Foreign Film, a form of soft power cultural diplomacy that served to challenge the Reagan administration's support of the Contras and rejection of the Nicaraguan Sandinistas. Littin's second Nicaragua film, *Sandino* (Spain/Nicaragua/Cuba/Mexico/Italy/Chile, 1990), was even more ambitious. Originally a three-episode series made for Radio Televisión Española (RTVE), the production history of *Sandino* is complicated and surrounded by rumors. The Spanish press published a series of articles reporting on the financial scandals behind the project, including accusations about the ways in which RTVE's director had backed the series, the supposed "bacchanalian" parties during the shoot, the overwhelming presence of Littin's family members in key roles in the crew, the cheap salaries paid to Nicaraguan extras, and the withdrawing of Spanish stars from the project.[64] Littin defended himself by claiming these attacks were politically motivated and were meant to harm the potential massive success of a TV series and a film that would tell the story of Nicaragua's revolutionary hero, the leader of a popular rebellion against the US occupation of the Central American nation in the late 1920s.[65]

As these examples demonstrate, the conditions of production of Chilean exile films were sometimes exclusively tied to local spheres of action. This happened to filmmakers who occupied a rather marginal position in the industry either by force or by choice. For the most part, though, the making of exile films responded to varying degrees of transnationalism. Modes of circulation and distribution echoed these shifting levels of transnational exchange, sometimes amplifying them or at times reducing them back to a framework of national and local influence.

MODES OF CIRCULATION AND DISTRIBUTION

Festivals and retrospectives. Film festivals were the primary venue for Chilean exile films and a major platform for ensuring their visibility.[66] Across and beyond the Cold War divide, festivals like Cannes, Berlin, Leipzig, Moscow, New York, Karlovy Vary, San Sebastián, Tashkent, Rotterdam, and London included Chilean exile titles in their official competitions and parallel sections and later programmed special retrospectives devoted to Chilean cinema in exile and in Chile. A robust festival presence often implied the chance of securing theatrical distribution in select territories. For example, the wide festival circulation of Littín's *La tierra prometida* (The Promised Land, 1973), with stops in Moscow, Cannes, Pesaro, and New York, was crucial for the film's subsequent release in France, Italy, Spain, and many other nations. In other cases, a festival recognition occurred after the exile film's domestic release—and even after its domestic television broadcast—as in Locarno's inclusion of *Il n'y a pas d'oubli* (*There Is No Forgetting*, Rodrigo González, Marilú Mallet, Jorge Fajardo, 1975) at its twenty-ninth festival held in 1976, where it received an honorable mention.[67] In this case, the festival delay can be explained by the relative absence of québécois cinema from the metropolitan centers of the art film.

Limited theatrical distribution in the metropoles. Regardless of how ample or small their budgets were, Chilean exile feature-length fiction films enjoyed limited theatrical releases in their respective countries of production—often restricted to a few select cinemas in capitals like Paris, Berlin, Stockholm, Mexico City, and Madrid. Official cinema releases meant the potential securing of distribution deals for other territories beyond the national, television sales, and sometimes presales for filmmakers' next projects. Most importantly, a theatrical release could attract press coverage and reviews that would increase the visibility of exile films. Valeria Sarmiento's *Notre Mariage*, a French and Portuguese coproduction shot in Portugal in 1984, had its premiere at Locarno Film Festival in August 1985 before its theatrical release a month afterward in Paris. Endorsed by critics like Alain Bergala and Serge Daney, the film benefited from the ample press coverage and glorious reviews it received, which were disproportional to the limited number of theaters in which it was playing.[68]

Regional/continental distribution. In at least one anomalous case, Chilean exile films enjoyed forms of distribution that were arranged on a regional and supranational scale. It happened to Sebastián Alarcón, who developed his exile career in Moscow with films produced by Mosfilm and benefited from a network of theatrical distribution and television broadcasting that reached most territories of the Soviet bloc. While it was most certainly an unreal exaggeration, Alarcón would often pride himself on being the Chilean exile director "with the largest audience," estimating that his film *Night Over Chile* had been distributed with seventeen hundred 35mm prints and seen by close to eighty million film and television viewers.[69]

Radical distributors and cine-clubs. In the United States and Europe, the 1970s saw a rise of alternative distributors dedicated to militant and radical films from the Third World: Tricontinental Film Center and Third World Newsreel (TWN) in the United States, Development Education Center (DEC) in Canada, the Workers' Film Association in the United Kingdom, and Cineclub Vrijheidsfilms in the Netherlands. Radical film distributors followed different models, however. DEC and TWN were interested in expanding the alternative circuits of exhibition by screening 16mm prints—working with cine-clubs, college student groups, and unions—and in developing workshops and other forms of audiovisual pedagogy with and for their local communities.[70] Other distributors, such as Tricontinental Film Center, catered simultaneously to the academic market and to commercial releases in traditional theatrical venues.[71] Cineclub Vrijheidsfilms functioned simultaneously as alternative production company, radical distributor, and cine-club, establishing a sustainable network of national clubs in partnership with community centers and activist collectives.[72]

After the coup, and given the role played by Chile's history in the political imagination of the Left, numerous Chilean exile titles were added to these distributors' catalogues. *The Promised Land* and *The Battle of Chile* were some of the most successful. In a blurb included in one of Tricontinental's guides, Karen Cooper, director of Film Forum in NYC, claims that *The Battle of Chile* "sold out every screening and turned away hundreds of people," generating "the largest audience of any program in Film Forum's 8-year history."[73] Proving that Tricontinental Film Center also rented its films with a lower fee to student associations and other community groups, the same catalog includes another blurb by a University of Houston cine-club.[74] The club's representative claims that *The Battle of Chile* gave the club the rare exception of "breaking even," charging just $1.00 for students.[75]

Public access TV. As mentioned earlier, television was an active player in the production of Chilean exile films. Regardless of the nature and amount of their financial involvement, television networks broadcast the titles they produced or purchased, amplifying the number of viewers that exile films had on their limited theatrical releases, usually reaching newer audiences in smaller cities and towns. Public access television—in its noncommercial, community-oriented, and narrowcasting model—constituted another platform of circulation for Chilean exile films, however limited to a niche audience. CUNY TV, the public access channel of the City University of New York, is an example. Its program *Cinema Then, Cinema Now* screened Littin's *The Promised Land*, followed by a dialogue with filmmakers Sergio Castilla and Juan Andrés Racz, in the first season in 1986. CUNY TV also partnered with other arts and cultural organizations. In November 1987 the gallery Exit Art organized the special series *Raúl Ruiz: Works for and about French TV* with the French Institute-Alliance Française and CUNY TV.[76] The series consisted of four programs totaling seven videotapes that had not been exhibited in the United States—all rare works made for television under the auspices of INA, plus the video *Images de débats* (*Debates*, 1979), commissioned by the Centre Georges Pompidou in Paris. CUNY TV's participation in this series involved the world television premiere of *Debates*.[77]

Informal networks and bootlegging. The informal networks of distribution that Ramon Lobato calls the "shadow economies of cinema"—"unmeasured, unregulated, and extra-legal audiovisual commerce"—offered additional spaces of circulation for Chilean exile cinema.[78] These informal circuits were especially relevant for exile films and videos in their journeys back into the homeland. Starting in the 1980s with the first waves of return from exile, filmmakers brought with them VHS and Betacam tapes of some of their own exile films or those of their colleagues. Such tapes circulated "hand by hand" for the most part in small circles tied to the local audiovisual scene, though in some cases they reached filmmakers who were abroad. Right around the time Sergio Castilla was participating in the *Cinema Then, Cinema Now* CUNY TV program, he met with a Chilean friend who came to visit in New York. As Castilla recalls, this friend was carrying a bag with three pirated VHS tapes of the trilogy *The Battle of Chile*.[79] The anecdote highlights that the sharing of videotapes of exile films constituted an important form of their consumption, even for filmmakers like Castilla who had other opportunities to view them. Throughout the decade of the 1980s in Chile, groups and collectives such as Teleanálisis and ICTUS TV developed their own alternative distribution networks, seeking audiences in unions, churches, community groups in shantytowns, and student organizations.[80] While their catalogs were mostly devoted to their own video productions, these collectives did sometimes include tapes of Chilean exile films. Director Angelina Vázquez has shared the anecdote of meeting with people who told her they had seen her film *Gracias a la vida (o la pequeña historia de una mujer maltratada)* (*Thanks to Life*, Finland/Chile, 1979) in a Chilean church in the 1980s.[81]

At last, the production and distribution of Chilean exile cinema had a recurring actor: Cinemateca Chilena. As a fundamentally exilic and transnational organization with continuous presence in the routes and networks of exile cinema, as well as with significant influence across overlapping spheres of production, circulation, safeguarding, archiving, and criticism, Cinemateca Chilena demands more dedicated attention.

CINEMATECA CHILENA AS TRANSNATIONAL ARCHIVE

Devoted to cataloging, archiving, and promoting Chilean cinema, Cinemateca Chilena en el Exilio (Chilean Cinematheque in Exile) was founded in April 1974 by filmmakers Pedro Chaskel and Gastón Ancelovici.[82] The organization was also called Cinemateca Chilena de la Resistencia (Chilean Cinematheque of Resistance). In fact, different accounts, including some by its two founders, indicate that the cinematheque's first name had the key word *resistance* in the title, though "after a few years" it would be changed to exile.[83] Archival sources offer contradictory information with regard to the founding and naming of this organization, which is further discussed in chapter 4. But one thing is certain: already by late 1974, both names were used in early official documents.[84] Given this simultaneity, in what follows I refer to the cinematheque simply as Cinemateca Chilena to avoid the confusion arising from its dual name.

In the Encuentro de Cineastas Latinoamericanos en Solidaridad con el Pueblo y los Cineastas de Chile (Encounter of Latin American Filmmakers in Solidarity with the People and Filmmakers from Chile), an event held in Caracas, Venezuela, in September 1974, Chaskel defined Cinemateca Chilena as the "logical continuation" of Cineteca de la Universidad de Chile (University of Chile's Cinematheque).[85] Founded in 1961 as the first public film archive in the country, the cinematheque was closely attached to the university's Center for Experimental Cinema (Cine Experimental), headed by Chaskel at the time of its dismantlement by the military.[86] Due to this position, Chaskel was also the secretary general of Unión de Cinematecas de América Latina (UCAL; Union of Latin American Cinematheques), an organization that grouped together the film archives of the region and that was instrumental for the development of the NLAC.[87] It is in this particular role that Chaskel, who at the time was relocating to Havana to edit *The Battle of Chile*, sent a note to address his peers in the Caracas encounter. Evaluating the difficulties faced by archives in the nations of the Southern Cone that were under military rule, Chaskel spoke of Cinemateca Chilena as the future center for collecting Chilean cinema. The declaration included in the proceedings of the Caracas encounter was similar to the one delivered during the Montreal *rencontres*, just a few months earlier in June 1974. There, Chaskel had claimed that Cinemateca Chilena's mission was to "reunite all filmic materials from or about Chile for their preservation, classification, safeguarding, and dissemination."[88] Thanks to the solidarity of Cuba's ICAIC, Cinemateca Chilena's holdings would be kept in Cinemateca de Cuba, the Cuban Film Archive. The first prints came from the Staatliches Filmarchiv der Deutschen (GDR State Archive) due to an exchange agreement with its director, Wolfgang Klaue, a deal secured after the eighteenth Leipzig film festival in 1975.[89]

Gastón Ancelovici's main contributions to Cinemateca Chilena were on the side of researching and cataloging the films produced in exile. In 1979, while living in Madrid, he created the Centro de Documentación de la Cinemateca Chilena del Exilio (Documentation Center of the Chilean Cinematheque in Exile). With the collaboration of scholars like Zuzana Pick (based in Ottawa, Canada) and Paulo Antonio Paranaguá (based in Toulouse), Ancelovici wrote pieces about Chilean cinema during Allende's UP government, worked on a series of exile filmographies, and initiated a critical reflection on the experience of Chilean exile filmmakers through articles and essays published in magazines and books.[90] The most important result of this research process was the annotated filmography authored by Pick in 1984 with the help of documents and materials gathered by Cinemateca Chilena.[91]

Even if the organization created in Madrid was a "research center," it also kept prints of twenty-five documentaries from the Allende years, which by 1981 were deposited in the collections of Filmoteca Española by Cinemateca Chilena's contributor Juan José Mendy.[92] Later, Ancelovici began working in the Médiathèque de Trois Mondes and established himself in Paris.[93] In this new phase the research center was located within the Médiathèque, which would serve as a larger institution from which to organize special film programs throughout the 1980s. Simultaneously, Cinemateca Chilena signed as production company of some Chilean exile films, such as *Recado de Chile* and *Chile, no invoco tu nombre en vano* (*Chile, I Don't Invoke Your Name in Vain*, Colectivo Cine Ojo, 1983). To further complicate things, a new entity emerged in the 1980s, Les amis de la Cinémathèque Chilienne, a not-for-profit institution that would function in reality as a production and distribution company. Ancelovici was its first director, but after he moved to Montreal in the mid-1980s the institution transitioned to an organizational structure led by a board.[94]

Summarizing, Cinemateca Chilena is difficult to classify under traditional labels because it adopted different forms (a film archive, a center for documentation and research, a production and distribution company, a not-for-profit foundation) and operated simultaneously in several countries (Cuba, France, Spain, Canada). Sharing multiple locations while lacking any fixed position, Cinemateca Chilena was by definition a transnational and exilic institution.

Evaluations of the work of Cinemateca Chilena are usually dismissive. The institution is described as a chimera, "un archivo de papel" (an archive solely in paper) whose impact and legacy were minimal, reduced exclusively to its two founders and no one else.[95] While there are aspects in the history of Cinemateca Chilena that remain nebulous (especially the proliferation of sister organizations tied to it), such a critical perception seems unfair. It disregards a crucial institutional effort to articulate Chilean exile cinema despite its inherently scattered nature. Cinemateca Chilena kept prints in film archives in Cuba and Spain, some of which would later return to Cineteca de la Universidad de Chile and to Cineteca Nacional de Chile (see chapter 7). It issued press kits and dossiers to facilitate the promotion of exile films. And it managed to produce dialogue between filmmakers, keeping track of what every director was doing regardless of their location. Ancelovici and Chaskel, together with their most frequent collaborators, interviewed directors and published essays; without these documents the study of Chilean exile cinema today would be practically impossible. The organization's structure—and especially its status as an extension of the dismantled University of Chile's Cinematheque—allowed Cinemateca Chilena to relate institutionally with film festivals, production and distribution companies, solidarity groups with Chile, and film archives. Two facets should be highlighted here.

First, in terms of circulation and exhibition, Cinemateca Chilena organized numerous screenings and special series across Europe and North America—whether in theaters in the form of regular film distribution, in solidarity activities happening in cine-clubs or at soirées, or as part of film festivals.[96] It is undeniable that this programming activity gave

Chaskel and Ancelovici a strong curatorial power in terms of the specific vision of Chilean cinema that was to be promoted. This vision can be mostly identified with what was called a "cinema of resistance"—films that denounced the crimes of the military Junta and forged the image of a people in struggle.[97]

Second, regarding relations with international archives, Chaskel presented the mission and work of Cinemateca Chilena in a report read during the general assembly of the thirty-first Fédération internationale des archives du film (FIAF; International Federation of Film Archives) congress held in Turin, Italy, in May–June 1975. The report focused mostly on the political violence suffered by the Chilean film community in the aftermath of the coup and therefore functioned as an update on the statements delivered the previous year in Montreal and Caracas.[98] In the following FIAF congress held in Mexico City in 1976, Chaskel chaired an open forum devoted to the relations between FIAF and UCAL; delivered a paper in a symposium on Latin American cinema; and showed the documentary *Fists against the Cannons*, one of the early films coproduced by Cinemateca Chilena.[99]

Even if participation in these congresses was marginal, Cinemateca Chilena's institutional presence in FIAF meetings should not be dismissed. It illustrates the need to be visible in global archival networks together with the desire to act as an official representative of the "Chilean" archival institutions, but in and from the transnational spaces of exile. In this regard, Cinemateca Chilena must be read as a bridge—an attempt to establish an institutional continuity resisting the radical rupture marked by the coup. It is clear that the work of Cinemateca Chilena, especially through the papers and documents produced by its research center, was geared toward the future—the moment in which democracy would be regained and the cultural apparatus of the state would be rebuilt on Chilean soil. Chaskel's figure is strategic as he himself embodies this institutional bridge: first as director of Cineteca de la Universidad de Chile before the coup, then as head of Cinemateca Chilena together with Gastón Ancelovici in exile, and later once again as director of the university's cinematheque when it reopened in Chile in 2008.

. . .

The "standard narrative" in the historiography of Chilean exile film and video claims that exile enforces a sense of isolation among filmmakers. The making of exile cinema is the product of individual efforts carried out by directors who are not in contact with one another and who are doing pretty much "their own thing."[100] It is true that the exile filmmakers living in the USSR or Mozambique were not always aware of what their peers in Canada or Venezuela were doing. But the focus on the isolation that exile filmmakers faced has served to obscure the personal and professional ties that several of them strengthened in exile. It has also obscured the dialogue between those who stayed in Chile—*inxiles* or "internal exiles"—and those who were forced to leave—exiles—reinforcing the idea that Chilean cinema during the 1970s and 1980s was comprised of "two streams" with total "lack of communication" between them.[101] The making of films like *Recado de Chile* evidences a series of transnational networks of support that included an active dialogue between those who remained in the country and those who left. Similarly, the assumption that the dominant logic among exile filmmakers was individualism has effaced the multiple connections that filmmakers and institutions sought to establish not only with other actors in Chile but with their peers in the diaspora. Cinemateca Chilena emerges as one of the most relevant efforts to develop transnational bonds between filmmakers, communities, and film institutions.

Through the work of Cinemateca Chilena we can also conclude the following. Even if the routes of Chilean exile cinema were varied enough and operative on almost every continent in the world, some places played a more important role than others. These were the nodes or poles of attraction of Chilean exile cinema: Berlin (East and West), Havana, Montreal, Paris, and Stockholm. In the circulation of Chilean exile cinema there were neither "centers" nor "peripheries." Nodes do not necessarily correspond to places where the largest number of Chilean exile films were produced. Similarly, cities that would traditionally be understood as peripheral, such as Helsinki and Maputo, acquired temporary relevance despite their geographic and linguistic isolation, mainly due to the dialogues created by filmmakers like Vázquez and Gonçalves with neighboring territories. There are cities that guided the interactions and exchanges within a regional and continental area, such as Caracas or Mexico City in Latin America; nonetheless, they did not become significant actors on a global scale. Madrid was a crucial site as well, but its status as a node of exile cinema was not stable. Finally, there were places that functioned as symbolic nodes: Nicaragua, as the new promised land of revolutionary processes, and Santiago in Chile, as the centripetal force calling exile filmmakers to return home.

Berlin, Havana, Montreal, Paris, and Stockholm became nodes because of the conjunction of several elements: film institutions' support (national offices and other funding structures), policies of solidarity with Chileans at the level of the state, the presence of a critical mass (various exile filmmakers residing in countries where large communities of Chilean exiles live), and the agency of specific individuals and the organizations they created. In the case of Paris, there was a symbolic function as well, for throughout the twentieth century it functioned as a center for cultural legitimation for Latin American intellectuals and artists, especially novelists.[102] Adding another layer for arguing for the relevance of Cinemateca Chilena, the nodes of Chilean exile cinema mostly coincide with the location and travels of both Chaskel and Ancelovici (the latter moved from East Germany to Spain, France, and then Canada).

As I have argued throughout this chapter, Chilean exile cinema should be seen as a process of forging multiple relations of aesthetic, political, and cultural production that operated on different but overlapping scales: local, national, regional, and transnational. The cine-geography of exile traversed these scales according to historically specific routes and movements. Chilean exile cinema functioned as a network of exchanges in which certain nodal points appeared. These were not fixed; rather, they moved in space and in time, following the transits of relevant actors such as Cinemateca Chilena, malleably adapting to different ideas and practices of solidarity.

CHAPTER 2

The Production of Solidarity

Genre, Geopolitics, Internationalism

In October 1973, five weeks after the coup, a solidarity soirée took place in the city hall of Saint-Ouen-sur-Seine, in the northern suburbs of Paris. The event included a musical performance by famous Chilean folk band Quilapayún; a poetry reading and homage to Pablo Neruda; and the screening of *El diálogo de América* (*The Dialogue of America*, Álvaro Covacevich, 1972), a documentary of an extended conversation between Fidel Castro and Salvador Allende made during the former's visit to Chile in November 1971.[1] The poster advertising the soirée included a red stain evoking a splash of blood. At the top were the words, "Everyone is concerned," and at the bottom, "No one can remain indifferent." Events like this were happening in every corner of the world in the weeks that followed the coup, and they would continue to take place throughout the 1970s and 1980s.[2] In big urban metropoles like London and Caracas, or in smaller towns like Bergen in Norway or Edmonton in Canada, these solidarity events proliferated quickly.[3] Some were planned specifically as either musical concerts, film screenings, poetry readings, or assemblies of speeches; others were conceived in the tradition of the soirée or the "week of solidarity" as evenings that mixed different kinds of art practices together with strategic forms of political organization.[4] Such was the case in Iraq's "Week of Solidarity with Chile," which included art exhibits, live music, and theater and took place at the Society of Iraqi Plastic Artists in Baghdad in June 1974.[5]

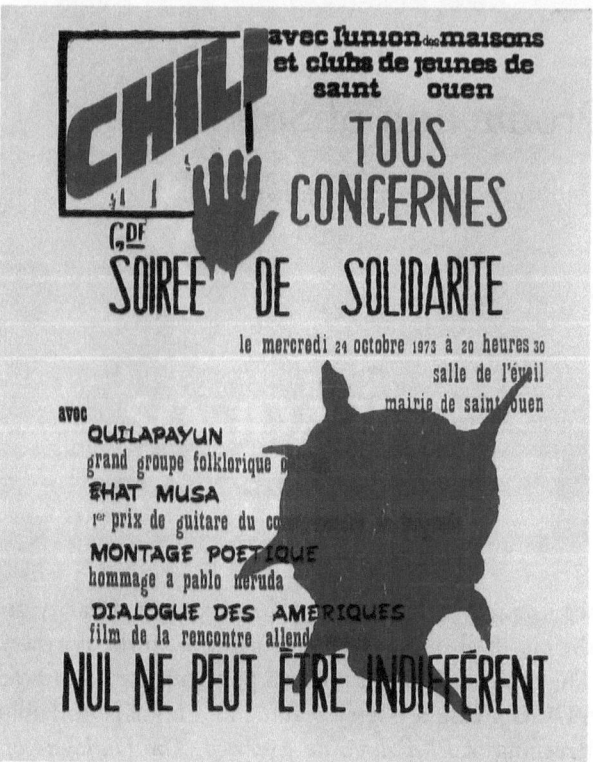

FIGURE 10. Poster for a solidarity soirée in Saint-Ouen-sur-Seine, October 1973. Fondo Eduardo Carrasco, colección Museo de la Memoria y los Derechos Humanos. Courtesy of MMDH.

The Saint-Ouen soirée was thus not unique, but the image that promoted it poignantly summarized the powers of solidarity for the Chilean exile experience.[6] Solidarity was expressed in the making and sharing of art and in the gathering of a community of different individuals reunited for a common political goal. The poster called for action and sought to evoke an emotional response from its plural subject, the "everyone" who would become a collectivity by participating in the solidarity soirée. Accounts of the Iraqi Week of Solidarity state that the cultural events "reverberated to such an extent" that they prompted authorities to impose "a set of measures against the participating artists so that the event's profound emotional and ideological effects would not be repeated."[7] The events of June 1974 in Baghdad highlight that the response that solidarity seeks is political as much as it is affective.

As developed in the introduction, by *solidarity* I mean a concept: the keyword in the lexicon of exiles, based on unity in the struggle against the dictatorship; a set of social practices—like boycotts, strikes, mass demonstrations, group fasts, the organization of cultural events or soirées, and the creation of "solidarity committees"; and a mode of political subjectivity—a community transcending national borders.[8] Transnational cinema solidarity, as an overarching term, bridges these three different realms with a wide range of solidarity actions that are specific to the film world.

The production and circulation history of most Chilean exile films is tied in one way or another to the building and sustaining of transnational networks of solidarity—that, in a nutshell, is the main argument of this book. This chapter examines some of the more precise meanings that solidarity adopted for the production of Chilean exile film and video. In particular, the chapter develops five variances of cinema solidarity: as a distinct film genre; as a form of geopolitics, as seen in the relations between Chile and the GDR; as the bridging of different cultural contexts such as Portuguese labor immigration, Québécois nationalism, and Chilean political exiles in Canada's NFB; as the "lived experience" and work ethos of a filmmaker like Angelina Vázquez; and as a mode of internationalism via a close engagement with the Nicaraguan revolution. The journey proposed in this chapter moves from a narrow sense of transnational cinema solidarity—both in its strictly filmic dimension and in terms of its tight connection to the Chilean exile experience—to a broader understanding that challenges state-centric, top-down models of solidarity. At the same time, this broader conception calls for an expanded cine-geography of solidarity in which Chile is no longer at the forefront and dissolves into other revolutionary struggles.[9]

SOLIDARITY AS GENRE

Whether in the ciphered form of a faux documentary in *L'ambassade* (The Embassy, Chris Marker, France, 1973) or as part of the militant tradition in *Lördags Chile* (Chile Film, Peter Nestler, Sweden, 1974) or *El tigre saltó y mató, pero morirá ... morirá ...* (The Tiger Leaps and Kills, but It Will Die ... It Will Die, Santiago Álvarez, Cuba, 1973), the solidarity film was fertile terrain for a variety of international directors interested in the situation of Chile.[10] The East German duo Walter Heynowski and Gerhard Scheumann were a clear example of this commitment, making four shorts and six feature-length documentary films about Chile between 1974 and 1985. The engagement of all these foreign filmmakers with the Chilean cause needs to be framed as part of a broader transnational and longitudinal history of solidarity filmmaking that, according to Rossen Djagalov, dates back to the films that Joris Ivens and Roman Karmen made about the Spanish Civil War in the 1930s.[11] Although there is still scholarly work to be done in terms of offering a comprehensive approach to the Chile films made by foreign directors, this section concentrates on the genre of solidarity films made by Chilean exiles themselves.

Several Chilean exile films, especially those that were produced in the wake of the coup, embody solidarity as a distinct film genre. The genre is most clearly at work in the documentary mode. These films are "about" solidarity on a thematic level; they strategically employ a series of visual and sonic codes that heighten an emotional impact on viewers; and they build a structure that conveys an understanding of solidarity, a "breaking down" of the concept into practices that are enacted on screen following a particular narrative logic. How solidarity works as a genre in Chilean exile film and video can only be defined through the combination of these three levels. However, a brief explanation of each of them separately is necessary to better understand how this articulation operates.

Solidarity as theme is the most straightforward of these levels. *Sången lever generaler!* (*The Song Doesn't Die, Generals!*, Claudio Sapiaín, Sweden, 1975) shows a series of music concerts and soirées organized by Swedish citizens in support of the resistance against the dictatorship. *Desaparecidos* (Missing Persons, Jaime Barrios, Penne Bender, Donna Bertaccini, Mónika R. Villaseca, US, 1979) concentrates on the testimony of three Chilean women during a short stay in New York to present the case of their disappeared relatives before the United Nations. In these films, solidarity functions as an overarching theme. That these films are "about" solidarity can quickly be seen by reading their synopses; such short texts condense the film's narratives into solidarity actions like demonstrating on the streets and organizing musical events or group fasts.[12]

The second level refers to the use of a recurring arsenal of visual and aural signs that are recognizable and read as emblematic by viewers. People with fists raised in the air, the bombardment of the presidential palace, the Hawker Hunter jets flying over the city, images of crowds marching and protesting, dead bodies near the Mapocho River, the recording of Allende's last speech, songs like "Venceremos" or "El pueblo unido"—these are all unavoidably present in Chilean exile films that fall under the solidarity genre. For Zuzana M. Pick, these "images . . . and sounds ... provided an emblematic set of affective and political codes through which the past could be safeguarded and preserved."[13] These signs situate viewers in a particular history—they allude, for instance, to the day of the coup—and they function as "identification devices" seeking a "dramatic and emotional charge" that surpasses their mere cinematic value.[14] Pick's last point indicates that the organization of this set of codes into a narrative ordering with a goal—moving viewers into political action—constitutes the third feature of the solidarity genre and is its most defining one. The study of solidarity as genre is therefore aligned with well-known forms of film genre analysis, such as Rick Altman's "semantic/syntactic" approach, which privileges the differentiation of the common traits or "building blocks" of a genre (semantic elements like a specific type of shot, character, or location) in dialogue with an examination of the structures (the particular kind of syntax) into which these building blocks are arranged.[15]

In Chilean exile cinema, the narrative structuring tends to mobilize a simple idea: the people, united in solidarity, will defeat the dictatorship. This idea adopts several variations. Some films are structured as musical documentaries tied to a "solidarity event." In films like *Canto Libre* (*Free Song*, Claudio Sapiaín, Sweden, 1979) and *Jag give dej en song* (*I Give You a Song*, Leonardo Céspeces, Juan Soto, Gastón Ocampo, Sweden, 1980), the performances of folk bands and singers constitute the films' narrative core, even if the concerts themselves are intertwined with other elements. Some films follow the "letter from Chile" structure, in which the goal is to deliver a message by the Chilean resistance, articulated from within Chilean territory, and disseminate it as truthful information to be spread throughout the world. This concept is already built into the titles of such films: *A los pueblos del mundo* (To the Peoples of the World, Latin American Film Project, 1975), *Lettre du Chili* (*Letter from Chile*, Marcos Galo, France, 1978), *Recado de Chile* (*Message from Chile*, Collective, 1979), and *Chile, no invoco tu nombre en vano* (*Chile, I Don't Invoke Your Name in Vain*, Colectivo Cine-Ojo, 1983).

Other solidarity films adopt a less prescriptive narrative structure, impossible to reduce to a single subgenre. *Matan a mi mañungo* (*They Kill My Manuel*, Jorge Fajardo, Canada, 1978) is a direct cinema documentary portraying a group of Chilean exiles and Canadians in Montreal to raise awareness of the crimes of the military junta. Most of the film is reserved for the everyday routines of the people going through the hunger strike and to the clashes that emerge between them. In addition to capturing the inner dynamics of a human group testing the limits of their bodies, the film addresses the conflicts arising between the Québécois "radicals" and the community of exiled Chileans. In *They Kill My Manuel* solidarity is neither totally dismissed nor celebrated in an uncritical fashion. The film makes clear that solidarity as a social practice may be the ground for divergent political projects, especially if these are shaped by asymmetries of class and race.

Missing Persons, in turn, was made in 1979 with the double purpose of transmitting the message that emanates from Chile in the fight against the dictatorship and to make visible the needs of that fight in the international arena. The film was coproduced by Chile Democrático (based in Rome and one of the leading organizations coordinating the political action of Chilean exiles against the dictatorship, with chapters and liaisons throughout the world, including one in New York) and Donna Bertaccini (at that time a film and television student at New York University).[16] It was made in two versions, one with voice-over in English and the other in Spanish, and it was codirected by Bertaccini, Mónika R. Villaseca (from Chile Democrático New York), educator and historian Pennee Bender, and Jaime Barrios. Barrios was a Chilean experimental filmmaker who had been working in the New York underground since the mid-1960s.[17] With Rodger Larson and Lynn Hoffer, he was also one of the founders of the Young Filmmakers Foundation in 1968, an association dedicated to creating film workshops for the youth in neighborhoods like the Lower East Side.[18] After the coup in 1973 and following the arrival of the first wave of exiles in New York, Barrios became more radically involved in the Chilean cause.[19]

The production conditions of *Missing Persons* evidence Barrios's permanent interest in collaboration as a creative strategy, as well as the need to bring political activism together with social movements, education, and audiovisual media. The film itself is a valuable piece of denunciation and political pedagogy centered on the figure of the *disappeared*.[20] The story focuses on the testimony of three Chilean women—Gabriela Bravo, Ulda Ortiz, and Ana González (the latter also appears in *They Kill My Manuel*)—who were present in New York to speak before the United Nations.[21] The interviews with the three women bring together the communicative and educational dimension of the testimony (transmitting a message to the viewer) with its affective dimension (moving the viewer and inspiring them to carry out solidarity actions). The moment in which González describes the horror of repeatedly visiting the Servicio Médico Legal (SML; Medical Legal Institute) to see if the corpses that arrived there correspond to those of her relatives summarizes the power of both dimensions. When González utters the phrase "Medical Legal Institute," a voice is heard behind the camera (presumably Barrios's) asking her to explain what institution that is. This interruption forces González to suspend for a few seconds the emotionality of her story for the sake of adequate communication for an international audience. Besides these testimonies and in addition to reporting on the functioning of the secret police Dirección de Inteligencia Nacional (DINA; National Intelligence Directorate), *Missing Persons* focuses on the political relationship between Chile and the United States. This reinforces the fact that every exile film is almost always a film on the local level, and that the solidarity documentary is necessarily about its own constituency.[22] In this case, the film aims to intervene in a specific field: critiquing and denouncing the role of the United States as a commercial ally of the Chilean dictatorship.[23]

Films like *Matan a mi Mañungo* and *Missing Persons* show how solidarity films turned to the denunciation of human rights abuses as one of their main goals.[24] In his transnational history of the genre, Djagalov explains the shift from "socialist transformation" to memory and human rights as the product of the historical defeat of leftist projects. Films that had been keen on the celebration of the building of socialism gave way to documentaries that memorialized this process or that emphasized social and collective memory as a strategy of resistance. In Chilean exile films, however, both dimensions are interlocked from the very beginning. Most solidarity films function simultaneously as a celebration of the socialist project of Allende and his UP coalition and as a denunciation of the crimes of the dictatorship—and therefore, as injunctions to remember by engaging in practices of solidarity. With its attention to diplomatic and commercial exchanges between the United States and Pinochet's dictatorship in Chile, *Missing Persons* also shows that the geopolitics of cinema solidarity vary in different contexts. The next section focuses on the relations between Chile and the GDR to closely examine the geopolitics of exile cinema and its broader cultural implications.

GEOPOLITICS OF TRANSNATIONAL CINEMA SOLIDARITY

As Claudia Rojas Mira and Alessandro Santoni claim, the Chilean exile experience transcended the polar divisions of the Cold War, in that exiles benefited from the solidarity of communist and socialist countries; capitalist nations; countries ruled by Social Democrats, Christian Democrats, and Laborist governments; and Third World nations in Africa, Asia, and the Arab world.[25] But the political meanings of solidarity inevitably varied in each context. The solidarity of Latin American countries united in anti-imperialist sentiments is not equivalent to the solidarity of the social democracies of Northern Europe, nor is it equivalent to the socialist countries of the Eastern bloc, which organized solidarity with Chile through the official apparatus of the state.[26]

Solidarity in the GDR combined the strictly geopolitical realm—establishing Third Worldist alliances as a means to defy the isolation imposed by the German Federal Republic (GFR)—with that of subjectivation—producing a particular form of subjectivity dictated by the state.[27] Caroline Moine recalls that the population was constantly reminded of the mandate of "solidarity with the oppressed peoples of the world" via a "festive mise en scène" of international solidarity, manifested in youth festivals, concerts, and film screenings.[28] The place of Chile in the discourses of solidarity in the GDR was indeed relevant, especially with Allende's electoral triumph in 1970 and later with the coup, which resulted in a dedicated "Chilean Center" within the structure of their solidarity committees.[29] Even though, as Moine has argued, the GDR strategically designed its apparatuses of solidarity as NGOs to give the impression of a noninstitutionalized movement, driven only by the commitment of its citizens, the truth is that solidarity with Chile was a top-down, state-sponsored policy in the GDR. It involved every level of the state apparatus, from the base to the Honeckers themselves—Erich, the general secretary of the Socialist Unity Party and leader of the GDR, and Margot, his wife and minister of education. The GDR provided support for a great number of exiles: jobs, apartments, and free education for their children.[30] East German citizens were actively involved in the solidarity committees and the "anti-fascist leagues," working closely in collaboration with the Chilean community.

This work coalesced in the international campaign to free a Chilean Communist leader imprisoned by the dictatorship: Luis Corvalán, the Communist Party's general secretary. Corvalán was one of the heads of the Chilean Left and probably the top political prisoner of Pinochet's dictatorship. After extended negotiations, he was exchanged for the Soviet dissident Vladimir Bukovsky and arrived in Moscow in late 1976, where he would live as an exile until 1983, when he returned clandestinely to Chile. Throughout his time in the Soviet Union he made frequent trips to East Germany, which had been a crucial nation in the international solidarity campaign to free him.[31] Two years earlier, the GDR had also received a visit from Gladys Marín, a young Communist congresswoman during Allende's government. After the coup, Marín sought asylum in the Dutch embassy in Santiago, where she would remain for eight months because the dictatorship denied her a safe-conduct. The DEFA studios produced two almost identical films about both figures' official visits to the GDR: *Gladys Marín* (Horst Winter, 1974) and *Wir werden siegen durch die Solidarität* (*We Will Triumph with Solidarity*, Joachim Hadaschik, 1977).[32] The films construct a double image of political perfection: the state that welcomes, adopts, and includes the exiles, demanding nothing from them and giving them everything in return; and the image of the model militant, the committed subject who goes to demonstrations, writes letters, and seeks funding—in short, the subject that enacts solidarity. In these films, the Chilean exile community appears briefly and near the end. The focus is on the East German nation as the bearer and producer of solidarity.

Both documentaries follow the same structure and are therefore perfect examples of the solidarity genre as developed by non-Chilean filmmakers. A model of the "visitor film" subgenre—leader-centric and bound to a circumscribed set of conventions including speeches and visits to factories—the narrative begins and ends at the airport.[33] The middle part consists of a succession of greetings and official ceremonies in which the lexicon and iconography of internationalism, solidarity, and anti-fascism are repeated like mantras. In *We Will Triumph with Solidarity*, the solidarity efforts of East Germans are shown to have a positive result: Luis Corvalán is freed from prison and arrives in East Berlin. An airplane lands, crowds wave flags, and the rescued figure descends and is greeted by state officials and lots of children. Joachim Hadaschik, its director, led the DEFA subdivision Camera DDR Group, responsible for making documentaries about Erich Honecker's official state visits around the world in the series *Begegnungen der Freundschaft* (Encounters of Friendship).[34] Only this time the film concentrates on a foreign visitor, and Honecker is the one who receives him. The narrative structure, nonetheless, is the same for all Camera DDR films. Compared to the Gladys Marín documentary, the mise-en-scène for Corvalán's arrival is much more impressive. The crowds are bigger and wait for Corvalán as his caravan passes through the streets of East Berlin. More than the quantity of the masses, it is the presence and weight of the state that feels more palpable in the film. Honecker greets Corvalán right after he descends from the plane. On a stage designed for the occasion and against a red backdrop, he speaks about the struggle against Western imperialism and utters, again and again, the sacred words: solidarity and anti-fascism. More speeches and official ceremonies follow, including a visit to a factory where East German workers give Corvalán a big check for the solidarity movement with Chile.

These DEFA films illustrate how solidarity transits from the abstract to the concrete. The image of solidarity they give is basic and works from the top to the bottom. Solidarity, as a concept, is broken down into a series of small events—going to demonstrations and rallies, raising funds, writing letters, and having children do drawings—all of which culminate in Corvalán's freedom. Even if "the people"—in the form of large crowds—and the organized citizenry—through the solidarity groups they have created—are present, the hierarchical differences between them and the party elite are quite explicit. The presence of the state and its leadership is inescapable, visually tied to an astonishing iconographic display of state power and aurally tied to the disembodied authority of the documentaries' "voice of god" narration.

After seeing these films, one could easily ridicule them as propaganda tools. This position fails to acknowledge the place that Chile had in the political narrative of the GDR and fails to understand the complexities behind the concept of solidarity in this context. As Jamie H. Trnka has argued, cultural objects produced in the GDR demand "a critical appraisal of solidarity without lapsing into a cynical dismissal of 'state solidarity' or an uncritical celebration of internationalism inattentive to the asymmetries of power within the international arena."[35] Reflecting on solidarity as a mode of political subjectivity shaped by affective dimensions is crucial in this critical appraisal, since the GDR expertly mobilized and mediatized this emotional aspect of solidarity. What Alberto Moreiras refers to as solidarity's "double conversion of us into other" can be seen in the relations between the GDR and Chile.[36] For the GDR, solidarity was functional to an official narrative predicated upon an openness out into the world, which in turn served to mask the politics of enclosing and surveillance within the East German state. But it was also functional to the narrative of Chilean exiles and of Chilean exile cinema. This narrative was based on the need to agglutinate individuals, groups, and nation-states under a common goal: to support the struggle of the Chilean people against Pinochet's regime. Once political strategies do not converge anymore, solidarity begins to crumble. Evidence of this is what happened when the Honeckers sought Chile's help.

The story of solidarity ties between the GDR and Chile spans forty years. Throughout these decades, important historical events took place:

Allende's socialist government, the coup that put an end to it in 1973, the exile of thousands of Chileans in the GDR, the fall of the Berlin wall, Germany's reunification, and Chile's return to democracy. These last three events coincided in the late 1980s and early 1990s. When Chilean exiles were going back to their homeland, Erich and Margot Honecker received asylum in Chile. This political history is also mixed with a family history, since a daughter of the Honeckers was married to a Chilean exile. The decision whether to give political asylum to Erich Honecker after he had faced a trial in Germany, and after he had spent two years in the Chilean embassy in Moscow, was Chile's first international conflict after the return to democracy in 1990.[37] Televised news reports show the brutal contrast between Corvalán's arrival in East Berlin in 1977, captured in *We Will Triumph with Solidarity*, and Honecker's arrival in Santiago in 1993:[38] no president to receive him, no grandiloquent speeches, no masses in the streets. The austerity of the mise-en-scène for his arrival shows how problematic the decision to offer asylum was, since the Chilean government faced pressure from the outside (Germany) and from within (the socialists in the government, who felt enormous gratitude toward the GDR because of how it had received and treated Chileans in exile). Now that political strategies were not equally convenient for both parties involved, a historical paradox began to reveal itself for Chileans: the state that had saved them from totalitarianism might have been totalitarian, too.

But throughout the 1970s and 1980s, the political strategies of Chilean exiles and the GDR state apparatus converged. Family memories found productive equivalences as well. The fate of Chileans—persecution, assassination, disappearance, and exile—activated how Germans were dealing with the aftermaths of the Holocaust. For the GDR, the rhetoric of anti-fascism, inseparable from the vocabulary of solidarity and struggle against imperialism, was another way to produce a "positive" image and to distinguish itself from West Germany. In relation to Chile, the GDR was quick to recognize the potentialities of these doubly affective memories, these mirror histories of displacement and anti-fascist struggle. As Jamie H. Trnka asks: "Where does East German antifascism stop, and Chilean antifascism begin?"[39]

Solidarity as a mode of political subjectivity remains trapped in the opacity of this double mirror, in which the GDR and Chile look at each other in fallacious equivalence. *Hitlerpinochet* (Juan Forch and Jörg Herrmann, 1975), a short DEFA animation film, this time codirected by a Chilean exile, epitomizes the convergences suggested by the anti-fascist

FIGURE 11. Still from *Hitlerpinochet* (Jörg Herrmann and Juan Forch, GDR, 1975). ©DEFA-Stiftung/Peter Pohler.

struggle. With cut out and stop motion animation techniques using paper, cards, and photographs, Hitler enters a picture frame with swastikas. He moves his mouth, and speech bubbles appear to communicate his message in German, Spanish, English, and French: "I shall eradicate Communism." A zoom in to his mouth leads to images of fire and destruction. Hitler disappears, but his jaw remains. A paper figure of Pinochet enters the picture frame, this time showing logos from transnational corporations, tanks, and jets. He grabs the jaw, puts it in his mouth, and delivers the same message as Hitler in the same languages. The paper figure turns into a shadow; the jaw remains white for a few seconds, then disappears. Fists emerge against a red backdrop, and the word *Venceremos* appears on top. The meaning of the short film is so obvious it is impossible to miss. Both dictators, although using different tools, are equivalents in their fascism. The final message of hope serves both Chilean exiles and the GDR: solidarity will defeat Pinochet, and it will make East Germany stronger.

These DEFA-made films replicate a state-centric understanding of solidarity. But not all modes of cinema solidarity followed the top-down structure evident in the state policies of the GDR. The next section investigates the production and reception history of the documentary *Les Borges* (Marilú Mallet, Canada, 1978) to examine how a public agency like the NFB mediated the meanings that solidarity could adopt in the local context of Quebec.

SOLIDARITY IN THE NFB'S *LES BORGES*

Les Borges (1978) was directed by Chilean exile Marilú Mallet and produced by the NFB, a cultural agency of the Canadian government whose legal mandate is "to produce and distribute films that aim to interpret Canada for Canadians and other nations."[40] More specifically, Mallet's documentary was made under the NFB's social activism program Challenge for Change (or Societé nouvelle in French). Between 1967 and 1980, Challenge for Change was an audacious experiment whose initial goal was to utilize film as a tool for social change, specifically by tackling the problem of "poverty in Canada through the production and dissemination of documentary cinema."[41] Democratizing the media, producing alternative video programs made by citizens themselves, and spreading the work of the NFB across all Canadian regions were some of its main achievements.[42]

A documentary about Portuguese immigration in Quebec, *Les Borges* focuses on the family of Manuel Borges, who arrived in Montreal in 1967. Favoring observation and eschewing voice-over commentary, the film addresses the conflicts surrounding migration through a generational perspective (offering a counterpoint between the father, a factory worker who never learned French, and one of the sons, an insurance salesman more adapted to Quebecois society). The film incorporates a gendered perspective as well, reflecting on the nature of domestic work and on the many migrant women who form the cheap labor force of industry in Montreal. In what follows I discuss some aspects of the film's production, distribution, and reception, since they shed light on the relations between exile, the local, and the transnational. They also point to the role of the NFB as a public agency framing the social meanings that migration and solidarity can have in the Quebecois context.

Les Borges is spoken in French and Portuguese, it is directed by a Chilean exile living in Montreal, it focuses on the topic of labor migration, and it documents the lives of Portuguese subjects. As such, the film is an example of what Hamid Naficy has called the "interstitial mode of production" of accented cinemas.[43] Primary sources dealing with *Les Borges* show how this interstitial position reveals itself through the strategy conceived by the NFB for the film's distribution. One document, dated April 1979 and sent to "all distribution agents in Quebec," includes a chronology of the film's exhibition history, a list of the community organizations that made use of it (plus others that could be potentially contacted), an interview with Mallet, and a description of every character and member of the Borges family.[44] These materials were accompanied by a pedagogical kit that further examined the social relevance of immigration, particularly focusing on the reasons for coming to Quebec and on the dilemma that several immigrants faced regarding staying or leaving.[45]

According to the exhibition chronology, a work print was screened during the Week of Quebecois Cinema in April 1978; that was *Les Borges*'s first public showing. Its official premiere took place a month later in the art house theater Cinéma Outrement as part of the Portuguese Cinema Festival. In June 1978 it screened during the Week of Cultural Heritage held in the National Library. In January 1979 it was shown for the first time on the national television channel Radio-Canada on a Sunday afternoon, and a few weeks later the film was shown at the Cinémathèque québécoise. However, these documents show that the main goal of the NFB was to reach out to local social organizations: schools, universities, centers for immigrants, governmental offices and social services, Christian groups, and unions.[46] The bonds with unions were particularly productive. In April 1979 a screening of the film was one of the central activities of the annual colloquium organized by the Fédération des travailleurs du Québec (FTQ; Federation of Workers of Quebec). The title and theme of the encounter was "A Common Country: Solidarity."[47] After the positive response from the workers, the federation decided to use the film in its network of unions to introduce its members to the problem of immigration.

The community-oriented use that was given to *Les Borges* demonstrates that, even if the film's production was marked by transnationality, its sphere of action was primarily local. Several reports commented on this trait. One review signaled that *Les Borges* "was not a film destined for the Portuguese; it is addressed to the Quebecois."[48] For Jean-Pierre Tadros, that nuance was fundamental for understanding the gaze at work in the film. In another article, critic Pierre Demers summarized the social relevance of the film in the following terms: "Our ignorance of international reality is such (and by our I mean the Quebecois), that we have cultivated for generations a certain xenophobia that we could quickly equate to what is considered racism in other countries."[49] It is worth considering this emphasis on the Quebecois collectivity as the ultimate ideal viewer of the film, since it challenges the assumption that Chilean exile filmmakers were directing works with Chileans in mind, that their "natural audience," as Pick claimed, were Chileans in exile and eventually Chileans in Chile after the end of the dictatorship.[50] Identifying the Quebecois as the ideal spectators of *Les Borges* also invites questioning what kind of role director Marilú Mallet played in this cultural landscape.

Mallet's first audiovisual work in exile was the video *Je ne sais pas* (I Don't Know, 1974), a thirty-minute piece that consisted of four testimonies with exiles who had been tortured in Chile. *Je ne sais pas* was produced and distributed by Vidéographe, a subsidiary of Challenge for Change/Societé nouvelle that has been described as the NFB's "subversive godchild."[51] Founded in 1971 as the "first independent alternative video production house in North America," Vidéographe became a model for future grassroots organizations working with video and favoring structures of self-representation by ordinary citizens and nonprofessional filmmakers.[52] Due to the high volume of proposals that Vidéographe received in its first years, the rejection rate was high. However, according to Scott MacKenzie, some projects received "special aid," and it is likely that *Je ne sais pas* was one of them, given the numerous expressions of solidarity with Chile that Canadians and the Quebecois had shown.[53] While Mallet was making this video she was also applying for funding to the NFB for her next project, the omnibus feature *Il n'y a pas d'oubli (There Is No Forgetting*, Rodrigo González, Marilú Mallet, Jorge Fajardo, 1975), for which she directed the middle segment, titled *Lentement (Slowly)*.[54] Zuzana M. Pick notes that the film's production was also the result of practices of solidarity, since the different unions of the NFB pressured the organization to grant funding for the project.[55] Mallet's third exile film was *Les Borges*, which led to her making *À force des points* (1979), another video about women immigrants and their labor conditions, this time produced for the Ministry of Immigration. Mallet's early career in Canada was thus tied both to the support of the NFB and to the subject of migration.

All documents of the NFB and every press report about *Les Borges* highlighted the exile condition of its director. The phrase "a film by the young Chilean refugee Marilú Mallet" was repeated with slight variations.[56] I want to emphasize three aspects of this phrase. First, the NFB—and in particular its more radical project Challenge for Change—needed to show migration from within. Already in 1974, when she was seeking

NFB funding for *Lentement*, Mallet criticized that Canadian films always portray "international communities from the outside (they are seen and studied by a gaze that is foreign to them)."[57] Her involvement with other communities' histories of immigration, such as the Portuguese, can be understood as a gesture of solidarity rooted in her desire to find alternative aesthetic paths to explore displacement. The second aspect regards Mallet's own position. The Chilean filmmaker was able to direct these early films and videos in exile precisely because of her refugee condition. She would quickly be typecast as someone who (only) made films about migration and displacement, and as someone who made them in the "social documentary" tradition of the NFB, of which she would later become quite critical. The third aspect of the phrase "a film by the young Chilean refugee Marilú Mallet" is perhaps the most important, as it suggests commonalities and solidarity ties between the Chilean exile experience, Portuguese immigration, and Quebecois nationalism. In interviews following the release of the film, Mallet would say: "I feel like an exile, of course, but the Quebecois also feel like exiles in this North American and Anglo-speaking continent, as if they were living in a mistaken land."[58] In fact, Quebec offers some particularities in this intersection between the local and the transnational. The linguistic exception, the sovereignty movement of certain sectors of society, selective policies of immigration, and a multicultural landscape in which numerous national communities coexist are all factors that constitute a complex social context for the identitarian definition of exiles and migrants, for their respective processes of transculturation, for the social positioning of their artistic practices, and for the possibilities of solidarity actions across different histories of displacement.[59]

While centering on a family of Portuguese immigrants living in Montreal, *Les Borges* establishes subtle connections between Portuguese labor migration, the Chilean exile experience, and the nationalist movement in the Quebecois society of the late 1970s. As its producer and distributor, the NFB and its Challenge for Change program mediate the transnational exchanges present in *Les Borges* and frame how the film can be understood. Focusing on the distribution and critical reception of this documentary shows how cultural agencies like the NFB played a relevant role in the making of Chilean exile film and video, not only because they enabled their funding and production. Institutions like the NFB determined the spaces through which these exile films could circulate—unions, libraries and weeks of cultural heritage, film festivals tied to national communities, television programs about migration—and negotiated their possible horizons of meaning. While transnational, the label "solidarity" is inevitably permeated here by the local: the specific political and cultural context of Quebec.

The previous sections have discussed solidarity in the form of geopolitical relations and as constitutive of the modes of production and distribution of a national cultural agency such as the NFB. The next section turns to Finland-based filmmaker Angelina Vázquez, whose approach to working in exile constitutes a compelling alternative model of transnational cinema solidarity.

ANGELINA VÁZQUEZ, COLLABORATION, AND "LIVED SOLIDARITY"

After the coup, Angelina Vázquez spent two years living clandestinely in Chile. As a militant of the MIR, she performed political duties as part of the internal resistance against the dictatorship. In March 1975 she left for Finland, where she lived for almost a decade. She later moved to Spain in the mid-1980s, before returning to Chile a few years after the end of the dictatorship in the early 1990s. The route she followed—Santiago, Helsinki, Madrid, Santiago—is inseparable from the way Vázquez explains her life: a daughter of Spaniard exiles and a filmmaker who ended her own exile in Spain as a form of closing the circle of uprooting that her parents had begun in 1939. Vázquez's movements were no accidents: Madrid responded to a deeper need to connect with the history of her family following the Spanish Civil War, and Helsinki was the result of her previous collaboration with EPIDEM, a Finnish production company for which she had worked when it made a couple of documentaries in Chile during Allende's government. Vázquez decided to live her exile in Finland because she thought this previous professional experience would help her when relocating to a foreign media industry. It did; her films were coproduced by EPIDEM and aired by Yleisradio, the Finnish public television network.[60]

In the middle of one of these films, *Gracias a la vida (o la pequeña historia de una mujer maltratada)* (*Thanks to Life, or the Little Story of a Mistreated Woman*, Angelina Vázquez, Finland, 1979), the main character, Silvia, sits in her living room and plays some music. She listens to Julio Rodríguez's "Otra historia de amor," a classic bolero of nostalgia for a lover who has moved on. A Chilean exile recently arrived in Finland, Silvia deals with the troubles of adjusting to a new home and of resuming her relationship with her husband, who has been waiting for her

FIGURE 12. Exile filmmaker Angelina Vázquez (right) departing from Santiago's Pudahuel Airport, March 1975. Courtesy of Angelina Vázquez.

in Finland while working for the Chilean resistance. In addition, Silvia carries a baby—conceived when she was raped by one of her torturers. As Silvia listens to the music, she looks lost in her thought. Her close-up is followed by seventeen short takes featuring unidentified places and characters: street vendors, children playing, people sitting in bars, façades, faces. Nothing unites these images except the fact that they seem to come from the same place and that everyone in them looks at the camera, as in an individual or collective portrait. Are these remembrances, fleeting visions from the past, an eruption of the distant home in Finnish land? If anything, as viewers we know this: a foreign world has taken over the diegesis, even if for a moment. No narrative explanation follows, and the sequence ends with Silvia's absorbed look, as she sits in her living room.

Another narrative emerges if one delves into the personal archive of the filmmaker. "What I liked the most about my film," said Angelina Vázquez in the Cuban magazine *Cine Guía*, "was the lived experience of solidarity amongst many Chilean, Latin American, and Finnish *compañeros* during the film shoot, and the enormous joy brought to me by that 4,000 feet can sent by my Chilean brothers."[61] What did she mean by this expression, "lived experience of solidarity"? Vázquez had asked her friend and filmmaker Pablo Perelman for images shot in Chile. In a letter

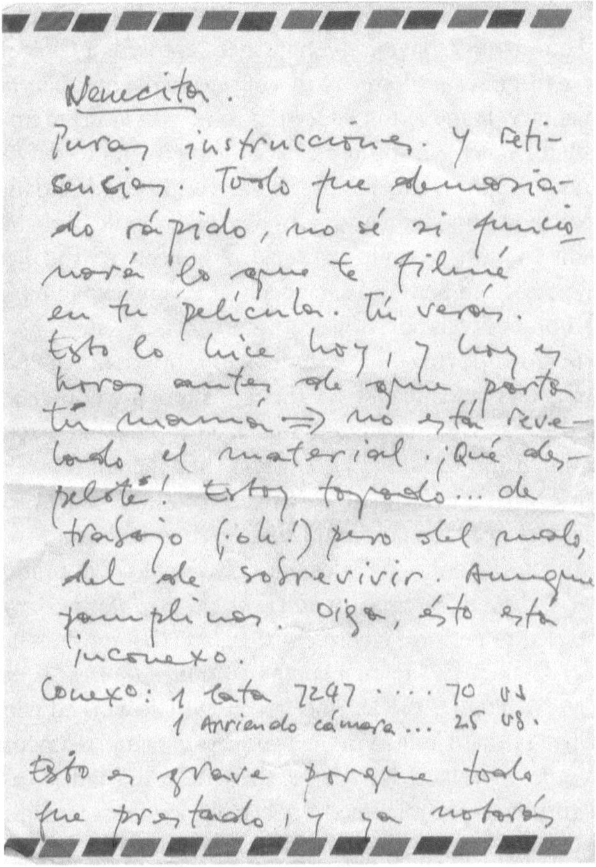

FIGURE 13. Letter from Pablo Perelman to Angelina Vázquez, November 1979. Courtesy of Angelina Vázquez.

she proudly keeps as testimony of friendship and cinematic commitment, Perelman wrote: "It was all too fast. I don't know if what I shot for your film will work. I did this today, hours before your mother left. The material isn't processed yet—what a mess! ... How to send you an invoice? I could, but today I can't."[62]

Letters such as this one challenge the "standard account" of Chilean exile cinema, a narrative that stubbornly separates those who stayed in Chile from those who left, concentrating on the isolation and individual efforts of filmmakers living far away from each other. Finland, not exactly the center of European film production, enhanced the sense of remoteness that the filmmaker experienced ("I am based in the Northern Pole," she used to say). But this is why she actively chose to fight against this isolation. For Vázquez, having these images captured in Chile in *Thanks to Life*, or returning clandestinely in 1983 to make her own homecoming documentary, *Fragmentos de un diario inacabado* (Fragments from an Unfinished Diary), constituted cinematic strategies to defy exilic distance.[63] Fundamentally, these strategies allowed her to remain engaged with her colleagues in Chile and with her fellow exile filmmakers—the only way she found to rebuild the sense of collectivity the dictatorship had taken away from her. And she achieved this by expanding the ways in which labor and collaboration are usually conceived.

In *Thanks to Life*, Angelina Vázquez did more than reach out to her fellow filmmakers in Chile and ask them to shoot a whole sequence and send it all the way to Finland. She managed to demand a requirement in the film's division of labor, a condition that she would subsequently stipulate in every exile film she made: the production had to hire another Chilean exile filmmaker and bring them to Helsinki to work with Vázquez. And so Rodolfo Wedeles, an occasional collaborator of Raúl Ruiz in Paris, flew to Finland to edit *Thanks to Life* in 1979; Shenda Román traveled to perform in *Presencia lejana* (Distant Presence, 1982); and Pedro Chaskel flew from Havana to edit *Apuntes nicaragüenses* (*Sketches on Nicaragua*, 1982). Since the crews she worked with were so small, having another Chilean in the production team "really made a difference," Vázquez explained in a letter she sent from Madrid to Santiago, addressed to the recently formed Asociación de Profesionales y Técnicos del Cine (APTA; Association of Film Professionals and Technicians), a sort of proto-union formed in Chile in the mid-1980s.[64] In this letter, Vázquez summarized her professional experience in Finland, but she also elaborated on that particular choice of hers regarding how to form a team. This decision was deeply tied to the meanings of exile and solidarity as well as to the experience of loss, in which the loss of a political project, a homeland, friends, and family is mirrored in the loss of a sense of collective work: "Never again have I had the feeling that I'm really part of a team. . . . I feel robbed of the continuity of growing together."[65]

Not being able to grow together: perhaps this was the definitive rift of exile, the most open of its wounds. It should not strike readers that this moving paragraph of private ruminations is included in a letter to an organization that will eventually become a union. These sentences remind us that, in exile, the domain of work is inseparable from the domain of emotions. They also tell us that exile forever erases the boundaries between private and public, personal and collective, family and colleagues.

Bringing other Chileans into the making of her films was not the solution to exile, but it opened the possibility to transform it.

Vázquez could not do this in her first film, *Dos años en Finlandia* (*Two Years in Finland*, 1975). Feeling simply lucky for having the chance to make it, she was in no position to demand anything. But by *Thanks to Life* she knew this production demand was as important as anything in the narrative or stylistics of the film. She knew this requirement spoke of exile as much as her story did. As Hamid Naficy claims, exile films internalize the conditions of their own production and become an allegory for the experience of their makers.[66] One of the central characteristics of exilic cinema, Naficy suggests, is its ability to subvert and transform the media structures that have allowed its existence in the first place. Vázquez understood this problem early on, and thus she chose to obliterate the distance that separated her from her exile colleagues and to subvert the marginality she experienced in her media environment by infiltrating it with other Chilean exiles. The goal was no other than to transform an isolated exilic film practice into the collaborative labor atmosphere she experienced before the coup.[67] In the practice of lived solidarity, to "work" is to make a film at the same time that it is a shared experience of learning through the dialogue between different political histories and different conceptions of cinema.[68]

A key factor in this endeavor was her complicity and friendship with regular crew member Anita Mikkonen, who plays an immigration officer in *Thanks to Life*, performs the voice-over narration in *Fragments from an Unfinished Diary*, and plays a protagonist role in Vázquez's subsequent *Sketches on Nicaragua*.[69] Mikkonnen's experience as a Finnish volunteer in Nicaragua's literacy campaign after the 1979 Sandinista revolution configured the narrative core of this new film. Its title indicates that the film is meant to function not as a "documentary" about Nicaragua but as a series of tentative "notes" or "sketches" producing a multiplicity of views on everyday life in the country.[70]

Developing the idea for this film, Vázquez wrote that her goal was to make spectators comprehend the relevance and necessity of their solidarity actions. The team behind the film understood "solidarity actions" as the "comprehension of the needs of others in relation to the cultural, social, and political framework in which the demand for that 'other' is raised."[71] *Sketches on Nicaragua* was thus conceived as a project to enact lived solidarity on multiple levels. The first and most obvious level is thematic, since the literacy campaign as an action of solidarity structures the narrative. Second, the production of the film responds to the need to build networks of solidarity, as evidenced by the demand to collaborate with Pedro Chaskel as an editor, who also brings his perspective on Nicaragua as an exile based in Cuba. Third, solidarity plays a definitive role in the film in political and pedagogical terms, since the main concept behind its making was the notion of traveling to understand and learn from a political project "other than one's own."[72] As I have shown, this double process of identification is at the heart of an understanding of solidarity as a mode of political subjectivity based on transnational "communities of feeling." Fourth, geopolitically, the exchanges between Santiago, Helsinki, Havana, and Managua that are present in the film account for the shifting geography of leftist projects in the context of the Cold War and highlight the relevance of Cuba, Chile, and Nicaragua in the political imagination of Latin America and the Third World.

EXILE, INTERNATIONALISM, AND THE NICARAGUAN REVOLUTION

Rossen Djagalov's work shows how throughout the twentieth century the cine-geography of anti-colonial, anti-imperialist, and anti-fascist solidarity filmmaking is a shifting one. Via major exponents like Joris Ivens and Roman Karmen, the solidarity genre travels from Civil War Spain to China, Indonesia, Vietnam, Cuba, and Chile.[73] These become centers of attention for leftist-oriented filmmakers, who travel to these nations to make films that seek to understand and promote their respective political projects. Chile (both in the hopeful UP years and after the bloody violence of the dictatorship) is one of the places and political processes that capture the attention of filmmakers as varied as Breny Cuenca, Allan Frankovich, Walter Heynowski and Gerhard Scheumann, Chris Marker, Peter Nestler, and Roman Karmen.

But Chilean exile cinema was also reinvigorated by its own internationalist endeavors. Rodrigo Gonçalves spent almost the entire decade of the 1980s making films in Mozambique, which had gained independence from Portugal in 1975 and had established a socialist state led by the Mozambican Liberation Front (Frente de Libertação de Moçambique, FRELIMO). Gonçalves's presence in Maputo evidences how intertwined the histories of solidarity filmmaking were. Initially an exile in Sweden, after his involvement with German filmmaker Peter Nestler codirecting *Así golpea la represión* (*This Is How the Repression Hits*, 1982) and later making his own *Rebelión ahora* (*Rebellion Now*, 1983)—both shot clandestinely in Chile—Gonçalves received support from the National

Film Institute in Mozambique. It offered its postproduction spaces for him to complete *Rebellion Now*, and then he remained in Maputo making a series of short documentaries for the institute.[74] These included a history of Mozambique from colonial times to the present told through painting in *Pintores mozambicanos* (*Mozambican Painters*, 1986), a film about the educational policies of the new socialist state in *Let the Flowers Survive* (1987), or a film focusing on the repatriation of Mozambican refugees due to the war with the apartheid regime of South Africa in *Espungabera: A New Dawn* (1987). In addition to Gonçalves in Mozambique, Pedro Chaskel made a series of didactic short films about Che Guevara for Cuba's ICAIC. In *Una foto recorre el mundo* (*A Photo Travels through the World*, 1981), *Constructor cada día, compañero* (*Constructor Every Day, Comrade*, 1982), and *Che, hoy y siempre* (*Che, Today and Always*, 1983), the celebration of socialism and internationalist solidarity is already entangled with the memorialization of the revolution through the figure of its most famous martyr.[75]

As seen in the previous chapter with Miguel Littín's Nicaraguan superproductions, Chilean exile cinema's own internationalism was particularly activated by the Sandinista program.[76] The Sandinistas, in turn, were inspired by the resonance of the global solidarity movement with Chile, encouraging the creation of solidarity groups and committees in different parts of the world.[77] The Sandinistas were also keenly aware of the power of cinema and other forms of visual culture and used them as integral elements of their insurrectional process.[78] After the 1979 revolution in which the Frente Sandinista de Liberación Nacional (FSLN; Sandinista National Liberation Front) defeated the thirty-year dictatorship of Anastasio Somoza, Nicaragua became a pole of solidarity film and videomaking.[79] While this step in the cine-geography of solidarity has been left out of previous historical accounts, the paragraphs that follow contribute to a recent and growing body of scholarship that considers Nicaragua as a key part in the development of internationalist film efforts and in the histories of global and Latin American political cinemas.[80]

The Chilean exile documentaries in and about Nicaragua begin with *Aufenthalt auf Erden* (*Residency on Earth*, Orlando Lübbert and Christiane Barckhausen, GDR, 1979), a documentary about East German militants who have fought during the Sandinista insurrection and later are recovering from their wounds in a Berlin hospital, and Marilú Mallet's *L'évangile à Solentiname* (*Gospel in Solentiname*, Canada, 1979), which focuses on the everyday life of the Christian community founded by priest and poet Ernesto Cardenal on the island of Solentiname. Produced by the NFB, and with Uruguayan director Mario Handler as cameraman and Mallet's then husband Michael Rubbo as sound recordist, *Gospel in Solentiname* ends right before the Sandinista takeover, with the premonition that Cardenal will become an important figure in the future revolution. Once the Sandinistas gain control of Nicaragua, other Chilean exiles travel to Central America to produce several films about the revolution, as seen previously with Vázquez's *Sketches on Nicaragua*.

Leutén Rojas and Leopoldo Gutiérrez, based in Canada, made *Nicaragua: The Dream of Sandino* (1982), a monumental historical and political analysis of the early years of the government of the FSLN.[81] The revolution is presented as the culmination of a long and complex process of independence, achieved by the unity of peasants and workers. Since it attempts a comprehensive overview of the process, interviewing and documenting the actions of every relevant actor in the revolution—the FSLN, the Christian groups, the peasants, the workers who organize factory collectives, the ministers of government—*The Dream of Sandino* paints a multilayered portrait of emergent social and political changes. Like many films that fall under what Djagalov calls the "socialism-in-construction" solidarity subgenre, Rojas's and Gutiérrez's work reproduces the official rhetoric of the FSLN, as exposed in interviews with several of its leaders.[82] Nonetheless, *The Dream of Sandino* allows room, if not for open dissent, at least for the uttering of doubts and caveats. At the level of form and structure, these doubts find expression in the constant cross-cutting between a plurality of social actors and viewpoints, and through a scarcity of voice of God documentary narration. The possibility of a counterpoint is also exposed via the more experimental musical choice of the German electronic band Kraftwerk, whose music adds an eerie quality to the revolutionary process and to the recurring images of the masses in the streets.

While the aforementioned works constitute examples of solidarity engagement with Nicaragua on the basis of limited and individual projects, the case of Wolfgang Tirado shows a long-standing commitment to the Sandinista revolution (like Gonçalves in Mozambique and Chaskel in Cuba). His Nicaraguan work also evidences the increasing role played by video and NGOs in the production of solidarity filmmaking. Tirado was a Chilean exile based in the United Kingdom with his partner, Jackie Reiter. Together they had made a film about indigenous people in Colombia called *Guambianos* (1981), then shifted their attention to Nicaragua. Their first project was a 16mm documentary produced by their company Tercer Cine (an obvious nod to the militant tradition of

Third Cinema), INPRHU (Nicaraguan Institute of Human Promotion, the oldest nonprofit NGO in the country), and CONFER (Conferencia de Religiosos de Nicaragua; Nicaragua National Conference of Religious, grouping a variety of Catholic organizations). *Gracias a Dios y a la Revolución* (*Thank God and the Revolution*, 1981) was made collectively by Tirado, Reiter, and Roberto Burgos. The film centers on the role of Catholic organizations in the Sandinista revolution and on the early years of the FSLN government. The documentary adopts the official rhetoric that celebrates the integration of Marxist principles with those of the Catholic Church—particularly via the Theology of Liberation school, of which Ernesto Cardenal was a foremost practitioner.[83] *Thank God and the Revolution* mixes observational sequences with peasants at work and women who organize in a cooperative to create a supermarket, with conventional interviews with leaders of the revolutionary government. The extended testimony of Mary Hartman, a nun from the United States, serves the double purpose of showcasing Nicaragua as a hub for international solidarity efforts (and a critique of US sanctions against Nicaragua) and of introducing the violence of the Somoza dictatorship. The montage sequence of the many Nicaraguans disappeared by the previous regime calls for an immediate connection to Chile. The footage of bombardments and planes flying over the city, together with Chilean Víctor Jara's song "Plegaria a un Labrador" (Prayer to a Peasant) playing on the soundtrack (all part of the repertory of affective and political codes of Chilean exile cinema, according to Pick), presents a vital solidarity link with Chile's ongoing struggle of resistance against the military dictatorship.

Thank God and the Revolution opened the doors of the country for Tirado and Reiter, who continued making documentaries about the revolutionary process and its challenges in Nicaragua. The subsequent works were all shot on video (Tirado and Reiter's company was relabeled Videonic), and they were also increasingly funded by a proliferation of NGOs and developmentalist funds of various kinds, including Oxfam America and CAFOD (Catholic Agency for Overseas Development), an international development charity. *Nicaragua, la otra invasión* (*Nicaragua, the Other Invasion*, 1984), made collectively by Tirado, Reiter, Mike Alcalay, Amina Luna, Oscar Ortiz, and Roberto Álvarez, focuses on the health policies of the Sandinista government. Its title offers a reversal of the concept of the "invasion," used here to refer to a "bombardment of solidarity," in the words of revolutionary leader Tomás Borge, who alludes with this invasion to the arrival of a delegation of medical doctors and nurses from the United States. The film weaves reenactments (showing how doctors treated peasants under the Somoza dictatorship), observational moments in which the community self-organizes, and interviews with members of the health brigades. The white US Americans who are interviewed are all severely critical of their country's war against Nicaragua. Yet the vocabulary of "aid" and "help" that they use, and which the video mobilizes via images of "gifts" being handed to the Nicaraguan doctors, illustrates a drastic transition from solidarity to charity.

This shift is also a direct manifestation of the different funding sources, rooted in the developmentalist tradition, that are backing these video-making efforts. Something similar occurs in *Nicaragua, Development under Fire* (Wolfgang Tirado and Jackie Reiter, 1986), which offers an in-depth examination of the economic effects of the Contra war against Nicaragua, and particularly of the mining of the Port of Corinto by the Central Intelligence Agency and US Navy Seals in 1983.[84] With funding from UK-based anti-poverty developmental agencies and charities like War on Want and Christian Aid, this video situates economic reconstruction (and the work of foreign aid) at the center of the narrative. Images of poverty such as naked children running around impoverished houses and streets resemble what Colombian filmmakers Luis Ospina and Carlos Mayolo famously termed *pornomiseria* (poverty porn).[85] These sequences dominate the beginnings and endings of *Nicaragua, the Other Invasion* and *Nicaragua, Development under Fire* and frame their narratives under an overarching logic of economic aid. In this regard, both the production conditions and the narrative structure of these videos reinforce the shift from internationalist solidarity based on shared leftist alliances to a model more akin to charity.

. . .

In this chapter I have discussed cinema solidarity as a distinct documentary genre, as a form of geopolitics, as an instance of social change in the work of a national cultural agency like the NFB in Canada, as a method of political understanding and redistribution of labor in the career of filmmaker Angelina Vázquez, and as a mode of internationalism through the engagement of Chilean film directors with the Sandinista revolution. In doing so, I have shown that the meanings of transnational cinema solidarity are plural and heterodox. Rather than being confined to a single political function—the denunciation of the military dictatorship and the call for international support—the practice of solidarity transforms itself depending on the political contexts it traverses and on the media structures it permeates. Likewise, the analysis has shown that the cine-geography of exile and solidarity is a shifting one, traveling between and across continents. The resurgence of Chilean exile cinema's internationalism with the advent of the Sandinista revolution in Nicaragua demonstrates as well that these were not separate plights "competing" for the financial support and solidarity actions of richer nations; rather, they constitute interlocked transnational histories of leftist alliances. The examples in this chapter have examined transnational cinema solidarity by playing close attention to modes of production and distribution. The next chapter looks at the cine-geography of exile and solidarity by focusing on exhibition and circulation via film festivals.

CHAPTER 3

A Film Festival Road Map

The Oberhausen Short Film Festival had a special program titled Solidarity with Chile in April 1974, which screened eleven short films about the nation's recent events. The selection included *La primera página* (*The First Page*, USSR, 1974), in which exile director Sebastián Alarcón reflected about Chile and the coup from his perspective as a film student at the VGIK, a short that received one of the International Federation of Film Critics (Fédération Internationale de la Presse Cinématographique, FIPRESCI) awards that year.[1] As Mónica Villarroel and Isabel Mardones note, during the festival a group of Chilean filmmakers signing under the name Chilenischer Widerstand–Kinofront (Chilean Resistance–Cinema Front) issued a manifesto in which they denounced the incarceration and torture of Chilean actors and other members of the film world. They also made an explicit call for solidarity: "In the name of all of us who are part of this front, we thank you for the solidarity you have shown us. We also thank you in the name of those who use cinema as an arm of liberation and in service of the revolution. Chile does not give up! *Venceremos!*"[2]

Chilean cinema held a unique position in the film festival circuit due to the widespread nature of the global movement of solidarity with the country. The presence of exile filmmakers at various film festivals, alongside the issuing of statements and manifestos like the one just cited, was frequent throughout the 1970s and 1980s. So was the vital discussion about solidarity and resistance that took place at these events, together with debates about the meaning of making and exhibiting films abroad as exile directors. Film festivals play an important part in the transnational history of cinema solidarity that this book recounts. They can be seen as one distinctive instance of the traveling geography of exile cinema that moves between and across Latin America, North America, Europe, and Asia—and between and across the First, Second, and Third Worlds.

This chapter presents a festival road map that begins in Caracas, Venezuela (1974) and ends in San Sebastián, Spain (1987), with stops in Pesaro, Italy (1974–75), Havana in Cuba and Moscow in the Soviet Union (both in 1979), and Leipzig, East Germany (1983). These festivals became crucial tools through which Chilean exile filmmakers navigated the fraught geopolitical map of the 1970s and 1980s—a map largely shaped by the Cold War, though the transnational exchanges that enabled the exhibition of Chilean exile films and videos in film festivals exceeded the hegemonic division of the East/West binary. For this reason, a study of the presence of Chilean exile cinema at global film festivals—and of the alliances and encounters that mediated this presence—needs to go beyond the model of cultural diplomacy "where state objectives determine the value of cultural exchange."[3] Questions of international relations play a vital role, especially in the socialist film festival circuit, but so do festivals as institutional markers of taste, as mediators of the political significance of films, as professional meetings for industry players, and as ephemeral gatherings suited to the social performance of solidarity.

In this chapter I argue that film festivals were instrumental for Chilean exile cinema as exhibition platforms, as places of encounter between exile filmmakers, and as sites for aesthetic and political discussion. In tracing this main argument and in following the road map from Caracas to San Sebastián, the chapter discusses three overlapping issues. First is the work of programmers and festival organizers, whose curatorial decisions shaped the ongoing discussions carried on by exile directors. Second is the affective domain of festivals, as events where filmmakers renewed ties of friendship and built new bonds, especially with critics, producers, and scholars, who would turn out to be key figures in the global circulation of their films. Third is the debates between filmmakers regarding how to conceive of the political nature of cinema under life in exile. The main idea in this debate is the notion of a cinema of resistance, which filmmakers opposed to that of an exile cinema.

Certainly other festivals played a significant function in the circulation of Chilean exile films and videos, besides those highlighted in this chapter. Cannes was a highly visible forum in 1974, and both its main competition and its Quinzaine des réalisateurs (Directors' Fortnight) section screened films by Patricio Guzmán, Raúl Ruiz, and Miguel Littin throughout the 1970s and 1980s.[4] With a more decided emphasis on experimental narrative forms, Locarno and Rotterdam were particularly important for Ruiz's career.[5] The Internationales Forum des Jungen Films (International Forum of Young Cinema) section of the Berlinale (also known as Forum), organized by the Arsenal-Institut für Film und Videokunst (Arsenal Institute for Film and Video Art) since 1971, deserves a special mention, as Chilean exile films and videos were regularly programmed in this parallel section of the festival. This presence was a direct result of the wide-ranging solidarity ties between West German and Chilean filmmakers, and particularly of Arsenal's long-standing commitment to preserving and promoting Chilean cinema.[6]

While the history of Chilean exile films and videos in film festivals cannot ignore these examples, the purpose of this chapter is to discuss a broader range of festivals that moves beyond well-known A-list events like Cannes and Berlin and beyond an auteurist approach that privileges festivals' engagement with specific directors or with specific films.[7] In pursuing this goal, I favor the dialogues that can be traced from one event to the other throughout two decades and across different continents and geopolitical regions. Besides the availability of archival documents, recounting how ideas of exile cinema and solidarity traveled and were reprised in later events has been a key principle in deciding which festivals to focus on. The chapter is devoted to festivals as a specific type of cinematic gathering and market, but the road map presented here also includes other kinds of film meetings, such as the Encounter of Latin American Filmmakers held in Caracas 1974, as well as other programs not necessarily tied to a festival, like the Antifascist Week of Cinema that took place in Volgograd in 1975. Kodwo Eshun's and Ros Gray's idea of a *cine-geography* is once again relevant in this regard, particularly for their emphasis on the "discursive platforms" that various film meetings, gatherings, and manifestos enable.[8] Film festivals and encounters are thus part of the transnational connections that "make thinkable" the expanded cine-geography of a politically oriented cinema like Chilean exile film and video.[9]

The festival road map that follows works as a double history. It is an inquiry into film festivals as cultural and geopolitical actors in the making of world cinema, as well as into their function as "contact zones" allowing for the unstable encounter and clash between disparate cultures, languages, cinematic traditions, and political formations.[10] In addition, the chapter presents a history of Chilean exile film and video told *through* film festivals. This is why the choice of festivals includes the events that took place at the Leipzig 1983 and San Sebastián 1987 festivals—which screened the largest special retrospectives—and others like Pesaro and Havana, which were instrumental in the programmatic framing of this cinema as an example of radical exilic filmmaking. The third Viña del mar International Film Festival, which took place in Chile in 1990, is also fundamental in a history of Chilean exile cinema told through film festivals. But given that its creation and its discursive framing were tied to issues of return—the return to democracy, the homecoming of exile directors who had not been in the country since they left after the coup, the "return" of films that had never screened in Chile—this festival is discussed separately in chapter 6 to examine it as a site of institutional homecoming.

Finally, the history of Chilean exile cinema at film festivals is also the discursive history of how exile filmmakers conceived their work. As Zuzana M. Pick explains, in order to accept the heterogeneity of their cinematic practice, exile directors had to "pass through a stage of bitter polemics."[11] These polemics—about how to relate to the transnational movement of solidarity with Chile, how to define a cinema of exile and resistance, what kind of stories to tell, how to participate in coproduction exchanges with television networks or in emerging festival markets—expressed themselves quite clearly in many festivals, and this chapter traces some of the most relevant iterations moving from one event to the other, and from one geographical region to the next.

CARACAS 1974 (LATIN AMERICA)

The Encuentro de Cineastas Latinoamericanos en Solidaridad con el Pueblo y los Cineastas de Chile (Encounter of Latin American Filmmakers in Solidarity with the People and Filmmakers from Chile) in Caracas, Venezuela, was the culmination of a series of recent experiences—meetings at which radical filmmakers from the Third World discussed the challenges of film production and distribution in tandem with their national struggles of liberation and decolonization. The Caracas encounter would not have occurred without these precedents, gatherings where the notion of solidarity was ubiquitous and overdetermined the cinematic and political discourse. For example, the published resolutions of the Third World Filmmakers Meeting in Algiers in December 1973 included a condemnation of the Chilean coup, as well as a recommendation for coproductions within the countries of the Third World to manifest "anti-imperialist solidarity."[12] The next Third World Filmmakers Meeting in Buenos Aires (May 1974) included similar resolutions, and so did the following tricontinental gathering—the Rencontres internationales pour un nouveau cinéma in Montréal (International Encounter for a New Cinema in Montreal) in June 1974.[13] Mariano Mestman's account of this event highlights the presence of Chilean exiles. Besides the already frequent denunciations of the coup and violence exerted by the dictatorship, in the Montreal *rencontres* Chilean exile filmmakers participated as directors, polemists, archivists, and distributors. Miguel Littin screened his *La tierra prometida* (The Promised Land, 1973) and had a debate with Argentine Fernando Solanas, codirector *of La hora de los hornos* (The Hour of the Furnaces, 1968). Pedro Chaskel sent documents and resolutions in his role of director of Cinemateca Chilena.[14] Juan Andrés Racz worked for the celebrated radical distributor Tricontinental Film Center, which distributed two Chilean films that screened during the Montreal encounter: *The Promised Land* and *Cuando despierta el pueblo* (When the People Awakens, 1973), a documentary made before the coup by the Latin American Film Project collective, which included Racz.[15]

When more than forty Latin American filmmakers thus gathered in Caracas (September 5–11, 1974) for their *encuentro*, they sought to situate themselves within this recent tradition of Third World meetings. They also sought to reaffirm a particular genealogy of the NLAC. Following the events held in Viña del Mar, Chile, in 1967 and 1969, and in Mérida, Venezuela, in 1968, Caracas presented itself as the fourth installment in a series of gatherings in which Latin American filmmakers defined their practice as a cinema of cultural decolonization and national liberation. Regarding tricontinental meetings, the introduction to the statement issued by the filmmakers attending Caracas mentioned these encounters only in passing, downplaying the Third Worldist impetus that guided them.[16] In Caracas, the creation of the specifically *Latin American* Filmmakers Committee—echoing but independent from the Third World Cinema Committee founded in Algiers—thus signaled a move from tricontinentalism to continentalism.

In this shift, the encounter of different peripheries became less important than the affirmation of Latin America as its own center. The recent proliferation of military dictatorships in the Southern Cone had changed the geopolitical landscape.[17] In this new context, filmmakers claimed that the Latin American Filmmakers Committee opened an organized front of struggle with urgent tasks to accomplish. "Our responsibility is to demarcate, in every one of our countries, the line separating imperialism and its intermediaries from all those forces struggling for true national liberation."[18] In this struggle, the Chilean case—with the contested experience of Chilefilms as a state-owned film production company; the right wing's ideological control of the media; and the imprisonment, torture, and exile suffered by many members of the film world—served as the most recent cautionary tale for Latin American filmmakers.

As the title of the event indicates, the Caracas encounter was an expression of what organizers called "militant solidarity."[19] The event was planned to coincide with the first anniversary of the coup and with worldwide manifestations to denounce the junta, with the explicit understanding that "the struggle of the Chilean people is the struggle of all peoples of the world."[20] "Before filmmakers," the text stated in an echo of the Chilean manifesto written by Littin in the wake of the 1970 election, "we are militants of the struggles of our peoples."[21] As seen in the previous chapters, in these different invocations of solidarity the term entailed concrete tasks: devising actions of support for fellow exile filmmakers, integrating them into their respective host nations and film industries; and organizing public campaigns to get Chilean filmmakers out of prison and out of torture centers.

The last aspect of the Caracas encounter is discernible in Miguel Littin's long speech about Chilean cinema and the government of the UP. Littin intervened by virtue of his triple status: as an exile in Mexico, as the former director of Chilefilms during the first year of Allende's presidency, and as one of the newly appointed members of the Latin American Filmmakers Committee. In his talk, Littin explained what he saw as the failures of revolutionary cinema under Allende. He claimed that filmmakers could not turn Chilefilms into a "centralized organ with real power" and therefore had to deal with the limitations of producing a "revolutionary cinema within the apparatus of the bourgeois state."[22] Littin also introduced an idea that was to become dominant for filmmakers and historians. (It was replicated almost word by word by Patricio Guzmán in a statement published a few days afterwards in Pesaro.) Right before the coup, Littin argued, the process of class struggle was reaching such a level of acuteness and the acceleration of historical events was such that the cinematic medium as an instrument in direct service of a revolutionary process became obsolete.[23]

Littin concluded his speech with a reflection on the role of artists and intellectuals under the current political situation. He mentioned that Chilean filmmakers had organized themselves in a Front of Resistance, echoing the strategies of popular resistance devised by the masses in Chile. He proposed a series of tasks to be undertaken by filmmakers throughout the world, which included organizing screening series devoted to Latin American cinema to raise funds for the Chilean resistance and working to facilitate conditions so that every Chilean exile director could make the film that "the Chilean Resistance demands."[24]

What did this demand mean? In his words, it meant all films that "have as a priority to forge the image of a people in struggle and with faith in victory" and those "that analyze different periods of the life of the country so as to rightfully comprehend recent events and project the future."[25] This was a work-in-progress definition that avoided the phrase "exile cinema" and that was to be complemented a few days afterward in Pesaro.

PESARO 1974 AND 1975 (EUROPE)

Consider the last paragraph of a statement read aloud on stage by the Chilean delegation present at the 10th Mostra Internazionale del Nuovo Cinema de Pesaro (10th Pesaro International Film Festival of New Cinema) in 1974, which ran September 12–19, immediately after the meeting in Caracas. Instead of a cautious avoidance of the term, *exile* is formulated in conceptual opposition to the idea of resistance: "In agreement with the resolution adopted in Caracas, we define our movement as that of *a cinema of resistance in opposition to a cinema in exile devoid of real contact with the struggle of our people*" (emphasis added).[26]

Directors Miguel Littin, Raúl Ruiz, and Valeria Sarmiento and actor Nelson Villagra formed the Chilean delegation at Pesaro. Besides explicitly mentioning the Caracas encounter in a previous passage in the Pesaro statement, a number of elements indicate a continuity with the declaration offered only days earlier in Venezuela. Among them are the reference to the 1970 manifesto as the document that defined the foundations for the cinema to come, the political analysis of the UP, the summary of tasks achieved by Chilefilms, the call to free imprisoned directors and actors, and the tendency to situate ideological struggle at the center of historical analysis. These aspects also suggest that the author of the Pesaro statement was most likely Miguel Littin.

To reflect on the emergence of Chilean exile cinema in terms of solidarity, resistance, and anti-imperialist struggle was logical, almost inevitable, in an encounter such as the one in Caracas, which owed its existence to that kind of discursive entanglement. But Pesaro 1974 proves that the framing of Chilean exile cinema under the concepts of solidarity and resistance was no question of Chilean and Latin American filmmakers alone; it was supported and encouraged by European critics and programmers in their roles as mediators and promoters of this cinema. In a lengthy two-volume study devoted to Chilean cinema during the 1960s, Verónica Cortínez and Manfred Engelbert are particularly harsh about the role of critics "motivated by the immediate and contingent actuality, where the political vision of the international left at the time had a primary role."[27] Their statement assumes a unified vision of the European Left, fails to acknowledge the reasons behind these critics and programmers' motivations in working with Latin American cinema, and does not account for the political and affective powers of transnational solidarity. Still, Cortínez and Engelbert are right in pointing out the role of these cultural actors and in inviting a more serious analysis of the implications derived from their work as cultural interpreters.[28]

Founded in 1965, the Mostra quickly acquired a crucial role as an international encounter of the many different traditions of political and militant filmmaking, especially after the global waves of unrest in 1968.[29] Pesaro was seen by various commentators as *the* festival that took up the challenge to think about the relations between cinema and politics, while its organizers embarked upon a revision of Italian national film history. For instance, the 1974 program of Chilean cinema under Allende and in exile coincided with a massive retrospective on Italian neorealism; the following year, the retrospectives were devoted to Brazilian Cinema Novo and Italian cinema under fascism.

Defining characteristics of the festival were its audience—a mix of students, cinephiles, and political activists; its emphasis on various documents aiming to provide cultural and historical context—translations, interviews, short texts, and manifestos; and its active engagement with networks of solidarity and with the struggles of the Third World.[30] The NLAC occupied a primary role in this regard.[31] A large series of Latin American cinema was the focus of Pesaro's retrospective in 1973, which began just one day after the September 11 coup in Chile. Since the coup and the ninth festival overlapped, there was no room to alter the 1973 program in a significant way. But the fact that the organizers chose to devote the next festival to Chilean cinema indicates that the plight of Chile was indeed at the forefront of Pesaro's efforts to mobilize support for nations experiencing dictatorships and for other struggles of the Third World. As Don Ranvaud has claimed, this support was evident in their working toward the release of political prisoners, setting up broad distribution networks, and lobbying state cultural organizations on behalf of Chilean exiles.[32]

This support manifested itself in Pesaro's programmatic decisions, too. As mentioned, the 1974 festival had a special retrospective of Chilean cinema under Allende: *Una testimonianza sul cinema di Allende*. The following year, the festival programmed many of the first films made by Chileans in exile together with the first part of Guzmán's *The Battle of Chile* (1975), therefore establishing "a continuing emphasis on Chilean cinema and an opportunity to seriously consider the options and prospects of an exiled film movement."[33] Solidarity was once again a keyword in these two editions of the festival: in the films themselves, pairing Chilean works with "solidarity films" directed by foreign filmmakers, like Heynowski and Scheumann's *Der Krieg der Mumien* (The War of the Mummies, 1974); in the roundtables and debates that took place there, as seen in the statement read by the Chilean delegation; and in the writings of Italian and European critics and programmers.

For the 1974 festival, in addition to a number of films produced during the UP—a "bombardment of short documentaries," as Pick refers to it—the series included *The Promised Land*, completed but never exhibited in Chile before the coup, and *Diálogo de exiliados* (Dialogues of Exiles, Raúl Ruiz, 1974), which had its world premiere in Pesaro that year.[34] As I develop in the following chapter (and as critics like Pick were quick to notice), these were not just any films, but works that opened up two radically different paths for Chilean exile cinema.

The Pesaro festival published a booklet entitled *Materiali sul cinema cileno* (Materials on Chilean Cinema). The booklet reprinted articles, documents, and interviews previously published in Latin American and European journals and included an annotated filmography that functioned as a catalog. The booklet's definitive contribution resided in its original materials. The anonymous prologue functions as the clearest manifestation of the vitality of the concepts of solidarity and resistance, which are tied to two demands: (1) unity and (2) a revision of the past enabling the imagination of a new future. "Chilean cinema will continue to exist in those filmmakers who are spread throughout the world in a painful diaspora. This cinema will maintain its unity and solidarity, affirming, in spite of all hardships, the political choice that no *coup* can erase or change."[35] Unity and solidarity are invoked here as antidotes to the difficulties that exile's dispersion provokes. Francesco Bolzoni's piece is a little more skeptical regarding these hardships. It claims that for Chilean cinema to survive in exile, it will have to overcome "the most difficult obstacles." Even though it does not specify what those obstacles are, Bolzoni implies that they are tied to the fate of Third Worldism and tricontinental solidarity in Europe.[36] The anonymous prologue provides clues by claiming that the revision of the past proposed by the series programmed in Pesaro only "acquires meaning if it also becomes an incentive for imagining the future of workers, and if it serves in some way the Chilean Resistance and the Chilean filmmakers who, aligned with yesterday's cultural and political practices, are now part of that Resistance."[37]

This means that the Italian programmers, in their official introduction to the cinema of the UP (a cinema "read" a posteriori, after its defeat), reproduce and give legitimacy to the rhetoric offered by Chilean filmmakers in exile. The official discourse allows no misinterpretation: cinema as an artistic practice is aligned—equated—with a social practice (a people that *resists*), and cinema ought to be a tool (in service of solidarity and resistance). The inclusion of Guzmán's essay in the booklet only reaffirms this alignment, adding another layer. It highlights Chilean exile filmmakers' discursive unity—at least when presented to the public—since his words replicate Littín's intervention in Caracas. Guzmán concludes that the acceleration of historical events and the heightening of class struggle before the coup had revealed "the caducity of cinema as an effective medium in service of the revolutionary process."[38] And he ends the essay with a brief paragraph in which he declares that cinema must work as a tool in direct service of resistance.[39]

But the reactions to the screening of *Dialogues of Exiles* show the initial fissures of this supposed unity, as well as the difficulties of aligning exile cinema with an artistic practice in service of resistance and solidarity. *Dialogues of Exiles* was made in early 1974 in a situation of great financial and emotional precarity both for the director and the participants, with many Chilean exiles having just landed in Paris and choosing to take part in the game of "ideological introspection" proposed by Ruiz. Actors played a version of themselves, one that was not virtuous, as some of the characters were presented as thieves and opportunists. The film functioned as a humorous ethnography of the exile community, so dark in its portrayal that it was immediately received by the audience in Pesaro as a provocation.

The forum that took place after the film's premiere was heated. In her book *Los años chilenos de Raúl Ruiz* (2019; The Chilean Years of Raúl Ruiz), journalist Yenny Cáceres collects numerous testimonies from people who were present that day in Pesaro.[40] Cubans Alfredo Guevara and Julio García Espinosa labeled it as politically inappropriate. Chilean actor Nelson Villagra, who at the time oversaw cultural affairs for the MIR party in exile, protested the "excessive" jokes about mishandling solidarity funds and reproached Ruiz for having succumbed to his "ego" as an artist. Most Chilean exiles in the audience were angry and wanted a piece of Ruiz, to the point that one night he had to hide in Littín's hotel room. A press conference took place the day after the premiere, at which Littín, who also disagreed with the appropriateness of the film given the political context of exile and dictatorial violence, nonetheless defended Ruiz's right to artistic freedom. Valeria Sarmiento later considered what happened in Pesaro a kind of "political trial."[41]

The legend of *Dialogues of Exiles* began in Pesaro. Beyond the "myths" surrounding the threats and harassment experienced by Ruiz in the wake of the film's first screenings, the premiere in Pesaro is relevant because it pointed to a debate that Chilean exile filmmakers would keep having for years: What were the aesthetic forms appropriate for the political urgency of exile and resistance?[42] This question was not only expressed in the films Chilean exiles were making. It was also mobilized by film festivals in their programming and in the spaces for critical discussion they facilitated.

Pesaro 1974 thus became a key site in the discursive production of Chilean exile cinema because it combined four realms: the cinematic dimension (the films screened in the retrospective), the critical dimension (in the form of the various translations, articles, and program notes included in the booklet and the debates that took place after the films' projection), the polemical dimension (especially in the case of *Dialogues of Exiles*), and the activist dimension (a kind of political work that relies on the lexicon of solidarity and resistance, as seen in the statement of the Chilean delegation).

VOLGOGRAD 1975, TASHKENT 1976, MOSCOW 1979 (SOVIET SPHERES I)

In 1975 the Week of Anti-Fascist Cinema took place to commemorate the thirtieth anniversary of the Soviet victory against Nazi forces in the Battle of Stalingrad (a city later renamed Volgograd). At this onetime festival, Chile was given "a place of honor" with a delegation that included filmmakers Patricio Guzmán (who screened the first part of *The Battle of Chile*), Claudio Sapiaín, Pedro Chaskel, Eduardo Labarca, and Joan Jara (the widow of the brutally murdered folk singer Víctor Jara).[43]

As predominant throughout different kinds of film festivals, the Chilean selection included representative works made during Allende's government prior to the coup, together with some of the recent new films made in exile—like Castilla's *Quisiera, quisiera tener un hijo* (*I Wish, I Wish I Had a Son*, Sweden, 1974). Unique to this festival, however, was the programmatic narrative constructing "a clear line" of anti-fascist struggle "from the Spanish Civil War through the Second World War to Indochina and, finally, Chile."[44]

The Volgograd event demonstrates that the cinema of solidarity with Chile and the films made by Chilean exiles moved beyond Western Europe and also traveled through the geopolitical spaces of the Eastern bloc, negotiating varying degrees of Soviet spheres of influence and moving from Central and Eastern Europe to Central Asia in festivals like Leipzig, Karlovy Vary, Moscow, and Tashkent. As Masha Salazkina has claimed, the Soviet Union and the radical aesthetic and political project of the NLAC were not close allies. The canonical films of the movement were most often absent from the programming in these festivals—except for Leipzig, which remained a hub for the cinemas of internationalist solidarity and which maintained close connections with Cuba's ICAIC as a beacon of radical filmmaking. This absence of the canonical films of the NLAC from the festivals of the Eastern bloc mirrors their absence from Soviet commercial screens.[45] Djagalov even suggests that Latin American cinema may have been the greatest casualty of Soviet political censorship.[46]

In this general framework, Chilean filmmakers occupied a "unique and ideologically privileged place on the socialist film festival circuit."[47] A range of factors contributed to creating this privileged position: the top-down, state-centered model of solidarity with Chile that the USSR adopted as well as its expert mobilization of anti-fascist rhetoric and emotions through the apparatus of the state; the strong ties between the respective Communist Parties; the presence of Chilean exiled politicians, intellectuals, and artists in Moscow; the role of solidarity committees in successful campaigns freeing political prisoners; and preexisting film-exchange agreements between Chile and the Soviet Union.

These ties between the Soviet Union and Chile's political and artistic circles explain the role of Chilean exile cinema at festivals like Tashkent and Moscow. While short lived—ten biennial festivals took place between 1968 and 1988—the Tashkent Festival of African, Asian, and Latin American Cinema in the capital of Uzbekistan became a major site for the interconnectivity of the cinemas of these three continents, as Razlogova, Djagalov, and Salazkina have each detailed in their respective painstaking historical reconstructions of the festival.[48] The cinemas of the so-called peripheries had secured important platforms in various European festivals, but the sheer geographical scope and the scale of Tashkent were unprecedented; the 1976 festival, for instance, included more than four hundred guests representing seventy-three different nation-states.[49] Even before Latin American cinema was officially included at Tashkent (its practitioners were observers in 1974 and full participants in 1976), Chilean films had already been a part of the festival. In 1972 the festival screened Álvaro Covacevich's *El diálogo de América* (*The Dialogue of America*, 1972). In 1974 Sebastián Alarcón's VGIK graduation film *La primera página* (*The First Page*), which had already played in Moscow, Oberhausen, and Leipzig, was included in the selection. Chilean exiles Guzmán, Littin, Alarcón, and Rodrigo Gonçalves participated as guests in several iterations of the festival throughout the 1970s and 1980s.[50]

The fifth festival, in 1976, had the greatest presence of Chilean exile filmmakers, with programming choices that reflected Tashkent's internationalist orientation: the medium-length documentaries *Sången lever generaler!* (*The Song Doesn't Die, Generals!*, Claudio Sapiaín, 1975), *Dentro de cada sombra crece un vuelo* (*Within Every Shadow There Grows a Flight*, Douglas Hübner, 1975), and *Dulce Patria* (*Sweet Homeland*, Beatriz González, 1975), plus the historical epic *Actas de Marusia* (*Letters from Marusia*, Miguel Littin, 1975) and the second part of the landmark *The Battle of Chile*. Littin, Guzmán, Sapiaín, Hübner, Alarcón, and cinematographer Cristián Valdés—another VGIK graduate—were in attendance, and Beatriz González was the only woman filmmaker participating as a guest at that festival. As Salazkina recounts, the "Chilean Patriotic Forces"—as the Chilean delegation was often called on the socialist festival circuit—present at Tashkent 1976 coincided with a series of other "embattled fronts" of the Third World, including Palestine and Angola.[51]

If Tashkent had a tricontinental mission, the Moscow International Film Festival often reserved most of its programming for "serious" art films, especially European. Due to its ideological position in the Soviet world, Chilean cinema also had a close connection to the Moscow festival. Its seventh iteration in 1971 featured a week of Chilean films, including the classic titles that gave birth to the New Chilean Cinema—*Caliche sangriento* (*Bloody Nitrate*, Helvio Soto, 1969), *Valparaíso, mi amor* (*Valparaíso, My Love*, Aldo Francia, 1969), and *El chacal de*

Nahueltoro (The Jackal of Nahueltoro, Miguel Littin, 1969). During the Moscow festival in July 1973, Miguel Littin's *The Promised Land* had its world premiere in the main competition. A mere five weeks before September 11, this was its only screening prior to the coup—almost a year before playing in New York as part of MoMA's and the Film Society of Lincoln Center's *New Directors/New Films* series in March–April 1974, and before its widely discussed screenings at Cannes, the Montreal *rencontres*, and Pesaro in May, June, and September 1974, respectively. Moscow's ninth festival in 1977 included the world premiere of Sebastián Alarcón's *Noch nad Chili* (Night over Chile, 1977), a historical reconstruction of the coup that subsequently entered the Soviet canon and received wide-ranging theatrical distribution throughout the Eastern and Soviet bloc.

The next festival, in 1979, had a different kind of participation by Chilean exile directors, one that is directly linked to debates held in Caracas and Pesaro. The organization invited a group of filmmakers and writers to be on a panel entitled "Orientation and Perspectives on Chilean Cinema." Participants included novelist José Donoso and directors Jaime Barrios, Orlando Lübbert, and Miguel Littin, who came from Madrid, New York, East Berlin, and Mexico City, respectively. A few local figures, exiled in Moscow, joined the panel: Sebastián Alarcón, Cristián Valdés, Eduardo Labarca, and novelist José Miguel Varas, who acted as a moderator.[52] A conceptual opposition was proposed at the beginning of this conversation. On one side, "resistance" would follow the politically committed tradition of the cinema produced during the Popular Unity and seek to further the idea of Third Cinema as a "guardian of popular memory."[53] On the other side, "exile cinema" would be a cinema that would eschew that commitment, avoid didacticism and explicit politics, and search for stories in individual rather than collective dramas.[54]

It was a forced opposition that obscured a great deal of common ground. All participants in the roundtable ended up agreeing that the cinema produced in exile had opened multiple and simultaneous aesthetics and themes, and that sustained political denunciation of the Junta and active support of the popular resistance in Chile were still urgent. At the same time, they all recognized that there was an encroaching "exhaustion of material," in the words of Sebastián Alarcón.[55] Barrios, in turn, complained that they were encountering great difficulties, especially in capitalist countries, in convincing producers to make films about Chilean politics.[56]

The conceptualization of a cinema of resistance sketched by Littin in Moscow—and previously asserted by him and other directors like Guzmán in places like Caracas and Pesaro—implied a lag in the political temporality of the exile subject. Resistance is antithetical to exile, in that the latter refers to the present conditions that define one's subjectivity. As developed in the next chapter, there were other notions of resistance that privileged its connection to present struggles. But in the conceptual opposition expressed in Moscow, the rhetoric of resistance moves from the present to the past. Its focus is on the UP, not exile. In short, resistance points back tow the time when cinema was defined as a revolutionary art. It restores continuity to an aesthetic project and to a political temporality broken by the coup. What matters in the context of this film festival road map is that such a conceptualization finds an equivalency in most festivals' programming, and especially in the ones that were part of the socialist circuit. These events tended to privilege the screening of the political films made during Allende's government, while the exile films—except those produced in unmistakable militant fashion—occupied a more secondary position.

The Moscow roundtable showed that Chilean exile filmmakers understood resistance as the undying bond to the past and exile as an opening toward the uncertainties of the present. Reading the transcript of the Moscow debate, one gets the growing feeling that the participants knew that something had just changed or was changing in front of their eyes, but they could not state exactly what it was. The ready-made phrases proliferating in their language did not account for the depth of their own work or that of their fellow filmmakers. The constantly reiterated concepts—solidarity, resistance, revolutionary cinema—did not describe the complexity of the historical crux in which they were: exile.

HAVANA 1979 (LATIN AMERICA)

"Dear brothers of our America: In Havana, Cuba's capital, we begin today, December 3, 1979, the First Festival of the New Latin American Cinema."[57] With these words, Alfredo Guevara, director of ICAIC and first president of the festival, inaugurated the event, which lasted eight days, screened 254 films, and hosted 655 guests from Latin America and the Caribbean.[58] Latin American film scholarship has overwhelmingly seen the founding of the Havana festival as the moment of institutionalization of the radical impulses of the NLAC.[59] In fact, the festival was explicitly founded as a continuation of the 1967 and 1969 Viña del mar

Film Festivals in Chile and the one held in 1968 in Mérida, Venezuela—all three usually seen as marking the birth of the NLAC. The founding of the Havana festival was also in direct dialogue with the Fourth and Fifth Encounters of Latin American Filmmakers, held in Caracas 1974 and in Mérida in 1977.[60] As mentioned earlier, the Caracas gathering was framed as a special instance of solidarity with the struggle of the Chilean people one year after the coup. The 1977 Mérida encounter extended this continental solidarity to all nations undergoing military dictatorships and continued Latin American filmmakers' denunciation of US imperialism.[61] Under the auspices of ICAIC and Cuba's Ministry of Culture, the Havana festival was created with the precise mission of guaranteeing a sustained and ongoing exchange between Latin American filmmakers. Though not explicitly stated, the festival also implied a decided redrawing of the geography of Latin American cinemas, situating Havana at their center.

In addition to the main competition of the various fiction, documentary, and animation sections, the festival included a seminar devoted to the discussion of theoretical, critical, and production challenges—aligned with previous experiences like those at Karlovy Vary, Pesaro, and Tashkent—special retrospectives, and the Mercado del Nuevo Cine Latinoamericano (MECLA; Market of the New Latin American Cinema). Over the years, the seminar created a space of open dialogue—sometimes polemic—between filmmakers, critics, scholars, and programmers. Often some of the key mediators between Chilean exile cinema and European and North American audiences were there: scholars Zuzana M. Pick (Canada), Julianne Burton (US), and Michael Chanan (UK); and critics/programmers Lino Miccichè (Pesaro) and Paulo Antonio Paranaguá (Toulouse/San Sebastián), among many others. The structure of the festival highlights the moment of crisis and transformation that the cinemas of the region were undergoing, marked by brutal dictatorships and domestic censorship, exile, and, consequently, the moving away from dominant militant approaches to a wider heterogeneity of aesthetic and political projects. The creation of MECLA was symptomatic in this sense; it was a clear acknowledgment that thinking about coproduction agreements, global sales, and distribution challenges was crucial for the survival of the cinema of the region.

In this context, the presence of Chilean exile film and video at the Havana festivals is once again significant. Chile's privileged position can be quickly seen by examining the first festival in 1979. Miguel Littín was a member of the jury for the fictional competition—presided over by acclaimed Colombian writer Gabriel García Márquez—while Pedro Chaskel served in the same position for the documentary section, presided over by Santiago Álvarez, former director of ICAIC's newsreel division and a legend of political documentary. Chileans received several awards that year. The Grand Coral Award was given to Guzmán's *The Battle of Chile*, which was exhibited in its entire three parts during the festival. Another Coral Award was given to the "ensemble of documentaries of Resistance in the Southern Cone," which included the exile films *Recado de Chile* (*Message from Chile*, Collective, 1979) and *Die Fäuste vor der Kanone* (*Fists against the Cannons*, Orlando Lübbert and Gastón Ancelovici, 1972/1974). In the fictional competition, a special mention was given to *Prisioneros desaparecidos* (Missing Prisoners, Sergio Castilla, 1979), a coproduction of Cuba's ICAIC and the Swedish Film Institute.[62]

The first seminar that accompanied the festival also had a direct link to Chile. At the discussion "The Role of Transnational Companies and the Penetration of Cultural Imperialism in Latin America and the Caribbean," its main speakers were French scholars Armand and Michèle Mattelart, both of whom had built their ideas on mass media and communication based on their work in Chile in the years leading up to the coup.[63] During the Encounter of Latin American Filmmakers (the sixth gathering if following the chronology initiated at Viña del mar 1967), statements about the film industry of many countries were delivered, including the Chilean report read by Miguel Littin.[64] The meeting of UCAL, over which Chilean Pedro Chaskel presided, also took place during the Havana festival to mark a continuation with the previous gatherings in Caracas and Mérida.[65]

Havana 1979 also gave a privileged space to two other cinemas. The first special retrospective of the festival was devoted to Chicano cinema and included many of the canonical films of this emerging body of work.[66] With this decision, Havana extended its political commitment to the Latin American migrants in the United States, where these films had found little recognition at the time. The other place of honor was given to Nicaragua. After the 1979 revolution, the Sandinistas created their national film institute, INCINE, modeled after Cuba's ICAIC. The inaugural session of the Havana festival began with INCINE's very first newsreel, followed by a standing ovation that lasted minutes.[67] This decision stresses the new geography of revolutionary struggles on the continent and predicts the role that Nicaragua would play in the cinemas of solidarity worldwide, particularly for Chilean exile filmmakers (as discussed in the previous chapter).

LEIPZIG 1983 (EASTERN BLOC AND SOVIET SPHERES II)

In 1983 the Internationale Leipziger Dokumentar- und Kurzfilmwoche für Kino und Fernsehen (International Leipzig Documentary and Short Film Week for Cinema and Television) devoted a series to Chile, entitled *Film im Freiheitskampf der Völker: Chile* (Cinema in the Struggle for the Liberation of the Peoples: Chile). Leipzig, founded in 1955 as a festival for East German documentaries, went international in 1960. The festival is an invaluable window into the geopolitics of solidarity during the Cold War.[68] "Films by Third World countries or liberation movements always found a home" in Leipzig, as Victor Grossman suggested in a review for *Cinéaste*.[69] The festival had a tradition of cooperation with Chile and support of its cinema that dated back to the late 1960s. Several Chilean short films produced before the coup, such as *Venceremos* (Pedro Chaskel and Héctor Ríos, 1970), had received awards there. Later, Chilean exile films and films from different nations about Chile and its politics found a place in their programming. In 1973 the festival started the Day of Anti-imperialist Solidarity.[70] In the opening ceremony, a statement condemning the Chilean coup was read, followed by a performance of the folk band Quilapayún, who sang, together with the audience, the *Venceremos* anthem. Thus the 1983 program, defined as a retrospective opposed to the oppression of the Chilean people and in support of the international solidarity movement with Chile, was one more step in a long history of socialist friendships.

Folders kept in the Federal Archive in Berlin contain numerous documents detailing the preparation of this retrospective.[71] The 1983 Chile series involved four years of exchanges between the festival, Chilean filmmakers, international archives, distribution companies, and solidarity committees throughout the world, plus a trip made by a Leipzig representative who traveled to Havana, met with Pedro Chaskel, and discussed the materials kept by Cinemateca Chilena in the Cuban Film Archive.[72] From the start, Leipzig organizers explained that they were looking for films under four categories: films produced before the UP government, films produced during the UP, Chilean exile films, and international films about Chile and the solidarity movement.[73] Gastón Ancelovici, from Cinemateca Chilena, proposed a more thematic approach: solidarity with Chile, Chilean exile films, documentaries about the Chilean labor movement, and Chilean solidarity with the people of Nicaragua.[74] This last strand evidences once again the symbolic and political weight that the Sandinista revolution had for Chilean exile cinema and for radical cinemas in Latin America and beyond. While the thematic framework suggested by Ancelovici was not chosen, in their letters of invitation to dozens of Chilean exile filmmakers, Leipzig organizers highlighted the fact that the retrospective was prepared in close cooperation with the solidarity committee run by the office of Chile Antifascista, and with Cinemateca Chilena. The desire to showcase the cinema under the UP and Chilean exile cinema was explicitly framed with the reasoning that those films "represent an important part of the anti-fascist documentary movement."[75] This reasoning is articulated in more dramatic terms in the book that was published to accompany the program: "This retrospective is part of the memory of Latin American revolutionary cinema. You are contributing to the solidarity cause. Solidarity with Chilean artists, solidarity with the Chilean people."[76]

The direct address to "you," together with the call to be fused with the "them" of the Chilean people, reinforces the affective dimension of international solidarity (not only a policy of collaboration between nation-states, institutions, and individuals, but an experience that is *lived* and *felt*) and highlights the presence of a shared history marked by anti-fascist struggle. In this regard, Pedro Chaskel's biography—part of his family was able to escape from the Nazis, relocating to Chile when he was a child—was an obvious reminder to the Leipzig organizers that there was a common thread uniting both historical experiences, the German past and Chile's present.

The official statement published in the book also reminds us that the circulation of Chilean exile films is produced and modified by specific political and ideological contexts. The Leipzig retrospective coincided with the tenth anniversary of the Chilean coup, a moment used by the GDR state to reposition the discourses of anti-fascism and international solidarity through the example of Chile. In a critical examination of the Leipzig retrospective, a celebration of the internationalism involved in its organization needs to be reconciled with the weight of the state, which persists as a powerful agent articulating the circulation of films, and whose ideology is more than visible in the final program. The series exhibited few works made by Chilean exiles and gave more space to films from the Allende years and to foreign films about Chile—examples of a cinematic internationalism. Most importantly, except for Pedro Chaskel's *Los ojos como mi papá* (*Eyes Like My Dad*, Cuba, 1979), the selection excluded all the exile films that did not fit the more dogmatic idea of resistance against the Pinochet dictatorship and international solidarity.[77]

The retrospective itself—with screenings preceded or followed by live music, testimonies, and political speeches—functioned as an opportunity for the social performance of solidarity guided by the state.[78]

SAN SEBASTIÁN 1987 (IBERIAN WORLDS)

The thirtieth San Sebastián International Film Festival, held in September 1987, programmed the largest and most ambitious series of Chilean cinema to take place at an international festival, screening a total of forty-one films and videos. In addition to its specific political orientation in celebrating a national cinema conducted in exile and under a military dictatorship, the series needs to be understood in the context of emerging cinematic dialogues between Spain and Latin America, expressed in festivals like Benalmádena and Huelva, and in various programs organized by Filmoteca Española in Madrid.[79] By the late 1980s, in anticipation of the celebrations of five hundred years of the so-called discovery of Latin America, these cinematic exchanges were increased.[80] In fact, the Chile series at San Sebastián in 1987 predates the huge showcase ABC de América Latina, held the following year, at which more than fifty Latin American films were screened.[81]

The organizers of the 1987 Chile series at San Sebastián faced some difficulties while putting together the program. Taking a great number of precautions, most film and video makers who were traveling from Chile waited until the very last moment to confirm their attendance. The presence of some of them required the intervention of diplomatic officials. The Spanish embassy and its cultural attaché in Chile had to find a way to officially invite video maker Hernán Castro, who had been prosecuted recently for participating as a cameraman on Patricio Guzmán's *En nombre de Dios* (In the Name of God, Spain, 1987). Programmed by José Riba, a champion of Latin American cinema who had been a part of the festival since 1982 and who would later head Cannes's Critics' Week, the series was impressive for the breadth of its curatorial choices. The program included various subsections, some of which were thematic, while others responded more to conditions and places of production: "Chile Documentaries," "Popular Music," "Resistances," "The Church," "The Coup," "Cinema and the Dictatorship," and "Fiction." Though the series made room for a few films made before the coup—in an homage to Sergio Bravo, founder of the University of Chile's Cine Experimental Group in 1957—the bulk was devoted to works made after the coup, both in exile and in Chile.[82] As in most special retrospectives, some films about Chile made by foreign directors were also included, while the work of women exile filmmakers was altogether absent.[83] Instead, the San Sebastián program paid special attention to the rich output of the alternative video scene in Chile, including clandestine newsreels, testimonies, music videos, and works that focused on protests and strategies of popular resistance. Yessica Ulloa, who had published in 1985 a thoroughly researched book on the production, circulation, and reception of independent video in Chile, was an adviser for the video section.[84] Her expertise is reflected in the heterogenous nature of this section of the program, which was more diverse than any previous festival selection of Chilean video.

The introductory text included in the festival catalog is short and presents few ideas for understanding programmatic decisions, other than the anniversaries—thirty years since the founding of Cine Experimental and eighty-five years after the "birth" of cinema in Chile—and other than the desire to offer a wide showcase of a cinema that survived "in spite of all."[85] Yet a range of ancillary documents, especially the daily newspaper that was published throughout the ten days of the festival, offers more clues.[86] In an interview and in a short article titled "Images of Exile," Paulo Antonio Paranaguá—a frequent San Sebastián collaborator and a mediating figure in the cinematic relations between Europe and Latin America—further elaborated on some of the artistic and political pathways followed by Chilean exile filmmakers. In an echo of the Moscow debate, Paranaguá described that these diasporic directors had been facing in recent years the conditions of their own present, in an expansion of practices and notions of "militant" cinema toward a "solid and reflective search for cultural identity in the widest possible sense."[87]

The interviews published in the festival's newspaper also stress some of the points that would be debated in the colloquium with Chilean filmmakers that took place during the festival. Sergio Bravo spoke of the multiple "rebirths" and "resurrections" of Chilean cinema.[88] Hernán Castro discussed the political necessity of making documentaries and alternative video newsreels, highlighting their wide distribution among churches, unions, and human rights organizations—an idea reprised by Patricio Guzmán when detailing the "semi-legal" premiere of *In the Name of God* and the fifty video copies that circulated through the same type of alternative distribution network.[89] The panel assembled for the Chilean colloquium expanded on these issues and resumed some of the topics debated in the Moscow roundtable, though its composition was more diverse. Panelists included the exile directors Guzmán, Orlando Lübbert, and Jorge Triviño; the Chilean-based Bravo, Castro, Ricardo Correa, and Leonardo Kocking; the East German filmmaker Walter Heynowski; and the Chilean actresses Érica Ramos and Shlomit Baytelman—the only female participants in the group, masking the absence of women filmmakers from the program.[90] The conversation was moderated by Paranaguá. All participants agreed that the ultimate goal that moved them was the recuperation of democracy, and that exile cinema had meant the chance to disseminate information with a level of global reach that would have never been possible for filmmakers working "from the inside." Correa also noted that this exile cinema had found a way of permeating the national border and circulating through informal networks, which had strengthened the bonds between those in Chile and in exile.

Beyond these words of politeness, there was a stark opposition between the video makers—committed to the project of countering the misinformation of Chilean mass media and newspapers—and the independent filmmakers who made a living doing advertisements and occasionally shot their fiction features. For Castro, one had to choose a space: working either on commercials or against the dictatorship. There were discussions about cinematic forms, the "exhaustion" of certain strategies (to go back to Alarcón's words in Moscow), and how to engage with industry trends: festival markets, coproduction agreements, global sales, and problems of distribution. In fact, when the debate became heated, actress Baytelman softened the discussion by reading aloud a message she had brought from the newly created Chilean Association of Film Producers, which called for international aid and support in establishing coproductions with directors based in Chile.

The conversation ended when Bravo—the oldest in the group—raised the most poignant issue: "We don't know what we want to be once we overcome the dictatorship."[91] The question was left unanswered, but it would preoccupy Chilean filmmakers for the next few years. In these debates as well as in its programmatic choices—particularly the need to bridge the work carried out inside Chile and that made abroad in exile—the San Sebastián retrospective anticipated and prefigured the "re-encounter" that would take place three years later at the Viña del mar film festival in Chile (see chapter 6).

. . .

The road map traced throughout this chapter demonstrates that film festivals are charged with an affective surplus. Entangled with market-oriented goals—like discussing the relationship between cinema and television, a recurring topic at San Sebastián and later at Viña—festivals constituted social gatherings of an emotional order. In the case of Chilean exile cinema, this emotional domain was mobilized in tandem with political beliefs centered on notions of solidarity. This intertwinement adopted several forms—whether the large-scale display of state solidarity by way of songs and speeches in festivals like Leipzig or in round panels that moved from dialogue to passionate debate and then segued into moral and political accusations, as in Moscow and San Sebastián.

If what is "sold" at festivals is "membership of the small band of accredited regulators" that determine and "police" how films are to be consumed and understood, as Paul Willemen has claimed, then this festival journey also charts an ongoing rearrangement of this elite circle.[92] The movement from festival to festival implies an expansion of the circle's affiliates—by including Chilean critics and filmmakers who had been distanced from the discussions shaped by international festivals and critics in Europe and North America. The festival journey also traces a recentering of the main concerns of filmmakers, from how to sustain and benefit from transnational solidarity in the 1970s to a more "national" framework in the late 1980s in San Sebastián, where most conversations were now about the future of Chilean cinema *in* Chile.

In the end, this road map evidences the sustained and ongoing conversation that Chilean exile filmmakers had for two decades throughout various festivals. The thread of the conversation carries over from one event to another, especially with regard to the political stakes behind an exilic film practice. The various booklets and catalogs published by these festivals are a material record of this conversation, as most of them recirculated and translated the same interviews, short texts, manifestos, and filmographies. Beyond solidarity, the key word for understanding the politics of Chilean exile cinema is *resistance*. The second part of this book is devoted to examining how these politics translated and moved from the discourse filmmakers constructed around resistance and exile to their cinematic expression—that is, from statements, manifestos, speeches, and words said in interviews or in festival round panels to the films themselves.

PART II

The Politics of Exile Cinema

CHAPTER 4

Cinemas of Resistance, Cinemas of Exile

In 1971 Salvador Allende invited artists to engage with the radical changes undertaken by his government and promote them throughout the world. As part of the "counter-information" campaign known as Operación Verdad (Operation Truth), Spanish art critic José María Moreno Galván and Italian painter Carlo Levi, together with artist José Balmes, who had arrived in Chile as a refugee following the Spanish Civil War in the late 1930s, thought about how the art world could express its support to the political project of the UP.[1] They eventually proposed the foundation of a museum of contemporary art based in Santiago, Chile. The result was a unique institution in the art world. To the socialist experiment of a government and its people, the museum responded with a utopian desire grounded in solidarity. Artists donated nearly five hundred pieces for its creation, including original artworks by the likes of Frank Stella, Joan Miró, David Siqueiros, and Sol LeWitt.[2] The name highlighted the political ethos behind the project, Museo de la Solidaridad (Museum of Solidarity), and affirmed the central role that discourses of internationalism had in its founding. Both in the act of donation and in the naming of the museum, solidarity was used in an "eminently ethical and humanist sense," as claimed by the committee in charge of executing the project.[3] "Happy ideas are like this: neither before nor after their time, they are born under the sign of history," said Brazilian exile Mário Pedrosa, first director of the museum, at the opening of its first exhibition in 1972.[4]

After the coup, and facing the loss of countless pieces, the museum had to rearticulate itself in exile. Art historian Carla Macchiavelo notes that this process took a few years of exploratory possibilities between two different nodes of the museum that were based in Paris and Havana.[5] In Cuba, the cultural organization Casa de las Américas and Miria Contreras—who was Allende's secretary and had interacted with the museum while managing donations from the presidential palace prior to the coup—became crucial figures in this process of reorganization.[6] In its second phase, the museum operated under a different name in recognition that the solidarity that was offered to a popular government had multiplied when its destination was a people in resistance. As Contreras said in a letter addressed to the artists and intellectuals of the world, written in Havana in 1979, "The passage from a process of liberation to a monstrous regime of oppression obliges us to initiate another phase of struggle and to create new institutions supporting the resistance of the Chilean people."[7] Museo de la Solidaridad became Museo Internacional de la Resistencia Salvador Allende (MIRSA; International Museum of Resistance Salvador Allende).

Solidarity gives way to resistance and to a different degree of institutional experimentation. What was this, in the end: a collection with no seat, an archive, a museum in exile? For Moreno Galván, its material existence was less relevant than its conceptual status. This institution was, above all, an *idea*: "Just like the UP, the museum is an idea that no *momio* (mummy) can kill."[8] The organization continued to live, receiving more donations and programming exhibits in Havana, Madrid, Paris, Valencia, and Stockholm.[9] Much later, under a new historical context signaled by the recuperation of democracy, the museum returned to Chile and to the use of the word solidarity present in its original name. In 1991 it was reopened as Museo de la Solidaridad Salvador Allende (MSSA; Museum of Solidarity Salvador Allende). From solidarity to resistance and then once again back to solidarity.

The case of Cinemateca Chilena offers a variation of this conceptual shift, one that confronts resistance with the historical condition of exile. As seen in chapter 1, this institution was founded in exile by Pedro Chaskel and Gastón Ancelovici in 1974 and was devoted to archiving and promoting Chilean cinema.[10] While the purpose of the organization was clear from the start, its name was not.[11] Some documents indicate a constant oscillation between two names—Cinemateca Chilena de la Resistencia (Chilean Cinematheque of Resistance) and Cinemateca Chilena en el Exilio (Chilean Cinematheque in Exile).[12] In most cases, though, founders Chaskel and Ancelovici explained that the cinematheque's first name was Cinemateca Chilena de la Resistencia and "after a few years" it was changed to Cinemateca Chilena en el Exilio.[13] However, in documents ranging from 1979 to at least 1983, the organization is referred to by its original name, and the logo Cinemateca Chilena de la Resistencia is clearly visible in letters and official communications between Ancelovici and other film archives.[14] Furthermore, films such as *Recado de Chile* (*Message from Chile*, Collective, 1979) and *Chile, no invoco tu nombre en vano* (Colectivo Cine Ojo, 1983) include title credits that read "Cinemateca Chilena de la Resistencia presents."

These details evidence that neither the institutional renaming nor its timeline is clear. The misunderstandings stem in part from the nature of this institution and the various sister organizations that were tied to it: the archive in Cuba, the center of documentation (first in Madrid and then in Paris), the film production company, and later the not-for-profit foundation. All these organizations were related to Cinemateca Chilena and used slight variations on its name. A few years before his death, Ancelovici reaffirmed that the name changed in the 1970s, albeit without providing a specific date or a rationale for the switch from resistance to exile.[15]

If we follow the case of the Museum of Solidarity, the shift in the name is clearly explained in its official narrative and in the archives containing its history. The coup marked a historical and hermeneutic break. A cultural effort legible under the prism of Third Worldist admiration needed to be reinterpreted in light of a new and urgent political goal: defeating the dictatorship. Thus solidarity leads to resistance. Resistance is understood here as a "call to action" through gestures of solidarity that can be enacted on a variety of fronts.[16] In the vocabulary of exile and solidarity, resistance is conceived of almost exclusively as struggle. The concept presupposes a subject or group that fights oppression and implies that the worlds of art and cinema participate in the range of practices of social and political confrontation that Chileans developed in defiance of the military rule.

The change of Cinemateca Chilena's name is more opaque. It suggests that exile is understood as a new phase, different from the one intelligible under the name resistance. The shift implies a passage—at the very least a discursive move—from resistance to exile. This transit is aligned with the dominant historical view of the trajectory of Chilean exile cinema, one that sees the late 1970s and early 1980s as a move away from an activist phase—a cinema of resistance—to a more diverse aesthetic and thematic body of films—a cinema of exile.[17] This transit presupposes also a new "regime of historicity," a change that is temporal (from the past to the present) as much as it is political (from cultural struggle to an emphasis on national identity in exile).[18] But the view of a shift or transition from resistance to exile is incorrect. Both approaches coexist from the very beginning of the phenomenon of Chilean exile cinema.

As the previous chapter on film festivals has shown, the understandings of resistance and exile were fraught. In exile filmmakers' rhetoric—in speeches, interviews, statements, and manifestos—resistance is situated in stark opposition to exile. Consider a short document that Pedro Chaskel sent to Zuzana M. Pick, precisely to explain this issue, at some point in 1974. Chaskel claims that exile is associated with a "permanent" condition. Furthermore, *exile* is a noun that means being "outside," while *resistance* suggests a verb that carries action. Resistance rejects the permanency of exile and functions as a form of communion with those who are "inside" performing actions of struggle. Chaskel goes on to say that there have been plenty of exile filmmakers in the history of cinema, but experiences in which those directors have been able to preserve a practice of cinematic resistance in their new environments have been less common. Exile filmmakers want to remain tied to the "definitive liberation of our people." It is in this sense—a vital commitment to the struggle of the Chilean people—that they understand the notion of a cinema of resistance, and this is why they prefer it over a cinema of exile.[19]

More than a teleological transit from resistance to exile, archival documents such as Chaskel's note tell a story of constant opposition between resistance and exile. Beyond filmmakers' rhetoric, this opposition also finds expression in their cinematic practice. The meanings of resistance lie at the heart of this conflict. As mentioned in the film festival history discussed in the previous chapter, director Miguel Littin spoke in Caracas one year after the coup and defined the cinema of resistance as those films that "have as a priority to forge the image of a people in struggle and with faith in victory" and those "that analyze different periods of the life of the country so as to rightfully comprehend recent events and project the future."[20] This double notion can be taken as the standard definition of a cinema of resistance. But a closer look at the films that exile directors made reveals a more nuanced account. Resistance came to name radical cinematic practices that were quite different from each other.

The real struggle that the notion of a cinema of resistance evidences is one over the politics of exile cinema—over the political nature of cinema under life in exile. This chapter draws on a variety of films together with primary sources to call into question this hegemonic definition and explore the plural meanings of resistance in all their aesthetic and political richness. It focuses on films made and released between 1974 and 1976 precisely to show that a cinema of exile did not come after a cinema of resistance. Rather, these conflicting approaches were happening simultaneously and early in the history of Chilean exile film and video. The chapter ends by considering the emergence of an exilic discourse as an alternative to the rhetoric of resistance with *Il n'y a pas d'oubli* (*There Is No Forgetting*, Rodrigo González, Marilú Mallet, and Jorge Fajardo, 1975) and the film's original funding proposal submitted to the NFB, both of which constitute a veritable theory of exile. By examining a wide range of strategies associated with the cinemas of resistance, this chapter challenges monolithic accounts of the politics of exile cinema.

RESISTANCE, OR A PEOPLE IN STRUGGLE

The image of the multitude—the people, the masses, the crowds, the many—was inherent in the cinema made in Chile during the UP.[21] The documentary short *Venceremos* (Pedro Chaskel and Héctor Ríos, Chile, 1970) ends with the masses rushing into the streets to celebrate Allende's electoral triumph and with an arresting final image. The crowds perform all the gestures of a festive demonstration: they jump, chant, dance, wave hands, and pounce at the shaking camera, placed in close proximity to the action.[22] The last image captures a multitude in the making, but one that in its coming together has already surpassed the camera, already left it behind as if knowing that the apparatus can record but not contain, never enclose, such a powerful collective force.[23] The "people" thus became a protagonist in the films produced during the three brief years of Allende's government, as a mythical community that enacts, celebrates, and defends the political transformations, and as one that resists the advances of the reactionary forces preparing their assault on the country.[24]

The notion of resistance ties itself to an image of the people and to a sense of struggle, an association made explicit in the subtitle of *The Battle of Chile*—"The Struggle of a People without Arms"—and in the titles of other exile films made in 1975, such as *La historia es nuestra y la hacen los pueblos* (*History Is Ours and It Is Made by the People*, Álvaro Ramírez, GDR) and *A los pueblos del mundo* (To the Peoples of the World, Latin American Film Project, US). This temporal coincidence suggests that invoking a people that *resists* was a fundamental goal for Chilean filmmakers in the early years of exile. Understood as a cinematic objective, resistance speaks to Octavio Getino's definition of militant cinema as an "internal category" of Third Cinema, for the Argentine director conceived of militant filmmaking as an "instrument, complement or support of a specific political goal."[25] A "more specific" variation on Third Cinema, militant films could adopt a variety of genres—like the essay, the pamphlet, the informational film, or the agitational film—and would emerge out of the vital dialogue with their "concrete" audience.[26] In this sense, Getino posited inconclusiveness as an intrinsic attribute of militant cinema, since in the end the filmic practice was to be redefined "on the basis of each concrete historical circumstance."[27] This understanding of militant cinema finds strong resonance in Chilean exile films, for the agitational logic subordinated to a political goal was certainly one of their driving characteristics. Yet the condition of forced political displacement poses challenges to a definition of militant filmmaking that assigns such an important role to the audience, for in exile said audience transforms itself into an indeterminate collective.

Consider the early work of Sergio Castilla. A few months after the coup and while exiled in Sweden, Castilla began working on a couple of brief pieces of agitation and denunciation, produced by the Swedish Film Institute and meant to be exhibited on television. Brevity and immediacy reveal themselves as crucial characteristics, and they remind us of Colombian filmmaker Carlos Alvarez's maxim that political filmmaking must be the "cinema of four minutes."[28] Likewise, the historical proximity between the event of the coup, the director's exile, and the making of these short pieces recalls another Álvarez in his plea for haste in the vital relation between art and commitment. Famous Cuban documentarian Santiago Álvarez claimed: "Without fear of producing a minor or inferior artistic work, the filmmaker must approach reality with urgency and anxiety."[29] And this is what Castilla did. Using children's drawings and a famous photograph of Pinochet with sunglasses, Castilla crafted a four-minute animation that achieved its goal—according to him—just by virtue of appearing in the TV guide.[30] The film gains meaning in the uttering of its title: *Pinochet: Fascista, asesino, traidor, agente del imperialismo* (*Pinochet: Fascist, Murderer, Traitor, Agent of Imperialism*, Sweden, 1974)—epithets that are repeated by the stark voice-over of a woman on the soundtrack. Near the end the woman's voice "speaks" the credits and informs viewers that "Latin American children's drawings were used" in the making of the film. The verb matters: the drawing is *used* to charge it with meaning with the help of a voice that admits only a single interpretation. Heir to the rich tradition of militancy outlined

FIGURE 14. Still from *Pinochet: Fascista, asesino, traidor, agente del imperialismo* (*Pinochet: Fascist, Murderer, Traitor, Agent of Imperialism*, Sergio Castilla, Sweden, 1974).

by Getino, the film's purpose is clear: to agitate and denounce. The ultimate goal is to deliver a message by the Chilean resistance and spread it to the world. With the background of a Chilean flag colored by children, the last words of the voice-over claim: "The Chilean people will crush fascism."

Castilla's next short film, *Quisiera, quisiera tener un hijo* (*I Wish, I Wish I Had a Son*, 1974), also uses children's illustrations to sustain its visual narrative. In this case it is a little girl who speaks throughout the film, informing the audience at the beginning that they are seeing "drawings made by children who witnessed the 1973 coup." Several devices mark these drawings with dramatic and symbolic force: sound effects (bombs and explosions), inflections of the voice that accentuate key words, rapid and shaky camera pans, and repetitions (of camera movements and of several words that are read).[31] The film ends once again with a similar message of hope: "The children, women, and men from Chile prepare themselves for the struggle. We will struggle until we overcome." In this short film we hear the voice of a child, but it works as a prosthetic voice corresponding to an invisible social body (the people that will triumph). An aural social body—absent from the visuals—speaks in the first-person plural to invoke the solidarity of the people it alludes to. Like the dominant rhetoric of resistance, this aural social body convinces viewers that, through unity, the people will crush fascism. The informational and agitational functions of Castilla's shorts point back to two of the militant film "genres" as conceptualized by Getino. But the *instrumental* function of militancy is even more relevant here: the goal is to contribute to the spreading of the message of the Chilean resistance by simultaneously alluding to the absent image of a people in struggle and to the missing national audience in exile. This absence marks the new historical conjuncture that redefines the diasporic practice of militant cinema, and thus these two short films work primarily in the mode of infiltration—hijacking the public television network by uttering the words that call to action.

Agitational films such as these, we are repeatedly told in interviews, short texts, and round panels in film festivals, are the works that the Chilean Resistance demands—Resistance with a capital "R," the main concept under which to interpret the historical moment Chilean filmmakers were facing.[32] The insistence on the capital "R" is indicative of the explicit logic of subordination behind the demands of resistance. I have shown throughout the previous chapter that the rhetoric of resistance implies equivalence between artistic and sociopolitical practices, but what really dominates is a principle of subservience. As Nelly Richard has argued with regard to the art world, "The Chilean traditional Left has always thought of the relation between culture and politics as one of instrumental subordination."[33] In this case, cinema is thought of as a "front" of struggle in service of resistance, and this is why this front is inevitably anchored to a mythical collective "we": the people that enacts solidarity, struggles, and resists.

As for the "rightful comprehension of events" that Littin identified in his Caracas talk as the second demand of the Chilean Resistance—besides forging the image of a people in struggle—*Die Fäuste vor der Kanone* (Fists against the Cannons, Orlando Lübbert and Gastón Ancelovici, West Germany, 1972/1974) provides a good example. Coproduced by Cinemateca Chilena, it begins with a title card that reads: "Production of this film began in Chile with the support of Chilean workers. It was completed outside of Chile with the help of the International Solidarity movement in support of the struggle of the Chilean people." Initiated during the UP, the film was meant to be a history of the labor movement in Chile from the late nineteenth century onward. The coup and the completion of the film in exile did not change the documentary's nature—a story of the labor movement is what viewers get through archival photographs and a conventional voice-over narration—but the new context did change the film's narrative structure and historical interpretation.

Fists against the Cannons works as counter-history. Against the dominant narratives of the Chilean oligarchy, the film proposes an exercise of popular memory and an immersion in the archive of workers' struggle. The coup adds an extra layer of retrospective reading. The film sees the army's insurrection in 1973 as an "instrument of multinational capitalism," suggesting that Pinochet's dictatorship is not a radical break but only one instantiation in a long history of economic and political oppression. In its *longue durée* historiographical analysis, *Fists against the Cannons* offers a "more rightful" understanding of events and, in so doing, enables the imagination of a new future by the collective "we" invoked in exile.

Despite its didactic function, this strand of resistance was not restricted to documentary alone. Littin himself had pioneered what this cinema could look like in the realm of fiction with *La tierra prometida* (The Promised Land, 1973). After resigning as president of Chilefilms in 1971, Littin began a project that would materialize the ideas about national and popular culture he had sketched out in the 1970 manifesto, which proclaimed: "Let us no longer allow the dominant classes to uproot the symbols which the people have produced in the course of their long struggle for liberation."[34] The result was an impressive epic examining the intersection of history and folk culture—"perhaps the most ambitious undertaking in the history of Latin American militant cinema," as Julianne Burton claimed in a review for *Film Quarterly*.[35] *The Promised Land* focuses on a group of landless peasants and their leader José Durán in Chile's countryside in the early 1930s. Taking over uninhabited government land, they found the Palmilla settlement. Excited by the news that the socialist republic of Marmaduque Grove has reached the nation's presidency, Durán leads his men to the local town of Huique to overthrow the provincial government. After finding out that the socialist presidency was quickly toppled, lasting only two weeks in power, the group's leader hesitates about how to proceed: whether to continue the peasants' takeover or initiate a dialogue with the local authorities. But the landlords and oligarchs know exactly how to proceed. They have no doubts, and they order the military to massacre the peasants. Durán and his group retreat to the valley, where they are slaughtered in a spectacular final sequence.

Though the film was shot and completed prior to the coup, its reception was tied to the condition of exile. As mentioned in the previous chapter, *The Promised Land* had its world premiere in Moscow in June 1973, two months before the coup, but all its subsequent festival screenings, theatrical releases, and nontheatrical showings took place in and after 1974. In his *Cahiers du cinéma* review following the film's Parisian opening, Serge Toubiana is explicit about this fact: "*The Promised Land* comes to us Europeans . . . as a film of exile, which has been uprooted from the countryside and the shantytowns where it would have had quite a different impact."[36] Toubiana was quick to recognize that this uprooting expands the temporality and the ideological analyses that can be derived from the relations between the film's setting (in Chile in the 1930s), the moment of its production (Chile in 1972, under Allende's government), and the time of its first showings in 1974 (in exile while Chile was living under dictatorship).[37] This temporal opening differs from what happened with the making of *The Battle of Chile*, whose production includes exile, as Guzmán's documentary was shot in Chile but edited and completed after long years of work in Cuba. Aware of this difference, Toubiana warned against reading Littín's film only in light of the September 1973 coup, "suppressing its original conditions of production."[38] The temptation was strong, for how can we avoid interpreting the film's treatment of its protagonist's revolutionary hesitations as criticism of Allende's leadership and vocation for political dialogue with its opponents? And how can we eschew the film's display of the massacred naked body of actress Carmen Bueno, kidnapped and disappeared by the secret police right around the time of *The Promised Land*'s first European screenings?

Critics like Burton, Toubiana, and Pascal Bonitzer warned against the desire to yield to the film's deceivingly simple message and to "think that its lessons can be assimilated without difficulty."[39] The "simple message" was superbly summarized by Toubiana: "It consists in saying to the peasants of 1972: your forefathers did the same thing, forty years ago, when they occupied the Palmilla lands under the guidance of José Durán, and the rich men's army came and massacred them. Let this memory serve to avoid the errors of the past."[40] Besides functioning as a succinct recounting of the film's primordial idea, Toubiana's wording points once again to Littín's definition of a cinema of resistance as one that provides "a more rightful" comprehension of historical events, and that does so while it produces an image of "the people" in struggle. While this is unmistakably the film's message, its formal operations and distancing devices are far more complex, especially with regards to the tension between image and sound, between the voiceover split in a double-voice narrator, and between this polyphonic speech and the lyrics of the film's songs. *The Promised Land* offers an epic that looks at the peasantry and the process of land redistribution and agrarian reform in the country, while simultaneously providing a visual spectacle that does not shy away from investigating myth and forms of popular culture. Ultimately, the film examines the writing of history and who gets to enact it.

In a time of proliferation of theories and manifestos about the powers of "politically made films," *The Promised Land* was quickly seen as emblematic of Third Cinema's capacity to work as a "guardian of popular memory," in Teshome Gabriel's famous words.[41] There was a significant sequence toward the end that supported this critical reading. Patriot Arturo Prat (one of those nineteenth-century figures "uprooted" by the dominant classes to foster a nationalist narrative, according to Littín in the 1970 manifesto) emerges in the middle of the final battle to give his sword to young peasant Chirigüa. José, the leader of the revolt narrated by the film, returns from the dead, galloping, and also gives his firearm to Chirigüa. The message is once again unmistakable and simple: the scene suggests that political struggles exist in a continuum and that the Chilean people have history on their side.

But not everyone was as convinced as the critics previously quoted. After its Pesaro screening, and writing for the French magazine *Positif*, Zuzana M. Pick claimed: "Even if Pesaro . . . opened with *The Promised Land* . . . , it isn't perhaps until *Dialogues of Exiles* (1974) by Raúl Ruiz that we can realize the new meaning we should give to the struggles of liberation in Latin America. Because it is not enough for the revolution to pursue its course that survivors pick up the firearms of dead combatants, Raúl Ruiz shot last spring, in Paris, this Dialogue that is so much more than a film about the condition of Chilean exiles in France."[42] Perhaps there was another way to conceive of a cinema of resistance and another way to investigate the cinematic representation of the popular.

RESISTANCE AS INQUIRY

Although Raúl Ruiz was a militant member of the Socialist Party, he was against the category of the militant artist—in his words, "always a bad militant and a bad artist."[43] Ruiz's early films offered evidence of his political unorthodoxy, diverging from the more overt radical paths followed by his Chilean and Latin American peers. The critical concepts and theoretical notions about cinema that he began to develop in the mid-1960s also distanced Ruiz from his colleagues. In a well-known dialogue with writers Enrique Lihn and Federico Schopf, published in 1970, Ruiz established a counterpoint between his views and those of

Littin.⁴⁴ Apropos of the much-celebrated *El chacal de Nahueltoro* (The Jackal of Nahueltoro, Miguel Littin, 1969), Ruiz reproached Littin for insisting with that film on a trite idea of a popular subculture resisting a dominant one. Ruiz proposed instead what he called "un cine de indagación" (a cinema of inquiry).⁴⁵ Opposed to the didacticism of the likes of Solanas and Gettino, and to the allegorical work of someone like Glauber Rocha, Ruiz's cinema of inquiry was an effort in "ideological introspection," a search for the clues that would explain a given group or nation.⁴⁶

The notion of resistance is crucial to the politics behind a cinema of inquiry, but Ruiz understood the concept in a way that had nothing to do with Littin's and other exile filmmakers' use of it. For Ruiz, there was no culture of resistance because culture *is* resistance.⁴⁷ Resistance does not name the key concept under which to imagine practices of cultural struggle in exile; it names a series of "tactics of rejection of any given order."⁴⁸ A cinema of inquiry thus rejects all kinds of imperatives (therefore, it is a cinema that *resists*) and has the capacity to become an ideological exercise (*introspection*) for the whole crew that participates in making the film. Ruiz saw the practice of a cinema of inquiry as an alternative to two models of "political modernism."⁴⁹ One was what he called a "cinema of foundations," which he associated with Jean-Luc Godard—a cinema that asks itself about the meaning of making films. Ruiz called the second model a "cinema of discovery," and he associated it with Littin—a cinema that explores a terra incognita, the underworlds of the lower classes, to show it to the rest of the world.⁵⁰

Exile is sometimes seen as a rupture in Ruiz's career, but tracing the threads of a cinema of inquiry shows that several of his exile films retain the main characteristics of his Chilean work.⁵¹ It is nonetheless undeniable that exile meant a radicalization of certain aesthetic and political procedures, as Ruiz redefined his cinematic practice in a transatlantic dialogue between Latin America and Europe. One of these procedures regards the investigation of forms of popular speech and the ways in which Chileans use language to *resist* the duties imposed by the real world.⁵² Popular language—a meandering way of speaking, avoidance of verbs, repetition, jumping from one idea to the next without apparent logical connection—was part of these everyday strategies of resistance that cinema could turn into a vehicle of ideological introspection through the medium's "function of recognition."⁵³ This is something that Ruiz pursued in his first exile film, *Dialogue d'exilés* (*Dialogues of Exiles*, France, 1974), which is full of scenes in which the exiles interrogate their sense of self through conversations—sometimes paradoxical, sometimes nonsensical. They alternate between Spanish and French, and they debate politics and ideology as if they were still residing in the nation that expelled them. The fractures exposed by spoken language reveal what Ruiz referred to as exile's ability to produce "an excess of identity" as opposed to a loss of it.[54] As argued elsewhere, this emphasis on fractured speech as constitutive of the exile experience finds visual correlation in the device of the 360-degree pan, one of the defining mechanisms by which Ruiz explores the Parisian apartments in *Dialogues of Exiles*.[55] A circling camera, usually in a long take that lasts an entire sequence, moves around an apartment filled with exiles: children sitting on the floor and drawing, a woman ironing, a group of men discussing a press release about the situation in Chile, a man narrating one of his dreams. Another scene pushes the device one step further: exiles enter and exit the frame, opening and closing doors and room dividers as they move through an apartment whose spatial coordinates we do not fully understand, as the camera follows the characters' movements in a circle. This cinematic device fulfills an obvious descriptive purpose in showing the crowded houses of exiles, living in borrowed and temporary apartments where domestic life coexists with political organization and therapeutic conversations. But the circular take also reveals something deeper, which is the profoundly altered sense of space that exiles experience, wherein no room constitutes a single entity, everything is discontinuous, and each space is populated by a multiplicity of other spaces. In this, *Dialogues of Exiles* internalizes the conditions of its own production and becomes an allegory of its making, to borrow Hamid Naficy's formulation. At the time, the creative figures and participants in the film were living the experiences of their characters: crashing in other exiles' apartments, struggling with the language, debating politics in cramped spaces.[56]

Dialogues of Exiles responded to the question of how to make a political film as a refugee in France. As seen in the previous chapter regarding its negative reception during the 1974 Pesaro festival, the film resulted in Ruiz being ostracized, with no recourse for him other than to "become French."[57] There is likely some degree of exaggeration when Ruiz claims that he "was literally excised from all Chilean and Latin American organizations" after the film's first screenings.[58] Archival documents evidence, nonetheless, that the debate was real and heated in France as well.[59] The transcription of a postscreening conversation between the makers—director Ruiz, producer Percy Matas, cinematographer Luis Poirot, and actress Carla Cristi—a journalist from the newspaper *Libération*, and an audience composed of Latin American and Chilean exiles points to key problems for the politics of exile cinema, particularly for a strand of filmmaking that wants to engage with political problems by less conventional means. The viewers repeatedly insist on the question of purpose (What is the objective of making a film like this in a time like this?), the question of the audience (Who is this film made for? The French People? Chilean and Latin American exiles?), and the question of instrumentality (Don't you see that what the film depicts can be grossly misappropriated by the Right?). As the preceding sections of this chapter demonstrate, these questions provide the basis for all conceptualizations of radical cinemas since the 1960s. The condition of exile forces filmmakers to redefine their practice and adapt the aesthetic principles they were working with to a new context.

Ruiz's caustic critique of the Chilean exile experience was thought to be inappropriate for that new context. That is, by 1975, when the film was theatrically released in France—a moment at which the Chilean dictatorship's rates of imprisonment, torture, murders, and disappearance were at their highest—the priorities of Chilean exile cinema should be anything but internal critique. This was, at least, the position of the "cinema of resistance" in its dominant form. After seeing *Dialogues* in Pesaro, Littin confessed to Ruiz that he had "very much liked the film" but thought it was not the right time to make it.

By no means do I want to create an artificial opposition between Littin and Ruiz.[60] It is nevertheless relevant to sketch some of the counterpoints between them as they apply to different understandings of resistance. During the UP government, Littin was seen as the cinematic embodiment of the 1970 manifesto—in short, someone who conceived of cinema as an instrument, a tool in service of something much larger than cinema: the path toward socialism. Differing from Littin's acute sense of political responsibility, Ruiz considered his relationship with politics one of "irresponsibility" and "experimentation."[61] Once in exile, Littin responded to displacement through the logic of resistance with a capital "R," forging the image of a people in struggle. Ruiz in turn responded critically to what he called "the ideology of exile." Zuzana Pick argues that by this Ruiz meant the idealization of the past, the fetishization of the nation, and the easy reliance on "popular memory" and folk culture as ways to establish a closer link with the people.[62] These are all elements that can be associated with Littin's cinema, elements that Ruiz was highly suspicious of, as evidenced in *Dialogues of Exiles*.

In his *Dialogues*, Ruiz carried out a poetics of exile devoid of nostalgia and of any kind of romantic view about Chile. His attention to the vicissitudes of Chilean speech in a French setting, and his insistence on dissecting the inner dynamics of a closed group—the "ghetto" of exile—revealed an ethnographic impulse, one that explored behavioral relations in imaginative ways and in a fictive world. Ruiz's political intervention was to avoid completely the expectations of a film made by a Chilean exile one year after the coup. This refusal to talk the language of international solidarity and resistance against the military dictatorship was misunderstood for a lack of engagement with politics when it was in fact the opposite, a radical inquiry into the consequences of exile within a given community.[63]

THE FEMINIST GAZE AS RESISTANCE

Ruiz's cinema of inquiry was not the only challenge to the more hegemonic definitions of a cinema of resistance. Exile filmmakers Marilú Mallet, Angelina Vázquez, and Valeria Sarmiento developed an alternative way of conceiving of resistance by advancing a decidedly feminist gaze. As Elizabeth Ramírez-Soto and Catalina Donoso Pinto claim, their work functioned as a form of triple "rebellion": against traditional film genres, against a political imperative ("el deber ser de lo político"), and against expectations that European programmers and audiences had for Latin American cinema.[64] The production history of their early short films in Chile, and later that of their work in exile, evidences the material challenges faced in particular by women filmmakers in the diaspora.[65] These challenges forced them to find new modes of production—as discussed in chapter 2 about Vázquez's practice of "lived solidarity"—and new aesthetic avenues that *resisted* the dominant forms of understanding cinematic resistance. One of these avenues was the diary film as pursued by Mallet and Vázquez in the early 1980s with the goal of interrogating female subjectivity in exile, which will be the focus of a close analysis in the next chapter. But centering stories on women characters and finding formal strategies to propel a feminist perspective are traits common to their entire work. Mallet established a name for herself in the landscape of Quebecois and Canadian cinema by directing projects for the Ministry of Immigration and the NFB that had women labor migrants at their center, such as *À force de points* (1979) and *Les Borges* (1978)—the latter analyzed in chapter 2. Later in her career, she explored questions of home and domestic life in exile through a gendered lens—*Journal inachevé* (Unfinished Diary, 1982)—love and desire—*Chère Amérique* (*Dear America*, 1990) and *2, Rue de la mémoire* (2, Memory Street, 1996)—and the figure of the woman artist—*Double Portrait* (*Double Portrait*, 2001) and *Sur les Traces de Marguerite Yourcernar* (*Searching for Marguerite Yourcenar*, 2011).

Vázquez approached all her work through a feminist lens as well. Her 1982 films *Apuntes nicaragüenses* (*Sketches on Nicaragua*) and *Presencia lejana* (*Distant Presence*) examine internationalist and cross-cultural solidarity specifically by focusing on the histories of female brigade members and militants of leftist organizations. *Dos años en Finlandia* (*Two Years in Finland*, 1975) documents the experiences of the first groups of Chilean refugees in the Nordic country, but special attention is placed on women laborers who work in the industry sector and on motherhood. Likewise, the short didactic animation *Así nace un desaparecido* (*This Is How a Disappeared Is Born*, 1977) shows viewers the plight of the relatives of the disappeared and their struggle against a judicial system in complicity with the dictatorship. Such a plight stresses the experiences of women: women relatives who search for their missing sons, daughters, and husbands, and women detainees who face abhorrent forms of sexual abuse in clandestine prisons. The latter narrative thread is reformulated via fiction in *Gracias a la vida (o la pequeña historia de una mujer maltratada)* (*Thanks to Life*, 1979), in which the protagonist is Silvia, a survivor of sexual violence perpetrated by the state. She arrives in her exile in Finland pregnant with a baby engendered by her torturer. *Thanks to Life* makes clear that Silvia is not sure whether she wants to keep the baby or not, although her husband would really like her to. It is not the only conflict between the couple: he will want to return to Chile to join the subversive struggle against the dictatorship at home, and she will want to stay in Finland. There is a life for exile subjects beyond resistance, the film suggests.

The lives of exiles are torn by displacement, but they are not defined by the sole condition of their uprooting. This fact finds expression in the themes of several exile films made by women directors—and in the choices their characters make—as well as in these filmmakers' feminist practice. Valeria Sarmiento is a case in point, as her films explored topics, stories, and political processes that were unrelated to Chile or to exile.

Sarmiento is mostly known for offering a destabilization of the male gaze and an innovative subversion of melodrama in films such as *Amelia Lopes O'Neill* (France/Chile, 1990), *Rosa la China* (Cuba/Spain/Portugal/

France, 2002), and the most critically acclaimed of all, her feature-length fictional debut *Notre mariage* (Our Marriage, France/Portugal, 1984).[66] *Notre mariage* was based on the romance novella *Mi boda contigo* by Corín Tellado and borrowed from the traditions of American melodrama (Douglas Sirk in particular), Latin American radio and television soap operas, and the pulp novel. The result was a "deliciously immoral" tale of incestuous desire, narrated with a "perverse" gaze.[67] Such perversity refers to the director's ability to add hauntings layers of menace to familiar situations—what Sarmiento herself has called the "sinister" tone that hovers over her films.[68] Ramírez-Soto, who has provided the most comprehensive studies of Sarmiento's modes of production in exile, argues that this perversity constitutes one of the defining traits of Sarmiento as an auteur.[69]

Sarmiento's documentary work would prove to be equally "sinister" in projects of a different nature, for instance, in her experimental approach to the life of immigrants in the suburbs of Paris in *Gens de toutes parts . . . gens de nulle part* (1979) where she fragments the bodies of her interviewees; in her daring indictment of socialist Cuba through the relations between childhood, pedagogy, and the revolution in *El planeta de los niños* (The Planet of Children, 1990); or in her analysis of *machismo* through codified elements of Latin American popular culture in *El hombre cuando es hombre* (A Man, When He is a Man, 1982), probably her most famous film.[70]

Both Sarmiento's prolific documentary work and the few feature-length melodramas she was able to produce in exile clearly deviated from the "demands of the Chilean resistance."[71] It is worth highlighting in this regard her first short film in exile, *La femme au foyer* (*The Housewife*, 1976), because it was an early and bold example of this deviation: a film that wanted to address the historical and political situation exiles had just lived, but without insisting on the idea of resistance as cultural struggle.

Like her husband Ruiz in *Dialogues of Exiles*, Sarmiento did not renounce politics but adopted an "oblique" and tangential look at political processes.[72] *The Housewife* explores the complex world of middle-class and upper-middle-class women in Chile who opposed the government of Allende and the UP coalition, just before the coup.[73] The distribution materials of the organization that backed the production of the project—Groupe de Recherches et d'Essais Cinématographiques (GREC; Group of Investigations and Cinematic Essays)—stress this focus on the women of the "petite bourgeoisie." The dossier states in writing the questions that the film asks through its narrative form: "Who are these women and what is their point of view? How did they experience the process of the Popular Unity?"[74] These questions point back to the cinema of inquiry, although here the work of ideological introspection is filtered through a feminist angle.

As I have detailed elsewhere, Sarmiento's short film is set entirely within an enclosed space: an apartment in a rich borough of Santiago (with Paris serving as a faux Santiago), where women watch telenovelas, clean obsessively, and complain about their maids and about Allende's government.[75] The only exterior shot in *The Housewife* is its final one: from across the street, viewers see a woman smiling on her balcony as the soundtrack shifts to the sound of the Hawker Hunter jets flying overhead en route to attack La Moneda, the presidential palace. When most of her colleagues were obsessively using the footage of the bombardment of the palace as the visual signifier of the coup—including the first part of *The Battle of Chile*, *Fists against the Cannons*, and *To the People of the World*—Sarmiento chose instead to do away with its iconography, rendering the historical event as an aural reference.[76] When her exiled Chilean colleagues returned to the experience of the UP to glorify it, Sarmiento approached that experience instead by focusing on a group of bored middle-class women performing domestic tasks. If the common visual signs alluding to the Allende years were absent in her film, so was the collective subject that embodied them: "the people." In so doing, Sarmiento pointed to a different kind of ideological battle, one that was fought at the time not in the streets, but inside people's homes.

EXILE POETICS AND EXILIC DISCOURSE IN *IL N'Y A PAS D'OUBLI*

Home, the domestic sphere, and everyday life appear as vital concerns to filmmakers who attempt a different kind of politics of exile cinema. An early exile film proves that the dominant, overarching narrative of resistance coexisted with an emerging discourse of exile. Produced by the NFB in 1975, *Il n'y a pas d'oubli* (*There Is No Forgetting*) was conceived as a coherent whole made of three independent thirty-minute pieces directed by Chilean exile filmmakers: *J'explique certaines choses* (*I Explain a Few Things*) by Rodrigo González, *Lentement* (*Slowly*) by Marilú Mallet, and *Jours de fer* (*Steel Blues*) by Jorge Fajardo.[77] Each part developed its own aesthetics and its own thematic reflection about the condition of exile in general and the situation of Chilean exiles in

Montreal in particular.[78] As a whole, *There Is No Forgetting* proposes both an exile poetics—a distinct set of aesthetic and narrative devices to approach the experience of exile in cinema—and a properly exilic discourse: a "common imaginary construction" that seeks to make sense of the specific form of displacement that constitutes the exile experience.[79]

The first part is the most theatrical, dominated by speech and characters voicing the political rhetoric of the UP. As defined by González, *I Explain a Few Things* is an "anthropological study of a group" whose center is an exiled professor who falls ill.[80] Former students, friends, and acquaintances come see him and wait for his death in visits that quickly turn into meetings at which the characters talk politics and interact as a community redefining itself in exile: each person playing a role in this minitheater of the exile condition.[81] Made around the same time, although thousands of miles apart, *I Explain a Few Things* is thus similar to Ruiz's *Dialogues of Exiles*, in that it attempts "re-production more than narration."[82] Like Ruiz's cinema of inquiry, González wanted "un cine de constatación," a cinema that establishes and exposes language and its folds with the goal of comprehending the inner workings of a group.[83]

The second short film focuses on intercultural relationships and the troubles of assimilation by delving into the private life of a woman, Lucía Barahona, who starts dating a Quebecois hippie. They both look at themselves and at each other in a gaze marked by a double process of self-exoticization and othering. *Slowly* alternates between a documentary narrator—a voice in the third person that comments on the character and provides bits of historical and contextual information—and a more fictional narrative told through the point of view of the female protagonist. In a subplot, Chilean exiles pressure Lucía and encourage her to appear on television to talk about her experience of detention and torture. After much hesitation, she accepts. The final minutes of *Slowly* consist of Lucía's affected face and voice, the powerful rhetoric and performance of testimony.

With little dialogue and in an observational style reminiscent of the tradition of direct cinema documentaries, the third short is a bleak story of labor and immigration that provides *There Is No Forgetting* with a sense of circular closure. After playing Pablo, one of the students in *I Explain a Few Things*, actor Manuel Aránguiz reappears as a different Pablo in *Steel Blues*. In the closing short film, he is now a middle-class man who takes a job as an *ouvrier* in a factory while his family remains in Chile. Here, the pains of exile relate to the hardships of every experience of migration: inability to speak the language of the employer, uselessness of one's skills and previous professional experience, rejection, and discrimination, but also the solidarity of peers and strangers. The hardships faced by the protagonist find an echo in the style of the film, as Fajardo wanted his images to bridge the optical and the haptic. The reality they captured had to become tangible; the camera would be "the palm that explores everything like the palm of a blind man." The film's ultimate goal was to capture the "total sensation" of an exile working in a factory.[84]

As a whole, *There Is No Forgetting* paints a larger picture of the experience of Chilean exile. An unconfessed resistance to assimilation and the exiles' most acute sense of dislocation dominate the first segment. These characters are defined as a group and through the exclusive reproduction of the UP (a group of people who still live mentally in Chile while living in exile in Canada). The second segment leaves politics in the background and gives viewers something of a love story, or an interrogation on intercultural relationships in exile. One can anticipate that Lucía will live her life in exile and that she will integrate successfully into Quebecois culture. The third segment is a less optimistic portrait and reminds spectators that the exile drama is one of distance, separation (family is far away and present only in the form of epistolary exchange), and discrimination, and that all of this is exerted on a body (the immobile body of Pablo in the film's final freeze-frame).

In his study of Iranian television production in Los Angeles, Hamid Naficy, with the help of anthropologist Arnold Von Gennep's work on rites of passage, defined exile as a "process of becoming" involving three phases: separation from home, liminality or in-betweenness, and incorporation into the host society.[85] A few years prior to Naficy, Ana Vásquez and Ana María Araujo, in their pioneering research on Chileans, also identified three phases in this becoming exile. They called them "arrival, transculturation, and prolongation."[86] Trauma, mourning, and a deep feeling of guilt mark the phase of arrival. The exile is alive; the others are not. The exile is better off; the ones in Chile are the real martyrs. Transculturation refers to the ongoing negotiation between resistance to and integration into the host society.[87] Prolongation is the phase in which collective myths and personal beliefs collapse. Exiles question themselves and the social and political project they were part of. They must decide, when the moment comes, whether to return or not. But even if they do, the state of exile prolongs itself well after the long-awaited homecoming.

At the core of these phases in which subjects become exiles lies a question of positionality: Where are exile subjects located; from where can they speak? With the Chilean case in mind, Zuzana M. Pick conceived of exile as a "subject position produced by a series of political, social, and cultural conditions tending to disengage human activity in the public sphere."[88] Naficy, in turn, concluded that the state of in-betweenness defines the exiles' experience; their position is always interstitial and liminal. To be in exile is "to be traveling in the slipzone." These phases of exile, whatever the name we give to them, are simultaneous and not just consecutive. Hence, exile is a process of "perpetual" becoming.[89]

The three-part structure of *There Is No Forgetting* is reminiscent of this division into phases of the exile experience. Indeed, in their project proposal to the NFB the three filmmakers make explicit reference to this structure. González focuses on how a human group resists a foreign culture that, little by little, ends up "taking possession" of the group. Fajardo concludes that "le Québec s'impose" (Quebec ends up taking over). And Mallet, advancing a theory of displacement in 1974, only one year after her departure from Chile, argues that exile is constituted by three phases: "the ghetto, subsistence, and integration—the moment in which exile is finally transformed into the quotidian."[90] With this in mind, Gonzalez's piece can easily be thought of as the one representing the phase of the ghetto, since it is devoted to the relations between a community of exiles that can only speak the language of the past. Fajardo's closing film, focusing on the very first days of a man in Quebec who starts a new job, would address the period of subsistence. And Mallet's segment, with its focus on everyday life, would speak for the phase of integration.

There Is No Forgetting seems to prove Naficy's point that these phases are not consecutive, not linear or chronological. The placing of *Slowly* in the middle of the film and not at the end reaffirms the fact that these periods of exile can be reverted. The end, with Pablo's freeze-frame in Fajardo's film, is a new beginning. He is still in the ghetto, but his is a different one—the Quebecois working class of transnational labor migrants. Isn't he an immigrant like the Portuguese who work by his side? Lucía, in turn, does away with the ultimate aspiration of the exile—to return home—and clearly says she *wants* to stay. Thus the film challenges the official narratives and undoes this process of becoming.

A film like *There Is No Forgetting* proves that some filmmakers were elaborating both a discourse of exile and an exile poetics at the same time that their peers were privileging more explicit forms of political filmmaking. One—exile cinema—does not come after the other—cinema of resistance. They are both two sides of the same problem: how to pursue radical aesthetic forms under forced displacement. Exile directors respond through the agitational short film (Castilla), with documentaries that perform historiographical analyses (Lübbert and Ancelovici), and through the forging of a mythical collectivity known as the people (Littin). These practices fall under the dominant logic of resistance as a front of struggle against the dictatorship at home, but this chapter has shown that there were competing understandings of resistance. Ruiz's cinema of inquiry examines the inner workings of the exiles as a group: the intricacies of their functioning as a ghetto relying on the speech and language of the past. But as they continue to look for ideological introspection and a function of recognition, Ruiz's early exile films face the theoretical and material problem of a missing audience. Women exile directors like Mallet, Vázquez, and Sarmiento, in turn, expand both the themes covered by exile filmmakers and the range of their aesthetic forms. Privileging a feminist gaze often perceived as radical by male peers, their work challenges masculinist histories of cinemas of exile and resistance. Finally, *There Is No Forgetting* offers an attempt to think with and through the artistic and social challenges posed by displacement. Advancing a discourse of exile in 1975, the makers of this film respond to the "excess of identity"—Ruiz's words—caused by exile. At the center of this excess lie the question of exilic subjectivity and the cinematic form appropriate for its interrogation.

CHAPTER 5

Subjectivity and the Unfinished Diary

Patricio Guzmán delivered a talk titled "Latin American Cinema: Exile, Crisis, and Future" at a seminar on the topic of criticism organized during the 2nd Havana Film Festival in 1980. The published version in the journal *Cine Cubano* is an invaluable document, as Guzmán identifies an aesthetic stagnation: "Our cinema is going through a crisis of language.... We move ourselves with the premises of the decade of the 1960s, and we are entering the decade of the 1980s."[1] Most importantly, he suggests that this stagnation stems from the subordination of cinema to politics: "During a long time we have denied ourselves the use of aesthetics, the use of modern language.... We have denied ourselves the use of cinema as an art.... We have behaved as if political discourse was the solution to everything."[2] The critique may come as a surprise, considering this is the same filmmaker who, in the text published in the Pesaro 1974 booklet only six years earlier, had called for a Chilean cinema committed to the tasks of resistance. Guzmán may have simply been talking about himself, of his own desire for a new aesthetic pathway, given that the cycle of *The Battle of Chile* had just come to an end with the release of its third part in 1979.[3] But he chose his words with careful intention, and he exaggerated a dichotomy between politics and aesthetics, one that he knew to be false, to make a point: the task of exile filmmakers was to create aesthetic forms, too.

Guzmán's cry for new and inventive cinematic languages—without being overdetermined by political discourse—was a departure from the discussion carried out in the 1970s and an attempt to chart the territory of the future, for which exile filmmakers were ready. They had actually been ready since the beginning of exile, as demonstrated by films that examine the everyday life of displacement, such as *Il n'y a pas d'oubli* (*There Is No Forgetting*, Rodrigo González, Marilú Mallet, and Jorge Fajardo, Canada, 1975), discussed in the last section of the preceding chapter as an early example of exilic discourse. This emphasis on home and everyday life—what Mallet described as the exile phase of "integration"—would gain more prominence in the early years of the 1980s, coinciding with Guzmán's call for new aesthetic forms.[4]

Consider the way Marilú Mallet starts her *Journal inachevé* (Unfinished Diary, 1982). "In the beginning," Mallet's voice says as the film opens, "I would have liked someone to explain to me this very clean, very organized place." This, however, is not the actual beginning. The director's words have followed a brief prologue with still images flashing before the viewers' eyes, with black frame intervals accompanied by the click of a slide projector. This display of photos (which has left the domestic space to which it belongs and reached a public one) shows nothing except ordinary views from Montreal: streets and parks covered by snow. The last image corresponds to a residential street and its façades of red brick houses. After the film's title has been printed over this view, the camera zooms in toward the entrance of a house, a shot accompanied by the sounds of a guitar, and then Mallet's opening words, this "place" she speaks of and that spectators associate with a house they are not yet seeing, this home of which they only know its threshold. If the stills suggest a movement from the interior to the exterior, the zoom in implies the opposite—a movement inward. This is where Mallet begins her unfinished diary: at home.

In the beginning Mallet did not intend to make a diary film but a "letter-film."[5] Scholars like Zuzana M. Pick and Elizabeth Ramírez-Soto have each documented that the original plan was not one filmed letter but an epistolary exchange, a "cine-dialogue," as Mallet called it, between herself and Valeria Sarmiento.[6] If there is a beginning, it could be this. During a trip to France in 1978, Mallet and her husband at the time, Australian filmmaker Michael Rubbo, visited Sarmiento and her partner Raúl Ruiz. As the men talked, they realized they were both making films about elections in France. Rubbo ended up directing *Solzhenitsyn's Children Are Making a Lot of Noise in Paris* (1979) and appearing as a character in Ruiz's reflexive documentary puzzle, *De grands événements et des gens ordinaires* (Of Great Events and Ordinary People, Raúl Ruiz,

France, 1978 [1983]). The two women, in turn, remembered that the last time they had seen each other, in the days of the Allende government in Chile, they were working together on a project that didn't get produced.[7] In exile, they shared common interests once again. Sarmiento said that the letters and news she received from Chile obsessed her, and Mallet told her she was making a film about Nicaraguan poet and priest Ernesto Cardenal, which she planned on calling *Lettre à Carter*.[8] In these conversations, Mallet and Sarmiento started shaping a new idea. They were both questioning what it meant to be a woman filmmaker, and they were both studying diaries and letters as traditional "feminine" genres of expression.[9] Given that letters were the main form of communication in exile, they decided to exchange letter-films. One would shoot a letter-film, send it over, and the other would respond with a new one—a cinematic epistolary exchange.[10] The visit was over. Mallet and Rubbo returned to Montreal. Sarmiento began producing her letter, shot the first, and mailed it to Quebec.[11] Mallet began shooting, too, while working on a proposal to ask for funding from the NFB. In it, she wrote: "Two friends dialogue from a distance, and their subjectivity becomes the measure of everything."[12]

Their subjectivity becomes the measure of everything. In this succinct sentence, Mallet captured the core of her aesthetic quest. Starting from her subjectivity as a woman and as an exile, hers was to be a cinema anchored in intimacy and in the interrogation of the self. Such an aesthetic quest presupposes a locus of enunciation that is simultaneously subjective and historical, combining "a documentary impulse—an outward gaze upon the world—with an equally forceful reflex of self-interrogation."[13] For many Chilean exile directors, that world exerted all of its historical and political weight over their images—leaving them with little room for exercises of self-introspection. Hence the assertion "to have subjectivity be the measure of everything" not only defines the basic principles behind a personal cinema—Mallet's—it also points to the many debates about the nature of political cinema that Chilean exile filmmakers had in the late 1970s, as discussed in the previous chapters. To get to the core of the exile experience, filmmakers move away from resistance as a cinematic project of cultural struggle and turn inward. Exile cinema would imply beginning and ending with the ultimate bastions of the subject: voice, self, body.

This chapter is concerned with the cinematic rendition of exilic subjectivity. By *subjectivity* I mean the production of a social imagination of selfhood; consequently, by *exilic subjectivity* I mean a consciousness of the self that has been produced by the historical and political conditions of exile.[14] Exilic subjectivity expresses itself more clearly in films that are *about* the consciousness that has authored them—in other words, films in which filmmaker and main character, subject and object, coincide. This is the case in Mallet's *Unfinished Diary* and in two other films produced around the same time. All three share the desire for a radical subjectivity together with a main mode of address, the diary film: *Fragmentos de un diario inacabado* (Fragments from an Unfinished Diary, Angelina Vázquez, Finland/Chile, 1983) and *Wenn wir zusammen lebten . . . (If We Lived Together . . .* , Antonio Skármeta, West Germany, 1983). In *Unfinished Diary*, Mallet narrates her everyday life by focusing on the domestic space and on the interactions she has with the outside world in Montreal (with other Chilean exiles; with her husband, friends, and family members; and at work with the participants of another documentary she is filming). In *Fragments from an Unfinished Diary*, director Angelina Vázquez returns semiclandestinely to Chile to capture popular strategies of cultural resistance, documenting several forms of civic, artistic, and political organization. True to its title, and due to her being expelled from the country amid preproduction, the documentary is fragmentary—a collection of sequences that offer elliptical impressions of life in Chile. In *If we Lived Together . . .* , Antonio Skármeta provides a humorous take on the struggles of the everyday lives of exiles. Mixing painting, literature, theater, and cinema, this diary film focuses on the healing powers of art and on exile artists' need to work together, creating a collective consciousness through which they can express themselves.

Both the diary as a cinematic form and the search for exilic subjectivity as a political necessity relate to what cinema studies has variously called "autobiography in film," "first person film," and "cinema of me," or what literature and cultural studies have called "the subjective turn," the "era of intimacy," and the "autobiographical space."[15] Following Alisa Lebow, I prefer the use of "first-person" film because autobiography in these cinematic diaries is less relevant than their mode of address. These works "'speak' from the articulated point of view of the filmmaker who readily acknowledges her subjective position."[16] Coupling *graphy* with *bio*, writing and life, is secondary to locating a site of enunciation, secondary to affirming a subjectivity that speaks and films itself to address collective memory and exile as a historical phenomenon. In other words, these directors are less interested in framing their films as narratives of *their* own lives. Instead, they are more concerned with translating into sounds and images a process of subject positioning, as women and Latin American exiles in Canada and Finland (in the case of Mallet and Vázquez) and as a male writer turned filmmaker in West Germany (in the case of Skármeta). These films offer a gendered exploration of exile and the subjectivity that arises from exile. While the first two are examples of a feminist cinematic practice, the last one is shaped by the trope of the "artist at work," an archetype that is decidedly marked as masculine.

This chapter traces the transnational connections behind these three diary films. In doing so, it retains the traveling and archival impulses that guide this book, while adding a more detailed form of close analysis. I explore the development of the diary film by looking at the transnational movements of filmmakers and their ideas and by analyzing both the films and a series of ancillary documents. The transnational lens and the traveling impulse behind these three projects are at work in various movements inscribed into the making of the films themselves, and sometimes into their diegesis: transits between Canada and France in the origins of *Unfinished Diary*; between Finland and Chile in *Fragments from an Unfinished Diary*; and between Chile, Cuba, Belgium, France, and Germany in *If We Lived Together* . . . . These transnational movements also leave their trace in several paratextual elements coming from interviews gathered from the Fondo Zuzana Pick at the Cineteca Universidad de Chile in Santiago, the draft of the project *Les lettres* written by Mallet and kept at the Cinémathèque québécoise in Montreal, and the personal archive of filmmaker Angelina Vázquez.[17] The latter includes various letters that Vázquez wrote to her friend and collaborator Pablo Perelman, who remained in charge of shooting in Chile after she was deported back to Finland. These archival remnants offer vital insight for understanding what drove filmmakers to the diary form and what propelled them to inscribe the sign of exilic incompletion into their work.

A detailed mode of textual analysis will show that three aspects are central to these films: the unfinished nature of exile, the focus on the present and everyday life, and the elusiveness of first-person enunciation. I begin with the latter. In these first-person films, the *I* is never quite in sync with the voice that names it in language and with the body that renders it a material thing in the world. To fully comprehend this trait, I return to the beginning: Marilú Mallet's proposal for the NFB, entitled *Les Lettres*.

FROM LETTERS TO DIARIES (ON THE AUTO-DIALOGIC)

In her NFB proposal, Mallet expands on the medium of the letter as the "natural language" of exile as well as on the historical role letters played in the lives of women and in their literature. To write a letter is simultaneously to confess and to reveal, to *unveil* what is essential: "The correspondence translates the uncomfortable vision of those gestures and attitudes that hide beneath the ceremony of everyday life."[18] How can we render this unveiling visible, since cinema is not literature? Mallet proposes an atmosphere of intimacy and a "journey through the states of the soul."[19] She envisions a light, moving, and handheld camera, able to wander through the physical environment. The making of a fiction using documentary techniques is stated as a conscious aesthetic choice. Finally, she added the already quoted maxim: "Their subjectivity becomes the measure of everything."

The "their" in this sentence finally became a "her," since Sarmiento could not be part of the project. Ramírez-Soto has reconstructed the intricacies of this unfinished production history. Among other facts, the Canadian independent producer went bankrupt, and the INA in Paris lost interest after finding out that Sarmiento was the wife of Raúl Ruiz (who was involved with several INA projects at the time).[20] Sarmiento tried to move forward independently, without financial support, but could not sustain the effort for long and eventually withdrew from the project. Therefore, Mallet had to reformulate her initial idea and *Les lettres*, which began production in 1979, became *Unfinished Diary*, completed and released three years later in 1982.[21] This loss of a double authorial signature, the change from "they" to "she," implies a shift in the dialogic aspect that was so germane to Mallet when formulating her idea as an epistolary exchange and a "cine-dialogue." The dialogic in the letter becomes the "auto-dialogic function" in the intimate diary.[22] A diary, after all, is a series of letters one writes to oneself.[23]

Writing letters to oneself: this was a habit Angelina Vázquez developed during her exile in Finland. The letters were addressed to her fellow exile filmmakers, although perhaps they were secretly intended for her. This one was supposed to be sent to Pablo Perelman:

> Dear Pablo: This is not the letter I would like to write to you, after such a long silence. It is merely a brief summary of the so-called "objective" facts. The subjectivities, of already proven local flavor, will have to be left for next letters that will come in a conditional future.

> After long months of trying to put together the puzzle of the footage, we have a finished product of 57 minutes, very simple, almost ascetic I would say, where a lot of material was discarded but the parts that remained are intact.... Between unit and unit there are some pieces from my travel diary.[24]

In 1983 Vázquez decided to make her first, semiclandestine attempt to return to Chile.[25] She knew it would be difficult to remain in the country. As a militant of the MIR and one who had already lived clandestinely in Chile from 1973 to 1975, as a politically engaged and committed filmmaker, Vázquez was not the most suitable candidate for a successful homecoming, especially during a time in which exiles' return was still prohibited. But she had an advantage: a Spanish passport. Her collaborator Anita Mikkonen and her two sons traveled with her (with Finnish passports). The four of them were able to enter the country with no problems in April 1983. While preparing the shoot with a local team led by her friend, comrade, and colleague Pablo Perelman, Vázquez kept a diary in which she reflected on her homecoming and on what she saw in the country. Her trip coincided with the emergence of the first massive protests that began to shake the authoritarian regime in May 1983. It was a moment of explosion in which most actors of civic society decided they had had enough. "How many fragments make up the fabric of struggle?" she wrote in that diary. Understanding the threads of that struggle, the "soul" of the Chilean people's resistance to the dictatorship, was one of her goals with this film. Her return, however, was fragmentary and unfinished. After almost seven weeks, in early June the police found her and expelled her from the country. She left national soil without shooting a single foot of film. Perelman—the addressee of the unsent letter quoted earlier—remained in charge of the production following directions and guidelines from Vázquez, who went back to Finland. Since her travel diary was aborted with her expulsion, she aptly titled the film *Fragments from an Unfinished Diary*, which she completed and released in November 1983.

The body of the committed filmmaker could not inhabit the territory of the homeland, yet militant images could be smuggled out of that territory and later enter the spaces of the Finnish media industry. Angelina Vázquez's body is therefore absent—forced to leave Chilean territory and forced to remain outside of her film's images. Assuming, in practical terms, the role of the director while shooting the documentary, Perelman inhabited Vázquez. Perelman became Vázquez's way of defying her disembodiment. Thus when she wrote to him this letter he never received, whom was Vázquez really addressing? Pablo, her loyal assistant, or Pablo, the name for a body that should have been hers? Was this an actual letter, or was it a continuation of her travel diary?

I read Pablo as the name for the man in charge of production (Perelman), as well as the name for Vázquez's prosthetic self. Pablo is the name for that body that had to become Vázquez's, once her own was expelled from the country. Like Mallet's failed cine-dialogue, here we also find a transition from a letter to a diary. This is a letter Vázquez wrote to (and kept for) herself—therefore a diary entry, but one that can only be read as such if we believe that, in this letter/diary, author and addressee have turned into the same person. If I have played on this fictional transubstantiation, it is only to highlight what will become evident in the discussion of the films. An *I* can assume many figurations, especially if the voice that speaks this *I* is severed from the body rendering it visible.

A VOICE SEVERED FROM A BODY (SITES OF WRITING)

"Feminine écriture, writing with the body."[26] In light of the specific concerns of a subjectivity interrogated in exile, both Mallet and Vázquez gave a twist to this dictum of feminist criticism while retaining its radical potentialities. The practice of women writing diaries has often been understood as a retreat within oneself, in the loneliness of a private room, with the only company of "those forces that intimate, that demand, that penetrate."[27] Feminist discourse has thought of these practices of seclusion into writing as writings of and from the body, relying on that sense of the word intimacy that suggests the act of introducing oneself into a body (our own). Stella Bruzzi notes that for feminist theories, the linking of a woman's voice directly with her body and thoughts is a response to "patriarchy's over-reliance on seeing and looking."[28] Bruzzi also highlights how the question of women's narration "challenges the authority of traditional documentary representation. A woman filmmaker's voice is not the voice of universality but of specificity, and signals the impossibility and the lack that the single male voice-over frequently masks."[29]

For women, the "intimate" in the "intimate diary" involves writing from within; it demands an inner voice that speaks from that site of gendered *difference*—the body. Voice, body, and *I* are thus the triad calling into question the subject that emerges in writing. In their diary films, however, Vázquez and Mallet disentangled this triad to highlight the fractured condition of exile subjectivity.

Originally, Mallet wanted to have an actress play her role. Due to budget restrictions, she took on the task but still chose to split herself. Even if the film begins with the "tethering of voice to body" (through the opening voice-over that spectators soon ascribe to the body of the filmmaker), *Unfinished Diary*'s main operation is the excision of voice from body, sound from image.[30] The film explores the dichotomy between the author's *I* who speaks through the voice-over and the performative self who appears on screen—the director's body.[31] In this splitting, the frontiers dividing subjectivity and objectivity are effaced; the boundaries separating the consciousness behind the work and the work's object are blurred (since that object also corresponds to the film's *subject*). For Vázquez, in turn, the body is pure absence. It cannot inhabit national territory, nor can it be present in the territory of images. Furthermore, in *Fragments from an Unfinished Diary*, it is her collaborator Anita Mikkonen who performs and embodies Vázquez's voice. The filmmaker's *I*, the subjectivity invoked by the first-person narration, speaks from an other's *I* and in another language, since Mikkonen reads in Finnish the Spanish words written by the filmmaker in her diary.[32]

As I have argued elsewhere, the rich textual materiality of the final image of *Fragments from an Unfinished Diary* synthesizes this doubling of languages as well as a convergence of media and literary genres: the newspaper, the letter/diary, the song, the philosophical essay, the poem. Everything is there, in an image that absorbs at the same time that it stratifies the meanings embedded in it. Newspapers in Spanish refer to the news from home, the signs of a political present that distance renders inaccessible. Over the dry, "objective" language of news, the subjectivity of the *I* expresses itself through the confessional nature of the diary. The quote from an essay by Ortega y Gasset, typed over these images, summarizes two of the topics of the film: popular art (folklore) and exile (the transit from home to home). The Finnish subtitles, also typed over the images, highlight the multilingual nature of any exile film. Over the credits, Vázquez's words offer a final reflection in a poetic language. The voice-over, the same *I* that writes the letter, emerges on the soundtrack in the form of Mikkonnen's vocal chords: "I want to give you a poem, Santiago . . . / a soft song, an insolent whispering . . . / when I have yet to be assaulted / by the unsolved mysteries of your indicative present." The poem is heard as the final credits appear on screen and while Violeta Parra's song about returning to a lost adolescence is still heard on the soundtrack. The sum of voice, song, and image emphasize here the unfinished nature of exile and return—always unresolved, always to be reckoned with.[33]

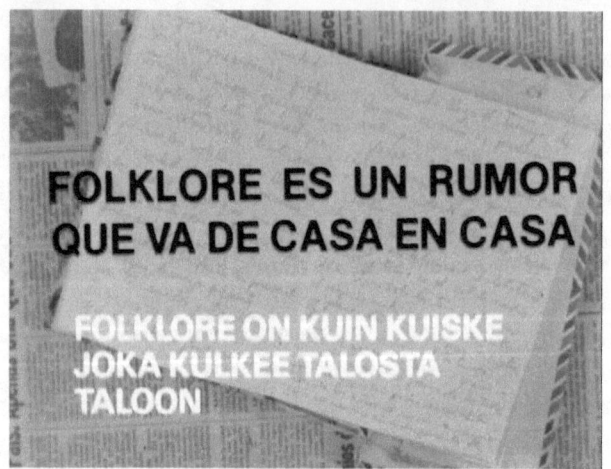

FIGURE 15. Still from *Fragmentos de un diario inacabado* (Fragments from an Unfinished Diary, Angelina Vázquez, Finland/Chile, 1983).

The site haunting all exiles—home—is transfigured into the site of writing. For Vázquez, écriture is the only possible home, the only place from which to elaborate exile and from which to deal with its subjectivation. The subjectivity emerging in this process, nonetheless, is marked by the impossibility of physical presence in her film and by the splitting of voice and body. The only solution is to borrow someone else's voice, to configure a self that is simultaneously hers and another's—a "vicarious self."[34]

Marilú Mallet's vicariousness, in turn, operates mainly through the effacement of the limits separating subject from object. Nowhere is this clearer than in the often cited and discussed climatic kitchen scene in *Unfinished Diary*, in which Mallet and her husband Michael Rubbo fight over the nature and narrative structure of the film viewers are seeing. Up to this point, Mallet hasn't explicitly exposed the rift between her voice and the bodily performance of herself. Even if the adding of sound and image favors the illusion of unity, of a unified self (voice + body = embodied voice, as opposed to the disembodied voice of Vázquez), *Unfinished Diary* is punctuated by the contrast between the more traditional documentary-style scenes and the interior monologue heard over scenes in which the camera wanders through every corner of Mallet's house. The moments in which Mallet's performative self interacts with others—when she acts like a documentarian, conversing with her friend Isabel

Allende (Salvador Allende's daughter) or visiting fellow Chilean exiles who struggle as they adapt to a foreign working-class environment—inevitably diverge from those moments in which, thanks to her inner voice, Mallet's subjectivity hovers over the images. This subjectivity, rendered visible through the aural image of her voice, seems to exist outside of the film's visuals; it resides in the site of writing, the writing of the text that has become a voice-over commentary.[35] But even if this contrast operates throughout the film, Mallet is in control of both the voice and her onscreen appearance.

The kitchen scene, instead, introduces the moment of "failure," the loss of her control over her object, that is, her own subject: *herself*.[36] Rubbo confronts her for failing to capture the essential drama of exile, which he locates in the figure of their son. He asks her if this kitchen scene (the one they are playing and that viewers are seeing) is in the script. After her negative answer, he faults her for improvising, then lectures her on the proper way to make a documentary: with characters, a conflict, a dramatic progression, and so on. Mallet defends herself, claiming that she needs to find *her* own way of making this film. She argues that she doesn't need to script the scene, since she knows what he is going to say. What she didn't expect was that he would shout that she couldn't reach the essence of the party scene because that moment, the materialization of the exile experience, was "too true." This demand of exacerbated truthfulness provokes what Rubbo asked for, a "too true" instant. The film cuts to a close-up of Mallet's affective response to Rubbo's injunction: she breaks down, she cries, she asks for the support she needs from her partner. In short, she loses control of herself as a performer. Here is the fundamental moment of "too truthfulness": when the onscreen body matches the consciousness behind the camera, when the performer becomes the exile artist, when subject and object finally merge into a single, porous entity.

Not only does reflexivity in this sequence evidence the "assertion of a radical subjectivity as a source of enunciation."[37] The kitchen scene also situates Mallet's explicit critique of what she called the "objective socio-political formula of the NFB."[38] In the challenge posed by first-person address to the discourse of social documentary, we find the seeds of what Stella Bruzzi has termed the "performative documentary," a kind of film that reflexively draws attention to the "impossibility of authentic documentary representation."[39] For Bruzzi, the documentary film "is given meaning by the interaction between performance and reality."[40] This is what happens in *Unfinished Diary*'s kitchen scene. The director has staged a moment of confrontation between her performative self and the character of her husband (Rubbo). But in the actual production of this moment (in the encounter between performance and reality), the excised nature of the director's subjectivity is made patently visible. Her onscreen bodily figure reveals itself as a mask of sorts.

MASKS (PERFORMING THE SELF)

A series of masks hang on a white wall in Mallet's apartment. As Seth Feldman notes, this wall and its masks figure as the backdrop against which three crucial moments in *Unfinished Diary* take place.[41] In the first one, Rubbo talks to the camera as if responding to a questionnaire, introducing basic aspects of his life: the country he was born in (Australia), his parents' occupations, his college education, his passion for film, and his decision to come to the NFB. In the second moment, midway through the film, Mallet has joined Rubbo and both are standing in front of the camera, with the masks on their backs. This shot lasts just a few seconds, and Mallet only has time to say "I was born in Santiago, and then . . . let's say," before the film cuts away to the image and sound of an organ grinder (the music of childhood and nostalgia). The last iteration takes place briefly after the climatic kitchen scene. Here, Rubbo announces: "And now, we're probably going to get a divorce." These three instances have been devised as masked interviews. Facing a frontal camera, the characters are supposed to provide the film (and its spectators) with background information about their lives. These constitute the moments of (auto)biography, but a biography that reveals itself in all its representational artificiality. Rubbo's biographical facts are predated by a shot, probably the most tender one in the film, in which Mallet whispers something to his ear and we hear both of them smiling, followed by this conversation:

Rubbo: About what?
Mallet: About love.
Rubbo: Love! Why?
Mallet: Why not?

Viewers understand that Mallet is playfully telling her husband/character what to talk about (and in the process letting viewers know about this "agreement" between wife/husband and filmmaker/subject) only to then offer an "interview" with Rubbo that has nothing to do with "love." Mallet's biographical account, in turn, follows a brief moment in

FIGURE 16. Director Marilú Mallet and her husband Michael Rubbo in a still from *Journal inachevé* (Unfinished Diary, Marilú Mallet, Canada, 1982).

which she is laughing and saying, as if apologizing for messing up the shot: "In any case, I can start all over again." Rubbo's final intervention against this wall full of masks also follows a similar dialogue, one in which he asks (supposedly talking to Mallet, behind the camera): "Come on . . . you want the true situation now, or you want the . . . what?" The revelation to come—the announcement of a likely divorce—is thus immediately cast under suspicion, since spectators don't know whether it belongs to the domain of the "true situation" or to another one, referred to by an ambiguous "what," and that comes to be associated with the domain of storytelling and representation.

Moments that highlight both the performativity of documentary representation and the artifices configuring every narrative, including an "autobiographical" one, have therefore predated all these "interviews" taking place against a wall full of masks. Thus, on the one hand, masks work as icons of narrative artifice; on the other, they are the visual embodiment of the gap between the biographical subject and the "real" person, between the voice behind the camera and the embodiment of that voice appearing onscreen.

These three moments can also be understood as a succinct summary of the "love story" between Mallet and Rubbo, with a beginning (introduction to the characters), middle (when they are together and smiling), and end (the announcement of a divorce).[42] These three masked interviews are complemented by another visual artifact: a painting of their wedding day done by Mallet's mother. In the middle of the film, the camera, wandering around the apartment's walls, moves closer to the painting, while the couple talk about it. Over the details of the painting, Mallet's voice says that she has the strangest face: "I have nothing but a hole there." Indeed, her mother has painted her with no eyes—it is a blank face, a mold of herself, a mask. Masks have punctuated the film all along the way: literally, as exotic objects hanging on a wall; figuratively, as the empty face in a painting; and metonymically, in the climatic kitchen scene, when the "hole" in the mother's painting is given a face—Mallet's close-up, the mask of her subjectivity. Ultimately, masks stress the point that the subject is unattainable—the film can only offer us a self in the shadows.

I have already noted how Vázquez's self is performed in *Fragments from an Unfinished Diary*. There, the mask is aural—it is through someone else's rendering of Vázquez's words in her travel diary that viewers gain access to the director's subjective world. But it is also worth looking at how other subjects perform their own selves when they are interviewed for this film. These performances clearly differ from the ones by Rubbo and Mallet in *Unfinished Diary*. Since Vázquez's purpose was to emphasize popular strategies of cultural resistance, the "content" of her interviewees' words becomes much more important. This factual information on their lives, however, is neither transparent nor direct. It is mediated, first, by a confessional attitude (the performance of a confession in front of the camera), and second, by editing devices that punctuate, interrupt, and fragment the testimonies.[43]

The film presents us with strategies of cultural resistance by documenting groups and individuals attempting to produce "popular art": art with a didactic function, made together with the people, and with the intention to reflect on questions of national and cultural identity as well as on the pressing issues experienced by Chileans under military rule. Midway through the film, we are introduced to Isabel Aldunate, a woman folk singer who, in a long sequence, discusses for the camera her own life path: the transition from the model citizen-consumer to the model militant artist who asks herself how to change her life to produce, in collaboration with others, a change in the political situation of the country. It should be noted that Isabel is introduced as a performer. First she is seen singing—passionately, even theatrically—and then sitting in a café, talking to the camera. She doesn't seem to be responding to predetermined questions; at least we don't hear those questions.

Instead, she appears to be releasing an accumulation of thoughts and emotions. Aldunate is benefiting from the presence of the camera to make sense of her life, to confess.[44] Confession is here not so much a matter of power dynamics (not a confession in front of a judging authority). It operates simply in its therapeutic function: confession as a "therapy of self-examination."[45]

Aldunate begins by saying: "I am a singer, I am 33 years old, and it is a bit strange for me to be doing this because I never planned it. I am also a lawyer. And before that I wanted to be a dancer." The alternative lives that this subject could have had are mentioned from the beginning, and what follows is an attempt to give coherence to that life and to explain the decisions she has made in her life. In contrast with the playful and deceptive nature of the interviews in *Unfinished Diary*, here we witness a subject telling difficult things, things one only confesses to oneself or to a therapist: the pains of romantic breakups, separation from her children, crises of identity—in short, the rifts and breaks of Aldunate's life. The affective power of this long testimony/confession lies in the communion between her and the camera that records it. It is a communion predicated on the recognition and immediate effacement of the apparatus's presence. Aldunate acknowledges the presence of the camera, but she does not talk to the camera to address an imaginary audience, nor does she talk to the people who are interviewing her (behind the camera). She looks at the camera's lens as if she were looking at herself in a mirror. What we see is Aldunate's personal and private confession, disguised, *masked* as an interview.

If the confessional tone suggests an element of performativity in Aldunate's narration of her life, the editing in this sequence also works in favor of highlighting the mediations operating in any given testimony. The recurrent fade to black—which alludes to the turning of pages in a journal, to the passage of days in one's life, and to the film itself as a living organism that breathes—does not diminish the confessional tone of the testimony, but it punctuates and fragments its narration.[46] This fragmentation is not yet a break, not a radical rupture, but the effect is doubled by the inclusion of a freeze-frame in the middle of the interview, a still image that lasts for quite a few seconds and that viewers experience in its temporal detention as they keep on listening to Aldunate's words on the soundtrack. This temporal arrest, followed by its reanimation, evidences the discontinuities of every biography and of every historical narrative. This is especially poignant for those lives and histories that have been marked by the ruptures of a coup. "Everything was interrupted on September 11" is, indeed, one of the first things Aldunate says as she begins to articulate her confession.

The procedure of the freeze-frame is replicated later in the film when introducing Héctor Noguera, a renowned actor who teaches a theater workshop to young men and women. Spectators first hear Noguera's voice, directly addressing Vázquez ("I am recording for *you* from a car") while we see the gray Santiago streets from the vehicle's window. This moving shot gives way to an interview with Noguera that begins with a freeze-frame that captures the actor in a reflexive pose: sorrowful, absorbed, his hand on his forehead. This moment is neither a proper interview nor a proper confession. In its direct address to the absent body of the film's director, Noguera is filming a letter for Vázquez.[47]

In these sequences, Vázquez's words—filtered through Mikkonnen's voice—are absent. The director effaces herself so that others can assume the place of the *I*'s voice, the site of the consciousness behind the organization of the narrative. Here, the performance of the subject is no artifice and no game of reflexivity. What matters for Vázquez is the desire to chronicle modes in which lives resist: subjectivities fighting both the exterior world and the roles that they themselves have assigned for their lives. The subject, here, only has meaning if it is opened to the speech of others. It is only meaningful if it allows those others to usurp the site of enunciation that was reserved to the director's *I*. In so doing, it is the director, too, who speaks through them. In *Fragments from an Unfinished Diary*, Vázquez speaks through another's voice (Mikkonnen) and from and through other bodies (Aldunate, Noguera).

TOGETHER IN EXILE (PERFORMING THE COLLECTIVE SELF)

If in *Fragments from an Unfinished Diary* confession works as therapy, in *If We Lived Together . . .* therapy comes via humor. When comparing this documentary to those of Mallet and Vázquez, the first element that strikes the viewer is the humorous tone of *If We Lived Together . . .*, enabled by Skármeta's performance of himself: playful, ludic, immune to ridicule, devoid of any sense of shame. Here is a filmmaker who presents himself as a buffoon in the comedy of his life, the comedy of exile. As mentioned earlier, the performance of subjectivity is very much gendered in these three films. Mallet and Vázquez confronted what it meant to be both a "Latin American woman" in exile and a "woman filmmaker," and they chose to do it through traditional genres of female expression:

letters and diaries. Not only was the fact that they were filming to expose the fractures of their subjectivities as women explicit in how both directors framed their projects (as we can see from the discussion of Mallet's proposal for the NFB); feminine writing as the site from which to imagine exile was indeed the central element organizing their cinematic narratives. If it were possible to say that every intimate diary adopts a fundamentally feminine position of enunciation, as Nora Catelli has argued, one would have to push the argument too far to claim this for Skármeta's diary.[48] Not only are women absent from the constellation of artists Skármeta brings together to perform the making of a collective film, but Skármeta's humorous performance of himself—and humor works here in contrast to the meditative and melancholic qualities of Mallet's and Vázquez's feminine voices—is constantly enacting masculinity through the archetype of the male writer.[49]

This is not to say that the film trivializes the exile experience. Its lightness is strategic: humor works as a prosthesis with which to mask the pains of displacement. Through humor Skármeta performs a version of himself, but one that does not aim to reach the inner depths of his subjectivity. The director masks his subjectivity as a unique person under the performance of a larger trope: the exile artist. In the film we see him constantly performing the figures of the filmmaker and the writer. But he is not alone in this task, and in fact the film argues that he cannot be. Skármeta's onscreen appearance, his body, is there only as a magnet for other bodies, other exile artists. A humorous performance of the self serves him as a political tool, in that both Skármeta and the film become hubs around which to convoke other actors, musicians, and filmmakers to foster a sense of brotherhood and collectivity. Together in exile, united by a hopeful attitude toward the present and the future, they will make the film they would have made, *if they lived together* in their homeland.

Performance is a structural element in *If We Lived Together . . .* , in which three different levels of performativity overlap: first, the performance of the diary form; second, Skármeta's performance of himself; and third, the performance of the making of a collective film. They are all intertwined, but I discuss them here separately.

In the prologue, a group of old ladies sit on benches in a public square. The handheld camera comes close and scans them slowly from left to right, while they say things like "He's only pretending to film us." The movement ends when the camera gets to Skármeta, who pretends to be unaware of its presence, and whose pose and gesture parodies the look of the introspective filmmaker. Without cutting, the camera moves back

FIGURE 17. Director Antonio Skármeta in a still from *Wenn wir zusammen lebten...* (*If We Lived Together...*, Antonio Skármeta, GFR, 1983).

to the left and the ladies continue laughing at the whole scene: "Can we stick our tongues out? We're still fresh as daisies." The camera moves once again to the right, only to find Skármeta now looking straight at the lens, smiling. If there is any expectation of a dense exile tale, the opening sets a tone of levity and play.

As if to immediately undo this lightness, an abrupt cut takes viewers from Skármeta's smiling close-up to a medium shot of him at night in the middle of a busy street corner with neon lights and advertisements in the background. Here, he also looks and talks straight into the camera, presenting himself (a Chilean, an exile writer who has lived with his family in West Berlin for eight years) and introducing the basic historical context conditioning the facts of his life (the Allende government, the coup, the dictatorship, exile). "When they asked me to film a diary of my life," he says, only to be interrupted by another abrupt cut to a moving train on which Skármeta, again with his smiley face, reads from a diary and continues the sentence where the previous shot left off: "I thought about music.... That's why I talked to my friend Sergio Vesely, who lives in Esslingen, and asked him to write a song for this film. I didn't know exactly what the film was going to be like, but I knew two things: I wanted to start with a song, and the title would be *If We Lived Together*. Vesely asked me: 'But what's the song about?' 'The same as the title,' I answered. 'Just write a song that starts like this.'" At this point,

Skármeta starts humming an imaginary tune, and his hands begin to move following a beat and a rhythm spectators will only hear when the film cuts away, again abruptly, to a shot of Vesely playing and singing the song in a recording studio, accompanied by a group of musicians. This scene is followed by images of Berlin streets captured from the window of the moving train. The film's title is printed over these images, with the caption "a diary film by Antonio Skármeta."

This is the kind of performativity whereby speech and act coincide; the prologue "says" of itself that it is a diary film at the same time that it enacts two qualities of the diary form: the first-person enunciation of its mode of address and its obsession with the present. What is enacted in this prologue, with its abrupt edits and its spatiotemporal dislocations, is the sense of the fragmentary—our own lives' discontinuities. Even if the diary might refer to the past, it is the present tense that orders and gives meaning to everything that is narrated. In this prologue, there is no measure of the past, no sense of chronology, and no foreseeable future tense: only the instant, the fugacity of a present that always escapes us. As P. A. Sitney argues, this feature of the diary film differs from autobiography per se, which always "demands that aspect of 'later.'"[50] The diary film, instead, "does not choose a fictive vantage point to reflect upon the past; in fact, it has next to no reference to the past. It would offer, instead, a series of discontinuous presents."[51] *If We Lived Together . . .* offers us nothing but a series of discontinuous presents; it gives us the everyday of life in all its disjointedness and not in its chronology—a life understandable only through the articulation of the subject who is living and telling it.

The film's second performative dimension—Skármeta's ludic performance of himself—is present in this prologue, too. Since this is the film's beginning, his way of appearing onscreen functions as a "declaration of principles" of sorts for the film, which starts by saying that its director, in addition to being the target of jokes by a group of old ladies, is someone who can laugh at himself. Furthermore, in this initial shot the subjective positioning of a directorial gaze behind the camera is objectivized in Skármeta's body, who performs this gaze onscreen: he is silent, he doesn't move; he just *looks*, staring in an unknown direction. But then the second iteration of the camera's movement across the benches—panning from the ladies to Skármeta—reveals someone else. This version of "the director" *performs* for the camera—acting out its ludic look and laughter. Here, the performative buffoon replaces the documentary observer.

Skármeta's performance of himself continues in a sequence in which the collective nature of exile art is announced. In a moment that cannot be logically explained by anything in the diegesis of the film, Skármeta drives a car and stops right in front of the camera. Carrying a passport in his hand, he looks directly at viewers, smiles, and says: "Our story has nothing exceptional to it. We're professional emigrants. Our passport, suitcase, and address book are always ready. Our art, we make it with our daily life. And our daily life is individual, but also collective." These last two sentences point to the heart of the film, which simultaneously claims: "Exile life is the matter of exile art" and "all exile lives are collective." They are all lived in the first-person plural.

This double claim introduces the last salient feature of *If We Lived Together . . .*: the performance of the making of a collective film. There is no contradiction in the idea of having an intimate diary—Skármeta's diary, private, personal, subjective—be a collective one as well—a locus for the enunciation of a plurality of *I*s. The goal of the film is to affirm that, living in exile, no subjectivity belongs to the self. The only attainable subjectivity is the one resulting from the invocation of a social body, a collective self. An *I* can only account for the measure of a subject as long as it speaks as a *we*. This may be true "ontologically speaking" for several first-person films, as Alicia Lebow has noted, and as seen in the previous analysis of Mallet's and Vázquez's diary films.[52] But one aspect distinguishes Skármeta's documentary from other diaries and first-person films: here, the production of a first-person plural is the very object of the film. It is, of course, a political endeavor. Living in exile, in the ruins of a socialist project, Skármeta is asking how to formulate, under these conditions, a new politics of the subject. His response is to offer not a diary film by and about Skármeta, but a diary film made by many and about the making of this film by many.[53]

Actor Nelson Villagra travels to Berlin from Havana, and cinematographer Leonardo de la Barra from Brussels. Actor, playwright, and theater director Oscar Castro travels from Paris, and singer/songwriter Sergio Vesely from the German city of Esslingen, close to the border with Switzerland. This is a documentary by Antonio Skármeta as much as it is one by all of them—especially by Castro and Vesely, whose theater plays and songs occupy a significant portion of the film. Both artists were also survivors—political prisoners known for making art while being detained—and this topic will play a relevant role in the film, too.[54] In addition to their presence as characters and performers, the "many" who make the film bring with them the mark of intermediality.

By 1983 Skármeta was on the cusp of his creativity in exile. In previous years he had authored several screenplays for West German films directed by Peter Lilienthal and Christian Ziewer, and he had recently published the novels *No pasó nada* (1980) and *La insurrección* (1982, based on one of his own scripts for Lilienthal).[55] But it was with *Ardiente Paciencia* (Burning Patience, 1983) that Skármeta took his concern for self-adaptations and narrative re-mediations to another level. This fictive account of the relation between Pablo Neruda and his postman was written first as a script for a radio show, then adapted for the screen and directed by Skármeta himself (in 1983, the same year in which *If We Lived Together . . .* was made), then written as a theater play, and finally written as a novel (published in 1985).[56]

The premise of *If We Lived Together . . .* is to make a film that combines the subjectivities of different Chilean exile artists and art forms. This is a diary film as much as it is a documentary about the staging of a theater play, or a documentary capturing the performances of an exile musician. The combination of multiple subjectivities/multiple art forms presupposes various degrees of intermediality together with distinct regimes of visuality and representation. With few breaks between them, as if the transition from one medium to the other was the most natural and smooth thing in the world, the film juxtaposes paintings with dramatizations of those paintings and the visual and sonic signs of exile (suitcases, trains, inability to communicate) with the theatrical staging of the "rites of passage" of the exile. The film transports viewers from the medium of communication in exile (the letter) to the medium of self-introspection (the written and filmed diary); from a short story read by Skármeta in a public reading to the short film that adapts that story for the screen (and the entire short is inserted into the film); and from lyrics written on notebooks to performed music. In these ongoing passages between different ontologies of the image and re-mediations of signs, Skármeta's performance of himself and Oscar Castro's as the figure of "the actor" play a key role.

Indeed, the "car scene" that I described earlier, with Skármeta addressing the camera to explain the stuff of exile art (daily life) and its authorial nature (collective), is situated in between two moments that highlight both intermediality and collectivity. Earlier in the film viewers have seen Oscar Castro wandering around the streets, carrying his suitcase, in scenes that mimic the paintings by Chilean exile artist Cecilia Boisier—paintings that the film has taken the time to show, one by one. But from these dramatizations of the exilic imagery the film moves to an actual theater play—*La triste e increíble historia del general Peñaloza y el exiliado Mateluna* (first staged in Paris by Castro's troupe Grupo Aleph in 1980).[57] Oscar Castro, together with other performers, acts (on a theater stage, but for the camera) a scene in which he calls someone on the phone and asks for an address. Since his German is very poor, he can't communicate well. The dialogue is repeated over and over again, until the character angrily hangs up the phone. Then the film cuts to Skármeta's already described car scene, which is immediately followed by a scene that takes place in the moving train. Here, Skármeta teaches Castro how to say the lines in German that we just heard him say in his play. Castro's language skills are limited, and the two artists laugh about it. Has Skármeta helped his friend by rehearsing with him the lines he needs to learn how to pronounce in his play? The production date of the play (1980) suggests that Skármeta has seen the performance and invented this funny moment in the train to stress both the difficulties of making art while in exile and the sense of brotherhood among exile artists. But the film's viewer does not know this fact, and the nonchronological linearity of the sequence reinforces that the opposite interpretation is also possible (the train scene is a more conventional documentary moment: an actual rehearsal of the lines in German so that Castro can learn how to pronounce them in the play). What matters is that the editing together of these three scenes has enacted the intermediality of the film (painting, theater, performative documentary, diary film) and its collective authorship. For who writes whom here? And how can we distinguish between the novelist and the playwright, theater director and filmmaker, film director and actor, and actor and character?

As if to stress the point one last time, Skármeta ends the film by placing himself in front of the typewriter, performing once again as "the writer" and saying/writing/typing/reading out loud: "In order to make this film, many friends from different parts of Europe came to West Berlin. None of them can live in Chile. Making this film with them has been like an anticipation of what we will do when we live together in our homeland." After this scene, the film cuts to a final credits sequence, in which the characters/artists are dancing, in the park, to the music that Vesely plays. When the song ends, the film ends as well: the image centers on Skármeta, who performs one last time, for his cameraman and for viewers, the gesture of "cut." Music and image, life and art, seem to coincide in the moment of closure. And exilic closure, too, the film seems to say, will have to be performed by this collective self.

Skármeta's festive ending suggests that no matter what, life in exile goes on. The diary is a privileged genre for articulating relations between life and cinema. In the films discussed in this chapter, those relations are marked by fragmentation, incompletion, and openness. Structured by the discontinuities of life in the present tense, the diary as a mode of address favors those three aspects. The same can be said of all exile lives: exile is "a discontinuous state of being," as Edward Said once said.[58] Both discontinuities meet in the diary form. The lives of exiles, with their physical, imaginary, and psychological displacements, match the cinematic diary. With its spatiotemporal rearrangements and configurations, the diary film gives visual expression to that discontinuous state of being at the same time that it offers a chance for exile subjects to imagine alternative lives for themselves.

But is this *I* really locatable, or is it only the shadow of a subjectivity that cannot be pinned down? Are we left with the subject, or only with the mask of the *I* through which it speaks? "We don't possess any definitive instrument to catch the subject—Nora Catelli stresses—that is the sign of the era of intimacy."[59] In these films we don't reach an exilic subject or self. We see, in turn, the processes by which exiles self-objectify themselves—the means by which subjectivity is caught into being. Since exile filmmakers themselves reveal the rifts and fractures that enable their subjective positioning, the desire to expose their subjectivity (as if they were performing an incision that opens their bodies up for all of us to see) is more important than the predictable result of an unattainable self.

EXILE AND THE UNFINISHED

Despite Skármeta's abrupt ending, these three films resist any sense of closure. By this I mean something other than the general idea of an "open work of art," going back to Umberto Eco's book *Opera aperta* (published in 1962).[60] I mean something other than the practices of narrative inconclusion and ambiguity prevalent in both European art cinema and the NLAC of the 1960s. And I mean something different than Third Cinema's insistence on inconclusion as a defining trait of militant cinemas—since it is the situated practice of viewing and discussing the work with a concrete audience that completes political films.[61] The sense of incompletion and lack of closure I am talking about here is more specific to the practices of exile cinema.

Both Mallet and Vázquez use the word *unfinished* in their titles; Vázquez has the word *fragments* in hers; while Skármeta adds the ellipsis at the end of the sentence *If We Lived Together . . .* , effectively undoing the gesture of "cut" that he performs in the last second of the film. In *Unfinished Diary*, the sign of incompletion refers to the elliptical and fragmentary nature of the diary as a narrative form, as well as to the unfinished project of transatlantic cine-dialogue that Mallet and Sarmiento had called *Les lettres*, *Unfinished Diary* being one of the surviving traces from that project that didn't get to be.[62] In Vázquez's case, the unfinished nature of her work refers to a specific circumstance. Expelled by the authorities a few weeks after having entered Chilean territory to preproduce and shoot her film, the writing of her diary and the making of the film she was reflecting on in that diary were interrupted. The film Vázquez ended up making is not the one she would have made had she been able to remain in Chile for the shoot. As Ramírez-Soto suggests, the sign of the unfinished is built into the film's "diffuse authorship," since in addition to Mikkonnen voicing Vázquez's words and assuming the director's vocal presence on the soundtrack, *Fragments from an Unfinished Diary* can also be seen as a series of cinematic letters sent by Perelman to Vázquez.[63] Indeed, in a letter sent to scholar Zuzana M. Pick, Vázquez lists the credits as: "Codirection, or something like this, with Pablo Perelman."[64] In this film, the unfinished is also part of its overall form, privileging a sense of discontinuity facilitated by recurring fades to black, freeze-frames, and a mosaic type of elliptical narrative structure.

As Alix Beeston and Stefan Solomon have recently argued, the unfinished is constitutive of feminist film history, partly due to incompletion being an aesthetic strategy favored by feminist filmmakers and partly due to the "wider structural inequities within particular film industries and cultures."[65] To this we should add that the unfinished is constitutive of exile cinema, and particularly of the work of female directors in exile. The number of projects that were interrupted—reformulated years later, unfinished, or simply unmade—first by the coup and later throughout the following decades—attests to the additional burden that the condition of exile supposed for Chilean women filmmakers.[66]

The sign of the unfinished is also constitutive of exile, plain and simple. After being forced to leave their countries, the lives of exiles are forever transformed—their previous selves remaining, as it were, incomplete. And once homecoming becomes a possibility, exiles soon find out that return offers no closure. *Fragments from an Unfinished Diary* already suggests that impossibility: all returns from exile are somehow partial, elusive, and fragmentary. As these three unfinished filmic diaries imply, and as the next chapter demonstrates, there is no after exile.

PART III

The Return and the Archive

CHAPTER 6

A Plurality of Cinematic Homecomings

Exile and return, just like exile and home, are "mutually defining" concepts.[1] One cannot be understood without the other. Return marks the telos of exile, giving it meaning and hearkening to the future. As Hamid Naficy said: "Return occupies a primary place in the minds of the exiles and a disproportionate amount of space in their films, for it is the dream of a glorious homecoming that structures exile."[2] Even if the exiles do not get to live their own homecoming, return is always present as an idea, permeating all levels of their imagination.

Chilean exiles found an image to summarize the power behind the drive to return home. Testimonies as well as studies of exiles' correspondence recall the all too frequent memory of packed suitcases stored underneath a bed.[3] Most exiles thought their displacement was going to be temporary. In a few months, maybe a few years, they would be ready to go back to Chile. The fierce repression that followed the coup, and later the successful attempt of the dictatorship to legitimize itself via a new constitution in 1980, proved otherwise. Exile was going to be a long, perhaps endless, experience. The awareness of the prolonged duration of exile produced an antinomy: "the desire to achieve complete integration" in tension with "the desire of an immediate return."[4] Thus the years go by and the bags remain under the bed, packed, as if tonight or tomorrow one could pick them up and take them to the airport to catch the next flight.

The exiles' invocation of a distant and irrecoverable homeland is temporal as much as it is spatial. The ongoing wish to return indicates the hope to set foot in the territory that one has been banned from and the desire to retrieve an often idealized past. In its telos, homecoming implies the end of uprootedness, an opportunity to leave behind exile as a "time lived in parenthesis."[5] Return seems to be what comes after exile, but there is no proper *after* exile because homecoming provides no closure.[6] Those who return quickly realize that home is always elsewhere and in another time. Herein lies the paradox of what Uruguayan writer Mario Benedetti called *desexilio* (literally: de-exile). Return from exile is yet another estrangement, another form of longing under the guise of counter-nostalgia.[7] As anticipated by the diary films studied in the previous chapter, exile must be thought of as an ongoing and fundamentally unfinished process. Far from being exile's closure, return functions as a new opening. Homecoming's intention to undo exile, to suture together the bonds broken in departure, is another act of dissolution, fissure, and loss. But even if it is doomed to fail in its quest, exile looks for completion in its striving for homecoming.[8] Fictional and documentary narratives of return find an endless source of creative inspiration in this apparent contradiction.

If this contradiction forms the basis of the exile imagination, what does return mean for an exile cinema? This chapter offers an answer in the form of an intertwined history, one in which the historical process of the return of the Chilean diaspora is linked to the waves of returns followed by exile directors, to the homecoming narratives they created, and to the sites of institutional returns they established. Chilean exile cinema involves a plurality of cinematic homecomings that go beyond return as a thematic and aesthetic inscription in their films. To understand this plural dimension, it is necessary to look at the transnational movements of filmmakers, their strategic modes of film and video production, and the entanglement between the return of an exile cinema and the return to democracy.

This chapter therefore explores the wealth of Chilean exile films and videos, especially documentaries, that focused on the question of return. These works proliferated beginning in the early 1980s, coinciding with the moment in which exile and return began to occupy a more prevalent position in human rights discourses and in the struggle for democracy. The way Chilean exile cinema deals with narratives of return is thus strictly tied to the historical and political process leading up to the return to democracy in 1990. I argue that cinematic homecomings reveal the impossibility of return signaled by the ceaseless nature of the exile condition. Far from idealization, in Chilean films of return "the dream of a glorious homecoming" is replaced by a critical and reflective stance on loss, displacement, and the experience of living in between cultures. The impossibility of return is also seen in the Viña del Mar Film Festival in 1990. This iteration of the festival was organized under the lens of a homecoming narrative and took place just a few months after the return to democracy. Entitled Reencuentro de Chile con su cine (Chile's Reencounter with Its Cinema), it explicitly sought to bridge the gaps between the filmmakers who had stayed in Chile and those who had lived in exile. In doing so, the 1990 Viña Festival became a living proof and institutional evidence of the wounds that exile had left on Chilean cinema.

A BRIEF HISTORY OF RETURN (1978–1994)

Exiles with Chilean passports had them stamped with a letter "L," meaning they were on a list with the names of those prohibited to return.[9] As Thomas Wright and Rody Oñate explain, legal return to the country was practically impossible after the dictatorship issued its Decree 81, dated November 1973, which required exiles to obtain permission from the Ministry of the Interior to enter Chile. Return policies remained unchallenged until 1978 and 1980, when the MIR and the Communist Party, respectively, began to introduce militants clandestinely for political work and armed resistance.[10] The first and marginal wave of return to Chile thus began in 1978. In addition to the MIR's Operación Retorno, by 1978 a limited number of people were also finding ways of going back home: women who had gone into exile following their husbands and later got divorced, children who were sent back to Chile to live with grandparents or other family members, and people who did not have the letter "L" on their passport and who had not adapted well to their new environment.[11]

Founded in 1978, the Comité Pro-Retorno de Exiliados (Committee for the Return of the Exiles) was instrumental in organizing and campaigning for the return of exiles.[12] The creation of this committee coincided with an emergence of various human rights organizations, most of them tied to the Church.[13] These were relevant institutions in the resistance against the dictatorship, particularly for their success in mobilizing and activating transnational networks of solidarity in the struggle for the defense of human rights (not to mention their involvement in networks of video production and circulation, as discussed later). The prohibition of return was indeed framed as a human rights violation, based on the 1948 Universal Declaration of Human Rights, which states, "Everyone has the right to leave any country, including his own, and to return to his country."[14] The Committee for the Return of the Exiles was able to instill the idea that the homecoming demand was a human rights demand through interventions in UN forums and through the 1980 and especially the 1983 Jornadas por el derecho de vivir en la patria (Conferences for the Right to Live in One's Homeland).[15] These events reunited various social actors with the goal of studying the cultural, political, economic, social, and psychological repercussions of return and had the ultimate objective of proposing new return policies and advocating for reparations for exiles.[16]

It would take a couple of years for these campaigns to produce concrete results. The September 1982 demonstrations protesting the Supreme Court's decision to prohibit the return of Jaime Castillo Velasco—a Christian Democrat, president of the Chilean Commission on Human Rights, and hardly a radical—helped to "broaden support for the return movement beyond the families" of militant exiles.[17] This event forced the military junta to revise its return policies. In December 1982 the junta issued the first of ten lists of persons authorized to return. These lists, however, proved to be a "cruel hoax."[18] Issued through October 1983, they contained names of dead persons and only a minimal number of actual exiles. This initial moment of return coincided with the wave of social unrest that began to shake the regime in the early 1980s. The demand for the right to return became an active component of the political struggle against the dictatorship and of the popular revolts, which, fueled by the 1981 economic crash that increased unemployment and poverty, led to national days of protests unfolding throughout 1983. In October that year, and as a response to these massive anti-government mobilizations, the dictatorship reversed its decision and went back to a total prohibition on return. But the change in the social and political climate had made it clear for leaders of the opposition that they needed to return from exile and participate in the organization against the regime from within the country. As Wright and Oñate explain, the campaign for the return of exiles intensified with the help of human rights organizations. Fundación de Ayuda Social de las Iglesias Cristianas (FASIC; Social Assistance Foundation of the Christian Churches), for instance, began publishing in 1983 a periodical called *Chile Retorno*, which reported on all matters related to the return of exiles. Several alternative media, such as the magazines *Hoy*, *Apsi*, and *Análisis*, and the latter's video version, *Teleanálisis*, increased their reporting of themes related to exile and return.

Facing pressure from multiple fronts, the dictatorship adopted a new policy, this time publishing lists with the names of those prohibited to enter the country. The first one, dated September 5, 1984, contained 4,942 names; the twelfth, dated March 15, 1987, included 1,471 individuals who could not go back to Chile.[19] Return policies were thus contradictory and highly dependent on current political upheavals and on the success of local and international pressure.

The dictatorship's return policies continued later in the decade with the publication of twenty-one lists allowing the return of 3,137 Chileans, published from late 1986 until 1988. Finally, on September 1, 1988, the military junta put an official end to exile via Decree 203 of the Ministry of the Interior, which left with no effect all previous decrees regarding prohibitions against returning to Chile.

Waves of return began to increase, especially after the victory of the "No" vote in the referendum that defeated Pinochet in October 1988, but they were never massive. One of the early measures of President Patricio Aylwin's government (1990–94), the first one after the end of the dictatorship, was the creation of the Oficina Nacional de Retorno (National Office of Return). This institution supported the return of exiles and guided them through the administrative, legal, and social hardships of the process. The closure of this office in 1994 coincided with the moment when the UNHCR put an end to the condition of refugee for Chilean exiles. That was the official, institutional end to the process of homecoming. Nonetheless, smaller waves of return continued well after that date.

Other thousands of exiles never returned, at least to live in Chile permanently. From the mid-1980s and throughout the 1990s, exiles were forced to confront return—the mythical project that had defined their lives—with a series of concrete conditions. If exile had been an imposition, return was a choice—and a difficult one.[20] Exiles had remarried. They did not want to separate themselves from their children who had been born in exile, or they did not want to put them through the experience of relocating to a foreign country. They had jobs they were not keen on quitting. They were skeptical of the incipient democracy in Chile. They traveled back and were not able to recognize the country they had left. They faced suspicious reactions from former friends and comrades, who considered them privileged because they had not experienced the dictatorship *directly*. They believed they were unwelcome: "I fear no one wants this resurrection of mine in Chile now," as one exile put it in a testimonial.[21]

When the National Office for Return closed in 1994, its records indicated that 56,000 people had returned to Chile, a minimal number compared to the official figure of 200,000 exiles.[22] Despite the figures, the significance of return for defining the experience of exile and for understanding the exiles' imagination should not be understated. This discrepancy between the official figures and the mythical status of return shows that homecoming constitutes, above all, an impossible project.

EXILE FILMMAKERS RETURN HOME

The story of the return of exile filmmakers to Chile echoes the broader history of the return of the Chilean diaspora sketched in the preceding section. On top of the dilemmas faced by all exiles, filmmakers had to consider the difficulties of relocating into a media environment that had little to do with the one they had known before 1973. The industry was sparse and lacked infrastructure, and most directors worked either in advertising or in the burgeoning alternative video scene. Still, the desire to come home was strong. There were directors and producers who began to return to reside permanently in Chile as soon as they were able to, starting in the late 1970s.

Throughout this book I have offered several lines of argument and examples that challenge one of the key points of the standard historical narrative of Chilean exile cinema, which sees a clear separation between *inxile* and exile. The process by which exile filmmakers began to return home together with their immediate contributions to the fields of film and media production, distribution, and education once again prove that the border between the inside and the outside was much more porous. The following examples illustrate that exile filmmakers played a crucial role in the reshaping of the audiovisual sphere in Chile in the years that preceded and followed the return to democracy.

Sergio Trabucco, who had created a distribution company with the Uruguayan producer Walter Achugar when they were both exiles in Venezuela, was among the first. He came back in 1978 and was later one of the figures behind the development of the guild of Chilean directors and producers.[23] Most filmmakers who had been based in the GDR returned early in the 1980s. The married couple Álvaro Ramírez and Beatriz González had a difficult time establishing themselves as part of the independent film industry once they returned. Ramírez worked mostly as an editor for Chilean directors who had remained in the country, while González served as head of production on a limited number of films, one of which was the highly influential documentary *Cien niños esperando un tren* (One Hundred Children Waiting for a Train, Ignacio Agüero, 1988). Upon returning from East Berlin in 1980, Douglas Hübner led the video division of one of the Catholic Church's many solidarity and human rights organizations, the Vicaría de la Pastoral Obrera (Workers' Pastoral Office).[24] This alternative video production and distribution network made more than thirty videos during the 1980s and reached an estimated audience of twenty thousand people. As well as overseeing the Pastoral's video division, Hübner directed twelve videos.

Also coming from the GDR, after having worked in the animation division at the DEFA studios throughout the 1970s, Juan Forch returned in the late 1970s and became an active figure in another strand of the video scene, one closer to video art. He was part of the avant-garde circles surrounding what critic Nelly Richard famously described as the Escena de Avanzada (Avant-Garde Scene) and codirected with her the video installation *Las cantatrices* (1980) by queer artist and performer Carlos Leppe.[25] One of Forch's early Chilean video pieces as sole director was both a homecoming narrative and an epistolary video documentary: *Papá te habla desde lejos* (*Dad Speaks to you from Afar*, 1982). Later, Forch was a regular participant in the numerous iterations of the Festival Franco Chileno de Video Arte (Franco-Chilean Festival of Video Art, 1981–92). Although it privileged experimentation and was sometimes excessively critical of the community-oriented and counterinformational practices of many Chilean video makers, the festival created a public sphere in which the different strands of the local alternative video scene were confronted.[26] As a returnee, Forch therefore occupies a privileged position as a figure who transited back and forth between cinema, video art, television, and advertising. In fact, a few years later he became one of the creatives behind the making of the "No" campaign for the 1988 referendum, for which he directed several sections and short videos.[27]

Another case worth highlighting is Pedro Chaskel, who returned in 1985 and became involved in the video scene rapidly developing in the country—codirecting with Pablo Salas videos like *Somos +* (We Are More, 1985) and *Por la vida* (For Life, 1987). Chaskel was later one of the first exile directors who began working for Chilean television in 1988 with the ethnographic series *Al sur del mundo* (To the South of the World, Canal 13, 1982–2001). Due to his vast experience as an editor, director, and archivist, Chaskel played the role of an informal mentor for several film and video makers of younger generations. With the creation of new film and media schools in the late 1980s and early 1990s, he would also become a professor in the more formal settings of higher education and would later lead the path toward the reopening of Cineteca Universidad de Chile in 2008—the same university cinematheque he had directed in the early 1960s, which had been dismantled after the coup.

All these homecoming trajectories stress that, while not necessarily massive, the early returns of exile filmmakers shaped the development of Chilean film and media in myriad ways, involving active engagement in the alternative scene of semiclandestine video newsreels, video art, independent filmmaking, television, advertising, and education.

STRATEGIC HOMECOMINGS (1982–1986)

The examples highlighted so far constitute some of the early cases of exile directors who returned to Chile to live there permanently. Throughout the 1980s, however, an important modality of return was not permanent but temporary. Various directors embarked upon a strategic mode of cinematic homecoming, which involved returning for a brief period for specific film projects that were shot in Chile but were later completed in their respective exile locations. This was the case for people like Rodrigo Gonçalves, Angelina Vázquez, and Raúl Ruiz, who had partial homecomings in 1982 and 1983, and later Miguel Littin, who first returned in 1985. Except for Ruiz's, all these returns were either fully clandestine or semiclandestine. They involved great danger, and in Vásquez's case, ended with her being expelled from the country.[28] This strategic mode of cinematic homecoming was responsible for some of the most original documentaries of return. Films like Vázquez's *Fragments from an Unfinished Diary* or Ruiz's short *Le retour d'un amateur de bibliothèques* (The Return of a Library Lover), both made in 1983, together with *Acta General de Chile* (*General Statement on Chile*, Miguel Littin, Spain, 1986) question what it means to come home while they reflect on the cinematic strategies used to represent homecoming. Since most of these films have been discussed at length elsewhere, I offer here only a few ideas regarding their conditions of production in relation to the question of strategic homecoming.[29]

On a short visit between 1982 and 1983, after ten years of exile, Ruiz returned to Chile and shot some 8mm images of his childhood home; the streets of Santiago, Valparaíso, and Quilpué; and conversations with friends. Then he went back to France and completed the film by adding sequences shot on 16mm and some folk songs. The thirteen minutes of *The Return of a Library Lover* were broadcast by the French network Antenne 2 as part of its series *Cinéma Cinémas: Lettres d'un Cinéaste*, which included other "letters" from filmmakers such as Wim Wenders and Alain Cavalier.[30] As discussed in the previous chapter, in *Fragments from an Unfinished Diary*, Vázquez was able to return to Chile in a semi-legal way, but she was soon expelled from national territory by the official authorities, even before a single frame had been filmed. A friend and filmmaker, Pablo Perelman, remained in charge of production, following instructions from Vázquez in Finland.[31] Rodrigo Gonçalves, in turn, had been an exile in Sweden until the early 1980s. His partial return to Chile to make the clandestine short film *Rebelión ahora* (Rebellion Now, 1983) had the consequence of propelling a second phase of his exile career, now in Africa. The recently created Instituto Nacional do Cinema in the People's Republic of Mozambique offered its postproduction spaces for him to complete the film, and he remained in Maputo for the rest of the decade, directing documentaries for the institute about the colonial and revolutionary history of Mozambique. In this case, Gonçalves's brief homecoming implied a detour that took him to a new continent and delayed his definitive return to Chile until the early 1990s.[32] After the recuperation of democracy, Gonçalves contributed to the building of bridges between *inxile* and exile filmmakers through the many interviews he conducted as part of his television program *Off the Record* throughout the 1990s and 2000s.[33]

As for Miguel Littín, he returned in 1985 to film the television documentary series *General Statement on Chile* for Spain's public network RTVE. For this project, Littín hired three foreign crews: Italian, French, and one whose members had different nationalities but all had Dutch credentials. He sent them to Chile to film "innocuous but plausible documentaries": one was about Italian immigration in Chile, the second focused on the country's landscapes and geography, and the third was devoted to the seismic history of the region.[34] The three crews did not know about the existence of each other. Littín communicated only with the head of production from each team, and they all called each other "Gabriel."[35] The three European crews were also not aware of Littín's main deception. In order to film this documentary, the director entered the country clandestinely and disguised himself as a Uruguayan executive. As such, he performed an identity that was not his own, one that forced him to be an exile in his own country. The result was a four-episode documentary series broadcast by RTVE in 1986.[36] A two-hour cut was produced for theatrical release, entitled *Actas de Chile*, and this was the version that circulated the most throughout the world, both in independent and repertory theaters, festivals, and other kinds of art spaces through networks of solidarity.[37]

Shot in 1985, *General Statement on Chile*'s worldwide recognition was enhanced by Gabriel García Márquez's chronicle *La aventura de Miguel Littín clandestino en Chile* (*Clandestine in Chile*), based on eighteen hours of interviews with the filmmaker upon his return to Madrid.[38] A first-person account in which García Márquez adopts Littín's voice, the book was published in 1986, coinciding with the first screenings of the film, though it had already circulated months earlier as a serialized novel published in various newspapers in Spain and other Spanish-speaking territories.[39] The failed assassination attempt on Pinochet in September 1986 brought even more attention to the film and the TV series, since the third episode contained an extended interview with members of the Frente Patriótico Manuel Rodríguez (FPMR; Manuel Rodríguez Patriotic Front)—a guerrilla group created in 1983 as the military branch of the Communist Party, which had adopted its "popular rebellion of the masses" policy and legitimized "all forms of struggle" against the dictatorship, including violent ones.[40] The inclusion of this interview proves that Littín's clandestine and political networks were strong, as he was able to successfully enter the deepest and most hidden circles of the Chilean resistance.[41]

In addition to García Márquez's account of Littín's trip, including all the details of the safety measures that enabled the making of the documentary—"the adventure" of his journey—at least two other paratexts should be mentioned. Hours before finalizing the production and leaving the country, Littín held an interview with journalist Patricia Collyer for the oppositional magazine *Análisis*. With the taunting title "Entrevista clandestina: Miguel Littín vino, filmó y se fue" (Clandestine Interview: Miguel Littín came, shot, and left), the article included a picture and appeared two days after the filmmaker's departure, in July 1985.[42] It was strategically designed to mock the dictatorship: one of the exiles whose names was on the lists of those prohibited from returning had indeed come home, made a film about it, and even broken into the presidential palace—"the dictator's lair"—disguised as a gaffer for the Italian crew.[43] The second paratext is the piece "El ojo en el corazón de Chile: Notas de una filmación clandestina" (Eyes on the Heart of Chile: Notes from a Clandestine Shoot), published in late 1985 in the exile journal *Araucaria de Chile*.[44] A first-person testimonial, the text is divided into twelve short entries that differ from the sense of adventure that García Márquez would later give to his book. In Littín's account, the privileged mode is nostalgia, and its narrative structure is that of a diary. Perhaps not entirely unlike Angelina Vázquez's travel diary, inscribed into the visuals and the diegesis of her *Fragments from an Unfinished Diary*, *General Statement on Chile*'s "clandestine narrator" returns to the tone essayed in this short piece: "I bring back with me the larch trees, the gigantic araucarias, the impenetrable forests, the wet paths covered by moss; I bring back love, the hidden substance of my land."[45] These "notes from a clandestine shoot" thus anticipate Littín's voice-over narration, especially in its nostalgic gesture of tying the nation with an image of the country's landscape from north to south—a recurring strategy in homecoming documentaries.

PERMANENT AND OTHER WAYS OF RETURNING HOME

Strategic homecomings were not the only way of returning home. Permanent returns continued with more intensity right before the end of the dictatorship and in the first years of democratic rule, roughly between 1987 and 1993. That was the case for the homecoming of filmmakers such as Orlando Lübbert, Carlos Puccio, Juan Andrés Racz, Antonio Skármeta, and many others. But returns did not end in the early years of the new democracy. Sergio Castilla, who had continued his career in the United States after living in Sweden and France, waited until 1997 to return and soon afterward made *Gringuito* (1998)—a fictional homecoming narrative centered on the experience of a child and his feelings of uprootedness while returning to Chile after living all his life in New York.[46] Several filmmakers simply continued to live in exile, returning only sporadically on trips that were often related to film projects or activities. Directors like Gastón Ancelovici, Patricio Guzmán, Patricio Henríquez, Marilú Mallet, Leutén Rojas, and Valeria Sarmiento fit under this category. Like many Chilean exiles, and for personal and professional reasons, these diasporic filmmakers began leading lives split between two countries. Other directors simply never came back to Chile, not even to film. Jorge Fajardo, with an extensive career in the independent circuits of Quebecois cinema, was one of them. And then there was Raúl Ruiz, whose multiple cinematic pathways of return evidence that homecoming is not always a clear bidirectional journey, or one that can be reduced to a single point in time.

Ruiz embodies the idea that the cinematic homecomings of Chilean exile cinema were plural and diverse. As already mentioned, Ruiz began making strategic returns at the end of 1982 for the shooting of *The Return of a Library Lover*. Then he came back several times throughout the 1980s, mostly to curate and introduce a selection of his works in different venues. Elizabeth Ramírez-Soto and I have argued elsewhere that these returns, insufficiently acknowledged in Ruiz's studies and in the historiography of Chilean exile cinema, constitute vital ways of coming home and engaging with local cinema structures, fellow filmmakers, and national audiences.[47] One of these instances of return, in 1986, was labeled by a critic as Chile's "greatest cinematic event in a long time."[48] Frequent brief return trips for specific projects continued throughout the late 1980s and early 1990s. These included the crucial year of 1990, when democracy was regained and Ruiz traveled to Chile for the double shooting of *La telenovela errante* (*The Wandering Soap Opera*, 1990–2017) and *A TV Dante (Cantos IX–XIV)* (1992), and also participated in the Viña del Mar Film Festival that year. Ruiz's returns gained in frequency and intensity starting in the early 2000s and continued until his death. They have even continued posthumously, since several of his unfinished films are being "returned" to life after being completed by Valeria Sarmiento and a team of close collaborators. For Ruiz, returning was a "critical and cinematic operation extended across four decades."[49] Throughout the years, he made several films that were sometimes loosely and sometimes more explicitly connected to the theme of return. In fact, many of these films—*The Return of a Library Lover*, *Las soledades* (The Solitudes, UK, 1992) and *Cofralandes* (Chile, 2002), to name but a few—bear striking similarities, as if they were only one large film about homecoming.[50] Ruiz's extended return undoes the chronology that conceives of homecoming as the "after" or the "end" of exile and emphasizes once again that incompleteness and the unfinished are fundamental qualities of the exile imagination.

FICTIONS OF RETURN

Narratives of return, or "homecoming journeys," as Naficy calls them, have a marginal presence in Chilean exile fiction films.[51] Miguel Littín waited until 1994 to create a fictional narrative about return in *Los náufragos* (The Shipwrecked), produced with funds from Chile, France, and Canada. *The Shipwrecked* qualifies as a more conventional homecoming narrative in which the protagonist goes back to Chile in the early years of the transition to democracy, only to find a country he does not recognize, even if he struggles to understand it. Luis Vera—who had already begun to return to Chile from Sweden when he directed *Hechos consumados* (Children of Fate, 1986), based on a play by Chilean playwright Juan Radrigán—made a feature-length fiction film about return called *Consuelo: En illusion* (Consuelo, 1988). Coproduced by several companies from Sweden and Chile, with support from the Swedish Film Institute, the film's production and release date needs to be noted. As I have explained, in the late 1980s the right to live in Chile was already a demand shared by many across the political spectrum, regardless of the inconsistent policies on return developed by the military junta. By September 1988, however, a month that coincided with the release of *Consuelo* in Swedish theaters, the ban on returning had already ended.[52]

The film is structured as a homecoming narrative, guided by a love triangle between Manuel (a Chilean exile), Lena (his fiancée in Sweden), and Consuelo (the woman he loved in Chile before he departed). The film begins in Stockholm and shows us Manuel "mentally absent, displaced, and always longing to return to Chile."[53] Eventually he does, and his return is as harsh as his first years in Sweden: he does not understand the country and cannot find a job. Flashbacks to his Swedish exile help reinforce the parallels between the two moments, highlighting the idea of return as a journey toward a new exile. Alienated from friends and family, Manuel finds his former girlfriend in Valparaíso, only to discover that she dances in a cabaret. The love affair resumes with striking ease, compared to everything else that Manuel faces upon returning. Near the end of the film, Lena's arrival in Chile complicates things, but Manuel ends their relationship. *Consuelo* has an open ending of sorts: the circle of displacement has apparently been closed with Manuel's return, yet he seems full of doubts and ambivalence. Neither he nor the viewers are ready to understand the implications of his return.

Shot on video, *Exilio y retorno* (*Exile and Return*, Sergio Navarro, 1987) tackles these implications in a more direct way. The dilemmas of return are presented via the story of two brothers, Juan and Pedro Milos. This is the kind of narrative José Donoso envisioned in the roundtable of Chilean filmmakers and writers that took place at the Moscow Film Festival in 1979.[54] In that discussion, Donoso spoke of the need to account for the divided reality of the country and thought of the story of two brothers: one staying in Chile and the other going into exile. Donoso came up with the idea as a metaphor for Chilean cinema—divided between the inside and the outside—and argued that a film like that had to be structured as two "parallel chronicles," one part shot in Chile and the other in exile.⁵⁵ *Exilio y Retorno* does away with the two-part structure but focuses on family relations that have been fractured by exile. The video tells a fictional story while retaining certain documentary elements, most notably the fact that brothers Juan and Pedro Milos play a version of themselves. *Exilio y Retorno* feels excessively didactic and performative: every action, every difficulty faced by Juan in his return, every conversation with his brother, appears to be there only to be displayed for the camera rather than because of its significance within a narrative structure. This is because the video was produced by a Christian community and was funded by FASIC. Created in 1975, FASIC had an ecumenical nature, and because of this characteristic, it was one of the largest human rights organizations tied to the various Christian churches in Chile. *Exilio y retorno*'s fictional narrative was mostly an excuse to stir up debate around the members of this Christian group. Its main function was to activate discussion within a community, and as such, it needs to be considered less as a strict fictional homecoming narrative and more as part of the prolific scene of community-based video and alternative film and video practices that developed in Chile during the 1980s.

ALTERNATIVE FILM AND VIDEO PRACTICES AND THE QUESTION OF RETURN

An important scene of alternative film and video developed in Chile throughout the 1980s.⁵⁶ The decade saw the proliferation of countless low-budget anti-dictatorship videos, which offered "an example of oppositional media at a time when any form of opposition amounted to a defiant and risky measure."⁵⁷ These practices not only documented forms of social and political resistance against the dictatorship but also constituted "a form of resistance in their own right."⁵⁸ Structured in collectives and groups, these organizations defied traditional forms of authorship and engaged in close dialogue with social and political institutions and NGOs in the struggle for democracy. Video collectives like Grupo Proceso, ICTUS, Teleanálisis, Vitel Noticias, and Vicaría de la Pastoral Obrera, among others, created a parallel media ecosystem of their own. These alternative media structures had a strong emphasis on the national circulation of their productions—beyond the capital Santiago—via grassroots networks that reached unions, churches, university campuses, cine-clubs, shantytowns, and even rural areas.⁵⁹

The film and video collectives emerging from this scene paid special attention to the struggle for the right to return. Colectivo Cine-Ojo—responsible for the magnificent *Chile, no invoco tu nombre en vano* (*Chile, I Don't Invoke Your Name in Vain*, Chile/France,1983) and *Días de Octubre* (*October Days*, Chile, 1989)—was one of these collectives. Shot in Chile and edited in Paris, *Chile, I Don't Invoke Your Name in Vain* was a groundbreaking effort in the dialogue between film and video makers residing in exile and those living in Chile. The film was censored by the dictatorship at home, though it enjoyed a wide circulation thanks to informal and alternative distribution networks.[60] Internationally, it premiered in the 1983 version of the Leipzig Film Festival as part of its Chilean retrospective that year (see chapter 3) and played in numerous countries, especially in solidarity events.[61] The formation of the group remained contested for many years, but the members included Mario Díaz, Jaime Reyes, Gastón Ancelovici, René Dávila, and Hernán Castro, who publicly assumed the leadership of the group in 1987.[62] As discussed in chapter 3, this was the year in which Castro was able to travel to the San Sebastián Film Festival after his involvement with Guzmán's *En nombre de Dios* and after working on a new collective initiative founded by Dragomir Yankovic, Vitel Nocticias.[63] Colectivo Cine-Ojo was formed by filmmakers who were living in exile and by others who resided in Chile. The conditions of production of these works determined their ultimate function, which was to operate as messages from the interior to be delivered to the world and then brought back to Chile through semi-clandestine distribution circuits.

In 1983, Colectivo Cine-Ojo made a film about the phenomenon of exile, simply titled *Exilio* (*Exile*). A hybrid oscillating between agitational short, news bulletin, and direct cinema style, *Exile* performs a radical form of political analysis in which the administrative, legal, and social implications of exile and return are exposed. The didactic voice-over frames exile as a tragedy and as the "extension of state repression; thus the struggle to live in one's homeland becomes crucial for Human Rights organizations." Members of the Committee for the Return of Exiles critique the dictatorship's initial and contradictory policies on return. Interviews with political leaders are juxtaposed with observational scenes in which the direct-cinema quality of the film reinforces the feeling of having privileged access to what occurs within the movement of resistance: the discussions in clandestine assemblies, in churches, and in schools. The film documents the social and political positioning of the question of return in late 1982. In this regard, it is worth noting that

Exile ends by aligning the demand for return with the struggle of resistance and the emergence of popular protests around the same time. Against the image of a truck burning in flames, shown on a TV screen, the voice-over says: "Just as the exiles can't wait, nor can the unemployed, those who suffer, those who are fearful.... Chile can't wait." That was, ultimately, the message to be disseminated abroad.

Alternative newsreels about the problems of exile and return had to circulate within Chile, too. *Teleanálisis*—the video version of the magazine *Análisis*—was a news bulletin distributed on VHS to an anonymous network of subscribers. The production and distribution of these videos was clandestine, though later in the 1980s they began listing full production credits and the names of onscreen reporters.[64] *Teleanálisis* devoted various short bulletins to the pressing issue of return: "Exilio: Un reencuentro pendiente" (*Teleanálisis* no. 3, 1984), "La causa de un regreso" (*Teleanálisis* no. 12, 1986), and "Retorno de exiliados: La fuerza de un derecho" (*Teleanálisis* no. 27 (1987). The titles show a progression from return understood as a "pending re-encounter" to return understood as a "powerful right."

Teleanálisis's "La causa de un regreso"—the second bulletin on return—focuses on artists' perspectives on exile while in a summer school in Mendoza, Argentina. Actor Julio Jung, songwriter Isabel Parra, and visual artist Nemesio Antúnez discuss the fractures produced by the coup in Chilean artistic and cultural life and talk about the role of international solidarity and of the creative impulse fueled by exile. The Rotterdam-based think tank Instituto para el Nuevo Chile (Institute for a New Chile) organized this summer school in 1986, in an exilic location close enough to the national territory to enable the participation of Chileans. This institute, founded in 1977, became an active think tank during the 1980s and constituted one example of the need for "renewal" experienced by the Chilean Left in exile.[65] This need for ideological renovation is best seen in the logic behind the publication of the journal *Plural*, whose first editorial in 1983 claimed: "The libertarian, egalitarian, and revolutionary utopia that mobilized our people, can only reemerge and be rooted in the respect for plurality. This presupposes differences and values them as legitimate."[66] The Institute for a New Chile reunited politicians, sociologists, and other academics and public intellectuals who researched the question of democracy and leaned toward the Scandinavian and Northern European models of social democracies. Beginning in 1981, they organized a summer school—Escuela Internacional de

Verano (ESIN)—inviting academics, students, and workers from Chile and Latin America living in various parts of the world.[67]

Art and cinema, as seen in "La causa de un regreso," was also a focus of attention for the think tank. Three years earlier, in 1983, it had funded a video workshop led by documentarian David Benavente, who resided in Chile. The result of this experience is one of the most fascinating examples of community-based video made during the decade: *Re-torno* (*Re-turn*, David Benavente, 1983). The participants in the workshop, ranging from teenagers to the elderly, gather in a classroom to talk about their experiences as exiles, reflecting on cultural identity and belonging, on the difficulties faced by their children, and especially on the fraught decisions surrounding return. These conversations are videotaped and screened on TV monitors to the participants of the workshop. Viewers of *Re-turn*, however, soon realize that they are witnessing a conversation between two groups, one based in Rotterdam and the other in Stockholm—a dialogue enabled by video. There are scenes in which the Rotterdam group watches the discussions that took place in Stockholm, and vice versa. But the conversation between the two does not take the form of a mere reaction to what the other group has videotaped; sometimes they directly address each other, as if they were sending video letters to specific members of the workshop. Furthermore, the exchange is not limited to the dialogue between Rotterdam and Stockholm. They also receive a letter from Chile, in which a woman says, "I am an exile in my own country. I live inside a pressure cooker. Sometimes I see a hole and I breathe. I am much less of a Chilean than you." This testimony produces a great impact on the participants and forces them to go deeper in their reflection on identity. *Re-turn*—simultaneously an instance of community-based video production as well as a video documentary on the process of that production—situates exile as a reflexive condition, an experience to be rationalized. Exile is constructed as an open and dialogic process of critical self-reflection, in a setting that resembles political discussions in the assembly style favored by grassroots organizations.

The last aspect stressed by the making of *Re-turn* is the ability to think about the mediated condition of images and testimonies. Participants discuss what happens to them when they see themselves and their friends on video. They recognize that the image video offers is not quite a self-portrait, but it is still an opportunity to gain a different knowledge of them from a position of exteriority and "outsideness"—a new understanding of their identity as exiles.[68]

UNDOING IDENTITY AND NOSTALGIA

This reflection on identity is acutely explored in the strategic homecomings of the already mentioned first-person documentaries *The Return of a Library Lover*, *Fragments from an Unfinished Diary*, and *General Statement on Chile*. More essayistic and performative in nature, all these films offer a radical consideration of the forms of nostalgia and counternostalgia that emerge in the process of returning home.

The cinematic treatment of nostalgia goes beyond fetishization or idealization. Svetlana Boym's work has been widely cited for her useful distinction between "restorative" and "reflexive" nostalgia. Restorative nostalgia favors an essentialist view of the nation, with an imagery relying on landscapes, rituals, and faces of people, in the hope that these images will spark a collective sense of popular memory. In this mode, the homeland is there to be recovered—restored to its "origin," before displacement and before the ravages of time turned it into a nebulous memory. Reflective nostalgia, in turn, distances these images from their immediate purpose of preservation. This form of nostalgia is suspicious of discourses of nationalism and of the possibility that there is something left to be recovered. If anything, what is left cannot be equated with the ideological constructs of nation and home. Reflective nostalgia favors irony, distancing, political analysis, and the fragmented subjectivity of the self as opposed to the collective remembrance of a people.[69] In the aforementioned films, both modes of nostalgia are in tension. But the critical stance of reflective nostalgia dominates insofar as these documentaries question the act of homecoming itself at the same time that they openly reflect on the aesthetic and narrative means with which to give form to homecoming.

One last example should be added to this group, a documentary journey of homecoming about the doubts, pains, and joys of a film director and his family's definitive return to Chile. In *Eran unos que venían de Chile* (They Were Some Who Came from Chile, 1986), Claudio Sapiaín goes back and forth between Sweden and Chile to capture his family's return over an extended period. Sapiaín had lived in Sweden for eleven years with his wife Vilma and their son Paulo, who was less than a year old when they left Chile after the coup. After the military junta began to allow the gradual return of exiles, the family decided to return and made a film about it. The narrative is thus structured around the return of this family to Chilean soil, featuring a constant first-person reflection on rootedness and what it means to belong to a homeland.

The spatiotemporal relations at work in the experience of exile—constantly exchanging the *here/now* with the *there/then*—appear from the outset. The title presents itself as a trap; it implies a positioning in and from exile, but the film tells the story of the return to Chile. Its story is that of a family *who came from Sweden*. The documentary is anchored by Sapiaín's voice-over. It is through his voice and thoughts that we gain access to the exile's mind full of doubts. Nevertheless, the story itself centers on the son Paulo. Throughout the film, Sapiaín makes a direct address to him. In fact, the documentary could be thought of as a letter-film sent by a father to his son.[70] The film is the director's way of coming to terms with his own return as well as a gift to his son's future self—like those letters that are only to be opened fifteen, twenty years from the present. The invocation of the future is felt through the explicit desire of both father and son to participate in the forging of a "better Chile," as they say. They are returning to be part of a future that, despite all the personal complications associated with homecoming, is filled with political hope. And yet that future is also the anticipation of a troubled memory. This is the "postmemory" of those children who feel the marks and wounds of traumatic events they experienced only through their parents.[71] The film expresses these marks poignantly in a scene when Paulo confesses to his father that he feels he's being watched. He is worried that at any point they might take Claudio. This is a fear produced by a memory that is not his own, perhaps a reenactment of a story he must have heard. In this, Sapiaín's film dialogues with a trend of Chilean exile film and video that centers on the relations between childhood and the experiences of exile and return—as seen in works like *Los ojos como mi papá* (*Eyes Like My Dad*, Pedro Chaskel, Cuba, 1979), *Llegué, me gustó, me quedo* (*I Came, I Liked It, I Stay*, Hogar el Encuentro, 1988), and *Aquí donde yo vivo* (*Here Where I Live*, Carlos Puccio, Germany, 1994).[72]

The final minutes of *They Were Some Who Came from Chile* explicitly discuss nostalgia and return, focusing on the attempt to rebuild a subjectivity that has been fragmented by displacement as well as on the need to give form to an image of the homeland that has been shaped by a dialogic encounter between cultures. The mentioning of the experience of the Conquista—with the usurpation of land and killing of indigenous people that came with it—links the pains of exile and return to a larger history of cultural struggle. Remote times and spaces find visual expression in the images of the cemeteries, the abandoned houses of the miners once enslaved, and the archaeological ruins of native peoples. Here, a set of private memories enables the configuration of a sense of popular memory. The voice-over highlights the idea of absence implied by the landscapes of ruins and forgotten stories of the Chilean north, by saying "eleven years of absence from the homeland, in time and in space." From that line onward, Sapiaín no longer addresses his son—the private letter is now directed to all viewers. His voice takes spectators from the personal to the collective, and the film's tracking shots take viewers on a geographical journey through emblematic images of the Chilean landscape and its people: mountains, the copper mines, fishermen in the south. "Eleven years with another culture, which gave us a different vision of our own. Exile was meant to be a punishment, and yet it gave us so much." Images of people walking the streets in downtown Santiago, farmers' markets, and women baking bread accompany these words. The voice concludes: "I don't know why, but I strongly feel that I belong to this."

The visual track works primarily in nostalgia's restorative mode. The film travels through the country to match the landscapes with the images that memory had built in the absence of the landscape itself. The *I* that speaks, however, focuses on what has been gained with exile. The affective display of the national territory is tied to a critical position allowed by cultural exchange. "Exile was meant to be a punishment, and yet it gave us so much" summarizes the experience of displacement as well as it redefines return under a more positive narrative of cultural encounter.

The circulation of *They Were Some Who Came from Chile* also needs to be considered here. Unlike other exile documentaries, the film and the character of Paulo acquired different afterlives. In "Los hijos del destierro" (The Children of Exile), a seven-minute piece included in episode 25 of *Teleanálisis* (1987), Paulo is profiled alongside other returnees. The value of the *Teleanálisis* artifact lies in how its counter-official stance breaks with the censorship of the news imposed by the dictatorship. The heart of the section is made up of testimonies of several returnee adolescents sharing their experiences on camera: estrangement, a lack of understanding, uncertainty about the future, and shock at the poverty they have seen in the country. An often-repeated sentiment has to do with contributing to shoring up Chile: they all want to help forge a new country.[73]

Sapiaín's film also got a different kind of mass media exposure when it was included in the September 7 episode of the 1988 campaign for the "No" vote, prior to the referendum that defeated Pinochet. Several exile films had been circulating hand-to-hand in bootlegged video copies, but a prime-time TV broadcast like this one, even if incomplete, was unprecedented. The episode included over four minutes excerpted from

They Were Some Who Came from Chile, which offered a summary of Pablo's story of return. The segment was followed by an onscreen testimonial by Moy de Tohá, the widow of Allende's former minister of defense, who expanded on the pains of the exile experience and on the challenges faced by people who were returning from exile. The broadcasting of the "No" campaign coincided with the military junta's lifting of its previous exile policies and prohibitions against return. Therefore, the excerpts from Sapiaín's documentary are situated as vital testimonies in the struggle for democracy and human rights, in a moment of key cultural significance such as the referendum and the media campaign for the "No" vote.

Sapiaín would continue to explore the experience of return in his next documentary—*Una vez más mi país* (Once again My Country, Sweden/Chile 1990)—in which the context of the referendum and the following transition to democratic rule would gain more prominence. The year 1990 was a watershed, filled with hope despite the fears provoked by the political power that the military retained, symbolized in Pinochet's unaltered status as commander in chief of the army. Still, the new democratic government took office in March that year. For exile filmmakers, it meant more opportunities to come home. For filmmakers in general, it coincided with a burgeoning moment of the local industry. Also in 1990 were the premiere of many fiction and documentary films and the slow rebuilding of cinema institutions and structures.[74] Initial coproduction agreements with television and early efforts to create a national film archive were part of this moment. Undoubtedly, though, the most significant cinematic event that year, and one that functioned as an institutional site of homecoming, was the Viña del Mar Film Festival.

SITES OF INSTITUTIONAL RETURN:
VIÑA DEL MAR 1990

It is widely acknowledged that the genealogy of the NLAC movement "begins," at least institutionally, with the first edition of the Viña del Mar International Film Festival in 1967.[75] This genealogy was explicitly invoked in the organization of the third festival, which took place October 12–20, 1990. Leonardo Kocking directed the festival, and among the organizing committee were Silvio Caiozzi, Ignacio Aliaga, Juan José Ulriksen, and Sergio Trabucco.[76] The labeling of the festival as "third" sought to establish a firm continuity between the foundational moment of the late 1960s and the refoundational moment signaled by the return

FIGURE 18. Marilú Mallet (left) and Valeria Sarmiento (right) during the third Viña del Mar International Film Festival, 1990. Photo by Zuzana M. Pick. Courtesy of Fondo Zuzana Pick—Cineteca Universidad de Chile.

to democracy earlier that year, in March 1990. Kocking put it like this: "It is actually the seventh edition of the Viña Festival, but if we called it that, the festival would have meant nothing."[77] Miguel Littin, who was not one of the organizers but whose participation in the festival did not go unnoticed, claimed in a round panel, "The truth is, we need to begin the history of Chilean cinema with the [Viña] festival."[78] The enormous twenty-year gap in between had an ambivalent effect on the festival. It highlighted the temporal discontinuity between the second and third edition at the same time that it affirmed the desire to restore continuity to a trajectory of the NLAC broken by the series of military dictatorships in the region. The desire for continuity is even clearer in the festival's subtitle, Reencuentro de Chile con su cine, a meeting between Chile and its cinema, the "re-encounter" between the two. The twenty-year gap is the mark of the dictatorship and, by extension, that of exile. The 1990 festival claims that it is time for Chilean cinema to reconcile its two streams: the films made in Chile with those made in exile. Sergio Trabucco summarized this double desire (historical continuity and therapeutic re-encounter) in an op-ed written for the magazine *Cine* after the festival was over: "There were the films ... and ... those who for years ... survived and gave everything to witness this ... wonderful parade. The debate and the talks, as dense as the smoke of cigarettes, returned us to Viña '67."[79]

As a crucial event in the history of Chilean and Latin American cinema, the 1990 Viña Festival needs to be thought of as a site of institutional homecoming: the "official" instance that allowed the return from exile of directors whose work was largely unknown. As has been discussed throughout the chapter, exile filmmakers performed a plurality of cinematic homecomings during the 1980s. But this one had a different nature. Its "official" status, tied to a new institutional democracy, can be summarized by the invitation to visit the governmental palace of La Moneda and have dinner with Minister of the Interior Enrique Correa.[80] For the majority of the thirty-five directors who attended, this was the first time they were returning to a place symbolically charged with state violence and with the beginning of the dictatorship. A narrative of return was therefore fundamental not only for the way the festival was organized or for its curatorial choices, but also for its social existence beyond the confines of the film world.

The press coverage of the festival paid attention to this opportunity to watch Chilean exilic production and foregrounded the "emotional weight" in the homecomings of those who had not had the chance to return to Chile during the dictatorship, like Sebastián Alarcón and Sergio Castilla.[81] The festival became a chance "to share the collective experience of recovering for ourselves the cinema that belongs to us."[82]

Most reports on the festival were optimistic, as indicated in Hans Ehrmann's review: "The festival was a valuable and revitalizing collective experience."[83] Some filmmakers shared this feeling. Orlando Lübbert, for instance, claimed, "For those of us who have been outside, the essential thing has been to see our reflection in the culture of this country, to recognize that we were not alone, to acknowledge that the things that united us were stronger than we thought."[84] For others, however, the materialization of the festival proved that the fissure opened by the separation between *inxiles* and exiles was hard to suture—the wounds were still open. Directors from the inside and the outside looked at each other with suspicion.

People like Silvio Caiozzi—responsible for some of the most celebrated feature-length fiction films produced in Chile during the dictatorship, such as *Julio comienza en Julio* (1978) and *La luna en el espejo* (1990)—felt that those who came from exile did not value the hard work in the film sphere in Chile.[85] Exiles, in turn, had the same need for recognition. They felt their work was disregarded either for the supposed privileges granted by filming in developed countries or for being "too political." The selection of films in the program was contentious. Balancing

Chilean and exilic production—the latter outnumbered the former by far—became an insurmountable trap. The work of women filmmakers in exile was once again minimally present. The fragile political climate of the early months of the transition to democracy left its mark in the program, too: films that were either overtly or allegorically political were for the most part excluded, something that limited the range of exilic films.[86] Another delicate issue was the resentment about not living in the country or about not wanting to live in the country. As Sebastián Alarcón recognized, "most exile filmmakers want to continue living abroad, and simply come to Chile to shoot."[87]

The debates were more heated in the round panels. There was one between Chilean critics that was deemed disappointing by the filmmakers who attended, who hoped to discuss the status of film criticism in Chile and its relationship with film production. As Olave tells with a dose of humor, the general audience also found the panel deeply disappointing, since they were expecting to see "the filmmakers kill the critics rather than seeing the critics kill each other."[88] The real polemics, nonetheless, were reserved for the talks and conversations between filmmakers.

Exiles disagreed among themselves, and certain filmmakers were resentful of others—especially of Miguel Littín—for trying to "appropriate" the phenomenon of exile cinema and for reducing its heterogeneity to one or two names. The atmosphere was already stormy by the time Littín had to speak, and some, as Sergio Trabucco recalls, wanted to prevent him from reading his talk.[89] This was perhaps because Littín prefaced the talk with a short response to German critic Peter Schumann, reprimanding him for insisting on a trite narrative of the "crisis" of Latin American filmmakers who have renounced their revolutionary spirit.[90] Littín delivered a paper titled "Se sabe que el que vuelve no se fue" (It Is Known that He Who Returns Has Not Left): "It is a tough exercise to be coming and going, to be far and to dream of the homeland, idealizing the sea . . . , to dream of returning to the time when everything began. For what holds the exile together if not nostalgia?"[91]

Littín's talk took everyone back to the most naïve version of what Boym called "restorative nostalgia." Furthermore, his address felt like a professor lecturing his students, teaching a film history lesson in which he was the hero. "Nostalgics and Apocalyptics Viewing the Sea"—as Olave titled his festival report for *Apsi*—had not fully reconciled. The festival's failure—perhaps because of the high expectations involved in a "glorious homecoming"—was best summarized by scholar Zuzana M. Pick in a recent testimonial, several decades after the event: "What was promoted as an 'encounter for Chilean cinema' ended up, paradoxically, being a dis-encounter that forced me to question the premises of my study."[92]

The dual evaluations of the festival—some positive and others, like Pick's, extremely negative—reveal the open fractures between Chilean filmmakers. The 1990 Viña Festival shows that "re-encounter" and homecoming had to mean something more than simply gathering in front of a screen to see films that had not been seen before. As Naficy would say, "It is possible for the exile to return, yet still not fully arrive."[93]

ONGOING RETURNS IN THE POSTDICTATORSHIP PERIOD

The organization of the Viña del Mar Festival in 1990 proved to be the culmination of a decade-long process of sustained dialogues between filmmakers and the struggle for democracy, as well as of sustained exchanges between exile directors and filmmakers who never left the country. But the festival also evidenced that the return and first public exhibitions of exile films, together with the homecoming of exile filmmakers, were not enough to produce a "re-encounter" between Chile and its cinema. This failure had little to do with the amount or type of titles shown, and more with the fact that the social and political fractures provoked by exile were still wide open in 1990, only months after Chile's return to democracy.

The analysis of narratives of homecoming throughout this chapter has demonstrated the prominent function return has in Chilean exiles' imagination, although less as the imperative of a "grand homecoming" in fiction films and more as an experience to be interrogated through the counter-informational logic of alternative media and the critical undoing of nostalgia in first-person documentaries. This subjective positioning vis-à-vis the historical processes the country was experiencing in its transition to democracy would become the norm in subsequent films dealing with the memories of exile and return. The early years of this transition configured a political period that, disguised by the apparent calm of a "democracy of agreements" between Left and Right, was effacing the traces of the country's recent past.[94] The memory of the disappeared and exercises of radical politics were left to the underground. The country had regained democracy and a parliament, but Pinochet was irremovable as a commander-in-chief of the army, his Constitution was unchangeable, and his neoliberal economic model was untouchable.[95]

In this context, exile filmmakers continued to return to the country: sometimes to reside in Chile permanently and sometimes to film a specific project (in a form that bears some resemblance to the earlier "strategic" homecomings, although without the clandestine part of it). Carmen Castillo, an exile in France, made a series of documentary films that examine postdictatorship Chile through a voice-over that links her own memory and biography with the lives of other leftist militants and the broader stories of political resistance that continued to shape the country.[96] Even if their focus is not exile, films like *La flaca Alejandra* (1994), *El país de mi padre* (1997), and *Calle Santa Fe* (2007) establish a confrontation between the past and the present that is guided by the gaze of an exile filmmaker who comes home.

Something similar can be said about Patricio Guzmán. He began to return in the late 1980s for the making of *En nombre de Dios* (1987), on which several members of the Chilean alternative video scene worked as cameramen and sound recorders. His more influential homecoming was delayed by a decade. As mentioned in this book's introduction, the year 1997 saw the first iteration of FIDOCS, the documentary film festival Guzmán created, at which both the three parts of *The Battle of Chile* and the homecoming documentary *Chile, Obstinate Memory* (1997) were screened, to much critical attention. In *Chile, Obstinate Memory*, Guzmán showed *The Battle of Chile* to high school and college students who had never heard of the landmark documentary and filmed the discussions that followed: heated debates reflecting a divided country and youthful repetitions of clichés heard from parents.[97] Since these found no room in the complex images of *The Battle of Chile*, new audiences were baffled and deeply *affected*. They cried. Their bodies shook in emotion, trembling. Their voices broke. With this film, Guzmán thus tied the investigation of the country's collective memory with a critical inquiry into his own documentary oeuvre and into the archival and political effects of these filmic images of the past. His more recent work continues this double inquiry. As I have argued elsewhere, in the trilogy made up of *Nostalgia de la luz* (Nostalgia for the Light, 2010), *El botón de nácar* (The Pearl Button, 2015) and *La cordillera de los sueños* (The Cordillera of Dreams, 2019), Guzmán retains the exterior gaze of the exile as a defining quality of the documentaries' point of view and narrative structure. The meditations on the intertwining of Chilean history and landscape function in these three films as a proxy for *returning* once again to the director's old obsessions. These include his lived experience of Allende's government, his making of *The Battle of Chile*, his being detained in the National Stadium, and, through his fraught re-encounter with the country after years in exile, the memory battles that persist in the present.[98]

Around the same time as Guzmán's return for *Chile, Obstinate Memory*, a different wave of cinematic homecomings began and continues to develop—that of the children of the diaspora. Films such as *Chile: A History in Exile* (Cecilia Araneda, Canada, 1998), *En algún lugar del Cielo* (Somewhere in Heaven, Alejandra Carmona, Chile, 2003), and *Generation Exile* (Rodrigo Dorfman, US, 2009) bear the marks of the "generation of postmemory" and concentrate on the myriad consequences that displacement had in the lives of their authors.[99] This ever-growing body of work has been widely discussed in the intersecting fields of documentary and memory studies as examples of first-person narratives that privilege familial and intergenerational conflicts derived from exile and that rely on autobiography, intimacy, and subjectivity.[100] As mentioned in this book's preface, the films of the generation of postmemory also rely on a variety of archival documents to examine the afterlives of the past in the present.

But what was the place of Chilean exile cinema in this archival turn to the filmic records of the past? Other than a few key titles, since the early 1990s the corpus had remained unknown to most audiences, including specialized publics formed by scholars, critics, and younger filmmakers. There was no official national film archive in the country until 2006, and thus most prints and copies remained in exile—dispersed among multiple archives throughout the world. The next and last chapter traces the material history of their unfinished return to Chilean archives and museums.

CHAPTER 7

Archival Returns and Digital Futures

The last chapter of this book is a call for a politicized remaking of world cinema from an archival perspective. What can the practice of transnational cinema solidarity offer if we devote our attention to film archives? How can archives work against the national, political, and cultural borders that shape world cinema? This chapter tells the story of the ongoing return of exile films and videos to Chilean archives and museums. At the same time, it intervenes in contemporary debates in three ways. First, it shifts the emphasis from memory as a thematic and aesthetic inscription in postdictatorship films to archives and their concrete role in shaping historical narratives and memories of exile.[1] Second, I move away from the kind of critical theory that interrogates "The Archive" as a singular noun—that site "where order is given" as Derrida famously claimed—and concentrate instead on the material histories of specific archives and their policies.[2] Issues of access, location, cataloging, curatorial practices, funding, cultural and political contexts, and institutional regulations constitute inescapable aspects to explore. Third, I contribute to an emerging field of archival scholarship that critiques the national paradigm that dominates the functioning of most film archives and that calls attention to power imbalances in global archiving networks.[3] Questions of restitution, reparation, repatriation, and return—the big "R" words, as discussed at the 7th International Conference at the EYE Filmmuseum in 2022—play a crucial role in this critique and invite us to redress the asymmetries that sustain the archival infrastructure of world cinema.

The final chapter of this book thus examines the challenges that exile—as a cultural and political experience of forced displacement—and exile cinema—as a mode of transnational media in perpetual movement and defiance of fixed locations—raise for archives. As I will show, these challenges remain at work even when archives, libraries, and museums want to operate under the principles of solidarity. Archival online platforms and what I call "digital returns" offer, nonetheless, possibilities that reimagine what return and repatriation may look like, proposing more equitable forms of transnational collaboration.

FROM MEMORY TO ARCHIVES

The year 2013 marked the fortieth anniversary of the military coup in Chile. Even more so than the thirtieth anniversary in 2003, the date was commemorated with an acute intensity in the public sphere.[4] Television shows, op-eds in newspapers, speeches, politicians asking for forgiveness, academic conferences, books, oral testimonies, art exhibits, and film programs were all part of a context in which the dictatorship and its legacies were once again debated. Several factors contributed to this reshaping of the relations between memory and citizens. As Michael Lazzara notes, the massive demonstrations of the 2011 student movement repoliticized the country and brought harsh new critical perspectives on the period known as transition to democracy. Human rights violations were prosecuted, and the Supreme Court issued a mea culpa for its previous blatant dismissal of the crimes of the military junta. Right-wing president Sebastián Piñera outed "passive accomplices," as he called those civilians from his own political sector who had supported the dictatorship. The idea of victimhood was gradually expanded. Besides murdered, disappeared, tortured, and exiled Chileans together with their relatives, figures like soldiers and civilians who were "forced" into doing the dirty work of the regime now claimed for themselves the label of victims and the right to reparations from the state.[5] Former detention centers and houses of torture were transformed into sites of memory. In the context of the bicentennial of the republic, Museo de la Memoria y los Derechos Humanos (MMDH; Museum of Memory and Human Rights) was created in 2010 with the mission of giving visibility to human rights violations committed by the state. Overall, the notion of memory was present as an ethical principle, as a "battleground" and confrontation of different narratives in social dispute, and as a living and embodied practice of testimony and performance.[6]

Exile and exile cinema also played a role in this renewed memory landscape in the years leading up to and following the 2013 anniversary. Even though various testimonies and sociological studies of exile had been published in the last years of the dictatorship and the beginning of the transition to democracy, these texts, just like the films made in exile throughout the 1970s and 1980s, had circulated in reduced circles and were still marked by the prejudices surrounding exile. Memories of displacement had always been troubling for both Right and Left. For the Right, exile was the just price many had to pay in order to protect Chile from its "Marxist cancer." For the Left, exile reactivated too many conflicting issues in those who stayed: resentment against those who had not experienced the dictatorship from "within"; skepticism toward those who had gone through an "ideological renovation" after residing in well-developed, capitalist countries; disbelief in the face of those exiles who were now critical of socialism after living in socialist nations of the Eastern bloc; and inability to deal with the criticism of *returnees*, who now saw Chile from the "privilege" of having lived in between cultures.[7] But if to be a returnee in the early and mid-1990s implied being the target of all kinds of suspicions from both ends of the political spectrum, the fortieth anniversary of the coup and the programs organized by MMDH provided a new platform for narratives of exile. The resurfacing of exile in public debates was also a generational process—the children of the diaspora have been the most invested group in recent years in critically reexamining exile as a cultural, political, and artistic phenomenon.[8]

The past two decades of Chilean cinema have seen a renewed thematic interest in exile that finds an aesthetic expression in what Elizabeth Ramírez-Soto has called the "cinema of affect"—films that seek to "elicit more sensorial" responses in viewers.[9] By turning to archival images and found footage, home movies, first-person voice-overs, and the essayistic, Chilean documentaries broadened the spectrum of relations between cinema, exile, and memory. Among many others, films like *El eco de las canciones* (The Echo of Songs, Antonia Rossi, 2010), *Vuelta y Vuelta* (Daniela Bichi and Markus Toth, 2013), and *Los descendientes* (The Descendants, Diego Zurita, 2013) gave visibility to diverse aspects of displacement, framing it as an experience that conditions the biographies of their makers since their early childhood. Exile, nonetheless, emerges here only as historical residue, as an enduring aftermath to be interrogated from the vantage point of "the generation of postmemory."[10]

An "archival impulse" was an essential aspect of this generational perspective.[11] Much as MMDH contributed to giving new value to a plurality of evidentiary sources often neglected in official historical narratives, these documentary films brought to the fore a range of archival images, sounds, manuscript documents, and material objects dealing with exile. The initial scene of *El edificio de los chilenos* (The Chilean Building, Macarena Aguiló with codirection by Susana Foxley, 2010) is particularly telling in this regard. In a literal rendition of historian Steve Stern's metaphor of Chile's "memory box," the director opens a small wooden trunk and grabs old letters, drawings, and notebooks from her childhood—the very materials that constitute the "stuff" of her memory and of her film's narrative.[12] In *The Chilean Building* there is even a sequence that includes footage from a rare Chilean exile film, *Éramos una vez* (*Once We Were*, Leonardo de la Barra, 1979).[13] While there is a connection between what is described in Aguiló's voice-over—a children's summer camp—and what viewers see in the archival images—a room with bunk beds—the sequence coming from de la Barra's short film is used less as a representational device and more as a textured and sensorial experience of the past. While these procedures were common in Chile's recent postdictatorship documentaries, the strategy of borrowing footage from an actual 1970s film made by a Chilean exile director constituted an exception.[14] The archives of exile cinema were largely unknown and remained, for the most part, in exile. This is the story of their unfinished return.

SITUATING THE PROBLEM

In 2013, and in the context of the commemorations of the fortieth anniversary of the coup, I was part of a team of six scholars who programmed a series called *Nomadías* (Nomadisms) for the twentieth Valdivia International Film Festival.[15] The series was devoted to three women filmmakers in exile, Marilú Mallet, Valeria Sarmiento, and Angelina Vázquez, whose work in Canada, France, and Finland remained largely unknown in Chile.[16] The program involved showing digital files of titles such as *La femme au foyer* (*The Housewife*, Valeria Sarmiento, 1976), *Chère Amérique* (*Dear America*, Marilú Mallet, 1990), and several other films that had never been screened in Chile and of which no local archive held copies. In a round panel held during the retrospective, director Angelina Vázquez claimed, "I returned in 1993, but my films have never returned."[17] Since she had just deposited most of her films in Cineteca Nacional de Chile, the national film archive, by this she could only have meant one thing: *my films are invisible*. Paraphrasing Hamid

Naficy and reprising an idea that was already present during the 1990 Viña Film Festival, Vázquez seemed to be saying, "An exile cinema may return, yet still not fully arrive."[18]

Since the mid-2000s, part of the corpus of Chilean exile cinema has begun its return to Chilean institutions—Cineteca Nacional de Chile, Cineteca de la Universidad de Chile, MMDH, and Archivo Ruiz-Sarmiento—through donations by filmmakers, the signing of international cooperation agreements, and the programming of special retrospectives. This last instrument is relevant because return cannot be reduced to the acts of depositing and storing films in an archive. When I speak of return, I am also talking about access and visibility. Exhibiting exile films in their theaters and lending them for series organized by other institutions and festivals has been the main way for these four archives and museums to bring this diasporic corpus closer to Chilean audiences, a significant goal considering that most exile films never received theatrical distribution in Chile and were never programmed on national television. In recent years, access has increased thanks to digitization projects and the inclusion of some of these films on the online platforms Cineteca Nacional Online (by Cineteca Nacional de Chile), Cineteca Virtual (by Cineteca de la Universidad de Chile), and MMDH's website.

The case of the *Nomadías* retrospective is illustrative in this regard. Programming the series in 2013 meant that most digital files that were brought for the first time to Chile were able to enter the collections of Cineteca Universidad de Chile and Archivo Ruiz-Sarmiento. The *Nomadías* program also led to a homonymous edited volume published three years later, a book that contributed greatly to the production of new knowledge on the work of Mallet, Sarmiento, and Vázquez.[19] The book implied an academic re-encounter with Zuzana M. Pick, pioneer scholar of Chilean exile cinema, who wrote the preface. In this context, Pick donated her personal archive to Cineteca Universidad de Chile, which is now digitizing her more than three thousand documents—correspondence, manuscripts, press clippings, handwritten notes, photographs, posters—related to Chilean exile cinema.[20] The "feminist May" of 2018, a series of massive protests against gender violence in Chile, together with the global "Me Too" movement, also led to a greater interest in the work of women exile directors. The films have been included in other series, they have aired on cable TV, and some of them are now part of the online platforms of both the Valdivia festival and Cineteca Nacional de Chile.[21] At the same time, and by virtue of the imperative need to challenge masculinist accounts of world cinema history, the films of Mallet, Sarmiento, and Vázquez have also found a place in international programs and exhibitions, such as *No Master Territories: Feminist Worldmaking and the Moving Image*, held at the Haus der Kulturen der Welt in Berlin in 2022.[22]

This brief account speaks to the long process required for acts of return to gain cultural legitimacy. Since most exile films remain unseen by Chilean audiences and scholars, the return of Chilean exile cinema has important implications for understanding the role of this corpus in national film history and for situating its material and symbolic function in the country fifty years after the coup and almost thirty years after the end of the dictatorship. This larger phenomenon is what I mean by *archival returns*: the process that has brought prints and copies of exile films to Chilean archives and museums, as well as the cultural demands, historical narratives, and memory debates activated by that process. *Return* is a tricky word to use in this archival context, and I shall soon explain why it is in fact the appropriate term rather than the more commonly used *film repatriation*. For the moment it suffices to go back to the previous chapter's idea that exile and return are mutually defining concepts: one cannot be understood without the other. In fact, to speak of archival returns is also to speak of what remains in exile. For the most part, Chilean exile films continue to be safeguarded in multiple archives across various continents. If Chilean exile cinema is a corpus, its parts are to be found in all corners of the world and in different kinds of archives.

In what follows I acknowledge such disparities by discussing a range of archives that currently store Chilean exile cinema and therefore impact the histories that can be written about it. The organizations that are discussed here are not homogeneous, as there are great differences between the highly professional and specialized archives in countries like France or Sweden and the "imperfect archives" of Latin America—those "orphans of the moving image archival infrastructure," as Janet Ceja Alcalá called them.[23] The main questions that lurk throughout this chapter are therefore political more than technological. Competing discourses of cultural heritage and transnational film history are at stake in the archival returns of Chilean exile cinema. These stakes derive from the nature of exile cinemas, which defy any sense of proper emplacement. The "interstitiality" of exile points to a fundamental aspect of the term *displacement*: being *out* of place, regardless of where exile subjects and cultural artifacts reside.[24] The following paradox emerges. While the archival presence of a film demands a specific positionality, no particular archival location can account for the multiplicity of geographic and cultural displacements evidenced by exile cinemas.

RETURN, OR THE CULTURAL POLITICS OF REPATRIATION

Exile destabilizes the logic that ties the discourse of cultural heritage to the nation as "a particular level of authority and power," as Caroline Frick has claimed.[25] Even if film archives have always collected "far more than their own countries' film productions," the symbolic and material power of the national dominates the policies and practices of most archival institutions—especially those that are called "national" film archives and cinematheques, which produce an indissoluble triad between national heritage, national film history, and the national archive.[26] In the world of museums and archives, discourses of repatriation have challenged the traditional understanding of heritage based on notions of possession and exclusivity, but they do not necessarily challenge the national paradigm within which archives work.[27] According to Paolo Cherchi Usai, the narrow and most frequently used definition of *repatriation* understands it as "the physical transfer of prints from one archive to the other on the basis of their nationality."[28] Etymologically, the Latin root *patria* adds enormous weight to the kind of exchanges present in repatriation projects, tied as they are to postwar and postcolonial contexts as well as to other situations of cultural and political violence.[29] Regardless of the specificity of the case, repatriation is intrinsically about nationhood, heritage, and belonging.

But where do exile films belong? And what (national) institutions can claim a right to them? Liminality is at the heart of the exile condition and is the main reason that repatriation is problematic as concept and as practice for dealing with exilic cultural production. It is true that many films can be found in archives that are located in countries that differ from the territory of their production or from the nationality of their filmmakers, and it is also true that the presence of an exile print in a particular archive responds to a series of circumstances that are also shared by nonexile films, such as coproduction agreements, festival programming, market sales, dubbing or subtitling of prints for specific international territories, and so on. However, Chilean and exile cinemas pose a specific kind of "anomaly" for the film archive, for two main reasons.[30] One refers to the political nature of exile as an experience of forced displacement, coupled with the explicit political project of a cinema of resistance against the dictatorship. In this regard, and as this book has made clear, the travels and movements of exile prints often respond to the intricacies of a circulatory network of transnational solidarities with the Chilean people, in which a range of actors that normally fall into the cracks of the archive intervene: solidarity committees, exile communities, embassies and consulates, labor organizations, film clubs, and so on. The second reason speaks to the question of belonging. If archival examples of war and postcolonial contexts configure a situation in which a work of art, material artifact, or film print *from* a particular nation has been usurped by a foreign power, in the case of exile cinemas that "from" remains ambiguous. Exile prints belong simultaneously *here* and *there*. Consider *Il n'y a pas d'oubli* (*There Is No Forgetting*, Rodrigo González, Marilú Mallet, and Jorge Fajardo, 1975), discussed in chapter 4. This is a film about the exile experience, made by three Chilean exile directors in Canada; produced by the NFB with a Canadian crew and a mix of Canadian and Chilean actors (including exiles playing a version of themselves); and spoken in Spanish, French, and English. The film is undoubtedly Canadian; however, even if it has never enjoyed a theatrical release or television broadcast in Chile, and even if no Chilean archive holds a print or digital file of it, *There Is No Forgetting*, for its portrayal of an emerging exilic community, bears an indelible bond with Chile—that country where it was not made, where it has not been shown, and where it is not safeguarded.

How do we speak of repatriation for exile cinemas, then? What right would a Chilean archive claim to hold a print of *There Is No Forgetting* as part of its collection? An alternative is raised by Cherchi Usai, for whom the safeguarding of "moral rights" presupposes a different repatriation scheme.[31] Arguing that "nationality is not necessarily a criterion for repatriation" allows for a much broader understanding of the repatriation process: "returning cinematic works to their community of origin for the purposes of collection development, preservation, public dissemination, or, for the protection of the community's cultural interests."[32] This definition could apply to the case of Chilean exile cinema, if it were clear that this cinema responded to the "community's cultural interests." But what community is invoked here? With repatriation we arrive at a dead end, because it is impossible to answer this question without falling back on a national (Chilean) or political allegiance (opponents to the dictatorship).

I prefer to speak of archival returns because return is the concept that connects the films as a form of cultural heritage, even as a form of cultural exchange property, with the specific historical condition that produced them—exile. The notion of archival returns points to the limitations of the institution of the archive when dealing with both exile as a cultural phenomenon and exile cinema as a transnational corpus. Archival safeguarding and preservation demand a precise location, a fixed positionality that does not reflect the core characteristics of transnationalism and exile: connectedness, mobility, and in-betweenness. The idea of an archival return does not solve these limitations; it could even be said that it reinforces them since return presupposes the homeland, a national site of origin, as the final destination for a cultural object that belongs to a place that is different from the one where it was produced. But the notion of an archival return redirects our attention to the archival infrastructures of world cinema and to the unequal relations that sustain them. Even if it does not do away with the weight of nationhood, the concept of archival returns charges the operation of cultural transfer and exchange with a sense of historical restitution. This is an archival angle for thinking about the widespread geography of political friendships that constitute what this book has called transnational cinema solidarity.

Returns from exile thus participate in an institutional and political landscape that negotiates the writing of transnational film history and the production of memories of the dictatorship. Following Kristen Weld in her understanding of archives as "instruments of political action" and "enablers of gaze and desire," I claim that the archival returns of Chilean exile cinema activate four desires.[33] First, they enable a desire for cultural and historical recognition; by returning to Chilean archives, it is acknowledged that these exile films belong *there*, where they had never resided in the first place. Second, they enable a desire for completion: the attempt to restore unity and continuity to Chilean cinema. This was a cinema supposed to be "split in two streams," divided between the films produced in exile and those that had been made in Chile under the dictatorship.[34] Third, they enable a desire to bear witness, to act as testimonies to the experience of exile—the desire to activate individual and collective memories of exile. Fourth and last, these returns imply a desire to radically reimagine what a truly "global approach to audiovisual heritage" might mean and do for world cinema history.[35] Since Chilean exile cinema is spread everywhere, its archival returns not only pose questions of national interest; they matter for the writing of world cinema history and for the building of more equitable global archival networks. This goal is only beginning to be forcefully articulated by heads of archives. As Giovanna Fossati claims, "We"—a plural form that includes archivists, scholars, and programmers—"need to ... support a structural system of collaboration and exchange between film archives worldwide."[36] The archival returns of Chilean exile cinema are part of this "global approach" to film archives. Explicitly seeking to "overcome national perspectives," this framework is now seen as a paramount task for redressing the inequalities of the archival field.[37]

THE SCATTERED BODY OF EXILE

Earlier I asked where exile films belong and what institutions can claim a right to them. In its most evident aspect, the question is about the frail and ambiguous positionality of exile and its cultural production. But it is also about how to understand world cinema through an archival lens. The archival locations of exile indicate allegiance to certain areas of the world (Latin America, Europe), and they allow for classifications under histories of national cinema (Chilean, French, Swedish, German, etc.). Most importantly, the archival locations of exile films point to broader political issues. Who stores the films leads to further questions concerning who has access to them and who benefits from said access, and ultimately about who can write history and thus benefit from that history. These questions do not take place in a purely conceptual sphere; they are shaped by the material conditions of archives and the structural inequalities between European and North American archives and their Latin American counterparts. The specific archival conditions and locations of Chilean exile cinema that I detail in this chapter must be understood within this broader context.

When one wishes to find the traces of Chilean exile cinema in international archives, the vastness of the corpus emerges as the first limitation. The most complete catalog to date was elaborated by Pick. Published in the US-based exile journal *Literatura Chilena: Creación y Crítica*, this filmography lists 176 titles and covers the first decade of exilic production (1973–1983).[38] Twenty years later, one of the first research projects undertaken by Cineteca Nacional de Chile soon after its founding in 2006 sought to find Chilean filmic materials in foreign archives and, whenever possible, to obtain copies and repatriate them.[39] However, exile did not constitute its exclusive focus. Since there was no proper national film archive in the country, the research team also looked for materials produced in Chile prior to the coup and after 1990, plus films and newsreels made by foreigners in Chile, regardless of their date. Published in 2008, the concluding report acknowledged great difficulties in accomplishing the research task, with regard to exilic production in particular. The main reasons cited were the dispersion in too many international archives, the diversity of film and video materials, and the lack of a detailed filmography.⁴⁰ The results were thus insufficient in the specific case of exile cinema, and the findings included errors and imprecision with regards to exile titles, the gauge of safeguarded materials, and the quantity of extant prints. Using these two catalogs as a starting point, the research I conducted in archives located in Canada, Chile, France, Germany, Mexico, Spain, Sweden, and the United States—plus the revision of the searchable online catalogs of various other international archives—allows me to estimate a total of over 230 Chilean exile films.⁴¹

Even if online archival databases have made the task easier, most of the difficulties listed in the 2008 report elaborated by Cineteca Nacional still persist. The second challenge is connected to the variety of modes of production and circulation of Chilean exile cinema. As developed in chapter 1, some works were made for television but were not broadcast (or records of their broadcasting have not been found); several films played at festivals but received limited theatrical distribution afterward; and while a good number of Chilean exile films had production and distribution companies behind them, for the most part these do not exist today (which is a problem when seeking rights and permissions to screen the films). It must be noted as well that a number of Chilean exile films now appear to be lost, or at least they are yet to be found.⁴² Since they were made in the margins of film industries and with little or no institutional support, these films were not deposited in any archive and were therefore not subject to their control and protection. This was not an uncommon fate for many Latin American films in the 1970s and 1980s.⁴³ The last challenge is the physical dispersal itself, what Ramírez-Soto calls the "scattered body" of Chilean exile cinema.⁴⁴

The vast majority of 16mm and 35mm viewing prints, copies, original negatives, sound elements, U-matic and VHS tapes, and other filmic materials corresponding to Chilean exile cinema are currently stored in national film archives and cinematheques, museums, production companies, television archives, university libraries, archives of political parties, and labor archives throughout the world—evidence of the geographic dispersion suffered by their makers and of the very different industrial conditions under which Chilean directors worked.⁴⁵

Institutions that escape the category of the national film archive, for example, constitute precious sources for locating marginal objects that generally fall under the label "orphan" film, understood here in the broad sense of "rare, unique or neglected films."⁴⁶ Orphan exile films can be found in television archives like France's INA—*J'ai rencontré l'arbre à pain* (Valeria Sarmiento, 1982)—or in university libraries like York University in Toronto—*Compañeros: From the Strings of My Guitar* (Leutén Rojas, 1981)—or at Duke University in Durham, North Carolina, which holds the Raúl Ruiz Film and Videotape Collection, 1960–1996. In accordance with the role played by Chile's history in the political imagination of the Left, several archives of political parties and social movements store Chilean exile films in their collections. Examples include the Fondazione Archivio Audiovisivo del Movimento Operaio e Democratico (AAMOD) in Rome and the International Institute of Social History (IISH) in Amsterdam. These collections evidence the extent to which politically oriented Chilean exile films traveled worldwide through alternative distribution networks run by cine-clubs and other associations like community groups and political organizations. A special archive in this regard is Arsenal Institut für Film und Videokunst (Arsenal) in Berlin, which holds 16mm political documentaries made during Allende's government, several U-matic tapes that give an account of the prolific video scene in Chile throughout the 1980s, and 16mm and 35mm prints of at least seventeen Chilean exile films.[47] National cinematheques and film archives in Europe and North America, however, store most Chilean exile titles, especially feature-length fiction films and documentaries. In addition to their role as archives, organizations that function as national institutes acted on several occasions as main commissioners, producers, or coproducers of Chilean exile films. This is why, for instance, the Swedish Film Institute (SFI; Svenska Filminstitutet) holds 35mm distribution prints plus original negatives and sound elements for *Prisioneros desaparecidos* (Sergio Castilla, 1979), a coproduction between SFI and Cuba's ICAIC. In plenty of other instances, Chilean exile films entered the collections of national cinematheques like Filmoteca Española in Madrid simply because they were programmed in their regular seasons or as part of special series.

The fact that a large percentage of exile films only remains safeguarded and available abroad, that is, still in exile, calls for a more active approach to the process of returning exile cinema to Chilean archives. These acts of return are mediated by instances of transnational cinema solidarity and are therefore part of the wider project of a politicized remaking of world cinema from the vantage point of archives.

RETURNING TO CHILEAN ARCHIVES

This section analyzes the presence of Chilean exile films in the collections of four institutions—Cineteca Nacional de Chile, Cineteca de la Universidad de Chile, MMDH, and Archivo Ruiz-Sarmiento. While these are not the sole film archives in the country, they have acted as key players in the return of Chilean exile cinema.[48] I focus here on the various mechanisms by which these four archives and museums have obtained 16mm and 35mm prints, videos, and digital files of this exilic corpus, as well as paper-based documentation relevant for the scholarly study of Chilean exile cinema.[49] A brief discussion of the nature of these institutions is necessary, since the approach each has taken toward safeguarding and presenting Chilean exile films can be explained to a large degree by their different histories, missions, archival practices, systems of governance, and sources of funding. As scholars have argued with regard to the Latin American archival scene, these features are not innocent, as they "determine the cultural policies of the institutions."[50] More broadly, all Chilean and Latin American archives share at least one common characteristic: "instability."[51] This instability is marked by a sense of ongoing financial precarity and a complicated relation with the state.[52] Often, nonetheless, heads of archives reclaim this lack of resources, as it allows them to question what the First World regards as universal practices of preservation. The "poverty" of Chilean and Latin American archives is the most evident face of a profound imbalance between "North" and "South" that is not merely infrastructural; rather, the imbalance suggests that different archival institutional cultures might be created to respond to specific political and historical contexts.[53]

Archivo Ruiz-Sarmiento is part of the Art Institute of the private university Pontificia Universidad Católica de Valparaíso. It was founded in 2013, two years after Raúl Ruiz's death, as an homage to Chile's most important director, who had taught cinema between 1969 and 1972 in the same university department that now houses the archive. Its mission concentrates on safeguarding the work of exile directors Raúl Ruiz and Valeria Sarmiento, who were married and developed intertwined careers as they collaborated on most of their films.[54] Although it possesses some DVD copies for on-site consultation, it cannot be considered a film or media archive properly speaking. Its focus is on manuscript and iconographic documentation donated by Sarmiento—seventy boxes containing unfinished projects, correspondence, press clippings and dossiers, photographs, screenplays, budgets, grant proposals, and so on. The physical location and overall mission of this institution resemble the rare manuscript section of a university library (its director, Bruno Cuneo, took the Beckett Collection at the University of Reading in the UK as a model).[55] But there is a difference: Archivo Ruiz-Sarmiento is run without overstressing the usual gateways and protocols that archives and libraries follow to guarantee the preservation of documents. This institution privileges access above anything else, and Cuneo has emphasized a vision of the archive as a sort of "bookstore" where scholars "come in and chat" and generate knowledge through collaborative conversations.[56] It is worth mentioning a foreign organization with regard to Archivo Ruiz-Sarmiento: the Institut Mémoires de l'édition contemporaines (IMEC; Institute for Contemporary Publishing Archives), located outside of Caen, France. IMEC has housed forty-two archival boxes of Ruiz documents since 2012.[57] Soon after the creation of Archivo Ruiz-Sarmiento, Cuneo and IMEC's director agreed on an instrument of cooperation, centered on the duplication of each institution's documentary holdings, which was in the end never implemented because it placed an impossible financial burden on the Chilean institution. This fact, together with the abysmal disparity in terms of physical settings—a very small university library room versus a monumental abbey—points to the already mentioned imbalance between archives in Europe and those in Latin America. Regardless, Archivo Ruiz-Sarmiento has developed a crucial role in bringing attention to a vast array of documentation that is allowing local scholars—for whom travel and access to European archives is more difficult—to produce new primary-source research on this couple of filmmakers.

The next university archive I discuss has a longer history. Founded in 1961, Cineteca de la Universidad de Chile became the first public film archive in the country. Its development has been closely entangled with the rise of political cinemas in Chile, especially through the university's Centro de Cine Experimental, which was one of the main hubs of Chilean film culture throughout the 1960s and early 1970s.[58] For this reason, the Cineteca was dismantled by the military soon after the coup. In 2004, after a series of internal negotiations, two university departments agreed on a protocol of collaboration and shared funding that eventually led to the reopening of the Cineteca in 2008 under the direction of legendary filmmaker Pedro Chaskel, who had also headed the institution in the early 1960s.[59] The immense temporal gap between Cineteca de la Universidad de Chile's official closure in 1976 and its reopening in 2008 evidences the financial and political difficulties in the rebuilding of the cultural apparatus of the state after the regaining of democracy in 1990.[60] Since its reopening, the Cineteca has managed to secure donations from exile filmmakers, especially those associated with Cine Experimental, like Chaskel. The state university cinematheque has also digitized a series of exile films that are part of its virtual platform and has organized, curated, and sponsored various film programs related to Chilean exile cinema.

MMDH differs from the other three, since it is a museum with a pedagogical and ethical mandate. As mentioned earlier, it was created in 2010 with the mission of giving visibility to human rights violations committed by the state of Chile between 1973 and 1990, so that "actions that affect the dignity of human beings are never again repeated."[61] Its Audiovisual Archive has existed since the creation of the museum and operates under the same mission. MMDH receives an annual direct subsidy from the state, regulated by the national budget act. This funding has come under scrutiny almost every year, which points to a still unachieved social and political consensus regarding the country's recent past and the museum's role in it. Frequent criticisms that center on the institution's strict temporal demarcation, its definition of who is a victim of human rights, and its fundamental conception as a project of "moral reparation" all suggest that it is the museum's very existence that is questioned.[62] The presence of Chilean exile titles in the collections of MMDH must therefore be understood within this broader landscape of memory as social narratives in dispute.[63]

Throughout the years, the museum has given space to the memories of exile in exhibits, websites, oral history projects, and video testimonials.[64] This interest peaked in 2014, when the entire programming was devoted to the topic of "exile and asylum," including two film series.[65] In terms of collection development, the legal mandate of the museum forbids the acquisition of documents, films, or artworks; it can only receive donations from individuals or institutions. For this reason, its audiovisual archive, composed of over twenty-five hundred titles, has been mostly created from filmmakers' personal donations. Rare exile titles like the video *Retorno* (*Re-turn*, David Benavente, 1983) and the film *Conversación en el exilio con Raúl Ampuero* (*Conversation in Exile with Raúl Ampuero*, Rafael Guzmán, 1986) are part of the museum's audiovisual collection.[66] Securing donations from international archives has also been a goal of MMDH, and this has been achieved thanks to institutional gestures of solidarity. Particularly relevant have been the efforts of television archives. European TV networks like the BBC, RAI, and ZDF, and national agencies such as France's INA, have provided plenty of interviews, newsreels, and television documentaries related to Chilean exiles.

MMDH's interest in films and other audiovisual works about exile exceeds Chilean exile cinema, if we understand the latter as those films made only by Chilean exile directors throughout the world, thus pointing to a much vaster media universe of the Chilean exile experience. In this museum, Chilean exile cinema is no different than other kinds of audiovisual pieces that are thematically connected to exile. The museum's lens for safeguarding and presenting exile cinema and media about exile is subjected to an ethical understanding of exile as a violation of human rights. Above all, it presents all exile films, whether fictional or not, exclusively as *documents* and evidentiary proof of the exile experience. This experiential approach has nonetheless a political advantage, as it favors the activation of social memories of exile that are geared toward the future. This is particularly evident in the museum's exhibition practice, which always involves some form of public discussion in which different generations of exiles and other victims of the dictatorship meet. Filmic returns are in this sense "embodied" in a collective re-elaboration of memory.

Cineteca Nacional de Chile was created in 2006 and immediately became the foremost film archive in the country. As Chile's National Film Archive, Cineteca Nacional has been a FIAF member since 2009. While theoretically a state institution, Cineteca Nacional depends on the Centro Cultural La Moneda, a private nonprofit foundation from which it receives a basic operational budget. Law 21.045, which created the Ministry of Cultures, the Arts, and Patrimony in 2017, includes Cineteca Nacional as one of the institutions that would become part of the National Service of Cultural Heritage and would therefore receive direct funding from the state. However, an official transfer has yet to occur.[67] Until that happens, Cineteca Nacional is forced to apply to various public funding instruments, competing with other local archives and museums to fund its preservation, exhibition, and educational programs.

Given this lack of resources, Chilean exile cinema has not been a priority for Cineteca Nacional, as the repatriation and restoration projects of early newsreels, the few extant silent features, and films produced by the national studio Chilefilms in the 1940s have been deemed more urgent. The corpus of Chilean exile cinema has entered the collections of Cineteca Nacional mostly thanks to donations from individual filmmakers, through a deposit agreement that regulates the safeguarding of the material and determines rights for public exhibition. At least fourteen Chilean exile filmmakers have donated DVDs, Betacam tapes, 16mm and 35mm prints, and original negatives and sound elements.[68] Another donation worth mentioning is the one from the Russian studio Mosfilm, which sent 35mm prints of all the features Sebastián Alarcón directed

FIGURE 19. Cineteca Nacional de Chile's vaults in 2020. Courtesy of Cineteca Nacional de Chile.

for the studio.[69] Due to its FIAF membership, Cineteca Nacional has also been able to sign contracts of collaboration, such as the 2009 agreement with ICAIC and Cinemateca de Cuba, which enabled the return of 35mm prints of Littín's *El recurso del método* (1978) and *Alsino y el Cóndor* (1982). In recent years, organizing film series has meant new agreements, such as the one signed with Cinémathèque française and INA in order to program *¡Celebremos a Ruiz!* in August 2016, a much smaller iteration of the seventy-film series devoted to Ruiz that Cinémathèque française had presented a few months earlier in Paris.[70]

The disparity in terms of the scope of these retrospectives, together with the fact that the Chilean version had to rely on digital screening files (since covering the costs of shipping prints was impossible for Cineteca Nacional), points once again to the structural inequalities that regulate the global archival field. All these instances of collaboration that led to the return of exile films to Chilean archives are predicated on a practice of transnational solidarity. But even if that is the case, these acts of solidarity do not necessarily imply a subversion of the power imbalances between archives in Latin America and those in Europe. Gestures of solidarity are regulated by contracts in which the holder of the original materials often retains advantages in terms of rights. For instance, the Cinémathèque française/INA and Cineteca Nacional agreement forbade the inclusion of the Ruiz films in the online platform of the Chilean archive. In fact, five of these titles were later uploaded to Cinémathèque française's streaming site Henri, shortly after its official launch in April 2020. Online platforms nonetheless offer possibilities that give new meaning to the idea of archival returns and that allow for at least a partial redress of the inequalities that shape the field of global audiovisual heritage.

ARCHIVAL ONLINE PLATFORMS

Most film archives currently have a website or digital platform highlighting titles from their collections. These films can be seen in their entirety and usually, though not always, without geographic restriction. The rise of online viewing sites run by archives is a consequence of a mixture of factors, including (1) the current emphasis on digitization projects, especially prevalent in archives with strong and steady public funding; (2) the need to open up to new publics and to understand digital access as a "core responsibility"; and (3) the industry turn toward streaming sites, especially accentuated after the COVID-19 pandemic in 2020.[71] Online viewability of what used to be rare archival materials, available only to a limited number of scholars, programmers, and archivists, constitutes a recent phenomenon that indicates a shift in archival practice compared to the situation ten years ago. In the case of Chilean exile films, the change is significant. To be able to watch a Chilean exile film, one had to get it directly from the filmmaker (who often did not have it) or had to travel. In 2013, for instance, I made a trip to archives in Montreal, Ottawa, and Toronto—the only way to watch the many films Chilean exiles had made in Canada. Years later, in 2017, *Il n'y a pas d'oubli* was digitized and uploaded to the website of the NFB, the organization that produced the film in 1975. This film is now searchable through its title or through keywords such as "Political Refugees," "Integration of Immigrants in Quebec," and "Lifestyle of Immigrants." Other digital platforms created by international archives that currently hold Chilean exile films include the SFI's Filmarkivet.se; the online website of Ciné Archives, the film archive of the French Communist Party; and the already mentioned Cinémathèque française's Henri.[72] These initiatives guarantee a greater access to Chilean exile cinema, both by a national audience in Chile and by diasporic communities abroad; however, not all difficulties have been resolved. The linguistic challenge remains, since all the international archives that I have mentioned do not offer Spanish subtitles or captions, and the curatorial gaze upon the films in question is dependent on the historical narrative proposed by the international archive (as seen by the keywords in the case of the NFB).

While there is an undeniable digitization divide between European/ North American and Latin American institutions—in terms of funding, infrastructure, scope, and number of projects—Chilean film archives have also been part of the boom of digital platforms.[73] Launched in 2011, the first was Cineteca de la Universidad de Chile's Cineteca Virtual, which uses a Creative Commons license and has a specific category dedicated to Chilean exile cinema that includes digital files of films such as Pedro Chaskel's *Eyes Like My Dad* (1979) and various other titles he directed for Cuba's ICAIC, as well as Rodrigo Gonçalves's works for the Instituto Nacional do Cinema in Maputo, Mozambique.[74] Privileging access over resolution, these online versions constitute an example of what Beatriz Tadeo Fuica and Julieta Keldjian have termed "palimpsestic digital copies," in which "different layers of material conversion" can be seen.[75] Like Cineteca Virtual, Cineteca Nacional de Chile's Cineteca Nacional Online followed in 2013, with the vision that there is no preservation if it does not go hand in hand with access.[76] The platform is part of the national film archive's broader digitization initiative, which has digitized 731 16mm and 35mm titles and more than 1,500 Super 8mm home movies using 2K and 4K scanners.[77] Films made in exile by directors like Orlando Lübbert, Miguel Littin, Leo Mendoza, and Angelina Vázquez, among many others, can be found here. During the COVID-19 pandemic, MMDH created Conectados con la memoria, a digital platform with a streaming component at which some Chilean exile films and other titles related to the experience of exile could be viewed. Currently, the platform does not exist as such and has been integrated into the museum's website.[78]

These three archives emphasize how digital platforms enable greater access to audiovisual heritage, especially in an excessively centralized country like Chile, where most cultural institutions function in the capital, Santiago. There are even more utopian visions, such as the one espoused by Luis Horta, head of Cineteca de la Universidad de Chile. Horta conceives the digital space as an opportunity to "re-signify the political use of the archive through education and outreach," with the understanding that the archive only exists as such once it is "appropriated by audiences."[79] What is missing in many of these comments is a more critical view of the neoliberal rhetoric of immediate "access" to "contents," terms that are loaded with ideology and that efface the material constitution of films as artifacts.[80] Furthermore, the films presented online by MMDH and Cineteca Virtual tend to be deprived of a curatorial and historical narrative. Curatorship is vital since its interpretative task is what "differentiates a collecting body from a mere repository of audiovisual content."[81] Cineteca Nacional Online favors interpretation through what it calls "online specials," thematic or historical groupings that are presented with a brief introductory text, like the one devoted to Chilean exile cinema that I coprogrammed in 2020.[82]

The fact that exile films hosted and safeguarded by a range of Chilean and international archives can be seen by anyone regardless of their geographical location points to the multiple material and digital migrations that allow films to be "made visible."[83] This availability gives new meaning to the idea of an archival homecoming. Archival online websites and streaming platforms enable what might be called *digital returns*: spaces of virtual collection and presentation that are not tied to a single location and that therefore might be more suited for an exile cinema with various national affiliations and cultural belongings.[84] The *digital* in digital return should also indicate a decentered archival practice in which more diverse actors and publics can participate.[85] The digitization, preservation, and exhibition of exile cinema implies in this sense a remaking of the global archival field.

DIGITAL FUTURES

In this chapter I have historicized the archival returns of exile cinema to Chilean archives and museums while also discussing the presence of this diasporic corpus in several international institutions. The cinematheques, museums, and film archives that have interested me here are the material spaces where technical and curatorial protocols are negotiated with particular institutional and administrative settings and with specific cultural expectations. Film archives are no mere repositories but fundamental "historical actors" that participate in wider social and cultural processes.[86] With this in mind I have demonstrated that the incomplete and unfinished phenomenon of archival return is due in great part to the difficulties that the exile corpus involves as well as to the specific nature and financial/political limitations of the Chilean institutions analyzed in this chapter. Archival returns have not responded to an official policy by the cultural apparatus of the state, nor have they been the result of a set of sustained curatorial guidelines of archives and museums addressing exile cinema as a whole. Rather, archival returns have taken place thanks to partial efforts related to projects involving particular films and the careers of a reduced number of filmmakers. Archivo Ruiz-Sarmiento favors an auteurist lens restricted to only two directorial figures. Cineteca de la Universidad de Chile espouses a vision of Chilean exile cinema that emphasizes the role of those individuals historically associated with the university cinematheque in the late 1960s and early 1970s. MMDH concentrates on the evidentiary power of Chilean exile films and on their ability to activate memories and transgenerational dialogue about the lasting effects of displacement. Cineteca Nacional de Chile favors the return of exile films whose themes or approach are more explicitly "Chilean," thus proving how challenging exile continues to be for an institutional film history still anchored within the geographical and ideological boundaries of the nation and its heritage.

The notion of archival returns stresses the various challenges that the transnationality, mobility, and inherent in-betweenness of exile cinemas pose for the institution of the archive. Archives and museums remain deeply rooted in the national as their main operative framework, even if they are not "national" archives properly speaking, and even if they engage in international exchanges via global networks like FIAF. As I previously suggested, the idea of an archival return does not do away with these challenges, as it will always presuppose, if not a homeland, at least a site of origin (even if this origin does not coincide with its actual place of production). In this regard, digital returns imply spaces of collection and presentation that do justice to the transnationality of exile and to its multiple cultural belongings. Furthermore, digital returns defy the hegemony of the national perspective in archival practice and call instead for a global approach to film and media preservation.

As Fossati has argued, audiovisual heritage that is not digitized "risks becoming invisible: not mapped, not researched, not curated, not seen."[87] But the task does not end with digitization and online visibility. Archival digital platforms and online spaces bring other opportunities. If geography and location are no longer factors in the online accessibility of exile films, this means that the national, linguistic, cultural, legal, and political borders that configure the field of audiovisual heritage in its current shape—in other words, the boundaries that tell us which objects belong *here* and which *there*—can and must be conceived anew. Active dialogue and support between scholars and archivists, as well as transnational collaboration projects between archives in the "North" and those in the "South," are the only ways of achieving this project.

The kind of collaboration I am speaking about here refers to global exchange projects that are founded on principles of transnational cinema solidarity—that is, projects in which those who are in a position of power are keenly aware of the imbalances that shape world cinema and

FIGURE 20. Still from *Färg mot fascismen!* (*Color against Fascism!*, Leonardo Céspedes, Peter Lund, and Kaj Mattson, 1978).

global archives and therefore *do* something to alleviate these inequities. I can offer as an example a collaborative project I led for Cineteca Nacional de Chile. Based on the archival research informing this book, I created for them a short filmography of exile prints that are currently only safeguarded in international archives and whose return should be deemed a priority. We have initiated a process of exchange with foreign archives that favors a model of digital returns. The first project involved a collaboration with SFI, which resulted in the digital return of seven films made by Chileans in Sweden. These include four works by Sergio Castilla—*La historia* (1973), *Pinochet: Fascista, asesino, traidor, agente del imperialismo* (1974), *Quisiera, quisiera tener un hijo* (1974), and *Prisioneros desaparecidos* (1979)—plus *Sången lever generaler!* (Claudio Sapiaín, 1975), *Åkersberga—Chillan tur och retur/ Åkerberga—Chillán ida y retorno* (Luis Vera, 1986), and *Färg mot fascismen!* (*Color against Fascism!*, Leonardo Céspedes, Peter Lund, and Kaj Mattson, 1978).

I want to highlight three aspects of this project. First, when Cineteca Nacional and I reached out to SFI through its senior curator Jon Wengström, the response was immediately positive, recognizing the importance of bringing these exile films to Chile and to a contemporary national audience. Wengström framed this response within the long history of solidarity ties between Sweden and Chile, acknowledging the presence and contributions of the large Chilean exile community that arrived there after the coup. Second, the terms of the exchange were not set by the Swedish archive; they were discussed in a series of conversations over the course of two years. We mused over several possibilities for moving forward, which were shaped by the material conditions of the prints and their status (original negatives plus other 16mm or 35mm prints considered master elements), the slowing of digitization workflows in Sweden due to the pandemic, and the financial limitations of the archive in Chile. In the end, we agreed on the following strategy: SFI would digitize at no cost all sound and image at their facilities and provide Cineteca Nacional with the raw 2K DPX sequences for the image and raw wav files for sound. Cineteca Nacional would sync and master the files and create digital viewing copies with new translations and subtitles. Both archives would have access to and safeguard the finished version of these seven films. Third, this collaboration constitutes a model of digital returns in which both the labor and results of the process of 2K scanning, syncing, mastering, translating, and subtitling are shared by the provider of the original materials and by Cineteca Nacional, its main beneficiary. As a model of digital returns, it can easily be replicated for other diasporic, exilic, and transnational contexts of filmmaking, and it can inspire related archival projects based on equitable forms of collaboration. In fact, the exchange with the SFI led to a second project currently underway with the EYE Filmmuseum in the Netherlands, where some of these newly digitized files were screened in 2022 and 2023. This project involved the digitization of Leonardo de la Barra's unseen raw footage of the day coup, discussed in this book's preface.

The practice of digital returns reinforces in a way the category of the national, in that it places a significant symbolic weight on the task of "activating" the archive *from* the cultural institutions of the homeland.[88] But this role should not be taken to mean that the national space functions as a new center. This book has made clear that the returns of Chilean exile cinema are still ongoing, and therefore that the history I have narrated here remains unfinished. The Chilean premiere of the seven films digitized thanks to the agreement with the SFI took place in September 2023, during the commemorations of the fiftieth anniversary of the coup. It remains to be seen what kind of effect this "embodied" form of digital return will have on national audiences. But if the screenings at the EYE Filmmuseum are any indication, they are sure to *move* the audiences, filling them with a renewed sense of emotional and political possibilities. Whenever I have programmed these films in different venues, I have seen the power of what Jane Gaines called "political mimesis" at work: bodies that move following the tunes of a revolutionary song, and minds and consciousnesses that are moved toward action.[89]

If I conclude in Amsterdam and not in Santiago, it is to reiterate that the returns I am talking about are more than nationally bounded. The new visibility of these exile films implies an actualization of their political potential; this is what historical restitution and reparation means. As *Transnational Cinema Solidarity* has also emphasized, Chilean exile cinema and its archival afterlives give shape to a transnational history that remakes the borders of world cinema. Archival online platforms and digital returns configure in this sense new transnational routes of circulation and exhibition that can be guided by principles of solidarity and that do not always end with a physical return to the homeland.

Epilogue

Exile, Solidarity, and World Cinema Otherwise

SOLIDARITY AND A POLITICIZED REMAKING OF WORLD CINEMA

The publication of issue n°811 of *Cahiers du cinéma* (July/August 2024) pops up on my social media as I write this epilogue. Titled "(Re)penser l'histoire du cinéma" (Rethinking Film History), the special issue examines some of the problems that scholars, critics, programmers, cinephiles, and archivists have been facing for quite a while: How do we move from a single—and usually Euro/American—film history to a plurality of film histories? How do we account for the feminist challenges to the masculinist canon and the patriarchal dimensions of the film archive? How do we define the "powers and functions" of film history to destabilize our present?[1] In a short piece written to address these questions, Nicole Brenez claims: "To completely reconfigure cinema histories through marginalized, minoritized, or ignored works does not consist in adding complementary chapters to an already existing film history as if it were the same one; it's about reconstructing the logic, the operative concepts, the instruments, and the methods. Not an improved history or a counter history, but a true history founded on the aesthetic relevance of the works, inseparable from their political pertinence and their critical potency."[2]

This book has made a similar argument in writing a film history based on solidarity and the travels of forced political displacement. Borrowing from scholars working on the histories of global solidarities, I have pushed for a politicized remaking of world cinema. By *world cinema* I mean here something other than a continental category (an area of the world that we can pin down) and something other than the nomadic dream of a world without roots or the cosmopolitan dream of taking equal part in a world that belongs to us all. I mean, quite simply, a cinema "of the world" that redraws the geopolitical boundaries that give meaning to the categories of national, exile, and transnational cinema. The transnational and liminal dimensions of exile cinema—moving across borders of different kinds yet remaining trapped in an ambiguous zone between homeland and host—reconfigure by force the clear-cut demarcations of world cinema histories. I have addressed Chilean exile cinema not only as an experience in the margins or in the interstices of other cinemas elsewhere (Canadian, German, French, Mexican, Mozambican, etc.) but as an experience that rearranges the geopolitical, aesthetic, and disciplinary parameters behind such partitions.

Consider one more time the work of Finland-based exile director Angelina Vázquez in a film like *Apuntes nicaragüenses* (*Sketches on Nicaragua*, 1982), discussed in chapter 2. This documentary enacts transnational cinema solidarity in its multiple forms: as the genre of a film dealing thematically with internationalism and literacy campaigns; as a production history that results from the building of personal and professional networks with fellow exile filmmakers and national film institutions in Cuba, Finland, and Nicaragua; and as the political and pedagogical goal of traveling to understand and learn from a political project "other than one's own," to quote from another of Brenez's articles.[3] I mention this example to highlight how the movements of cinema solidarity trace the politicized world cinema map this book is calling for. For what stable categories would make sense for a film that functions as the site for a series of cinematic and political exchanges between Santiago, Helsinki, Havana, and Managua? Where do we place this film in the known borders of world cinema?

This is the worldmaking power of transnational cinema solidarity: to propose a new cine-geography, a global articulation of film histories based on political friendships and struggles of cinematic resistance. A politicized remaking therefore implies a radical reimagining of the world through cinema histories of solidarity, exile, and migration.

As Brenez also pointed out, the task of reconstructing cinema histories is necessarily a collective endeavor.[4] This book can only do its small part. But we live in a world where newer and more complex forms of displacement coexist with state violence, genocidal wars, apartheid, economic dispossession, social expulsion, and climate migration. Global practices of solidarity, with their political and affective potency, are perhaps one of the only actions at our disposal to counteract these dominant modes of oppression. If we acknowledge these two facts, then as film scholars we must dive into old and contemporary cinemas of migration and solidarity cinemas, and we must reconsider what transnational networks of cinema solidarity might mean and do for understanding our present and its images.[5]

EXILE AND TRANS/NATIONAL FILM HISTORY

I have already highlighted the transnational dimensions of Chilean exile film and video as well as stressed the point that following networks of solidarity and the cinematic routes of forced displacement necessarily produces a reconfiguration of our world cinema histories. But it would be ludicrous to claim that this history is not a national one, too. When the transnational "turn" emerged in the discipline of film and media studies, scholars were quick to point out that transnationalism did not negate or supersede the sphere of the national; rather, it functioned as a method or lens for tracking the movements of cinema histories and industries across a diversity of borders. It might seem obvious, but I want to say it explicitly: Chilean exile cinema is a "Chilean" cinema, explained by historical conditions tied to the ideology, institutions, and symbolic force of the nation. And it is also something different. We may call it "transnational" cinema, or "world" cinema, or we may conclude that the multiple, divergent, and sometimes contradictory pathways of exile and solidarity render these notions less "operative," to go back to Brenez's call for another film history: world cinema *otherwise*.

In the introduction I mentioned that Chilean exile cinema sometimes attaches itself to the nation through a sort of umbilical cord and sometimes only wishes to distance itself from Chile. Part of my purpose has therefore been tied to a double movement: to return this cinema to Chilean/Latin American film history and to simultaneously return it to this alternative world cinema history. For the former, I have privileged issues such as the multiple dialogues between those filmmakers who had remained in the country during the dictatorship and those who fled it; the homecoming journeys of exile directors; and the archival returns of film prints and videotapes that have been entering the collections of national archives/museums and finding new audiences in the process. As for returning this diasporic cultural practice to a world cinema history, I have privileged historicizing transnational modes of production and circulation, networks and practices of cinema solidarity, the travels of political and aesthetic debates via film festivals, and the challenging of the ideological and infrastructural parameters that shape the global archiving field.

This is an unfinished trans/national history: a living one, still in the making. As such, it remains to be seen how Chilean exile cinema, now that it is more widely accessible than ever before, will begin to impact the field of Chilean film culture and its history. Will local filmmakers, especially in documentary, incorporate the archival images of exile into their projects? Will they find a renewed sense of inspiration in the feminist practices of their predecessors? Will general audiences turn to these films to challenge their political and historical preconceptions?

THE LANGUAGE OF RESISTANCE

It also remains to be seen whether this transnational exilic practice finds echo in contemporary forms of cinema solidarity and in newer fields of artistic and cultural struggle against oppression taking place in other parts of the world. This book has devoted many of its pages to better historicizing the political and aesthetic language of resistance. Solidarity and resistance functioned as keywords in the lexicon of exile filmmakers, attached as these concepts were to the social practice of joining forces to defeat the dictatorship at home. Having focused on the myriad meanings adopted by resistance and on the different approaches to the politics of exile cinema, I hope to have contributed to long-standing debates about the features of rebellious, militant, radical, revolutionary, didactic, agitational, counter-informational, and Third Cinemas. And I hope that the stories of these filmmakers—who in many cases suffered abhorrent forms of state violence—their exile travels, and their commitment to political struggle as expressed in their films will inspire other scholars to rethink what a practice of cinematic resistance might imply today. In other words, I see the transnational cinema solidarity of Chilean exile film and video as a vital step in the long history of political cinemas and as one that can trigger new understandings of global solidarity cinemas, past and present.

FORGOTTEN FILMS, PROGRAMMING, AND THE ARCHIVES OF EXILE

Several of the films I have talked about in this book remain relatively unknown to audiences in Chile and abroad—even to specialized publics.

In various chapters, but especially in the last one on archival returns, I discuss some of the reasons behind such unknowability and silencing. Except for names like Patricio Guzmán, Miguel Littin, and Raúl Ruiz, and apart from one or two other feature-length fiction films, this is an orphan corpus in that several works are of a more unclassifiable nature: short films; pieces made for television; videos moving freely between the experimental, documentary, and fictional modes. It is also an orphaned corpus—not always in the sense of lacking institutional belonging and safeguarding—but in the more crucial aspect of having been deprived of a history and of the appropriate context to make sense of it. Due to its pathways of production and circulation, and given its exilic and transnational nature, it has also been archivally neglected: the fragile and poor conditions of its filmic and video records constitute material evidence of a forgotten history of exile and cinema solidarity.

But the "unseen" nature of Chilean exile cinema has been gradually changing in recent years. This renewed visibility has been largely the result of—sometimes concerted, sometimes unconcerted but parallel— efforts between scholars, archivists, and programmers. As mentioned in chapter 7, the archival returns of exile cinema bear little meaning if they are not accompanied by possibilities of seeing, debating, and engaging with this work. Acts of return, at least in the way that I have conceived them here, as shaped by the forces of transnational solidarity, can also contribute to reimagining the archival field. Much as film history is being rethought today alongside the politicized lines described by Brenez's quote, the field of global archiving is also being radically reconceptualized to not only make room for and preserve neglected materials, but also reconfigure what practices of archival repatriation and reparation *do*. In this regard, to facilitate the archival returns of exile is to *restore* these films and videos, and this history of transnational cinema solidarity, to their full political potentiality.[6]

Notes

NOTE ON SOURCES

Archival Sources

This book quotes from several archival unpublished sources. These are listed here.
  Angelina Vázquez (Personal Archive)
    Letter from Angelina Vázquez to APTA, Madrid, July 1985
    Letter from Angelina Vázquez to Pablo Perelman, Helsinki, 1983
    Letter from Pablo Perelman to Angelina Vázquez, Santiago, November 1979
  Archivo MMDH, Museo de la Memoria y los Derechos Humanos (Santiago, Chile)
    Fondo Eduardo Carrasco, CL MMDH 00000164
    Fondo Hernán Castro, CL MMDH 00000428
    Fondo Sergio Insunza Barrios, CL MMDH 00000632
  Archivo Ruiz-Sarmiento, Instituto de Arte, Pontificia Universidad Católica de Valparaíso (Viña del mar, Chile)
    RR-27-1-4-3, "Conversación con Libération"
    RR-27-1-4-4, "Respuesta a críticas Diálogo de exiliados"
    RR-27-1-5-1, "La utopía/El cuerpo repartido"
    RR-43-1-1-6, "Aquí van las respuestas que les quedé debiendo"
    VS-1-1-1-3, "GREC, Séance Promotionnelle"

Berkeley Art Museum and Pacific Film Archive (BAMPFA, Berkeley, CA, United States)
 "Acta General de Chile," Q&A recording, September 2, 1987, BAMPFA Film Library & Study Center Audio Collection
 "*The Battle of Chile*," Tricontinental Film Center, press kit, 1977
 "Snakes and Ladders," Q&A recording, April 29, 1990, BAMPFA Film Library & Study Center Audio Collection

Bundesarchiv (Berlin, Germany)
 BArch DR 140-299/DR 140-365, Retrospektive "Film im Freiheitskampf der Völker: Chile"
  "Letter from Manfred Lichtenstein to Volodia Teitelboim."
  "Letter from Gastón Ancelovici to Manfred Lichtenstein."
  "Letter from Manfred Lichtenstein to Valeria Sarmiento."

Cinémathèque québécoise (Montreal, Canada)
 Dossier *Chère Amérique*, 1989
 Dossier *Les Borges*, 1984.0082.27.AR
  "Communiqué—Les Borges."
  "Memorandum *Les Borges*—distribution."
  "Partir ou rester."
 Gastón Ancelovici, "Document de préproduction: *Chili in transition*," 2000.0365.72.AR
 "Les Lettres: Scénario," 1979, 1984.0082.26.SC
 Parler d'Amérique: Une série de neuf moyens métrages documentaires sur les mythes américains, 1989
 Projet *Il n'y a pas d'oubli*, Jorge Fajardo, Marilú Mallet, Rodrigo González, 1974, 1990.0181.13.SC
 Scénario du film *Lentement*, 1984.0019.05.SC

Cinémathèque française (France)
 FEST LOC 76 (Catalogues Locarno Film Festival)
  Festival internazionale del film, Locarno, 29, 1976
 FEST RES 115 (Catalogues Cannes Film Festival)
  Festival international du film, Cannes, 31, 1978
  Quinzaine des réalisateurs, Cannes, 6, 1974; 7, 1975; 8, 1979; 15, 1983
  Semaine internationale de la critique française, Cannes, 13, 1974

Cineteca Universidad de Chile—Fondo Zuzana Pick
 "Apuntes Nicaragüenses," ca. 1981
 "Carta abierta a la Cineteca de la Universidad de Chile," 2016
 Chaskel, "Définition," 1974
 "Entrevista con Angelina Vázquez," 1981
 Jean-Pierre Tadros, "L'immigration vécue par une famille portugaise," 1978
 Letter from Angelina Vázquez to Zuzana Pick, ca. 1983
 Normande Juneau, "La famille Borges n'attend plus rien: Elle vit," 1978
 Pierre Demers, "Le cinéma étranger québécois," 1980

Deutsche Kinemathek (Berlin, Germany)

26 Internationale Leipziger Dokumentar- und Kurzfilmwoche für Kino und Fernsehen
    Festival Journal, 1983
    "Preisträger 1983"
    "Protokoll," 1983
Festival Internacional de Cine de San Sebastián (Donostia-San Sebastian, Spain)
    Fondo Fotográfico, Fl0047, "Distintos cineastas durante la rueda de prensa por la Retrospectiva Chile," Artxiboa.
    Diario del XXXV Festival Internacional de Cine de San Sebastián 2, 4, 5, 7, 8, 9 (September 18, 20, 21, 23, 24, 25, 1987), Artxiboa.
Filmoteca Española—Centro de Documentación (Madrid, Spain)
    Dossier *Sandino*, 1990
The Getty Research Institute (Los Angeles, CA, United States)
    "Program for Art on Film (New York, N.Y.), Records 1951–1999, undated, bulk 1984–1997," IA.20008, 20004
Institut national de l'audiovisuel (INA) (Paris, France)
    Fonds Production et co-production, INA 14225-0001, dossier no. 3, "Botaniques"
    Fonds Production et co-production, INA 14225-0025, dossier no. 69, "Rues des Archives."
RGALI (Russian State Archive of Literature and Art) (Moscow, Russia)
    ["Week of Anti-Fascist Cinema, Volgograd, 1975"], RGALI, f. 3064, op. 1, d. 150

Published Sources

For published sources, full bibliographical information is included when they are cited for the first time in the notes. Subsequent mentions throughout the notes follow an abridged form of citation (author's last name, short title, and page number).

PREFACE, OR LETTERS FROM THE ARCHIVE

1. International Film Festival Rotterdam, "Focus: Chile in the Heart" (2024 program), accessed July 22, 2024, https://iffr.com/en/film?category=Focus%3A+Chile+in+the+Heart&edition=iffr-2024.

2. After studying in California, de la Barra worked as assistant to director Costa-Gavras on *State of Siege* (1972), shot in Chile, an experience that marked his filmmaking style. See Iván Pinto and Luis Horta, "Vías no realizadas en el cine político chileno: Parodia, extrañamiento y reflexividad," *Aisthesis*, no. 47 (2010): 135.

3. Luis Horta, "Películas olvidadas: *Queridos compañeros de Pablo de la Barra*," *Revista Séptimo Arte*, October 1, 2010, accessed July 22, 2024, https://r7afiles.blogspot.com/2010/10/peliculas-olvidadas-queridos-companeros_01.html.

4. Patricio Guzmán, in a piece originally written in November 1973 and revised in 2010, recounts that the day of the coup he was trying to go to Santiago's downtown, and amid the chaos, he ran into Pablo de la Barra, who told him, "It's okay if you can't shoot today. My brother is already out there filming." See Patricio Guzmán, *La batalla de Chile: Historia de una película* (Santiago: Catalonia, 2020), 107.

5. See María Teresa Cárdenas Maturana, "Leonardo de la Barra: El guión de la memoria," *Revista Sábado*, October 28, 2023, 6; and MMDH (@Museo-MemoriaCL), "Leonardo fue detenido y pasó varias semanas en el recinto de Londres 38 y en Villa Grimaldi. Al recuperar la libertad, salió al exilio," Twitter, July 7, 2024, 12:20 p.m., https://x.com/MuseoMemoriaCL/status/1809985814543090056; and Leonardo de la Barra, *En los repliegues del silencio* (Santiago: Ocho Libros, 2023), dust jacket.

6. Horta, "Películas olvidadas."

7. See Pinto and Horta, "Vías no realizadas en el cine político chileno," 136; and Heiner Ross's testimony, quoted in Mónica Villarroel and Isabel Mardones, *Señales contra el olvido: Cine chileno recobrado* (Santiago: LOM, 2011), 83.

8. Pablo de la Barra had contacts with the French cultural attaché from having worked on Costa Gavras's *State of Siege*. See Omar Mesones, "Pablo de la Barra: Episodio VIII," November 3, 2022, in *Voces del Cine Venezolano*, podcast, accessed July 22, 2024, https://shows.acast.com/alfredo-anzola-voces-del-cine-venezolano-episodio-1/episodes/pablo-de-la-barra-episodio-viii.

9. Yenny Cáceres, *Los años chilenos de Raúl Ruiz* (Santiago: Catalonia/UDP, 2019), 289, 291.

10. *Informe de la Comisión Nacional de Verdad y Reparación*, vol. 1, tomo 2, 794; Carlos Maldonado, "Álvaro de la Barra: La búsqueda que no termina," *The Clinic*, July 5, 2018, accessed July 22, 2024, www.theclinic.cl/2018/07/05/alvaro-la-barra-la-busqueda-no-termina/; and Marisol Águila, "Álvaro de la Barra: Chile, sin que sea un personaje en la película, también es parte de la búsqueda y quizás es lo que más sea contradictorio conmigo," *El Agente: Crítica de Cine*, December 6, 2017, accessed July 22, 2024, http://elagentecine.cl/entrevista/alvaro-de-la-barra-chile-sin-que-sea-un-personaje-en-la-pelicula-tambien-es-parte-de-la-busqueda-y-quizas-es-lo-que-mas-sea-contradictorio-conmigo/.

11. Horta, "Películas olvidadas."

12. Pinto and Horta, "Vías no realizadas en el cine político chileno," 137.

13. Hamid Naficy distinguishes between *film-letter* and *letter-film*. In the former, writing, receiving, and reading letters are actions undertaken by characters. Epistolarity, here, is inscribed into the diegesis. The letter-film, in turn, is structured by epistolarity: the epistle constitutes its narrative form. See Hamid Naficy, *An Accented Cinema: Exilic and Diasporic Filmmaking* (Princeton, NJ: University of Princeton Press, 2011), 101.

14. A similar point is made in Álvaro García, "Memorias, rescates (3): Queridos compañeros (Pablo de la Barra, 1973–78)," *El Agente: Crítica de Cine*, October 4, 2013, accessed July 22, 2024, http://elagentecine.cl/criticas-2/memorias-rescates-3-queridos-companeros-pablo-de-la-barra-1973-78/. For a more recent analysis in the context of the fiftieth anniversary of the coup, see Iván Pinto, "El

montaje de la memoria," *Palabra Pública*, August 24, 2023, accessed July 22, 2024, https://palabrapublica.uchile.cl/el-montaje-de-la-memoria/.

15. García, "Memorias, rescates (3)."

16. Marianne Hirsch, "The Generation of Postmemory," *Poetics Today* 29, no. 1 (2008): 103–28.

17. For a thorough analysis of Chilean postdictatorship documentary's turn to "a cinema of affect" that seeks to reveal the materiality of the past, see Elizabeth Ramírez-Soto, *(Un)veiling Bodies: A Trajectory of Chilean Post-Dictatorship Documentary* (Cambridge, UK: Legenda, 2019), 1–32.

18. Águila, "Álvaro de la Barra."

19. I use *revelation* in the sense used by Ramírez-Soto in her book *(Un)veiling Bodies*: as unearthing and bringing to light previously neglected filmic materials, words that are tied to a forensic dimension with strong resonances in countries with histories of military dictatorships and disappeared people. See Ramírez-Soto, *(Un)veiling Bodies*, 62–80.

20. A few other filmic records of the day of the coup exist, including one by Juan Ángel Torti that began to circulate more widely after the fortieth anniversary of the coup. See Claudia Bossay, "Las vidas del registro: El bombardeo al Palacio de La Moneda y sus usos contemporáneos" (n.d., unpublished paper); and Elizabeth Ramírez-Soto, "La cámara que tiembla: Sobre el bombardeo al Palacio de la Moneda y algunas imágenes que nos mueven," *Savoirs en prisme*, no. 9 (2018): 147–58.

21. Steve Stern, "Introduction to the Trilogy: The Memory Box of Pinochet's Chile," in *Remembering Pinochet's Chile: On the Eve of London 1998* (Durham, NC: Duke University Press, 2004), xx.

22. I use Steve Stern's metaphor of the "giant, collectively built memory box," which "sits in the living room, not in the attic" and which is a "holder of truths" about traumatic points in Chileans' personal and collective lives. Stern, "Introduction to the Trilogy," xxviii.

23. De la Barra, *En los repliegues del silencio*, 25.

24. De la Barra, *En los repliegues del silencio*, 49.

25. MMDH (@MuseoMemoriaCL), "Para lograr sacar la filmación del país, su hermano se la entregó a un ciudadano holandés y logró recuperar el registro solo una vez que estuvo en el exilio," Twitter, July 7, 2024, 12:20 p.m., https://x.com/MuseoMemoriaCL/status/1809985818561323122.

INTRODUCTION

1. The "Rest" refers to Stuart Hall's famous critique of the discursive opposition between the "West" and all those areas of the world that common language and dominant modes of representation situate as non-Western. Stuart Hall, "The West and the Rest," in *Essential Essays*, vol. 2, *Identity and Diaspora*, ed. and with an introduction by David Morley (1992; Durham, NC: Duke University Press, 2019), 141–46.

2. Ella Shohat and Robert Stam, *Unthinking Eurocentrism. Multiculturalism and the Media* (New York: Routledge, 1994), 13–54; Masha Salazkina, "World Cinema as Method," *Canadian Journal of Film Studies* 29, no. 2 (2020): 11; and

Nataša Ďurovičová, preface to *World Cinemas, Transnational Perspectives*, ed. Nataša Ďurovičová and Kathleen Newman (New York: Routledge, 2010), x.

3. For the raiding of Chile Films, see Pamela Biénzobas and Macarena Hernández, "El día en que las cámaras dejaron de rodar: Testimonios del golpe militar en el cine chileno" (thesis, Universidad de Chile, 1999), 42–96; and Jacqueline Mouesca, *Plano secuencia de la memoria de Chile: Veinticinco años de cine chileno (1960–1985)* (Madrid: Ediciones del Litoral, 1988), 138–39.

4. This summary relies on a series of details about the perils of making and saving *The Battle of Chile*, as told in Villarroel and Mardones, *Señales contra el olvido*, 80–81; Patricio Guzmán and Pedro Sempere, *Chile: El cine contra el fascismo* (Valencia: Fernando Torres, 1977), 91–96; Guzmán, *La batalla de Chile*, 112–31; and José Carlos Avellar, "Bonus: Interview with Patricio Guzmán," in *Five Films by Patricio Guzmán* (Icarus Films, 2015), DVD box set, disc 4.

5. One could also add here the previous solidarity efforts of Chris Marker, who sent plenty of film stock to Guzmán, circumventing the economic blockade imposed on Allende's government. See Guzmán, *La batalla de Chile*, 16–22.

6. Guzmán has remarked that, seeing what looked like a disorganized pile of reels that seemed to have been dumped in the room, his first reaction was not to thank the solidarity efforts but to think "What a mess!" and start doing an inventory with Elton right away. Not a single reel of film had been lost. See Avellar, "Bonus: Interview with Patricio Guzmán." I thank manuscript reviewer 2 for pointing me toward this anecdote.

7. Letter from Tom Luddy, then director of Berkeley's PFA, to Carlos Broullon, head of the distributor Tricontinental Film Center, August 10, 1977, included in "*The Battle of Chile*," press kit, 5, BAMPFA—Cine-Files, accessed July 22, 2024, https://cinefiles.bampfa.berkeley.edu/catalog/52830.

8. *Les murs de Santiago* (*The Walls of Santiago*, Carmen Castillo, Pierre Devert, Fabienne Servan-Schreiber, France, 1983) includes a scene in which the filmmakers project a videotape of *The Battle of Chile* to different audiences in Chile. I thank Elizabeth Ramírez-Soto for pointing me to this film.

9. FIDOCS, *Catálogo Primer Festival Internacional de Cine Documental: Primera Retrospectiva de Cine Documental Chileno* (Santiago: FIDOCS, 1997). See also Ramírez-Soto, *(Un)Veiling Bodies*, 44–46; and María Paz Peirano, "FIDOCS y la formación de un campo de cine documental en Chile en la década de 1990," *Cine Documental* 18 (2018): 71, 76–77, 79–80.

10. See especially Guzmán and Sempere, *Chile*; and Guzmán, *La batalla de Chile*.

11. For film studies, see Laura Marks, *The Skin of the Film: Intercultural Cinema, Embodiment, and the Senses* (Durham, NC: Duke University Press, 2000); Ella Shohat and Robert Stam, *Multiculturalism, Postcoloniality, and Transnational Media* (New Brunswick, NJ: Rutgers University Press, 2003); Naficy, *Accented Cinema*; David E. James, *The Most Typical Avant-Garde: History and Geography of Minor Cinemas in Los Angeles* (Berkeley: University of California Press, 2005); and Elizabeth Ramírez-Soto and Catalina Donoso Pinto, eds., *Nomadías: El cine de Marilú Mallet, Valeria Sarmiento y Agelina Vázquez* (Santiago: Metales Pesados, 2016). For critical theory, see Stuart Hall, "Thinking the Diaspora: Home-Thoughts from Abroad," in *Essential Essays*, 2: 206–26;

Édouard Glissant, *Poetics of Relation*, trans. Betsy Wing (Ann Arbor: University of Michigan Press, 1997); and Rossi Braidotti, *Nomadic Subjects: Embodiment and Sexual Difference in Contemporary Feminist Theory* (New York: Columbia University Press, 2011). For useful distinctions between some of these terms, see John Durham Peters, "Exile, Nomadism, and Diaspora: The Stakes of Mobility in the Western Canon," in *Home, Exile, Homeland. Film, Media, and the Politics of Place*, ed. Hamid Naficy (New York: Routledge, 1999), 17–41; and T. J. Demos, *The Migrant Image: The Art and Politics of Documentary during Global Crisis* (Durham, NC: Duke University Press, 2013), 1-20.

12. Khachig Tölölyan, "The Nation State and Its Others: In Lieu of a Preface," *Diaspora: A Journal of Transnational Studies* 1, no. 1 (1991): 4–5. Karen Elizabeth Bishop, on the other hand, argues for exile as an encompassing category including figures like the economic migrant, the asylum-seeker, the diasporic subject, the stateless, the expatriate, etc. Karen Elizabeth Bishop, "Introduction: The Cartographical Necessity of Exile," in *Cartographies of Exile. A New Spatial Literacy*, ed. Karen Elizabeth Bishop (New York: Routledge, 2016), 2.

13. Hamid Naficy, "Between Rocks and Hard Places: The Interstitial Mode of Production in Exilic Cinema," in *Home, Exile, Homeland. Film, Media, and the Politics of Place*, ed. Hamid Naficy (New York: Routledge, 1999), 132.

14. Naficy, *Accented Cinema*, 3–39.

15. Naficy, *Accented Cinema*, 22–26.

16. Seung-hoon Jeong sees this understanding of world cinema as a "rainbow community of multicultural differences," reinforcing a "Manichean dichotomy between 'bad' normative Hollywood and 'good' alternative rest." Seung-hoon Jeong, *Biopolitical Ethics in Global Cinema* (Oxford: Oxford University Press, 2023), 15.

17. Rob Stone et al., "Introduction: The Longitude and Latitude of World Cinema," in *The Routledge Companion to World Cinema*, ed. Rob Stone, Paul Cooke, Stephanie Dennison, and Alex Marlow-Mann (London: Routledge, 2018), 1. See also Peter Limbrick, *Arab Modernism as World Cinema: The Films of Moumen Smihi* (Oakland: University of California Press, 2020), 3.

18. Aihwa Ong, *Flexible Citizenship: The Cultural Logics of Transnationality* (Durham, NC: Duke University Press, 1999), 4.

19. Critiques of this descriptive use of the transnational have been made by various scholars. See Mette Hjort, "On the Plurality of Cinematic Transnationalism," in *World Cinemas, Transnational Perspectives*, ed. Nataša Ďurovičová and Kathleen Newman (New York: Routledge, 2010), 12–13; Will Higbee and Song Hwee Lim, "Concepts of Transnational Cinema: Towards a Critical Transnationalism in Film Studies," *Transnational Cinemas* 1, no. 1 (2010): 10; and JungBong Choi, "Of Transnational-Korean Cinematrix," *Transnational Cinemas* 3, no. 1 (2012): 8.

20. See Deborah Shaw, "Transnational Cinema: Mapping a Field of Study," in *The Routledge Companion to World Cinema*, ed. Rob Stone, Paul Cooke, Stephanie Dennison, and Alex Marlow-Mann (London: Routledge, 2018), 290–92; Higbee and Lim, "Concepts of Transnational Cinema," 9–10; and David Martin-Jones, "Transnational Turn or Turn to World Cinema?," *Transnational Screens* 10, no. 1 (2019): 13–22.

21. Robert Stam, *World Literature, Transnational Cinema, and Global Media: Towards a Transartistic Commons* (New York: Routledge, 2019), 131.

22. Salazkina, "World Cinema as Method," 15.

23. Among others, see Seth Fein, "Transnationalization and Cultural Collaboration: Mexican Film Propaganda during World War II," *Studies in Popular Latin American Culture* 17 (1998): 105–28; Adrián Pérez-Melgosa, *Cinema and Inter-American Relations: Tracking Transnational Affect* (New York: Routledge, 2012); and Ana Laura Lusnich, Alicia Aisemberg, and Andrea Cuarterolo, eds., *Pantallas transnacionales: El cine argentino y mexicano del período clásico* (Buenos Aires: Imago Mundi/Cineteca Nacional de México, 2017). For a summary of transnational approaches in the study of Latin American cinema, see Rielle Navitski and Nicolas Poppe, introduction to *Cosmopolitan Film Cultures in Latin America, 1896–1960*, ed. Rielle Navitski and Nicolas Poppe (Bloomington: Indiana University Press, 2017), 1–6.

24. Ana M. López, *Essays*, ed. and with an introduction by Laura Podalsky and Dolores Tierney (Albany: SUNY Press, 2023), esp. pt. 1.

25. Nilo Couret, "When New Waves Crash: The Friction of Transnational Film Distribution in Brazil, 1931–1959," *Film History* 31, no. 2 (2019): 93. See also López, *Essays*, 109–34, 163–82; and Jorge Rufinelli, "Bajo cinco banderas: El cine multinacional de Carlos Hugo Christensen," *Nuevo Texto Crítico* 11, nos. 21/22 (1998): 277–323.

26. Salazkina's call to consider "world cinema as method," that is, as a "manner of thinking about cinema geopolitically" and "an exploration of the uneven and heterogeneous processes that constitute the relations across, between, and within cinematic cultures globally," resonates strongly with my aims in this book. Salazkina, "World Cinema as Method," 12.

27. Zeina Maasri, Cathy Bergin, and Francesca Burke, "Introduction: Transnational Solidarity in the Long Sixties," in *Transnational Solidarity. Anticolonialism in the Global Sixties*, ed. Zeina Maasri, Cathy Bergin, and Francesca Burke (Manchester: Manchester University Press, 2022), 2. See also David Featherstone, *Solidarity: Hidden Histories and Geographies of Internationalism* (London: Zed Books, 2012); and Jessica Stites Mor, ed., *Human Rights and Transnational Solidarity in Cold War Latin America* (Madison: University of Wisconsin Press, 2013).

28. Maasri, Burgen, and Burke, "Introduction: Transnational Solidarity," 12; and Jessica Stites Mor and María del Carmen Suescun Pozas, "Introduction: Transnational Pathways of Empathy in the Americas," in *The Art of Solidarity. Visual and Performative Politics in Cold War Latin America*, ed. Jessica Stites Mor and María del Carmen Suescun Pozas (Austin: University of Texas Press, 2018), 2.

29. Maasri, Burgen, and Burke, "Introduction: Transnational Solidarity," 4; and Stites Mor and Suescun Pozas, "Introduction: Transnational Pathways," 2.

30. See Moira Cristiá, *AIDA: Una historia de solidaridad artística transnacional (1979–1985)* (Buenos Aires: Imago Mundi, 2021), xiii–xxiii; and Stites Mor and Suescun Pozas, eds., *Art of Solidarity*.

31. Mette Hjort, "The Ontological Transnationalism of the Filmmaker: Solidarity-Based Talent Development across Borders," *Transnational Screens* 10, no. 1 (2019): 55. See also "Editorial NECSUS," *NECSUS* 10, no. 1 (2021): 1–3.

32. Rossen Djagalov, *From Internationalism to Postcolonialism. Literature and Cinema Between the Second and the Third Worlds* (Montreal: McGill-Queen's University Press, 2020); and Masha Salazkina, *World Socialist Cinema. Alliances, Affinities, and Solidarities in the Global Cold War* (Oakland: University of California Press, 2023), 8.

33. Maasri, Bergin, and Burke, "Introduction: Transnational Solidarity," 4.

34. Historian Robin D. G. Kelley speaks of solidarity as worldmaking when discussing the history of Black-Palestinian solidarity alliances. See Robin D. G. Kelley, "From the River to the Sea to Every Mountain Top: Solidarity as Worldmaking," *Journal of Palestine Studies* 48, no. 4 (2019): 85.

35. Thomas Wright and Rody Oñate, "Chilean Political Exile," *Latin American Perspectives* 34, no. 4 (2007): 31–49.

36. Julie Shayne, *They Used to Call Us Witches: Chilean Exiles, Culture, and Feminism* (New York: Lexington Books, 2009), 63–87.

37. Among other studies, see Margaret Power, "The U.S. Movement in Solidarity with Chile in the 1970s," *Latin American Perspectives* 36, no. 6 (2009): 46–66; Margaret Power and Julie Charlip, "Introduction: On Solidarity," *Latin American Perspectives* 36, no. 6 (2009): 3–4; Del José Pozo Artigas, introducción to *Exiliados, emigrados y retornados: Chilenos en América y Europa, 1973–2004*, ed. José Del Pozo Artigas (Santiago: RIL, 2006), 9–12; Brenda Elsey, "'As the World Is My Witness': Transnational Chilean Solidarity and Popular Culture," in *Human Rights and Transnational Solidarity in Cold War Latin America*, ed. Jessica Stites Mor (Madison: University of Wisconsin Press, 2013),177–208; Caroline Moine, "Les mobilisations de solidarité avec le Chili: Militantisme transnational et stratégies médiatiques (années 1970 et 1980)," *Les Temps des Médias*, no. 33 (Winter 2019): 88–103; Fernando Camacho Padilla, *Suecia por Chile: Una historia visual del exilio y la solidaridad, 1970–1990* (Santiago: LOM, 2009); Claudia Rojas Mira, "La casa de Chile en México," in *Exiliados, emigrados y retornados*, 107–26; Michael D. Wilkinson, "The Chile Solidarity Campaign and British Government Policy towards Chile, 1973–1990," *European Review of Latin American and Caribbean Studies* 52 (1992): 57–74; Maurizio Rossi, *Solidarité d'en bas et raison d'État: Le Conseil fédéral et les réfugiés du Chili (septembre 1973–mai 1976)* (Neuchâtel, Switzerland: Alphil éditions, 2008); and Inga Emmerling, *Die DDR und Chile (1960–1989): Aussenpolitik, Aussenhandel und Solidarität* (Berlin: Ch. Links Verlag, 2013).

38. Kim Christiaens, Magaly Rodríguez García, and Idesbald Goddeeris, "A Global Perspective on the European Mobilization for Chile (1970s–1980s)," in *European Solidarity with Chile 1970s–1980s*, ed. Kim Christiaens, Idesbald Goddeeris, and Magaly Rodríguez García (Frankfurt: Peter Lang, 2014), 7.

39. Wright and Oñate, "Chilean Political Exile," 40.

40. Alice Médigue, *Mémoires latino-américaines contre l'oppression, Témoignages d'exilés du Cône sud (1960–2000)* (Paris: INDIGO, 2008), 107-119.

41. Glenda Sluga and Patricia Clavin, "Rethinking the History of Internationalism," in *Internationalisms: A Twentieth Century History*, ed. Glenda Sluga and Patricia Clavin (Cambridge: Cambridge University Press, 2017), 3–14; and Cristiá, *AIDA*, 1–28.

42. Nicole Brenez, "Political Cinema Today—The New Exigencies: For a Republic of Images," *Screening the Past* 37 (September 2013), accessed July 22, 2024, www.screeningthepast.com/2013/09/political-cinema-today-%E2%80%93-the-new-exigencies-for-a-republic-of-images/.

43. For an overview of various theories of solidarity, see Carol C. Gould, "Transnational Solidarities," *Journal of Social Philosophy* 38, no. 1 (2007): 150–52. See also Stites Mor and Suescun Pozas, "Introduction: Transnational Pathways," for the role of empathy in solidarity; Jodi Dean, *Solidarity of Strangers. Feminism after Identity Politics* (Berkeley: University of California Press, 1996), 3, particularly for how solidarity bridges principles of identity, difference, and universality; and Chandra Tapalde Mohanty, *Feminism without Borders: Decolonizing Theory, Practicing Solidarity* (Durham, NC: Duke University Press, 2003), 7, for solidarity as the construction of the "universal on the basis of particulars/differences."

44. Alberto Moreiras, *The Exhaustion of Difference: The Politics of Latin American Cultural Studies* (Durham, NC: Duke University Press, 2001), 215.

45. Lauren Berlant sees solidarity as being "affected and affecting" in a mode of "relationality and reciprocity." Deborah B. Gould claims that "solidarity is both an affective state . . . along with a set of practices of mutual assistance and support." David Featherstone speaks of "affective geographies of connection to refer to the 'more than rational' forms of identification, exchange and articulation produced through political spatial practices." See Lauren Berlant and Jordan Greenwald, "Affect in the End of Times: A Conversation with Lauren Berlant," *Qui Parle* 20, no. 2 (2012): 88; Deborah B. Gould, *Moving Politics: Emotion and ACT UP's Fight against AIDS* (Chicago: University of Chicago Press, 2009), 328; and David Featherstone, *Resistance, Space, and Political Identities: The Making of Counter-Global Networks* (Oxford: Wiley-Blackwell, 2008), 44-5.

46. Anne Garland Mahler, *From the Tricontinental to the Global South. Race, Radicalism, and Transnational Solidarity* (Durham, NC: Duke University Press, 2018), 10.

47. Margaret Randall, *Exporting Revolution. Cuba's Global Solidarity* (Durham, NC: Duke University Press, 2017), 1–21 and 98–110; and Christine Hatzky, "Cuba's Concept of 'Internationalist Solidarity': Political Discourse, South-South Cooperation with Angola, and the Molding of Transnational Identities," in Stites Mor, *Human Rights and Transnational Solidarity in Cold War Latin America*, 143–74.

48. Higbee and Lim, "Concepts of Transnational Cinema," 10.

49. See, among many others, Luis Garrido Soto, *La "vía chilena" al socialismo: Un itinerario geohistórico de la Unidad Popular en el sistema mundo* (Santiago: Ediciones UAH, 2015); Franck Gaudichaud, *Chili 1970–1973: Mille jours qui ébranlèrent le monde* (Rennes: Presses Universitaires de Rennes, 2013); and Jorge Magasich Airola, *Historia de la Unidad Popular*, vols. 1–4 (Santiago: LOM, 2020).

50. José Miguel Palacios, "Resistance vs. Exile: The Political Rhetoric of Chilean Exile Cinema," *Jump Cut*, no. 57 (Fall 2016), accessed September 27, 2024, www.ejumpcut.org/archive/jc57.2016/-PalaciosChile/index.html. See also Tanya

Harmer, *Allende's Chile and the Inter-American Cold War* (Chapel Hill: University of North Carolina Press, 2011); Margaret Power, *Right-Wing Women in Chile: Feminine Power and the Struggle against Allende, 1964–1973* (University Park: Pennsylvania State University Press, 2002); and Peter Winn, *Weavers of Revolution: The Yarur Workers and Chile's Road to Socialism* (Oxford: Oxford University Press, 1986).

51. Marcelo Casals, *El alba de una revolución: La izquierda y la construcción estratégica de la "vía chilena al socialismo," 1956–1970* (Santiago: LOM, 2010), 11. See also Marian E. Schlotterbeck, *Beyond the Vanguard: Everyday Revolutionaries in Allende's Chile* (Oakland: University of California Press, 2018), 1–14; and Michael Hardt, *The Subversive Seventies* (Oxford: Oxford University Press, 2023), 53–64.

52. For a more politically nuanced history of Chilean cinema in the 1960s, see Verónica Cortínez and Manfred Engelbert, *Evolución en Libertad: El cine chileno de fines de los sesenta, tomos 1 y 2* (Santiago: Cuarto Propio, 2014). For Centro de Cine Experimental, see Claudio Salinas Muñoz and Hans Stange, *Historia del cine experimental en la Universidad de Chile 1957–1973* (Santiago: Uqbar, 2008).

53. "Filmmakers and the Popular Government Political Manifesto," trans. Sylvia Harvey, in *Chilean Cinema*, ed. Michael Chanan (London: BFI, 1976), 83.

54. For a recent discussion, see Pablo Marín Castro, *Imaginémonos el caos: Cine, cultura y revolución en Chile, 1967–1973* (Santiago: FCE, 2023), 25–39.

55. For a reevaluation of the work of Chilefilms during the UP years, see Ignacio Del Valle Dávila, *Cámaras en trance: El nuevo cine latinoamericano, un proyecto cinematográfico subcontinental* (Santiago: Cuarto Propio, 2014), 361–77. For a feminist critique of this period, see Elizabeth Ramírez-Soto, "Women (Not) Making Movies under the Popular Unity in Chile (1970–1973)," in *Incomplete: The Feminist Possibilities of the Unfinished Film*, ed. Alix Beeston and Stefan Salomon (Oakland: University of California Press, 2023), 125–46.

56. Zuzana M. Pick, "Chilean Cinema: Ten Years of Exile (1973–1983)," *Jump Cut* 32 (1987), accessed July 22, 2024, www.ejumpcut.org/archive/onlinessays/JC32folder/ChileanFilmExile.html. For an example of these bitter polemics, see the dossier "Chili: Le cinéma de l'Unité Populaire," *Écran* 22 (1974): 13–20.

57. Luiz Alberto Sanz, a Brazilian exile in Chile and later in Sweden, is an example. See Anita Leandro, "Cinema do exílio: Entrevista com Luiz Alberto Sanz e Lars Säfström," *Aniki* 2, no. 2 (2015): 349–59.

58. For numbers and statistics of Chilean exiles see José Del Pozo Artigas, ed., *Exiliados, emigrados y retornados: Chilenos en América y Europa, 1973–2004* (Santiago: RIL, 2006); Anne Marie Gaillard, *Exils et retours: Itinéraires chiliens* (Paris: L'Harmattan, 1997); and Thomas Wright and Rody Oñate, *Flight from Chile Voices of Exile* (Albuquerque: University of New Mexico Press, 1998). For a general perspective on the regional phenomenon of exile in Latin America, see Luis Roniger and Mario Sznajder, *The Politics of Exile in Latin America* (Cambridge: Cambridge University Press, 2009).

59. Ana Vásquez and Ana María Araujo, *La maldición de Ulises: Repercusiones psicológicas del exilio* (Santiago: Editorial Sudamericana, 1990), 23–63.

60. After fifty years, a February 2024 Supreme Court ruling sentenced five members of the army to twenty years in prison for this crime. See Poder Judicial

de Chile, "Corte Suprema condena a agentes de la DINA por secuestro calificado de pareja de cineastas," accessed July 22, 2024, www.pjud.cl/prensa-y-comunicaciones/noticias-del-poder-judicial/105366.

61. For a continental overview, see Yanet Aguilera, ed., *Imagem e exílio: Cinema e arte na América Latina* (São Paulo: Discurso Editorial, 2015).

62. Mariano Mestman has also made these arguments in the prologue to a book on Argentine exile cinema by Javier Campo. See Mariano Mestman, prólogo to Javier Campo, *Revolución y democracia: El cine documental argentino del exilio (1976–1984)* (Buenos Aires: Ediciones Ciccus, 2017), 13.

63. This standard narrative is most clearly at work in: Jaime Larraín Ayuso, "Cine de resistencia," in Alfonso Gumucio Dragón, *Cine, censura y exilio en América Latina*, 2nd ed. (1979; La Paz: Film/Historia, 1984), 103–10; Peter Schumann, "The Chilean Cinema in Exile," *Framework* 10 (1979): 13–14; John King, "Chilean Cinema in Revolution and Exile," in *New Latin American Cinema*, ed. Michael T. Martin (Detroit: Wayne State University Press, 1997), 2:397–419; José Agustín Mahieu, "Cine chileno en el exilio," *Cuadernos Hispanoamericanos*, nos. 482–483 (1990): 241–56; Mouesca, *Plano secuencia de la memoria de Chile*, 137–58; and Jacqueline Mouesca, "El cine chileno en el exilio," *Cine Cubano* 109 (1984): 34–43.

64. In 1988 Grínor Rojo made a similar argument about the need to connect the history of Chilean exile with the history of its literature. Grínor Rojo, *Crítica del exilio: Ensayos sobre la literatura latinoamericana actual* (Santiago: Pehuén, 1988), 105.

65. Naficy stresses the idea that restrictive categorizations produce "discursive ghettos" with the aim to "delimit the meanings" films can have. Hamid Naficy, "Phobic Spaces and Liminal Panics: Independent Transnational Film Genre," in *Global/Local: Cultural Production in the Transnational Imaginary*, ed. Rob Wilson and Wimal Dissanayake (Durham, NC: Duke University Press, 2006), 120.

66. This argument has also been put forth by Elizabeth Ramírez-Soto, "Journeys of *Desexilio*: The Bridge between the Past and the Present," *Rethinking History* 18, no. 3 (2014): 439.

67. Mouesca, *Plano secuencia de la memoria de Chile*, 137–58; and Mouesca, "El cine chileno en el exilio," 34–43. Argentine scholar Javier Campo borrows from this way of understanding a trajectory of Chilean exile cinema and proposes two phases for the Argentine exilic output: the first was centered on questions of militancy and armed struggle, and the second on issues of human rights. See Campo, *Revolución y democracia*, 65–67.

68. Gumucio Dragón, *Cine, censura y exilio en América Latina*, 100.

69. Zuzana M. Pick, "Chilean Cinema in Exile (1973–1986): The Notion of Exile; a Field of Investigation and Its Conceptual Framework." *Framework* 34 (1988): 56.

70. Pick, "Chilean Cinema in Exile (1973–1986)."

71. A defense of Pick can be found in Lars Gustaf Andersson and John Sundholm, "Accented Cinema and Beyond: Latin American Minor Cinemas in Sweden, 1970–1990," *Studies in Spanish & Latin American Cinemas* 13, no. 3 (2016): 227–45.

72. Kodwo Eshun and Ros Gray, "The Militant Image: A Ciné-Geography," *Third Text* 25, no. 1 (2011): 1.
73. Eshun and Gray, "Militant Image," 1.
74. Miguel Littin, "Fragmentos del informe de la delegación chilena, presentado por Miguel Littin en el encuentro de cineastas latinoamericanos," in *Por un cine latinoamericano: Encuentro de cineastas latinoamericanos en solidaridad con el pueblo y los cineastas de Chile, Caracas, Septiembre de 1974* (Caracas: Rocinante, 1974), 50–51.
75. Marilú Mallet, "Les Lettres: Scénario," 1979, Cinémathèque québécoise, 1984.0082.26.SC, 6.
76. Hal Foster, "An Archival Impulse," *October* 110 (2004): 3–22.

CHAPTER 1. EXILE TRAVELS AND TRANSNATIONAL
FILM HISTORY

1. The most complete filmography of Chilean exile cinema only covers the first decade of production. See Zuzana M. Pick, "Cronología del cine chileno en el exilio 1973/1983," *Literatura Chilena: Creación y Crítica* 27 (1984): 15–21. Archival research conducted for this book allows me to estimate over 230 titles. See chapter 7 for more details.
2. Even if both *La triple muerte del tercer personaje* and *Gentille Alouette* retain elements that can be associated with the experiences of exile, torture, and the histories of the military dictatorships in Latin America, their narrative construction exceeds a strict association with Chile. See Jürgen E. Müller, "Das mediale Labyrinth des Films: Helvio Soto; *La triple mort du troisième personage*," in *Blick-Wechsel: Tendenzen im Spielfilm der 70-er und 80-er Jahre*, ed. Jürgen E. Müller and Markus Vorauer (Munster: Nodus Publikationen, 1992), 201–12; and Verónica Cortínez, "Cervantes y *Gentille Alouette* de Sergio Castilla," *Iberoromania* 83 (2016): 84–102.
3. Pick, "Chilean Cinema: Ten Years of Exile (1973–1983)." See also Pick, "Chilean Cinema in Exile (1973–1986)," 39–57; and Pick, "Cronología del cine chileno en el exilio 1973/1983," 27–31.
4. Higbee and Lim, "Concepts of Transnational Cinema," 7–21.
5. Bishop, "Introduction: The Cartographical Necessity of Exile," 1.
6. Eshun and Gray, "Militant Image," 1.
7. James Clifford's pairing of *root* and *route* is exemplary in cultural theory's thinking of identity through spatial metaphors. See James Clifford, "Diasporas," *Cultural Anthropology* 9, no. 3 (1994): 302–38. On the "spatial turn" in cultural theory, see Steve Pile and Nigel Thrift, introduction to *Mapping the Subject. Geographies of Cultural Transformation*, ed. Steve Pile and Nigel Thrift (London: Routledge, 1995), 9–12.
8. For the concept of network in film studies, see Marijke de Valck, *Film Festivals. From European Geopolitics to Global Cinephilia* (Amsterdam: Amsterdam University Press, 2007), 29–36.
9. Fernando Camacho Padilla, "La diáspora chilena y su confrontación con la embajada de Chile en Suecia, 1973–1982," in *Exiliados, emigrados y*

retornados: Chilenos en América y Europa, 1973–2004, ed. José Del Pozo Artigas (Santiago: RIL, 2006), 37–62.

10. I thank Masha Salazkina for reminding me to stress this point.

11. Arthur C. Danto, "Remembering Andre Racz," *American Art* 12, no. 2 (1998): 58–65.

12. Mariano Mestman, "Estados generales del tercer cine: Los documentos de Montreal, 1974," *Rehime: Cuadernos de la Red de Historia de los Medios* 3, no. 3 (2013/2014): 28; and *Rencontres internationales pour un nouveau cinéma* in Montréal, *Cahier no. 1: Projets et résolutions* (Montreal: Comité d'Action Cinématographique, 1975), 41. *To the Peoples of the World* did not include credits in the 16mm prints that circulated; however, a 1979 catalog of the Latin American Film Project, a production/distribution group directed by Barbara Margolis and Brazilian exile cinematographer Alfonso Beato, credits the film to the group and attributes the directing role to Margolis.

13. Claudia Sandberg, *Peter Lilienthal: A Cinema of Exile and Resistance* (New York: Berghahn Books, 2021), 61, 71, 101.

14. Villarroel and Mardones, *Señales contra el olvido*, 77; and Guzmán, *La batalla de Chile*, 129.

15. Verónica Cortínez, *Cine a la chilena: Las peripecias de Sergio Castilla* (Santiago: RIL Editores, 2001), 70; and Verónica Cortínez, "Sergio Castilla: The Emblematic Chilean Filmmaker," *Radical History Review* 124 (2016): 192–95.

16. Orlando Lübert, interview with the author, April 16, 2019. See also Villarroel and Mardones, *Señales contra el olvido*, 97–98. For Mexico's solidarity with Chile, see Rojas Mira, "Los anfitriones del exilio chileno en México, 1973–1993," *Historia Crítica* 60 (2016): 123–40.

17. Hans Ehrmann, "Sebastián Alarcón: El chileno desconocido," *Enfoque* 17 (December 1990): 20; "Orientación y perspectivas del cine chileno: Mesa redonda realizada en el Festival Internacional de Cine de Moscú 1979; Participantes: Sebastián Alarcón, Jaime Barrios, José Donoso, Eduardo Labarca, Miguel Littin, Orlando Lübbert, Cristián Valdés y José Miguel Varas (moderador)," *Araucaria de Chile* 11 (1980): 125–26, 131; and Djagalov, *From Internationalism to Postcolonialism*, 144, 150.

18. Djagalov notes that Soviet policies indicated that VGIK's international students on fellowships had to return to their home countries upon graduation. Given the circumstances of the coup, Soviet authorities exempted Alarcón from this rule, "thus making him one of the very few foreign-trained VGIK graduate to have had his cinematic career in the USSR." Djagalov, *From Internationalism to Postcolonialism*, 249.

19. Arsenal's online database and catalog does not list *Fists against the Cannons* as having been part of the 1974 Forum program, something "inexplicable" according to Ross. See Villarroel and Mardones, *Señales contra el olvido*, 97–98.

20. Villarroel and Mardones, *Señales contra el olvido*, 97–98.

21. Orlando Lübert, interview with the author, April 16, 2019. See also Villarroel and Mardones, *Señales contra el olvido*, 97–98.

22. Ramírez-Soto, "Journeys of *Desexilio*," 448.

23. Ramírez-Soto, "Journeys of *Desexilio*," 448.

24. *Recado* has a variety of meanings—among others, "message," "greeting," "regards," or "gift." The film's title alludes to Chilean poet Gabriela Mistral, who used the term *recado* to designate the short pieces and sketches she wrote for Latin American newspapers. See Jacqueline C. Nanfito, "Gabriela Mistral's Prose: The Poetic Mapping of Cultural Identities and Feminine Subjectivities," *Revista de Estudios Hispánicos* 26, no. 1 (1999): 117–18.

25. See chapter 3 for an account of this festival.

26. Ancelovici's NFB film had two versions: the one-hour original French version, *Mémoires d'une guerre cotidienne*, and the thirty-minute English-language *Memories of an Everyday War*. See Cinémathèque québécoise, "Récits d'une guerre cotidienne," accessed July 22, 2024, https://collections.cinematheque.qc.ca/recherche/oeuvres/fiche/31148-recits-dune-guerre-quotidienne.

27. "Snakes and Ladders," Q&A recording, April 29, 1990, BAMPFA Film Library & Study Center Audio Collection.

28. Martha C. Nussbaum, "Patriotism and Cosmopolitanism," in *For Love of Country: Debating the Limits of Patriotism* (Boston: Beacon, 1996), 4.

29. Bruce Robbins, "Introduction Part I: Actually Existing Cosmopolitanism," in *Cosmopolitics. Thinking and Feeling beyond the Nation*, ed. Pheng Cheah and Bruce Robbins (Minneapolis: University of Minnesota Press, 1998) 2. See also Mariano Siskind, *Cosmopolitan Desires. Global Modernity and World Literature in Latin America* (Evanston, IL: Northwestern University Press, 2014), 3.

30. Siskind, *Cosmopolitan Desires*, 3.

31. Siskind, *Cosmopolitan Desires*,6.

32. Navitski and Poppe, introduction, 3.

33. With Jean-Luc Larguier, Ruiz codirected La Maison de la Culture du Havre between 1985 and 1989. See Maison de la Culture du Havre, "Assemblés Générales," accessed July 22, 2024, https://asso-maisondelaculture.fr/association-maison-culture-havre/historique/.

34. Cáceres, *Los años chilenos de Raúl Ruiz*, 279–80; and Sandberg, *Peter Lilienthal*, 61, 71, 101.

35. Elizabeth Ramírez-Soto, "The Double Day of Valeria Sarmiento: Exile, Precariousness, and Cinema's Gendered Division of Labor," *Feminist Media Histories* 7, no. 3 (2021): 162.

36. Cáceres, *Los años chilenos de Raúl Ruiz*, 282.

37. In an unpublished paper, Ramírez-Soto offers more evidence of the troubled relationship between Ruiz and the ZDF when making *The Scattered Body and the World Upside Down*. Elizabeth Ramírez-Soto, "Tomar la pantalla por asalto: Raúl Ruiz en la televisión europea" (paper presented at the colloquium Raúl Ruiz desde Chile: Cartografías y metamorfosis, Santiago, July 26, 2016). See also Cáceres, *Los años chilenos de Raúl Ruiz*, 280–82.

38. For tensions with ZDF, see Archivo Ruiz Sarmiento, RR-27-1-5-1, "La utopía/El cuerpo repartido."

39. Serge Toubiana, "Le cas Ruiz," *Cahiers du Cinéma* 345 (1983): 5. See also Benoît Peeters and Guy Scarpetta, *Raoul Ruiz: Le magicien* (Brussels: Les Impressions Novelles, 2015).

40. *Les Destins de Manoel* was the title of the theatrical 140-minute version of this project, which also included the three-part French TV series *L'île aux merveilles de Manoel* or *Manuel na Ilha das Maravilhas* (*Manoel in the Island of Wonders*) and the four-part Portuguese TV version *Aventures au Madeira* (*Adventures in Madeira*).

41. Ruiz had had a brief but intense stay in the United States much earlier in his career, in 1965–1966. For a detailed account of Ruiz's stay in the United States and Mexico in the mid-1960s, see Verónica Cortínez and Manfred Engelbert, *La tristeza de los tigres y los misterios de Raúl Ruiz* (Santiago: Cuarto Propio, 2011), 152–67.

42. On Ruiz's video installation, see Francisca García Barriga, "Arqueologías de la mirada: Reactivación crítica de la videoinstalación *La expulsión de los moros* (1990) de Raúl Ruiz," *Revista 180* 48 (2021): 42–51; Francisca García Barriga, "Notas en torno a las instalaciones (1990–1996)," *la Fuga* 24 (2020), accessed July 22, 2024, www.lafuga.cl/notas-en-torno-a-las-instalaciones-1990-1996/1015; and Carol Ann Klonarides, "Raúl Ruiz," *BOMB* 34 (1991): 14–16. On the making of *The Golden Boat*, see James Schamus, "Raúl Ruiz Remembered by James Schamus," *Filmmaker Magazine*, August 19, 2011, accessed July 22, 2024, https://filmmakermagazine.com/28180-raul-ruiz-remembered-by-james-schamus/.

43. For the conference proceedings, including contributions by Moreiras and Ruiz, see Ministerio de Educación, *Utopía(s): Seminario Internacional* (Santiago: Ministerio de Educación, 1993).

44. Ignacio Albornoz and Iván Pinto, "Introducción: Presentación de los editores," in *Raúl Ruiz: Potencias de lo múltiple*, ed. Ignacio Albornoz and Iván Pinto (Santiago: Metales Pesados, 2023), 9.

45. As Ramírez-Soto argues, studies of Ruiz also elide or downplay the role played by his wife, editor, and creative partner Valeria Sarmiento. See Ramírez-Soto, "Double Day of Valeria Sarmiento," 154–77.

46. BAMPFA, "Snakes and Ladders."

47. For the artisanal mode in Latin American cinema, see Julianne Burton, "Film Artisans and Film Industries in Latin America, 1956–1980: Theoretical and Critical Implications of Variations in Modes of Filmic Production and Consumption," in *New Latin American Cinema*, ed. Michael T. Martin (Detroit: Wayne State University Press, 1997), 1:157–84. See also Zuzana M. Pick, "Hablan los cineastas," *Literatura Chilena: Creación y Crítica* 27 (1984): 28, in which exile filmmaker Leutén Rojas is quoted saying that when he first went into exile, in Honduras and later in Canada, all he knew was how to make an "artisanal cinema."

48. Little has been written on Toronto's Film League. Key members of the group were Glen Richards and Peggy Nash. Peter Steven refers to the Film League as "a documentary collective that created several innovative labor films." Peter Stevens, "The DEC Films Story: To Recover and Reclaim," *Jump Cut* 59 (Fall 2019), accessed July 22, 2024, www.ejumpcut.org/archive/jc59/2019/Steven-DEC/index.html.

49. Naficy, *Accented Cinema*, 43–56. In an earlier piece, Naficy describes accented cinemas as a mode of "interstitiality within social and economic

formations and marginality within the dominant film and media industries." See Naficy, "Between Rocks and Hard Places," 129.

50. Naficy, *Accented Cinema*, 46.

51. José Miguel Palacios and Catalina Donoso Pinto, "Infancia y exilio en el cine chileno," *Iberoamericana: América Latina—España—Portugal* 17, no. 65 (2017): 57–58.

52. Existing filmographies tend to date *Sotelo* as 1976. However, I am opting for the copyright date as seen in the film itself. Similarly, *Le mal du pays* is sometimes dated as 1980, whereas its official production date is 1979.

53. Ramírez-Soto quotes and translates from an interview with Sarmiento included in the TV program *Exiles* (BBC, 1988), in which the filmmaker says: "The first years were very hard settling in, because I didn't know French. . . . I did a bit of everything: I was a cleaning lady, we did everything just to survive. . . . And then we started to work in cinema." Ramírez-Soto, "Double Day of Valeria Sarmiento," 162.

54. Dalila Missero and Masha Salazkina, "CFP—Feminist Media Histories, "in "Gender, Media, and Developmentalism," special issue of *Feminist Media Histories*, accessed July 22, 2024, https://docs.google.com/document/d/12FMQtz XQqnffJLkvIoippmwvGIYagioKKeZMmTbT5HM/edit. See also chapter 2 for a discussion of the developmentalist mode in the series of documentary films and videos that Wolfgang Tirado and Jackie Reiter made in Nicaragua.

55. On the role of the Institut québécois du cinéma in dialogue with other public funding structures in Quebec, see "Claude Fournier: Président de l'Institut québécois du cinéma," *Séquences* 120 (1985): 15–19; and Christian Poirier, *Le cinéma québécois: À la recherche d'une identité*, tome 2, *Les Politiques Cinématographiques* (Sainte-Foy: Presses de l'Université du Québec, 2004), 86–97.

56. Elizabeth Ramírez-Soto, "Channel 4 and the South Series (1991–93): From the Third World to the Global South," *Historical Journal of Film, Radio, and Television* 44, no. 1 (2024): 168–94.

57. Stein quoted in Ramírez-Soto, "Channel 4 and the South Series (1991–93)," 171.

58. Dossier no. °69, "Rues des Archives," Fonds Production et co-production INA 14225-0025, Institut national de l'audiovisuel (INA); and dossier no. 3, "Botaniques," Fonds Production et co-production INA 14225-0001, Institut national de l'audiovisuel (INA).

59. See the monograph about this series published by the NFB, *Parler d'Amérique: Une série de neuf moyens métrages documentaires sur les mythes américains* (1989), and the dossier about Mallet's contribution *Chère Amérique* (1989), both held at Cinémathèque québécoise.

60. For minor cinemas, see David E. James, *Allegories of Cinema: American Film in the Sixties* (Princeton, NJ: Princeton University Press, 1989), 3–28; James, *Most Typical Avant-Garde*, 203–47; and Naficy, "Between Rocks and Hard Places," 132.

61. Ramírez-Soto, "Channel 4 and the South Series (1991–93)," 168–94.

62. Antonio Skármeta, "Europe: An Indispensable Link in the Production and Circulation of Latin American Cinema," in *New Latin American Cinema*, 1:263–69.

63. For a detailed analysis of the film, see Alexsandro de Sousa e Silva, *Cinema, política e exílio: O Caso Miguel Littin* (Foz do Iguaçu: CLAEC, 2021), 113–19.

64. Dossier *Sandino* (1990), Centro de Documentación, Filmoteca Española.

65. For more on the production history of *Sandino* and an analysis of the film, see Silva, *Cinema, política e exílio*, 182–97.

66. See chapter 3 for a detailed account of the relationship between Chilean exile cinema and film festivals.

67. FEST LOC 76, Festival internazionale del film, Locarno, 29, 1976, Cinémathèque française.

68. See Alain Bergala, "Sur le fil du rasoir," *Cahiers du cinéma* 375 (1985): 57–58; and Serge Daney, "*Notre mariage* tient vraiment bien la route," *Libération*, September 12, 1985. At least nine other French newspapers published reviews of *Notre mariage* in September 1985.

69. Ehrmann, "Sebastián Alarcón," 22; and Mouesca, *Plano secuencia de la memoria de Chile*, 149.

70. Stevens, "DEC Films Story."

71. Jonathan Buchsbaum, "Militant Third World Film Distribution in the United States," *Canadian Journal of Film Studies* 24, no. 2 (2015): 51–65.

72. Luna Hupperetz, "Cineclub Vrijheidsfilms: Restoring a Militant Cinema Network," *The Moving Image* 22, no. 1 (2022): 50.

73. Tricontinental Film Center, *Programmer's Guide to Third World Cinema* (New York: Tricontinental Film Center, 1980), 7.

74. For Tricontinental's scale of prices, see Buchsbaum, "Militant Third World Film Distribution," 56.

75. Tricontinental Film Center, *Programmer's Guide to Third World Cinema*, 7.

76. See the catalog in Exit Art, *Raúl Ruiz: Works for and about French TV* (New York: Exit Art, 1987).

77. "Program for Art on Film (New York, N.Y.), Records 1951–1999, undated, bulk 1984–1997," IA.20008, 20004, 14–40, The Getty Research Institute.

78. Ramon Lobato, *Shadow Economies of Cinema. Mapping Informal Film Distribution* (London: BFI, 2012), 1.

79. Castilla quoted in Guzmán, *La batalla de Chile*, 130.

80. Yessica Ulloa, *Video independiente en Chile* (Santiago: CENECA, 1985), 38–43; and Germán Liñero, *Apuntes para una historia del video en Chile* (Santiago: Ocho Libros, 2010), 77–84.

81. "Chile in the Heart Talk" (presented at International Film Festival Rotterdam, January 31, 2024).

82. Rencontres internationales pour un nouveau cinéma in Montréal, *Cahier no. 1: Projets et résolutions*, 40. See also Marcy Campos Pérez, "Le patrimoine chilien contemporain à la croisée des réseaux transnationaux des années 70," *L'histoire du temps présent en Amérique latine* 120 (2023), accessed July 22, 2024, https://journals.openedition.org/caravelle/14054.

83. Villarroel and Mardones, *Señales contra el olvido*, 113.

84. For the use of *exile*, see Rencontres internationales pour un nouveau cinéma in Montréal, *Cahier no. 1: Projets et résolutions*, 40. For *resistance*,

see Pedro Chaskel, "Informe de la secretaría general de UCAL al VII congreso: Caracas, 1974," in *Por un cine latinoamericano: Encuentro de cineastas latinoamericanos en solidaridad con el pueblo y los cineastas de Chile, Caracas, Septiembre de 1974* (Caracas: Rocinante, 1974), 67–68.

85. Chaskel, "Informe de la secretaría general de UCAL al VII congreso," 68. For a discussion of the Caracas event, see chapter 3.

86. Chaskel officiated as director of Cineteca de la Universidad de Chile between 1961 and 1963. Kerry Oñate became the new director and remained in the position until the department was finally closed by the military in 1976. See Salinas and Stange, *Historia del cine experimental en la Universidad de Chile*, 87–90.

87. For a history of UCAL, see Janet Ceja Alcalá, "Imperfect Archives and the Principle of Social Praxis in the History of Film Preservation in Latin America," *The Moving Image* 13, no. 1 (2013): 74–81; and Fabián Núñez, "Notas para um estudo sobre a Unión de Cinematecas de América Latina," *significação* 42, no. 44 (2015): 65–79.

88. Rencontres internationales pour un nouveau cinéma in Montréal, *Cahier no. 1: Projets et résolutions*, 40. Campos Pérez cites a May 2, 1974, letter from Chaskel to Saul Yelin, head of Cuba's cinematheque, with almost identical phrasing. See Campos Pérez, "Le patrimoine chilien contemporain."

89. Villarroel and Mardones, *Señales contra el olvido*, 110–13.

90. Among others, Gastón Ancelovici and Paulo Antonio Paranaguá, "Cine chileno del exilio," *Araucaria de Chile* 14 (1981): 196–97.

91. Pick, "Cronología del cine chileno en el Exilio 1973/1983," 15–21.

92. Villarroel and Mardones, *Señales contra el olvido*, 116. These titles remain in Filmoteca's collections in 16mm and 35mm prints. See Fondos Fílmicos, email to the author, December 3, 2018.

93. Médiathèque des trois mondes distributed and promoted films from the Third World in France. Archival resources about the Médiathèque can be found at BNF, Médiathèque des trois mondes, accessed July 22, 2024, https://data.bnf.fr/13946287/mediatheque_des_trois_mondes_paris/.

94. Gastón Ancelovici, "Document de préproduction: *Chili in transition*," 2000.0365.72.AR, Cinémathèque québécoise.

95. Peter Schumann, quoted in Villarroel and Mardones, *Señales contra el olvido*, 114.

96. See chapter 3 for a discussion of the retrospective "Film Im Freiheitskampf der Völker: Chile" (Cinema in the struggle for the liberation of the peoples: Chile) during the 1983 edition of the Leipzig Film Festival.

97. See chapter 4 for an analysis of the various meanings of "resistance" for Chilean exile cinema.

98. FIAF, "Rapport du secrétariat général de l'UCAL à l'assemblée générale du XXXI congrès de la FIAF," Torino, June 2–5, 1975, annex 8, appendices, 26–33, accessed July 22, 2024, www.fiafnet.org/images/tinyUpload/E-Resources/Official-Documents/Protected%20Files/Congress-Reports/1975-AppendicesRED.pdf.

99. FIAF, minutes of the Congress and General Meeting, Mexico City, May 24–27, 1976, accessed July 22, 2024, https://www.fiafnet.org/images

/tinyUpload/E-Resources/Official-Documents/Protected%20Files/Congress-Reports/1976-Mexico%20GA%20MinutesRED.

100. Peter Schumman, quoted in Villarroel and Mardones, *Señales contra el olvido*, 116.

101. The phrase "internal exiles" comes from Coco Fusco, *Internal Exiles: New Films and Videos from Chile* (New York: Third World Newsreel, 1990). The idea of "the two streams" was expressed in Ancelovici and Paranaguá, "Cine chileno del exilio," 197; Zuzana M. Pick, "Tradición y búsqueda," *Araucaria de Chile* 23 (1985): 103; and Pick, "Chilean Cinema: Ten Years of Exile (1973–1983)."

102. For the role of Paris in the cultural imagination of Latin American exiles, see Marcy E. Schwartz, "Cultural Exile and the Canon," in *Paradise Lost or Gained: The Literature of Hispanic Exile*, ed. Fernando Alegría and Jorge Ruffinelli (Houston: Arte Publico Press, 1990), 208.

CHAPTER 2. THE PRODUCTION OF SOLIDARITY

1. Fondo Eduardo Carrasco, CL MMDH 00000164, Archivo MMDH.

2. Alejandro Witker, ed., *La solidaridad mundial con Chile: Voces—imágenes—documentos* (Mexico City: Instituto Politécnico Nacional, 1989), 127–204.

3. Roberto Hervas Segovia, *Les organisations de solidarité avec le Chili* (Saint-Leonard, Quebec: 5 Continents, 2001).

4. Joan Simalchik, "The Material Culture of Chilean Exiles: A Transnational Dialogue," *Refuge. Canada's Journal on Refugees* 23, no. 2 (2006): 97–100.

5. Urok Shirhan, "A Loud Voice Never Dies," *The Derivative*, December 1, 2020, accessed July 23, 2024, https://thederivative.org/a-loud-voice-never-dies-songs-across-time-and-place/. See also Mysa Kafil-Hussain (@mysakh), "The catalogue/pamphlet cover from the Iraqi Plastic Arts Society Week of Solidarity with Chile in June 1974," Twitter, March 28, 2023, 5:51 a.m., https://twitter.com/mysakh/status/1640698007577403398.

6. For an analysis of solidarity posters, see Priscila Pilatowski Goñi and Amaia Cabranes, "Militancias gráficas: Carteles y solidaridad transnacional entre Francia y América Latina 1970–1980," *Secuencia* 108 (2020): 1–44; and Estela Aguirre and Sonia Chamorro, *"L": Memoria gráfica del exilio chileno 1973–1989* (Santiago: Ocho Libros, 2009).

7. Shirhan, "Loud Voice Never Dies." See also Ali Abdul Ameer, "Jaafar Hassan's Guitar," AliAbdulAmeer.com, November 25, 2009, accessed July 23, 2024, www.aliabdulameer.com/inp/view.asp?ID=256.

8. For solidarity committees, see Wright and Oñate, "Chilean Political Exile," 40–41; and Del Pozo, introducción, 9–12.

9. For cine-geography, see this book's introduction as well as Eshun and Gray, "Militant Image," 1–12.

10. Carolina Amaral de Aguiar, "O cinema latino-americano e a solidariedade ao Chile," in *Golpe de Vista: Cinema e ditadura militar na América do Sul*, ed. Nuno Cesar Abreu, Alfredo Suppia, and Marcius Freire (São Paulo: Alameda,

2016), 289–309; and Zuzana M. Pick, "A Special Section on Chilean Cinema," *Ciné-Tracts 9: A Journal of Film and Cultural Studies* 3, no. 1 (1980): 18.

11. Djagalov, *From Internationalism to Postcolonialism*, 173–209.
12. Pick, "Cronología del cine chileno en el exilio 1973/1983," 16, 18.
13. Zuzana M. Pick, *The New Latin American Cinema: A Continental Project* (Austin: University of Texas Press, 1993), 164.
14. Pick, "Chilean Cinema in Exile (1973–1986)," 50.
15. Rick Altman, "A Semantic/Syntactic Approach to Film Genre," *Cinema Journal* 23, no. 3 (Spring 1984): 10.
16. For Chile Democrático, see Wright and Oñate, "Chilean Political Exile," 40; Alessandro Santoni, "Comunistas y socialistas italianos frente a la causa chilena: Solidaridad y renovación (1973–1989)," *Revista Izquierdas* 19 (2014): 115–16; Jorge Arrate and Eduardo Rojas, *Memoria de la izquierda chilena (1970–2000)* (Santiago: Javier Vergara Editor, 2003), 262; and the Chile Democrático files in Fondo Sergio Insunza Barrios, CL MMDH 00000632, Archivo MMDH.
17. Julio Ramos, "Jaime Barrios: Introducción; un cineasta chileno en las fronteras del underground neoyorkino," *la Fuga* 21 (2018), accessed July 23, 2024, www.lafuga.cl/jaime-barrios-introduccion/899.
18. Jessica Gordon-Burroughs, "Re-editando al amateur: *Film Club* (1968–2004) de Jaime Barrios," *la Fuga* 21 (2018), accessed July 23, 2024, www.lafuga.cl/re-editando-al-amateur/901; and Jessica Gordon-Burroughs, "Looking Back and Away: Jaime Barrios' *Film Club*," *Discourse* 42, no. 3 (Fall 2020): 281–304.
19. Julio Sebastián Figueroa, "El documental político de Jaime Barrios," *la Fuga* 21 (2018), accessed July 23, 2024, www.lafuga.cl/el-documental-politico-de-jaime-barrios/903.
20. José Miguel Palacios, "Número de copias: Cero; Apuntes sobre una película huérfana, Jaime Barrios y el cine chileno del exilio," *la Fuga* 21 (2018), accessed July 23, 2024, www.lafuga.cl/numero-de-copias-cero/902.
21. Pranay Gupte, "3 Chileans Ask Return, Not Asylum," *New York Times*, November 26, 1977, 18.
22. Thomas Waugh, *The Conscience of Cinema: The Films of Joris Ivens 1912–1989* (Amsterdam: Amsterdam University Press, 2016), 526.
23. For Chile-U.S. relations, see Tanya Harmer, "Fractious Allies: Chile, the United States, and the Cold War, 1973–76," *Diplomatic History* 37, no. 1 (2013): 109–43.
24. See also Catherine Grant, "Camera solidaria," *Screen* 38, no. 4 (1997): 311–28.
25. Claudia Rojas Mira and Alessandro Santoni, "Geografía política del exilio chileno: Los diferentes rostros de la solidaridad," *Perfiles Latinoamericanos* 41 (2013): 127. For Third World and Arab World solidarity with Chile, see Eugenia Palieraki, "Chile, Algeria, and the Third World in the 1960s and 1970s: Revolutions Entangled," in *Latin America and the Global Cold War*, ed Thomas C. Field Jr., Stella Krepp, and Vanni Pettinà (Chapel Hill: University of North Carolina Press, 2020), 274–300; and Eugenia Palieraki, "Broadening the

Field of Perception and Struggle: Chilean Political Exiles in Algeria and Third World Cosmopolitanism," *African Identities* 16, no. 2 (2018): 205–18.

26. Rojas Mira and Santoni, "Geografía política del exilio chileno," 135. See also Alessandro Santoni, "El partido comunista italiano y el otro 'compromesso storico': Los significados políticos de la solidaridad con Chile," *Historia* 43 (2010): 523–46. See also Caroline Moine, "Denouncing or Supporting the Chilean Dictatorship in West Germany? Local Associations of Solidarity and Their Transnational Networks Since the 1970s," *Global Societies* 33, no. 3 (2019): 333.

27. On the GFR's Hallstein doctrine, which isolated the GDR in the global arena, see Caroline Moine, *Screened Encounters: The Leipzig Documentary Film Festival, 1955–1990* (New York: Berghahn Books, 2018), 33.

28. Caroline Moine, "La RDA à l'heure de la 'Solidarité internationale': Berlin-Est, août, 1973," in *La République démocratique allemande: La vitrine du socialisme et l'envers du miroir (1949–1989–2009)*, ed. Chantal Metzger (Brussels: Peter Lang, 2010), 289.

29. Moine, "La RDA à l'heure de la 'Solidarité internationale,'" 291. See also Emmerling, *Die DDR und Chile (1960–1989)*; and Antiimperialistisches Solidaritätskomitee für Afrika, Asien und Lateinamerika, *Solidarität mit Chile: Dokumente der internationalen Solidaritätsbewegung* (Berne: Verlag nicht ermittelbar, 1973).

30. For a critical perspective on the solidarity efforts of the GDR, see Jost Maurin, "Flüchtlinge als politisches Instrument—Chilenische Emigranten in der DDR 1973–1989," *Totalitarismus und Demokratie* 2 (2005): 345–74; and the landmark novel by Carlos Cerda, *Morir en Berlín* (Santiago: Planeta, 1996).

31. See his memoirs in Luis Corvalán, *De lo vivido y lo peleado: Memorias* (Santiago: LOM, 1997).

32. For a more in-depth discussion of *Gladys Marín*, see Palacios and Donoso Pinto, "Infancia y exilio en el cine chileno," 50–51.

33. Djagalov, *From Internationalism to Postcolonialism*, 191–92.

34. DEFA Film Library, "Foreign Ministry," accessed July 23, 2024, www.umass.edu/defa/research/genres/Foreign%20Ministry.

35. Jamie Trnka, "Choreographing Exile: Lothar Warneke's and Omar Saavedra Santis' *Blonder Tango*," *The German Quarterly* 84, no. 3 (Summer 2011): 315.

36. Moreiras, *Exhaustion of Difference*, 215.

37. Cristián E. Medina Valverde and Gustavo Gajardo Pavez, "Entre protectores y opositores: Labor política frente al caso Honecker," *Revista de Ciencia Política* 36, no. 3 (2016): 731–48.

38. Deutsche Fernsehgeschichte, "Erich Honecker flieht nach Chile (TV-Beitrag von 1993)," October 4, 2019, YouTube video, 3:34, accessed July 23, 2024, www.youtube.com/watch?v=GWl8rL5NbMA&t=7s&ab_channel=Deutsche Fernsehgeschichte.

39. Trnka, "Choreographing Exile," 313.

40. National Film Board of Canada, "Mandate and Values," accessed July 23, 2024, www.canada.ca/en/national-film-board/corporate/about/mandate-values.html.

41. Michael Brendan Baker, Thomas Waugh, and Ezra Winton, "Introduction: Forty Years Later ... a Space for Challenge for Change/Société nouvelle," in *Challenge for Change. Activist Documentary at the National Film Board of Canada*, ed. Thomas Waugh, Michael Brendan Baker, and Ezra Winton (Montreal: McGill-Queen's University Press, 2010), 4.

42. Baker, Waugh, and Winton, "Introduction: Forty Years Later," 3–14; and Deirdre Boyle, "O, Canada! George Stoney's Challenge," *Wide Angle* 21, no. 2 (1999): 49.

43. Naficy, *Accented Cinema*, 46.

44. "Memorandum *Les Borges*—distribution," included in Dossier *Les Borges*, Cinémathèque québécoise 1984.0082.27.AR.

45. "Partir ou rester," included in Dossier *Les Borges*, Cinémathèque québécoise 1984.0082.27.AR.

46. "Memorandum *Les Borges*—distribution."

47. Fédération des travailleurs du Québec, *Un pays en commun: La solidarité* (Montreal: Fédération des travailleurs du Québec, 1979).

48. Jean-Pierre Tadros, "L'immigration vécue par une famille portugaise," 1978, Cineteca Universidad de Chile—Fondo Zuzana Pick.

49. Pierre Demers, "Le cinéma étranger québécois," 1980, Cineteca Universidad de Chile—Fondo Zuzana Pick.

50. Pick, "Chilean Cinema: Ten Years of Exile (1973–1983)."

51. Thomas Waugh, "Introduction: Vidéographe," in *Vidéographe: Sélections vidéo/video selections* (Montreal: Vidéographe, 1989), 6.

52. Scott MacKenzie, "Le mouton noir: Vidéographe and the Legacy of Société nouvelle," in *Vidéographe: Sélections vidéo/video selections*, 136–37.

53. MacKenzie, "Le mouton noir," 138.

54. See chapter 4 for an analysis of this film.

55. Pick, "Chilean Cinema in Exile (1973–1986)," 40.

56. "Communiqué—Les Borges," included in Dossier *Les Borges*, Cinémathèque québécoise, 1984.0082.27.AR.

57. Scénario du film *Lentement*, Cinémathèque québécoise, 1984.0019.05.SC.

58. Normande Juneau, "La famille Borges n'attend plus rien: elle vit," 1978, Cineteca Universidad de Chile—Fondo Zuzana Pick.

59. See Elizabeth Dahab, *Voices of Exile in Contemporary Canadian Francophone Literature* (New York: Lexington Books, 2009), 3–5; and José del Pozo, "Exilio e identidad: El caso de los chilenos de Montreal, Canadá, observaciones preliminaries," *Revista Universum* 17 (2002): 72–75.

60. For an overview of Vázquez's career, see Laura Senio Blair, "Atravesando continentes y océanos: La obra fílmica de Angelina Vázquez," in *Nomadías: El cine de Marilú Mallet, Valeria Sarmiento y Agelina Vázquez* (Santiago: Metales Pesados, 2016), 181–206; Elizabeth Ramírez-Soto and Catalina Donoso Pinto, introducción to *Nomadías*, 13–37; and Elizabeth Ramírez-Soto, "Journeys of desexilio," 444–46.

61. Frank Padrón, "Angelina Vázquez: El cine chileno está vivo," *Cine Guía* 3, no. 3 (1981): 4.

62. Letter from Pablo Perelman to Angelina Vázquez, Santiago, November 1979, Angelina Vázquez, personal archive.

63. For an analysis of this film, see chapter 5.

64. Letter from Angelina Vázquez to APTA, Madrid, July 1985, 1, Angelina Vázquez, personal archive.

65. Letter from Angelina Vázquez to APTA, 3.

66. Naficy, "Between Rocks and Hard Places," 132.

67. A similar instance of labor and collaboration in exile was Antonio Skármeta's diary film *Wenn wir zusammen lebten* ... (*If We Lived Together* ..., West Germany, 1983). See chapter 5 for a detailed analysis.

68. "Entrevista con Angelina Vázquez," 3, Cineteca Universidad de Chile—Fondo Zuzana Pick.

69. For the relationship between Mikkonen and Vázquez, see Ramírez Soto, "Journeys of *desexilio*," 445. For Vázquez and ideas of friendship and collaboration more broadly, see Elizabeth Ramírez-Soto, "Why Didn't You Write to Me? On Friendship, Exile, and Transnational Collaboration," in *Feminist Worldmaking and the Moving Image*, ed. Erika Balsom, Hila Peleg, and Haus der Kulturen der Welt (Cambridge, MA: MIT Press, 2022), 267–85.

70. Angelina Vázquez, "Apuntes Nicaragüenses," Cineteca Universidad de Chile—Fondo Zuzana Pick.

71. Vázquez, "Apuntes Nicaragüenses."

72. See Brenez, "Political Cinema Today"; and this book's introduction.

73. Djagalov, *From Internationalism to Postcolonialism*, 208.

74. Rodrigo Gonçalves, *Imágenes de un retrato cinematográfico* (Santiago: J. C. Sáez, 2013), 29–36.

75. For more on Chaskel's didactic shorts in Cuba, see Andrea Chignoli and Catalina Donoso Pinto, *(Des)montando fábulas: El documental político de Pedro Chaskel* (Santiago: Uqbar, 2013).

76. See the discussion of the exilic super production in chapter 1, and Silva, *Cinema, política e exílio*, 113–19, 182–97.

77. Eline van Ommen, *Nicaragua Must Survive: Sandinista Revolutionary Diplomacy in the Global Cold War* (Oakland: University of California Press, 2023), 26.

78. Ana Daniela Nahmad Rodríguez, "Mexicans in Nicaragua: Revolution and Propaganda in Sandinista Documentaries of the University Center for Cinematographic Studies (CUEC-UNAM)," trans. Ana M. López, *Studies in Spanish & Latin American Cinemas* 17, no. 2 (2020): 235. See also John Hess, "Nicaragua and El Salvador: Origins of Revolutionary National Cinemas," in *New Latin American Cinema*, 2:193–208; and John Ramírez, "Introduction to the Sandinista Documentary Cinema," in *New Latin American Cinema*, 2:209–14.

79. See, among others, Carole Isaacs and Julia Lesage, "Learning from Our Compañeras," *Voices from Nicaragua: A U.S.-Based Journal of Culture in Reconstruction* 1, nos. 2–3 (1983): 3–6, 47–48; and Alfonso Gumucio Dragón, "Cine obrero Sandinista," in *Cuadernos de Comunicación Alternativa no. 1* (La Paz: CIMCA, 1983), 21–28.

80. Jonathan Buchsbaum, *Cinema and the Sandinistas: Filmmaking in Revolutionary Nicaragua* (Austin: University of Texas Press, 2003), offers a detailed history of Nicaragua's National Film Institute (INCINE), but dedicates few pages to the work of women and foreign filmmakers (other than the Cubans,

whose ICAIC functioned as a model for INCINE). Djagalov's *From Internationalism to Postcolonialism* includes Nicaragua in his transnational history of solidarity, but to a lesser extent than other territories. Recent work on internationalist cinema in Nicaragua includes Nahmad Rodríguez, "Mexicans in Nicaragua," 233–51; Marina Cavalcanti Tedesco, "Cineastas brasileñas que filmaron la revolución: Helena Solberg y Lucia Murat," *Cine Documental* 17 (2018): 24–41; María Lourdes Cortés, "Historia del cine nicaragüense," in *Diccionario del Cine Iberoamericano: España, Portugal y América*, tomo 6, ed. Joao Bénard da Costa, Iván Giroud, Carlos F. Heredero, and Eduardo Rodríguez Merchán (Madrid: SGAE, 2011), 267–72; and Claudia Ferman, "Mi país era América Latina: Testimonio de Jorge Denti, cineasta de la Revolución Sandinista," *Istmo. Revista virtual de estudios literarios y culturales centroamericanos* 20 (2010): 1–21.

81. For a history of the Nicaraguan revolution and the FSLN, see Salvador Martí I Puig and Carlos Figueroa Ibarra, *La izquierda revolucionaria en Centroamérica: De la lucha armada a la participación electoral* (Barcelona: Los Libros de la Catarata, 2006), 1–28; Mateo Jarquín, *The Sandinista Revolution: A Global Latin American History* (Chapel Hill: University of North Carolina Press, 2024); and van Ommen, *Nicaragua Must Survive*.

82. Djagalov, *From Internationalism to Postcolonialism*, 181.

83. Ernesto Cardenal, *The Gospel in Solentiname*, trans. Donald D. Walsh (Eugene: Wipf and Stock Publishers, 2010); and Mee-Ae Kim, "Liberation and Theology: A Pedagogical Challenge," *The History Teacher* 46, no. 4 (2013): 601–12.

84. Peter Kornbluh, "The Covert War," in *Reagan Versus the Sandinistas: The Undeclared War on Nicaragua*, ed. Thomas W. Walker (New York: Routledge, 1987).

85. Luis Ospina and Carlos Mayolo, "¿Qué es la pornomiseria?," accessed July 23, 2024, https://geografiavirtual.com/wp-content/uploads/2023/03/la-pornomiseria.webp.

CHAPTER 3. A FILM FESTIVAL ROAD MAP

1. Villarroel and Mardones, *Señales contra el olvido*, 85–86; and FIPRESCI, "20th International Short Film Festival Oberhausen," accessed July 23, 2024, https://fipresci.org/festival/20th-international-short-film-festival-oberhausen/.

2. Villarroel and Mardones, *Señales contra el olvido*, 87. This manifesto was similar to the "Stockholm Declaration" issued by Chilean filmmakers on February 1, 1974. See "Stockholm Declaration," *Cinéaste* 6, no. 2 (1974): 59.

3. Elena Razlogova, "World Cinema at Soviet Festivals: Cultural Diplomacy and Personal Ties," *Studies in European Cinemas* 17, no. 2 (2020): 142.

4. Cannes's Semaine international de la critique française (International Critics' Week) in 1974 programmed Miguel Littín's *La tierra prometida* (The Promised Land, 1973). That same year, the Quinzaine des réalisateurs (Directors' Fortnight) screened the Chilean films *Hay que matar al general* (The General Must Be Killed, Enrique Urteaga, 1972)—also known as *Operación Alfa*—and *La expropiación* (The Expropriation, Raúl Ruiz, 1971/1974). The

1975 and 1976 editions of the Quinzaine screened the first and second parts of Patricio Guzmán's *The Battle of Chile* (1975 and 1976). The main competition at Cannes in 1978 included *El recurso del método (¡Viva el Presidente!)* (The Recourse to the Method, Miguel Littin, 1978). In 1983 the Quinzaine turned once again to Guzmán's work with *La rosa de los vientos* (The Compass Rose, 1983). See FEST RES 115, Semaine internationale de la critique française, Cannes, 13, 1974; Quinzaine des réalisateurs, Cannes, 6, 7, 8, and 15 (1974, 1975, 1976, and 1983); and Festival international du film, Cannes, 31, 1978, Cinémathéque française. See also Carolina Amaral de Aguiar, "Cinema latino-americano, festivais europeus e redes de solidariedade," *Tempo e Argumento* 14, no. 35 (2022): 15–16.

5. The 1982 edition of the International Film Festival Rotterdam (IFFR) had a special focus on Rául Ruiz. Locarno, in turn, placed him on the map of world cinema in 1968 when *Tres tristes tigres* (Three Sad Tigers) won the Golden Leopard—the festival's top prize.

6. Villarroel and Mardones, *Señales contra el olvido*, 48–65; 85–117; and 149–159. See also Arsenal Institute for Film and Video, "The Berlinale Forum Archive 1971–2023," accessed July 23, 2024, www.arsenal-berlin.de/en/forum-forum-expanded/archive/.

7. For a recent example of an excellent study of solidarity and film festivals focusing on one single film, *The Battle of Chile*, see Carolina Amaral de Aguiar, "Cinéma et solidarité internationale: *La Bataille du Chili* dans les festivals," *Iberic@l: Revue d'études ibériques et ibéro-américaines* 23 (2023): 1–13.

8. Eshun and Gray, "Militant Image," 1.

9. Eshun and Gray, "Militant Image," 1.

10. For the original notion of contact zone, see Mary Louise Pratt, *Imperial Eyes: Travel Writing and Transculturation*, 2nd ed. (1992; New York: Routledge, 2008), 8. For its use in film festival studies, see Kathleen Newman, "Notes on Transnational Film Theory: Decentered Subjectivity, Decentered Capitalism," in *World Cinemas, Transnational Perspectives*, ed. Nataša Ďurovičová and Kathleen Newman (New York: Routledge, 2010), 9–10; and Masha Salazkina and Rossen Djagolov, "Tashkent '68: A Cinematic Contact Zone," *Slavic Review* 75, no. 2 (2016): 279–98.

11. Pick, "Chilean Cinema: Ten Years of Exile (1973–1983)."

12. "Resolutions of the Third World Filmmakers Meeting. Algiers, Dec. 5–14 (1973)," in *New Latin American Cinema*, 1:258 and 260. Chilean exile Sergio Castilla was part of the Committee 2: Production/Co-production group, which drafted that recommendation.

13. Mariano Mestman, "From Algiers to Buenos Aires: The Third World Cinema Committee (1973–74)," *New Cinemas: Journal of Contemporary Film* 1, no. 1 (2002): 43.

14. See chapter 1, 48.

15. Mestman, "Estados generales del tercer cine," 28; Rencontres internationales pour un nouveau cinéma in Montréal, *Cahier no. 1: Projets et résolutions*, 29–42, and "Programme." See also Buchsbaum, "Militant Third World Film Distribution," 51–65.

16. "Declaración del encuentro de cineastas latinoamericanos en Caracas," in *Por un cine latinoamericano: Encuentro de cineastas latinoamericanos en solidaridad con el pueblo y los cineastas de Chile, Caracas, Septiembre de 1974* (Caracas: Rocinante, 1974), 9–13.

17. See the section "From Revolution to Exile" in this book's introduction for more context on the different dictatorships in the Southern Cone.

18. "Declaración del encuentro de cineastas latinoamericanos," 13.

19. "Declaración del encuentro de cineastas latinoamericanos," 13.

20. Introducción to *Por un cine latinoamericano*, 7. For the discursive centrality of the denunciations of the Latin American coups in Caracas, see Salazkina, *World Socialist Cinema*, 108.

21. "Documento de la comisión sobre producción y coproducción," in *Por un cine latinoamericano*, 22. The Chilean manifesto in 1970 declared: "Before filmmakers we are men engaged within the political and social phenomenon of our people." See "Filmmakers and the Popular Government Political Manifesto," in *Chilean Cinema*, 83.

22. Littin, "Fragmentos del informe de la delegación chilena," in *Por un cine latinoamericano*, 32–33. This talk was also reprinted in Miguel Littin, "El cine chileno y la Unidad Popular," *Octubre* 2–3 (1975): 15–22.

23. Littin, "Fragmentos del informe de la delegación chilena," 41. Littin reiterated this idea in an interview: "Entretien avec Miguel Littin," *Cahiers du Cinéma*, no. 251–52 (1974): 61.

24. Littin, "Fragmentos del informe de la delegación chilena," 51.

25. Littin, "Fragmentos del informe de la delegación chilena," 50–51.

26. "Déclaration collective des cinéastes chiliens à Pesaro," *Positif* 164 (December 1974): 42.

27. Cortínez and Engelbert, *Evolución en libertad*, tomo 2, 839.

28. See, for example, Willemen's critique of the "euphoric internationalism" of Pesaro's cultural actors. Paul Willemen, "The Limitations and Strengths of a Cultural Policy," *Framework* 15/17 (1981): 97.

29. Mariano Mestman, "Archivos y documentos del cine político de América Latina: Consideración sobre el devenir de las fuentes," in *Cine chileno y latinoamericano: Antología de un encuentro*, ed. Mónica Villarroel (Santiago: LOM, 2019), 209.

30. Don Ranvaud, "Pesaro Revisited," *Framework* 18 (1982): 34.

31. Mariano Mestman, "From Italian Neorealism to the New Latin American Cinema: Ruptures and Continuities during the 1960s," in *Global Neorealism. The Transnational History of a Film Style*, ed. Robert Sklar and Saverio Giovacchini (Jackson: University Press of Mississippi, 2012), 171.

32. Ranvaud, "Pesaro Revisited," 34.

33. The 1975 program included the exile films *Quisiera, quisiera tener un hijo* (I Wish, I Wish I Had a Son, Sergio Castilla, 1974), *Dulce Patria* (Sweet Homeland, Beatriz González, 1975), *Los puños frente al cañón* (Fists against the Cannons, Orlando Lübbert and Gastón Ancelovici, 1972/1974), *La historia es nuestra y la hacen los pueblos* (History Is Ours and It Is Made by the People, Álvaro Ramírez, 1975), *Nombre de Guerra: Miguel Enríquez* (Nom de guerre:

Miguel Enríquez, Collective, 1974), and the first part of *The Battle of Chile*. See Julianne Burton, "The Old and the New: Latin American Cinema at the (Last?) Pesaro Festival," *Jump Cut* 9 (1975), accessed July 23, 2024, www.ejumpcut.org/archive/onlinessays/JC09folder/PesaroReport.html.

34. Zuzana M. Pick, "Pesaro à l'heure de la lutte contre le fascisme," *Positif* 164 (December 1974): 40.

35. Untitled and anonymous prologue to *Materiali sul cinema cileno: Quaderno informativo 61* (Pesaro: Mostra Internazionale del Nuovo Cinema, 1974), 4.

36. Francesco Bolzoni, "Una testimonianza sul cinema di Allende," in *Materiali sul cinema cileno*, 16.

37. Untitled and anonymous prologue to *Materiali sul cinema cileno*, 5.

38. Patricio Guzmán, "Il cinema cileno nel periodo del governo popolare," in *Materiali sul cinema cileno*, 22. Guzmán's article maintains the kind of political analysis he was developing while editing *The Battle of Chile*, dissecting his study of the Popular Unity in three main categories: ideology, politics, and the economy. Dated "May 1974," it is unclear whether Guzmán's article was written before Littin's in Caracas, or if it was shared among exile filmmakers prior to its translation and publication in the Pesaro booklet. What matters here is the absolute coincidence between the two and their almost simultaneous public release. For the Spanish version, see Patricio Guzmán, "Breve análisis del cine chileno durante el gobierno popular, 1970–1973," in *Hojas de cine: Testimonios y documentos del nuevo cine latinoamericano* (Mexico City: Secretaría de Educación Pública, Universidad Autónoma Metropolitana/Fundación Mexicana de Cineastas, 1988), 1:331–339.

39. Guzmán, "Il cinema cileno nel periodo del governo popolare," 23.

40. Cáceres, *Los años chilenos de Raúl Ruiz*, 295–98.

41. Cáceres, *Los años chilenos de Raúl Ruiz*, 297.

42. Cáceres narrates that in Pesaro, a group of Chileans asked Ruiz to burn the film's negative. Another tale goes like this: after Pesaro, a cell of MIR militants instructed the stealing of the print and the kidnapping of Ruiz. This "myth" is particularly ironic as one of the storylines in *Dialogues of Exiles* revolves around a group of exiles kidnapping a conservative Chilean singer in Paris. See Cáceres, *Los años chilenos de Raúl Ruiz*, 297, 301.

43. ["Week of Anti-Fascist Cinema, Volgograd, 1975"], f. 3064, op. 1, d. 150, l. 15, RGALI. I thank Elena Razlogova for generously sharing archival documents related to the Volgograd festival. See also Salazkina, *World Socialist Cinema*, 110.

44. Salazkina, *World Socialist Cinema*, 110.

45. Salazkina, *World Socialist Cinema*, 103.

46. Djagolov, *From Internationalism to Postcolonialism*, 168.

47. Salazkina, *World Socialist Cinema*, 108.

48. Razlogova, "World Cinema at Soviet Festivals," 140–54; Elena Razlogova, "Cinema in the Spirit of Bandung: The Afro-Asian Film Festival Circuit, 1957–1964," in *The Cultural Cold War and the Global South*, ed. Kerry Bystrom, Monica Popescu, and Katherine Zien (New York: Routledge, 2021); Elena Razlogova, "The Liberation Politics of Live Translation," *JCMS: Journal of Cinema and Media Studies* 59, no. 4 (2020): 183–88; Salazkina, *World*

Socialist Cinema; Djagolov, *From Internationalism to Postcolonialism*; and Salazkina and Djagolov, "Tashkent '68."

49. Razlogova, "World Cinema at Soviet Festivals," 144.
50. Djagolov, *From Internationalism to Postcolonialism*, 160.
51. Salazkina, *World Socialist Cinema*, 110.
52. Their conversation was transcribed and published one year later in the exile journal *Araucaria de Chile*. See "Orientación y perspectivas del cine chileno," *Araucaria de Chile* 11 (1980): 119–36.
53. Gabriel himself often used Littín's films as examples in his essays. See Teshome Gabriel, "Third Cinema as Guardian of Popular Memory: Towards a Third Aesthetics," in *Questions of Third Cinema*, ed. Jim Pines and Paul Willemen (London: BFI, 1989), 56–59.
54. For a more detailed analysis of this roundtable and conceptual opposition, see José Miguel Palacios, "Resistance vs. Exile."
55. "Orientación y perspectivas del cine chileno," 123–25.
56. "Orientación y perspectivas del cine chileno," 133.
57. *Festival Internacional del Nuevo Cine Latinoamericano, La Habana, Cuba, 1979—1988* (Havana: ICAIC, 1988), 13.
58. *Festival Internacional del Nuevo Cine Latinoamericano*.
59. See, among others, Del Valle Dávila, *Cámaras en trance*, 21; and Ana M. López, "An 'Other' History: The New Latin American Cinema," *Radical History Review* 41 (1988): 110.
60. *Festival Internacional del Nuevo Cine Latinoamericano*, 13.
61. *Por un cine latinoamericano, V Encuentro de cineastas latinoamericanos: Mérida 1977*, (Caracas: Rocinante, 1978), 6.
62. *Festival Internacional del Nuevo Cine Latinoamericano*, 15–17.
63. *Festival Internacional del Nuevo Cine Latinoamericano*, 18.
64. *Festival Internacional del Nuevo Cine Latinoamericano*, 21–22.
65. *Festival Internacional del Nuevo Cine Latinoamericano*, 21.
66. *Festival Internacional del Nuevo Cine Latinoamericano*, 20.
67. *Festival Internacional del Nuevo Cine Latinoamericano*, 13–14.
68. Caroline Moine, "Gone with the Eastern Wind: Glasnot in 1980s East European Film," *Film International* 8, no. 2 (2004): 6. See also Moine, *Screened Encounters*, 1–16.
69. Victor Grossman, "Left-Wing Documentaries at Leipzig Film Festival," *Cinéaste* 8, no. 4 (1978): 51.
70. Villarroel and Mardones, *Señales contra el olvido*, 120.
71. Retrospektive "Film im Freiheitskampf der Völker: Chile," BArch DR 140-299/DR 140-365. I am grateful to Isabel Mardones for sharing copies of parts of these archival materials with me.
72. In the daily bulletin published by the festival, a statement notes the difficulty of communicating with filmmakers and archives, and especially the difficulty of getting prints, as they were spread across too many countries. "In this process, not all our wishes came true." See "Retrospective Opened," *Festival Journal*, 26 Internationale Leipziger Dokumentar- und Kurzfilmwoche für Kino und Fernsehen, Deutsche Kinemathek.

73. "Letter from Manfred Lichtenstein to Volodia Teitelboim," BArch DR 140-299/DR 140-365.

74. "Letter from Gastón Ancelovici to Manfred Lichtenstein," BArch DR 140-299/DR 140-365.

75. "Letter from Manfred Lichtenstein to Valeria Sarmiento," BArch DR 140-299/DR 140-365.

76. Manfred Lichtenstein and Gerd Meier, eds., *Film im Freiheitskampf der Völker: Chile* (Berlin: Staatliches Filmarchiv der DDR, 1983), 2–3.

77. The Chilean exile films shown in the Leipzig special program were Álvaro Ramírez's *Lota '73* (1977) and *Los libertadores* (1978); *A los pueblos del mundo* (Latin American Film Project, 1975) and *Miguel Enríquez: El color de la sangre no se olvida* (Collective, 1975); *Fists against the Cannons*; the three parts of *The Battle of Chile*; Patricio Castilla's *La piedra crece donde cae la gota* (1977); *Message from Chile*; *Eyes Like My Dad*; Gonzalo Justiniano's *Inti Illimani: Une expérience de vie* (1981); Patricio Paniagua's *Quilapayún, peregrinos de la música* (1981); and Leutén Rojas's *Compañeros: Con las cuerdas de mi guitarra* (1981). There were two other exile films that played in Leipzig 1983 as part of the main competition: Carlos Puccio's *Cachencho* (1983) and Colectivo Cine Ojo's *Chile, no invoco tu nombre en vano* (1983)—the latter received a special prize from the jury. I have assembled this list by contrasting the following sources: "Preisträger 1983," *Festival Journal*, and "Protokoll," 26 Internationale Leipziger Dokumentar- und Kurzfilmwoche für Kino und Fernsehen; and Lichtenstein and Meier, *Film im Freiheitskampf der Völker*. See also Villarroel and Mardones, *Señales contra el olvido*, 197–98.

78. In the opening ceremony, Gastón Ancelovici gave a short speech about the overall situation of Chilean cinema both in Chile and in exile, followed by an "enthusiastic" musical performance by Dean Reed—a frequent Leipzig guest. See "Retrospective Opened" in *Festival Journal*.

79. José Agustín Mahieu, "Diálogo cultural entre España e Iberoamérica," *Cuadernos Hispanoamericanos* 390 (December 1982): 667–68; Festival Internacional de Cine de Huelva, "Ediciones anteriores," accessed July 23, 2024, https://festicinehuelva.com/ediciones-anteriores; Francisco Griñán, "50 años del festival que desafió la censura," accessed July 23, 2024, www.diariosur.es/sur-historia/anos-festival-desafio-20190224214048-nt.html; and Filmoteca Española/Festival de Cine Alcalá de Henares, *Raúl Ruiz* (Alcalá de Henares: Cine Club Nebrija de Alcalá de Henares y Filmoteca Nacional, 1983).

80. Mahieu, "Diálogo cultural entre España e Iberoamérica," 667–68.

81. Festival Internacional de Cine de San Sebastián, *ABC de América Latina* (San Sebastián: Quinto Centenario/Festival Internacional de Cine de San Sebastián, 1988).

82. The list of exile films and videos screened as part of the Chilean retrospective in San Sebastián 1987 included the U-matic videos *Testimonio Valenzuela* (Jorge Triviño, France, 1986), *Frente Patriótico Manuel Rodríguez* (Jorge Triviño, France, 1986), and *Chile, la cultura necesaria* (Orlando Lübbert, GFR, 1986); 16mm prints of *En nombre de Dios* (Patricio Guzmán, 1987), *Dulce Patria* (Juan Andrés Racz, Chile/Canada, 1985), *No eran nadie* (Sergio Bravo, Chile/France, 1982), *Ardiente paciencia* (Antonio Skármeta, GFR, 1983), and *Mémoires d'une*

guerre cotidienne (Gastón Ancelovici, Canada, 1986); and 35mm prints of *Queridos compañeros* (Pablo de la Barra, Chile/Venezuela, 1973/1978), *El paso* (Orlando Lübbert, GDR, 1978), *Prisioneros desaparecidos* (Sergio Castilla, Sweden/Cuba, 1979), and *El jaguar* (Sebastián Alarcón, Soviet Union, 1986).

83. Tatiana Gaviola, based in Chile, was the only woman included in the retrospective, with her short video *Yo no le tengo miedo a nada* (1984). See *XXXV Festival Internacional de Cine de San Sebastián* (San Sebastián: Festival Internacional de Cine de San Sebastián, 1987), 195–215.

84. Ulloa, *Video independiente en Chile*.

85. *XXXV Festival Internacional de Cine de San Sebastián*, 197.

86. The festival's archive can be found at Festival Internacional de Cine de San Sebastián, *Artxiboa*, accessed July 23, 2024, https://artxiboa.sansebastianfestival.com/?_gl=1*13y2jw2*_ga*MTIwNjU4Njg4LjE2ODY5MzUoOTA.*_ga_9SV35XL570*MTY5MDU2MDcwOS4xMC4xLjE2OTA1NjA3MzMu MC4wLjA.

87. Paulo Antonio Paranaguá, "Imágenes del exilio," *Diario del XXXV Festival Internacional de Cine de San Sebastián* 4 (September 20, 1987): 8; and Patricia García Ríos, "Chile: The Final Resurrection," *Diario del XXXV Festival Internacional de Cine de San Sebastián* 5 (September 21, 1987): 22.

88. Carmen Ruiz de Garibay, "Sergio Bravo: Desde Francia con Chile," *Diario del XXXV Festival Internacional de Cine de San Sebastián* 4 (September 20, 1987): 9.

89. Carmen Ruiz de Garibay, "Hernán Castro: El arte del documental comprometido," *Diario del XXXV Festival Internacional de Cine de San Sebastián* 2 (September 18, 1987): 12; and "Patricio Guzmán: En nombre de Chile," *Diario del XXXV Festival Internacional de Cine de San Sebastián* 9 (September 25, 1987): 8.

90. This list may not be accurate, as there are inconsistencies in the festival's reporting. A short piece published on the day of the panel but before it took place indicated that directors Sebastián Alarcón and Sergio Castilla would be present, but their names are excluded from the article published the day after the event. See "Realizadores chilenos: Juntos otro Septiembre," *Diario del XXXV Festival Internacional de Cine de San Sebastián* 7 (September 23, 1987): 9; and "El cine y el exilio chilenos," *Diario del XXXV Festival Internacional de Cine de San Sebastián* 8 (September 24, 1987): 7. I have used the list of panelists included in the latter, which is the same one that the official catalog of the festival's archive uses to annotate a photograph of the event. See "Distintos cineastas durante la rueda de prensa por la Retrospectiva Chile," Fondo Fotográfico, Fl0047, Festival Internacional de Cine de San Sebastián. It is not clear who G. Navarro is.

91. "El cine y el exilio chilenos," 7.

92. Willemen, "Limitations and Strengths of a Cultural Policy," 96.

CHAPTER 4. CINEMAS OF RESISTANCE, CINEMAS OF EXILE

1. Carla Macchiavello, "Weaving Forms of Resistance: The Museo de la Solidaridad and The Museo Internacional de la Resistencia Salvador Allende," *Arts* 9, no. 12 (2020): 3.

2. A catalog of donations can be found in *Museo de la solidaridad Chile: Fraternidad, Arte y Política 1971–1973* (Santiago: MSSA, 2013), 140–280.

3. Comité Internacional de Solidaridad Artística con Chile, "Declaración," in *A los Artistas del Mundo/To the Artists of the World: Museo de la Solidaridad Salvador Allende México/Chile 1971–1977* (Mexico City: MUAC, 2016), 53.

4. "Antecedentes del museo," in *Museo Internacional de la Resistencia Salvador Allende. Cuatro Años de Actividades* (Havana: MIRSA, 1979), 6.

5. Carla Macchiavello, "A Case of Collective Resistance: Museo de la Solidaridad Salvador Allende," in *A los Artistas del Mundo*, 85–86.

6. Macchiavello, "Weaving Forms of Resistance," 10.

7. "Antecedentes del museo," 6.

8. Francisco Moreno Galván, "Untitled," in *Chile-País Valencià* (Valencia: Conselleria de Cultura del País Valencià, 1978), 3. The word *momio* was a popular term to connote the conservatism and reactionary nature of the upper classes that rejected Allende's transformations.

9. The exile film *Färg mot fascismen!* (*Color against Fascism!*, Leonardo Céspedes, Peter Lund, and Kaj Mattson, 1978) documents one of these exhibits at the Moderna Museet in Stockholm in April 1978.

10. Chapter 1 offers a more detailed discussion of Cinemateca Chilena as a transnational archive and about its role in the history of Chilean exile cinema.

11. In her analysis of Cinemateca Chilena, Marcy Campos Pérez reaches a similar conclusion by examining a different set of documents. See Campos Pérez, "Le patrimoine chilien contemporain."

12. See both names in two documents from 1974: Rencontres Internationales pour un Nouveau Cinéma in Montréal, *Cahier no. 1: Projets et résolutions*, 40; and Chaskel, "Informe de la secretaría general de UCAL al VII congreso, Caracas, 1974," 67–68.

13. Villarroel and Mardones, *Señales contra el olvido*, 113; and Ancelovici and Paranaguá, "Cine chileno del exilio," 196.

14. See the exchanges in preparation for the Chilean retrospective organized in Leipzig in 1983 (discussed in chapter 3). BArch DR 140-299/DR 140-365.

15. "Des-exilio del cine chileno: 40 años de la Cinemateca Chilena del Exilio," in *Ciclo de cine sobre el exilio 2014* (Santiago: Museo de la Memoria y los Derechos Humanos, 2014), 8–10; and Villarroel and Mardones, *Señales contra el olvido*, 113.

16. Macchiavello, "Case of Collective Resistance," 86.

17. Jacqueline Mouesca claims that after five years of exile a new set of themes began to emerge, and that by 1983 the cycle of Chilean exile cinema was reaching an end. Peter B. Schumann and José Agustín Mahieu made similar claims. Sometime in the late 1970s, Chilean exile cinema opened to a variety of themes less concerned with Chilean politics. Michael Goddard has argued that the kind of ethnography of exile that Raúl Ruiz was practicing by 1974 would characterize a good deal of Chilean exile cinema, "but only at a later moment in time." Zuzana M. Pick does not make this evolutionary argument; nonetheless, her division of Chilean exile filmmakers into various generations implies that the younger directors show a broader range of thematic and political concerns.

Javier Campo adopts a similar progression for his study on Argentine exile cinema. See Mouesca, *Plano secuencia de la memoria de chile*, 147–55 and "El cine chileno en el exilio," 36; Schumann, "Chilean Cinema in Exile," 13–14; Mahieu, "Cine chileno en el exilio," 241–56; Michael Goddard, *The Cinema of Raúl Ruiz Impossible Cartographies* (New York: Columbia University Press, 2013), 32; Pick, "Chilean Cinema: Ten Years of Exile (1973-1983)"; and Campo, *Revolución y democracia*, 65-7.

18. Campos Pérez, "Le patrimoine chilien contemporain."

19. Chaskel, "Définition," Cineteca Universidad de Chile—Fondo Zuzana M. Pick.

20. Littin, "Fragmentos del informe de la delegación chilena," 50–51.

21. For different understandings of "the people" in Latin American cinema, see Mariano Mestman and Mirta Varela, "Presentación," in *Masas, pueblo, multitud en cine y televisión*, ed. Mariano Mestman and Mirta Varela (Buenos Aires, Eudeba, 2013), 7–17; and Gonzalo Aguilar, "El pueblo como lo 'real': Hacia una genealogía del cine latinoamericano," in *Más allá del pueblo: Imágenes, indicios y políticas del cine* (Buenos Aires: FCE, 2015), 179–94. For Chilean cinema, see Pablo Corro, *Retóricas del cine chileno: Ensayos con el realismo* (Santiago: Cuarto Propio, 2012), 67–76; and Héctor Oyarzún, "Masa y cine: Un ensayo visual," *la Fuga* 21 (2018), accessed July 23, 2024, https://lafuga.cl/masa-y-cine/913.

22. I am thinking here of the way Didi-Huberman conceives of "gestures of uprising" in his curatorial texts for the exhibition *Sublevaciones*. See Georges Didi-Huberman, "Sublevaciones," MUNTREF Centro de Arte Contemporáneo, Buenos Aires, June–August 2017, accessed July 23, 2024, chrome-extension://efaidnbmnnnibpcajpcglclefindmkaj/https://untref.edu.ar/muntref/sublevaciones/assets/gacetilla_didi.pdf.

23. The dichotomy between enclosing or freeing the people in its cinematic representation is developed in Georges Didi-Huberman, *Peuples exposés, peuples figurants* (Paris: Les Éditions de Minuit, 2012), 144.

24. For the idea of the people as community in Chilean cinema, see Carlos Ossa, *El ojo mecánico: Cine político y comunidad en América Latina* (Santiago: FCE, 2013), 11–48.

25. See Octavio Getino, "Militant Cinema: An Internal Category of Third Cinema" and "The Cinema as Political Fact," *Third Text* 25, no. 1 (2011): 52–53, 41.

26. Getino, "Cinema as Political Fact," 41–52.

27. Getino, "Cinema as Political Fact," 42.

28. Carlos Álvarez, "Postulados del tercer cine," in *Cine documental en América Latina*, ed. Paulo Antonio Paranaguá (Madrid: Cátedra, 2003), 466.

29. Santiago Álvarez, "Arte y compromiso," in *Cine documental en América Latina*, 458.

30. Cortínez, *Cine a la chilena*, 49.

31. Palacios and Donoso Pinto, "Infancia y exilio en el cine chileno," 53.

32. The conceptual abstraction of resistance began to acquire iconic presence in the walls of Chile under the form of an R inside a circle in the late 1970s.

People who opposed the dictatorship did not take it as an enigmatic sign; they knew it stood for Resistance. This circled R is captured in the exilic film *Recado de Chile* (Collective, 1979).

33. Nelly Richard, "Destrucción, reconstrucción y deconstrucción," in *Fracturas de la memoria: arte y pensamiento crítico* (Buenos Aires: Siglo XXI Editores, 2007), 32.

34. "Filmmakers and the Popular Government Political Manifesto," in *Chilean Cinema*, 83.

35. Julianne Burton, "The Promised Land," *Film Quarterly* 29, no. 1 (Autumn 1975): 57.

36. Serge Toubiana, "*The Promised Land*: The Power of Speech," trans. Jill Forbes, in *Cahiers du Cinéma*, vol. 4, *1973–1978: History, Ideology, Cultural Struggle*, ed. David Wilson (London: Routledge, 2000), 244.

37. Toubiana, "*The Promised Land*," 245.

38. Toubiana, "*The Promised Land*," 245.

39. Burton, "Promised Land," 57–61; Pascal Bonitzer, "The Voice Keeps Watch," in *Cahiers du Cinéma*, 4:249–51; and Toubiana, "*The Promised Land*," 244.

40. Toubiana, "*The Promised Land*," 245.

41. Jean-Luc Godard, "What Is to Be Done?," trans. Mo Teitelbaum, *Afterimage* 1 (1970): 10–16; and Gabriel, "Third Cinema as Guardian of Popular Memory," 56–59.

42. Pick, "Pesaro à l'heure de la lutte contre le fascisme," 39.

43. Christine Buci-Glucksmann and Fabrice Revault d'Allones, "Entretien avec Raoul Ruiz," in *Raoul Ruiz* (Paris: Éditions Dis Voir, 1987), 84–105.

44. Enrique Lihn y Federico Schopf, "Diálogo con Raúl Ruiz," *Atenea* 500 (2009): 270–72.

45. Lihn y Federico Schopf, "Diálogo con Raúl Ruiz," 276. For a discussion of Ruiz's notion of inquiry, see Cortínez and Engelbert, *La tristeza de los tigres*, 75–81; and Ignacio López-Vicuña and Andreea Marinescu, introduction to *Raúl Ruiz's Cinema of Inquiry* (Detroit: Wayne State University Press, 2017), 9–10.

46. Lihn y Schopf, "Diálogo con Raúl Ruiz," 277.

47. Lihn y Schopf, "Diálogo con Raúl Ruiz," 271.

48. Sergio Salinas et al., "Prefiero registrar antes que mistificar el proceso chileno," in *Ruiz: Entrevistas escogidas—filmografía comentada*, ed. Bruno Cuneo (Santiago: UDP, 2013), 36.

49. Borrowing from Sylvia Harvey, D. N. Rodowick defines "political modernism" as the "desire to combine semiotic and ideological analysis with the development of an avant-garde aesthetic practice dedicated to the production of radical social effects." See D. N. Rodowick, *The Crisis of Political Modernism: Criticism and Ideology in Contemporary Film Theory* (Berkeley: University of California Press, 1988), 1–2. For Latin American cinema, see Tomás Gutiérrez Alea, *Dialéctica del espectador* (Havana: Unión de Escritores y Artistas de Cuba, 1982), 39–51.

50. Lihn y Schopf, "Diálogo con Raúl Ruiz," 276.

51. For a summary of critical readings that interpret exile as a radical break in Ruiz's work, see Cortínez and Engelbert, *La tristeza de los tigres*, 96–8.

52. Andrés Claro, "Los cinco sentidos de Raúl Ruiz," *Pensar & Poetizar* 12 (2015): 138.
53. Salinas et al., "Prefiero registrar antes que mistificar el proceso chileno," 36.
54. Raúl Ruiz, "Aquí van las espuestas que les quedé debiendo," Archivo Ruiz-Sarmiento, RR-43-1-1-6.
55. This brief analysis comes from José Miguel Palacios, "Everything We Are Seeing We Have Already Seen: Citation in the Cinema of Raúl Ruiz," *Screen* 61, no. 4 (2020): 583–84.
56. See Cáceres, *Los años chilenos de Raúl Ruiz*, 284–85.
57. Raúl Ruiz, "Mi pequeña historia de O," in *Ruiz: Entrevistas escogidas*, 196.
58. Ruiz, "Mi pequeña historia de O," 196.
59. See "Conversación con Libération" and "Respuesta a críticas Diálogo de exiliados," Archivo Ruiz-Sarmiento, RR-27-1-4-3 and RR-27-1-4-4.
60. For an account of how critics and filmmakers have conceived this opposition between Littin and Ruiz, and how they have promoted an alleged rivalry between the two, see Cortínez and Engelbert, *Evolución en libertad*, tomo 2, 557–63.
61. Ian Christie and Malcom Coad, "Between Institutions: Interview with Raúl Ruiz," *Afterimage* 10 (1981): 103–5.
62. Pick, "Pesaro à l'heure de la lutte contre le fascisme," 39–40.
63. Palacios, "Everything We Are Seeing," 584.
64. Ramírez-Soto and Donoso Pinto, introducción to *Nomadías*, 32.
65. See Ramírez-Soto, "Women (Not) Making Movies"; and Elizabeth Ramírez-Soto, "'Why Didn't You Write to Me?': On Friendship, Exile, and Transnational Collaboration," in *Feminist Worldmaking and the Moving Image*, ed. Erika Balsom, Hila Peleg, and Haus der Kulturen der Welt (Cambridge, MA: MIT Press, 2022), 267–85.
66. Vania Barraza, "Melodrama, mujeres y mirada en el cine de Valeria Sarmiento," in *Nomadías*, 133–54. See also Mónica Ríos, "La comunidad en el ver: El lente melodramático de Valeria Sarmiento," in *Una mirada oblicua: El cine de Valeria Sarmiento*, ed. Bruno Cuneo and Fernando Pérez Villalón (Santiago: Ediciones Universidad Alberto Hurtado, 2021), 102–19.
67. Daney, "Notre *mariage* tient vraiment bien la route."
68. Zuzana M. Pick, "Entrevista a Valeria Sarmiento," Cineteca Universidad de Chile—Fondo Zuzana Pick.
69. See Ramírez-Soto, "Double Day of Valeria Sarmiento," 168–70; and Elizabeth Ramírez-Soto, "*Habanera*: De fragmentos y retornos inacabados," in *Una mirada oblicua*, 89–101.
70. For a detailed analysis of *El hombre cuando es hombre*, see Pick, *New Latin American Cinema*, 70–75.
71. For the conditions of production of Sarmiento's films and her overall "precarious mobility," see Ramírez-Soto, "Double Day of Valeria Sarmiento," 154–77.
72. Macarena García Moggia, "Una mujer oblicua," in *Una mirada oblicua*, 14–22.

73. For the role of conservative women during the Popular Unity years, see Power, *Right-Wing Women in Chile*.

74. Séance Promotionnelle, GREC, VS-1-1-1-3, Archivo Ruiz-Sarmiento.

75. For an extended discussion of *La femme au foyer*, see José Miguel Palacios, "Beyond Memory: An Introduction," *Film Quarterly* 77, no. 1 (2023): 43–44.

76. For the footage of the bombardment of La Moneda as a representational device that "sutured image and event," see César Barros, "Declassifying the Archive: The Bombardment of La Moneda Palace and the Political Economy of the Image," in *Technology, Literature, and Digital Culture in Latin America*, ed. Matthew Bush and Tania Gentic (New York: Routledge, 2016), 128.

77. The title of González's *J'explique certaines choses* functions as a citation of Neruda's famous poem "Explico algunas cosas," included in his book about the Spanish Civil War, *España en el corazón* (Santiago: Editorial Ercilla, 1937). Fajardo's short film, in turn, was the only one distributed on its own and in French and English versions: *Jours de Fer* and *Steel Blues*.

78. For a more detailed analysis, see José Miguel Palacios, "Del cine chileno del exilio a la inmigración portuguesa en Canadá: Un estudio sobre *Il n'y a pas d'oubli* (1975) y *Les Borges* (1978)," *Archivos de la Filmoteca* 75 (2018): 85–100.

79. Hamid Naficy, *The Making of Exile Cultures: Iranian Television in Los Angeles* (Minneapolis: University of Minnesota Press, 1993), 2. For the notion of poetics in cinema, especially in documentary, see Michael Renov, "Toward a Poetics of Documentary," in *Theorizing Documentary*, ed. Michael Renov (New York: Routledge, 1993), 12–21.

80. Projet *Il n'y a pas d'oubli*, Jorge Fajardo, Marilú Mallet, Rodrigo González, 1974, Cinémathèque québécoise, 1990.0181.13.SC.

81. When asked about the intentions behind the film, González linked theatricality with a form of liturgy and rituality: "I believe in Theatre, in the Ritual of Representation, in the Eucharist." See Alain Ergas, "A) Rodrigo González 'J'explique certaines choses,'" *Cinéma Québec* 4, nos. 9–10 (1975): 20.

82. Projet *Il n'y a pas d'oubli*.

83. Projet *Il n'y a pas d'oubli*.

84. Projet *Il n'y a pas d'oubli*.

85. Writing in the first decade of the twentieth century, Von Gennep conceived three phases for the rites of passage that accompanied every change of social position: separation from the community, the threshold, and reaggregation into the original community. Arnold Von Gennep, *The Rites of Passage* (London, Routledge, 2004), 11. See also Naficy, *Making of Exile Cultures*, xvi, 8.

86. Vásquez and Araujo, *La maldición de Ulises*, 22–68.

87. The authors prefer to speak of transculturation as opposed to "assimilation," which is always conceived from the standpoint of the dominant culture. See Vásquez and Araujo, *La maldición de Ulises*, 250.

88. Pick, "Chilean Cinema in Exile (1973–1986)," 44.

89. Naficy, *Making of Exile Cultures*, 7–10.

90. Projet *Il n'y a pas d'oubli*.

CHAPTER 5. SUBJECTIVITY AND THE UNFINISHED DIARY

1. Patricio Guzmán, "Cine latinoamericano: Exilio, crisis y futuro," *Cine Cubano* 99 (1981): 124.
2. Guzmán, "Cine latinoamericano," 125.
3. Guzmán has claimed that it was only when he finished the third part of *The Battle of Chile* that he went through the depression and sense of loss that most exiles experience years earlier, as soon as they leave the country. "When I completed the film, I realized I was an exile: I had no country, no themes, nowhere to go, no future: I had nothing; I had the film." The paper Guzmán delivered at the Havana symposium is tied both to this immense loss and to the desire for something new, to stop "living off the praise" that *The Battle of Chile* had received. See Avellar, "Bonus: Interview with Patricio Guzmán."
4. See the end of chapter 4 for a discussion of *There Is No Forgetting* and the theory of exile it proposes.
5. Naficy, *Accented Cinema*, 101. See note 13 in the preface for a distinction between *film-letter* and *letter-film*.
6. Pick, *New Latin American Cinema*, 162–63. For a more detailed historical reconstruction of the origins of this letter-film project, see Ramírez-Soto, "'Why Didn't You Write to Me?,'" 267–85. The concept of "cine-dialogue" comes from Mallet, "Les lettres: Scénario," 1979, 4, Cinémathèque québécoise, 1984.0082.26.SC.
7. The history of the unfinished project *Tres por tres*, an omnibus film by Mallet, Sarmiento, and Vázquez, has been narrated in Ramírez-Soto, "Women (Not) Making Movies," 125–46.
8. In the end, Mallet titled her documentary *L'évangile à Solentiname* (The gospel in Solentiname, Canada, 1979).
9. At the time, filmmakers like Mallet preferred the word *feminine* over the more loaded *feminist* label. For Chilean women directors' relationship with feminism, see Ramírez-Soto, "Women (Not) Making Movies," 125–46.
10. Mallet, "Les lettres: Scénario," 2–3.
11. Ramírez-Soto claims that in this first letter, which Sarmiento shot in black and white, she showed parts of her Parisian apartment to her friend Mallet. This 16mm letter appears to be lost, or at least it is yet to be found. See Ramírez-Soto, "'Why Didn't You Write to Me?,'" 273.
12. Mallet, "Les lettres: Scénario," 6.
13. Michael Renov, *The Subject of Documentary* (Minneapolis: University of Minnesota Press, 2004), 105.
14. I have expanded on some of the features of exilic subjectivity in José Miguel Palacios, "Chilean Exile Cinema and Its Homecoming Documentaries," in *Cinematic Homecomings: Exile and Return in Transnational Cinema*, ed. Rebecca Prime (New York: Bloomsbury, 2015), 153.
15. For autobiography, see among many others, P. A. Sitney, "Autobiography in Avant-Garde Film," *Millenium Film Journal* 1, no. 1 (Winter 1977–1978): 60–106; Elizabeth W. Bruss, "Eye for I: Making and Unmaking Autobiography in Film," in *Autobiography: Essays Theoretical and Critical*, ed. James Olney

(Princeton, NJ: Princeton University Press, 1980), 269–320; Philippe Lejeune, "Cine y autobiografía, problemas de vocabulario," in *Cineastas frente al espejo*, ed. Gregorio Martín Gutiérrez (Madrid: T & B, 2008), 13–26; and Michelle Bossy and Constanza Vergara, *Documentales autobiográficos chilenos: memoria y autorrepresentación* (Santiago: Fondo de Fomento Audiovisual del Consejo de la Cultura y las Artes, 2010). For subjective cinema, first-person films, and the cinema of me, see Laura Rascaroli, "Introduction: Subjective Cinema and the I/Eye of the Camera," in *The Personal Camera: Subjective Cinema and the Essay Film* (New York: Columbia University Press, 2014), 1–20; Alisa Lebow, *First Person Jewish* (Minneapolis: University of Minnesota Press, 2008); and Alisa Lebow, ed., *The Cinema of Me: The Self and Subjectivity in First Person Documentary* (New York: Columbia University Press, 2012). For literature and cultural studies, see Sylvia Molloy, *Acto de presencia: La escritura autobiográfica en Hispanoamérica* (Mexico City: FCE, 1996); Nora Catelli, *En la era de la intimidad: Seguido de El espacio autobiográfico* (Rosario, Argentina: Beatriz Viterbo Editora, 2007); and Beatriz Sarlo, *Tiempo pasado: Cultura de la memoria y giro subjetivo; Una discusión* (Buenos Aires: Siglo XXI, 2005).

16. Lebow, introduction to *The Cinema of Me: The Self and Subjectivity in First Person Documentary* (New York: Columbia University Press, 2012), 1.

17. In her account of the origins of the cine-dialogue between Sarmiento and Mallet, Ramírez-Soto also relies on a draft of the project kept by Sarmiento in Paris, a document to which I haven't had access. Ramírez-Soto, "'Why Didn't You Write to Me?,'" 267–85.

18. Mallet, "Les lettres: Scénario," 6.

19. Mallet, "Notes sur *Journal inachevé*," in *Femmes et cinéma québécois*, ed. Louise Carrière (Montreal: Boréal Express, 1983), 264.

20. Ramírez-Soto, "'Why Didn't You Write to Me?,'" 270–71.

21. Pick, *New Latin American Cinema*, 162–63.

22. Lise Gauvin, "La question des journaux intimes," *Études Françaises* 22, no. 3 (1987): 102.

23. If we consider the auto-dialogic through the lens of Mikhail Bakhtin, we could say that dialogism is inherently auto-dialogism. But it is so only if we acknowledge that in the diary the *I* addresses itself already as an other. Mikhail Bakhtin, "Author and Hero in Aesthetic Activity," in *Art and Answerability*, ed. Michael Holquist and Vadim Liapunov (Austin: University of Texas Press, 1990), 164.

24. Letter from Angelina Vázquez to Pablo Perelman, Helsinki, 1983, 1, Angelina Vázquez, personal archive.

25. Ramírez-Soto, "Journeys of *Desexilio*, 444.

26. Brenda Longfellow, "Feminist Writing in *Journal inachevé* and *Strass Café*," in *Words and Moving Images: Essays on Verbal and Visual Expression in Film and Television*, ed. William C. Wees and Michael Dorland (Montreal: Mediatexte, 1984), 86.

27. Nora Catelli, "El diario íntimo: Una posición femenina," in *En la era de la intimidad*, 51.

28. Stella Bruzzi, *New Documentary: A Critical Introduction* (London: Routledge, 2000), 66.

29. Bruzzi, *New Documentary*, 66.
30. Longfellow, "Feminist Writing in *Journal inachevé* and *Strass Café*," 80.
31. Pick had already noted this in her discussion of the film, in which she proposed to distinguish between "the authorial self (Mallet as producer and director) and the performing self (Marilú as main protagonist) of the film." Pick, *New Latin American Cinema*, 163.
32. Ramírez-Soto noted this as well in "Journeys of *Desexilio*," 445.
33. Palacios, "Chilean Exile Cinema and Its Homecoming Documentaries," 161.
34. Gonzalo Aguilar uses this expression ("vicarious self") to refer to the difficulties of defining the person in first-person films, insofar as the *I* is always in struggle with someone (parents, friends, family members) and something else (the social, the political, the historical). Gonzalo Aguilar, "The Documentary: Between Reality and Fiction, Between First and Third Person," in *New Argentine and Brazilian Cinema: Reality Effects*, ed. Jens Andermann and Manuel Álvarez Bravo (New York: Palgrave, 2013), 209.
35. The voice-over narration for the film was cowritten with writer Jean-Yves Collette and later published as a booklet authored by him. On the back cover, Collette defines the text as a preproduction document of *Unfinished Diary*, the result of ten days of work in June 1980. See Jean-Yves Collette, *Chère Valéria: Trame narrative du film Journal inachevé, de Marilú Mallet*, accessed July 23, 2024, chrome-extension://efaidnbmnnnibpcajpcglclefindmkaj/https://www.jycollette-bibliographie.org/src/pdf/CHERE%20VALERIA.pdf.
36. Longfellow, "Feminist Writing in *Journal inachevé* and *Strass Café*," 89.
37. Longfellow, "Feminist Writing in *Journal inachevé* and *Strass Café*," 86.
38. "Marilú Mallet: Un voyage par des états d'âme", *Format cinéma* 25 (March 1983): 3.
39. Bruzzi, *New Documentary*, 185.
40. Bruzzi, *New Documentary*, 186.
41. Seth Feldman, "Circling I's: Some Implications of the Filmmaker's Presence in Michael Rubbo's *Margaret Atwood: Once in August* and Marilú Mallet's *Journal inachevé*," in *Dialogue: cinéma canadien et québécois/Canadian and Quebec Cinema*, ed. Pierre Véronneau, Michael Dorland, and Seth Feldman (Montreal: Mediatexte/Cinémathèque québecoise, 1987), 249–51.
42. Feldman, "Circling I's: Some Implications of the Filmmaker's Presence," 250.
43. This confessional tone was already noted in Iván Pinto, "Lo incompleto: Desajuste y fractura en dos diarios fílmicos del exilio chileno," in *Prismas del cine latinoamericano*, ed. Wolfgang Bongers (Santiago, Chile: Cuarto Propio, 2012), 221.
44. Bakhtin claimed that confession, "an accounting rendered to oneself for one's own life," was "the first essential form of verbal objectification of life and personality." Bakhtin, "Author and Hero in Aesthetic Activity," 141.
45. Renov, *Subject of Documentary*, 194.
46. Iván Pinto suggests that this "breathing between the shots" marks the tone of the film. Pinto, "Lo incompleto," 220.
47. Ramírez-Soto, "Journeys of *Desexilio*," 446.

48. Catelli, "El diario íntimo," 45–58.
49. The exception is painter Cecilia Boisier, even though *If We Lived Together*... shows her paintings more than it shows her.
50. Sitney, "Autobiography in Avant-Garde Film," 65.
51. Sitney, "Autobiography in Avant-Garde Film," 103.
52. Lebow, introduction, 3. See also Bakhtin, "Author and Hero in Aesthetic Activity," 150–166; and Catelli, "Zombies en la academia," in *En la era de la intimidad*, 66.
53. Ramírez-Soto suggests that Mallet's *Unfinished Diary* also needs to be understood in terms of an expanded authorship including producer Dominique Pinel, cinematographer Guy Borremans, and cowriter Jean-Yves Colette. See Ramírez-Soto, "Why Didn't You Write to Me," 280–81.
54. Cristiá, *AIDA*, 24–25.
55. For Skármeta's collaborations with Lilienthal, see Sandberg, *Peter Lilienthal*, 60–136 and 173–79.
56. Rojo, *Crítica del exilio*, 116–39.
57. Fernando de Toro and Oscar Castro, "Entrevista de Fernando de Toro con Oscar Castro del Teatro Aleph," *Iberoamericana* 2/3 (1984): 153. See also Cristiá, *AIDA*, 25–26, for a detailed discussion of networks of solidarity supporting Castro and his Aleph group, and for the collective authorship behind the play.
58. Edward Said, "Reflections on Exile," in *Reflections on Exile and Other Essays* (Cambridge, MA: Harvard University Press, 2002), 177.
59. Catelli, introducción to *En la era de la intimidad*, 9.
60. Umberto Eco, *The Open Work*, trans. Anna Cancogni, with introduction by David Robey (1962; Cambridge, MA: Harvard University Press, 1989). I thank Masha Salazkina for pushing me to make this contextualization.
61. For inconclusion and militant films, see chapter 4, as well as Getino, "Cinema as Political Fact," 42.
62. Ramírez-Soto, "'Why Didn't You Write to Me?,'" 269.
63. Ramírez-Soto, "'Why Didn't You Write to Me?,'" 278–79.
64. Letter from Angelina Vázquez to Zuzana Pick, ca. 1983, Cineteca Universidad de Chile—Fondo Zuzana Pick.
65. Alix Beeston and Stefan Solomon, introduction to *Incomplete: The Feminist Possibilities of the Unfinished Film*, ed. Alix Beeston and Stefan Salomon (Oakland: University of California Press, 2023), 11.
66. See Ramírez-Soto, "'Why Didn't You Write to Me?,'" 267–85.

CHAPTER 6. A PLURALITY OF CINEMATIC HOMECOMINGS

1. Rebecca Prime, introduction to *Cinematic Homecomings: Exile and Return in Transnational Cinema*, ed. Rebecca Prime (New York: Bloomsbury, 2015), 1.
2. Naficy, *Accented Cinema*, 229.
3. Among others, see Eugenia Neves, "Vivir en París: Testimonios de un exilio," *Araucaria de Chile* 9 (1980): 157–70; María Angélia Celedón and Luz María Opazo, *Volver a empezar* (Santiago: Pehuén, 1987); Jaime Llambías-Wolff, *Notre exil pour parler: Les chiliens au Québéc* (Montreal, Fides, 1988);

Loreto Rebolledo, *Memorias del desarraigo: Testimonios de exilio y retorno de hombres y mujeres de Chile* (Santiago: Catalonia, 2006); Vásquez and Araujo, *La maldición de Ulises*; Mili Rodríguez Villouta, *Ya nunca me verás como me vieras: Doce testimonios vivos del exilio* (Santiago: Ediciones del Ornitorrinco, 1990); Wright and Oñate, *Flight from Chile*; and MMDH, "Memorias de exilio," accessed July 23, 2024, www.memoriasdeexilio.cl/.

4. Nicolás Prognon, "La diáspora chilena en Francia: De la acogida a la integración (1973 a 1994)," in *Exiliados, emigrados y retornados: Chilenos en América y Europa, 1973–2004*, ed. José Del Pozo Artigas (Santiago: RIL, 2006), 82.

5. Loreto Rebolledo, "Memorias del des/exilio," in *Exiliados, emigrados y retornados*, 167.

6. The oxymoronic nature of "after exile" has been discussed in Prime, introduction, 1; and Amy K. Kaminsky, *After Exile: Writing the Latin American Diaspora* (Minneapolis: University of Minnesota Press, 1999), 2–3, even if the author retains the paradoxes of the phrase for her book's title.

7. Mario Benedetti, *El desexilio y otras conjeturas* (Madrid: El País, 1984), 39–42. See also Ramírez Soto, "Journeys of *Desexilio*," 439.

8. Palacios, "Chilean Exile Cinema and Its Homecoming Documentaries," 153.

9. Aguirre and Chamorro, *"L": Memoria gráfica del exilio chileno*.

10. Wright and Oñate, *Flight from Chile*, 171.

11. Gaillard, *Exils et retours*, 13.

12. Mario Garcés and Nancy Nichols, *Para una historia de los DD.HH. en Chile: Historia institucional de la Fundación de Ayuda Social de las Iglesias Cristianas FASIC 1975–1991* (Santiago: LOM/FASIC, 2005), 182.

13. Among these are Vicaría de la Solidaridad, Comisión Chilena de Derechos Humanos, FASIC, Protección de la Infancia Dañada por los Estados de Emergencia (PIDEE; Protection of Youth Damaged by States of Emergency), and Hogar Juvenil "El Encuentro." Organizations that did not have ties to the Church and that played an important role in aiding the return of exiles were the World University Service (WUS) and the International Organization for Migration (IOM).

14. United Nations, "Universal Declaration of Human Rights," accessed July 23, 2024, http://www.un.org/en/universal-declaration-human-rights/.

15. See, for instance, Comité Pro-Retorno de Exiliados, *Documento Presentado a la Organización de las Naciones Unidas* (Santiago: Comité Pro-Retorno de Exiliados, 1980).

16. Gaillard, *Exils et retours*, 13. See also "El país debe indemnizar a los exiliados," *El Mercurio*, August 29, 1983.

17. Wright and Oñate, *Flight from Chile*, 172.

18. Wright and Oñate, *Flight from Chile*, 172.

19. Wright and Oñate, *Flight from Chile*, 174.

20. Vásquez and Araujo, *La maldición de Ulises*, 29.

21. Rebolledo, "Memorias del des/exilio," 172.

22. Prognon, "La diáspora chilena en Francia," 82–83; and Wright and Oñate, *Flight from Chile*, 200.

23. Sergio Trabucco Ponce, *Con los ojos abiertos: El nuevo cine chileno y el movimiento del Nuevo Cine latinoamericano* (Santiago: LOM, 2014), 394.

24. Biénzobas and Hernández, "El día en que las cámaras dejaron de rodar," 65.

25. The term was first coined in Nelly Richard, *Una mirada sobre el arte en Chile* (Santiago: Nelly Richard, 1981). For Forch's engagement with Richard and Leppe, see Nelly Richard, *Cuerpo correccional* (Santiago: Francisco Zegers, 1980).

26. Sebastián Vidal, "Festival Franco-Chileno de Video Arte: A Space of Resistance under Dictatorship and Expansion in Democracy," in *Encounters in Video Art in Latin America*, ed. Elena Shtromberg and Glenn Phillips (Los Angeles: Getty Research Institute, 2023), 163–80.

27. Liñero, *Apuntes para una historia del video en Chile*, 158–60.

28. See chapter 5.

29. See notes 28, 32–39, and 41–42.

30. A slightly different version was later broadcast by Channel 4 in the United Kingdom on March 20, 1985, as part of *Vision*'s third season, episode "Video Pioneers no. 3: Raúl Ruiz." See *Visions: Channel 4's Cinema Programme* (London: Large Door Ltd., 1985), 38–40. An off-air recording of this broadcast is "Visions—Raúl Ruiz—1985," August 20, 2011, YouTube video, accessed July 23, 2024, www.youtube.com/watch?v=2Wp9yWTVjEk&t=17s &ab_channel=PabloMartinez. For more on *The Return of a Library Lover*, see Palacios, "Chilean Exile Cinema and Its Homecoming Documentaries"; Andreea Marinescu, "Raúl Ruiz's Surrealist Documentary of Return: *Le retour d'un amateur de bibliothèques* (1983) and *Cofralandes* (2002)," in *Raúl Ruiz's Cinema of Inquiry* (Detroit, MI: Wayne State University Press, 2017), 177–96; and Valeria de los Ríos, *Metamorfosis: Aproximaciones al cine y la poética de Raúl Ruiz* (Santiago: Metales Pesados), 75–88.

31. For more on Vázquez's film, see chapter 5 and Ramírez-Soto, "Journeys of *Desexilio*," 444–46.

32. Gonçalves, *Imágenes de un retrato cinematográfico*.

33. A collection of several of these interviews can be found in Cineteca Nacional Online, "Cine Off: Entrevistas en *Off the Record*," accessed July 23, 2024, www.cclm.cl/colecciones/cine-off-entrevistas-en-off-the-record/.

34. Naficy, *Accented Cinema*, 280. See also Cristiá, *AIDA*, 219–20; and Silva, *Cinema, política e exílio*, 130–32.

35. "Acta General de Chile," Q&A recording, September 2, 1987, BAMPFA Film Library & Study Center Audio Collection.

36. See Gabriel, "Third Cinema as Guardian of Popular Memory," 58–59; Naficy, *Accented Cinema*, 279–82; and especially Silva, *Cinema, política e exílio*, 130–75, for a detailed analysis of the film and TV series.

37. See Cristiá, *AIDA*, 222–26, for a detailed account of the networks of solidarity facilitating the screenings of *General Statement on Chile* in Amsterdam.

38. Gabriel García Márquez, *Clandestine in Chile*, trans. Asa Zatz (New York: New York Review Books, 2010).

39. Casa de América, *Retrospectiva Miguel Littín* (Madrid: Casa de América, 1997), 9.

40. Jaime Reyes Soriano, "La autodefensa de masas y las Milicias Rodriguistas: Aprendizajes, experiencias y consolidación del trabajo militar de masas del Partido Comunista de Chile, 1982–1987," *revista Izquierdas* 26 (2016): 1–27.

41. Silva claims that Littin received political and logistical support from the Communist Party. See Silva, "Exilio y clandestinidad," in *Imagem e exílio: Cinema e arte na América Latina*, ed. Yanet Aguilera (São Paulo: Discurso Editorial, 2015), 322.

42. Patricia Collyer, "Entrevista clandestina: Miguel Littin vino, filmó y se fue," *Análisis* 8, no. 98 (July 1985): 29–31.

43. The phrase "the dictator's laid" comes from "Acta General de Chile," Q&A recording.

44. Miguel Littin, "El ojo en el corazón de Chile: Notas de una filmación clandestina," *Araucaria de Chile* 32 (1985): 71–80.

45. The idea of the "clandestine narrator" comes from Silva, *Cinema, política e exílio*, 130. The extended quote belongs to Littin, "El ojo en el corazón de Chile," 80.

46. For an analysis, see Camilo Trumper, "Displacement, Emplacement, and the Politics of Exilic Childhood in Sergio Castilla's *Gringuito*," in *Chilean Cinema in the Twenty-First Century World*, ed. Vania Barraza and Carl Fischer (Detroit: Wayne State University Press, 2020), 313–37.

47. José Miguel Palacios and Elizabeth Ramírez-Soto, "El eterno retorno de Raúl Ruiz: *A TV Dante (Cantos IX–XIV)* y *La telenovela errante*," in *Transiciones de lo real: Transformaciones políticas, estéticas y tecnológicas en el documental de Argentina, Chile y Uruguay*, ed. Paola Margulis (Buenos Aires: Libraria Ediciones, 2020), 138–39.

48. Pedro Labra, "Encuentro con Raúl Ruiz," *Revista Cosas*, May 15, 1986.

49. Palacios and Ramírez-Soto, "El eterno retorno de Raúl Ruiz," 139.

50. Palacios and Ramírez-Soto, "El eterno retorno de Raúl Ruiz," 138–39. See also Marinescu, "Raúl Ruiz's Surrealist Documentary of Return," 177–96.

51. Naficy, *Accented Cinema*, 229–37.

52. Swedish Film Institute, "Consuelo: En illusion," The Swedish Film Database, accessed October 6, 2024, www.svenskfilmdatabas.se/en/item/?type=film&itemid=17231#release-dates.

53. Andersson and Sundholm, "Accented Cinema and Beyond," 241.

54. For a discussion of this roundtable, see chapter 3 and Palacios, "Resistance vs. Exile."

55. "Orientación y perspectivas del cine chileno," *Araucaria de Chile* 11 (1980): 125.

56. Ulloa, *Video independiente en Chile*; and Liñero, *Apuntes para una historia del video en Chile*.

57. Antonio Traverso and Germán Liñero, "Chilean Political Documentary Video of the 1980s," in *New Documentaries in Latin America*, ed. Vinicius Navarro and Juan Carlos Rodríguez (New York: Palgrave, 2014), 168.

58. Traverso and Liñero, "Chilean Political Documentary Video."

59. Yéssica Ulloa's groundbreaking study of these distribution circuits, published in 1985, remains the definitive source on the topic. See the chapter "La circulación de videogramas" in Ulloa, *Video independiente en Chile*, 38–43.

60. For the official censor acts, see "Memorandum Interno no. 456" and "De: Presidente del H. Consejo de Calificación Cinematográfica," Fondo Hernán Castro, MMDH CL 00000428, Archivo MMDH.

61. An interview with the exile journal *Araucaria de Chile* sheds light on the collective's mode of production and their use of networks of solidarity. Jacqueline Moueca, "Rescatar la memoria popular," *Araucaria de Chile* 32 (1985): 80–82.

62. Mouesca, *Plano secuencia de la memoria de Chile*, 157; and Ramírez-Soto, "Journeys of *Desexilio*," 448.

63. For the presence of Hernán Castro in San Sebastián, see Ruiz de Garibay, "Hernán Castro," 12. For Vitel Nocticias, see Liñero, *Apuntes para una historia del video en Chile*, 65–66.

64. Traverso and Liñero note that "each installment of the video bulletin included production credits and onscreen reporters," however, an examination of multiple video copies of these programs reveals that the practice was not consistent and that there are several early editions that do not include credits. See Traverso and Liñero, "Chilean Political Documentary Video of the 1980s," 170.

65. On the political renovation of the Chilean Left in exile, see Mariana Perry Fauré, *Exilio y renovación: Transferencia política del socialismo chileno en Europa Occidental, 1973–1988* (Santiago: Ariadna Ediciones, 2021); Cristina Moyano, "Diálogos entre el exilio y el interior: Reflexiones en torno a la circulación de ideas en el proceso de renovación socialista, 1973–1990," *Revista Izquierdas* 9 (2011): 31–46; Alessandro Santoni, "Modelos y antimodelos de la renovación socialista: La revista Convergencia y la crisis del socialismo mundial (1981–1991)," *Historia* 46, no. 1 (2013): 153–76; and Pedro Isern, "Exilio y renovación de la izquierda chilena (Parte II)," *Letras Internacionales* 139-5 (2011), accessed July 23, 2024, https://revistas.ort.edu.uy/letras-internacionales/article/view/843.

66. Jorge Arrate etal., "Presentación," *Plural* 1 (1983): 3.

67. "El Instituto para el Nuevo Chile," *Plural* 1 (1983): 108.

68. Mikhail Bakhtin, "Response to a Question from the *Novy Mir* Editorial Staff," in *Speech Genres and Other Late Essays*, ed. Caryl Emerson and Michael Holquist (Austin: University of Texas Press, 1986), 1–9.

69. Svetlana Boym, *The Future of Nostalgia* (New York: Basic Books, 2001), xviii.

70. Palacios and Donoso Pinto, "Infancia y exilio en el cine chileno," 60–62.

71. Marianne Hirsch, "The Generation of Postmemory," *Poetics Today* 1, no. 29 (2008): 103–28.

72. For a detailed analysis of these films, see Palacios and Donoso Pinto, "Infancia y exilio en el cine chileno," 45–66.

73. Patricia Castillo and Alejandra González-Celis note this desire as well in their study about diaries, letters, and drawings made by children during the dictatorship period. See Castillo and González-Celis, "Infancia, dictadura y resistencia: Hijos e hijas de la izquierda chilena (1973–1989)," *Revista Latinoamericana de Ciencias Sociales, Niñez y Juventud* 13, no. 2 (2015): 917–18.

74. "Estrenos: Seis directores en cartelera," *Cine* 40 (1990): 4.

75. Cortínez and Engelbert, *Evolución en libertad*, tomo 1, 101; Aldo Francia, *Nuevo Cine Latinoamericano en Viña del Mar* (Santiago: CESOC/Chile-América, 1990), 120; López, "An 'Other' History," 106–7; Silvana Flores, *El nuevo cine latinoamericano y su dimensión continental: Regionalismo e integración cinematográfica* (Buenos Aires: Imago Mundi, 2013), 136; Del Valle Dávila, *Cámaras en trance*, 51–52; and Mestman, "From Italian Neorealism to New Latin American Cinema," 167–72.

76. *Cineastas Chilenos: III Festival Internacional de Cine de Viña del Mar; Documentos (Racconto de un encuentro)* (Santiago: Secretaría de Comunicación y Cultura, 1990), 4.

77. Daniel Olave, "Nostálgicos y apocalípticos con vista al mar: Festival de cine de Viña del Mar," *Apsi* 365, no. 15 (1990): 43.

78. Littin quoted in Trabucco Ponce, *Con los ojos abiertos*, 518.

79. Trabucco Ponce, *Con los ojos abiertos*, 513.

80. "Cena en La Moneda," in *III Festival Internacional de Cine de Viña del Mar*, 51.

81. Olave, "Nostálgicos y apocalípticos con vista al mar," 43; and Hans Ehrmann, "Festival de Viña del Mar: ¿Quo Vadis?," *Enfoque* 17 (December 1990): 19.

82. Olave, "Nostálgicos y apocalípticos con vista al mar," 42.

83. Ehrmann, "Festival de Viña del Mar," 19.

84. Trabucco Ponce, *Con los ojos abiertos*, 515.

85. Trabucco Ponce, *Con los ojos abiertos*, 395.

86. Sebastián Alarcón confessed that the organization of the festival told him it would not be wise to show films such as *Noche sobre Chile* (1977) or *Santa Esperanza* (1980) because they dealt with state repression. Alarcón, however, believed the festival did the right thing. See Ehrmann, "Sebastián Alarcón," 22.

87. Trabucco Ponce, *Con los ojos abiertos*, 515.

88. Olave, "Nostálgicos y apocalípticos con vista al mar," 46.

89. Trabucco Ponce, *Con los ojos abiertos*, 514.

90. Littin, "Introducción—Respuesta a Peter Schumann," in *III Festival Internacional de Cine de Viña del Mar*, 20.

91. Littin, "Se sabe que el que vuelve no se fue," in *III Festival Internacional de Cine de Viña del Mar*, 21.

92. Zuzana M. Pick, "Carta abierta a la Cineteca de la Universidad de Chile," Cineteca Universidad de Chile—Fondo Zuzana Pick.

93. Hamid Naficy, "Introduction: Framing Exile," in *Home, Exile, Homeland*, 3.

94. Nelly Richard, *Cultural Residues. Chile in Transition*, trans. Alan West-Durán and Theodore Quester (Minneapolis: University of Minnesota Press, 2004), 15. For discussions on the transition to democracy and the notion of post-dictatorship, see Nelly Richard and Alberto Moreiras, eds., *Pensar en/la Post-dictadura* (Santiago: Cuarto Propio, 2009); and Tomás Moulián, *Chile Actual: Anatomía de un mito* (Santiago: LOM, 1997).

95. José Miguel Palacios, "Residual Images and Political Time: Memory and History in *Chile, Obstinate Memory* and *City of Photographers*," in *New Documentaries in Latin America*, 114.

96. For the cinema of Carmen Castillo, see Felix Valdés García, Carla Valdés León, and Marco Álvarez Vergara, eds., *Los crepúsculos nunca vencerán a las autoras: Carmen Castillo; cine, memoria y revolución* (Havana: Editorial Filosofí@.cu, 2020); and Ramírez-Soto, "Memoria y desobediencia: Una aproximación a los documentales de Carmen Castillo," *la Fuga* 12 (2011), accessed July 23, 2024, www.lafuga.cl/memoria-y-desobediencia/450.

97. For an extended analysis, see José Miguel Palacios, "Obstinate Memories," in *Five Films by Patricio Guzmán* (Icarus Films, 2015), booklet accompanying the DVD box set; and Palacios, "Residual Images and Political Time," 107–20.

98. Palacios, "Beyond Memory," 39–40.

99. Further titles include, among others, *Eterno retorno* (Leonora González, 2003), *Rey Negro* (Sergio Vesely, 2003), *Vuelta y Vuelta* (Daniela Bichi and Markus Toth, 2013), *Los descendientes* (Diego Zurita, 2013), *Exilios chilenos, exils chiliens* (Michel Szempruch, 2013), *Exil-sur-scène* (Marina Paugam and Jean Michel Rodrigo, 2015), and *Me duele la memoria* (Lara Heredia and Bastien Genoux, 2018). Made by second generation exiles, these titles coexist with a proliferation of documentaries *about* the experience of exile and return of other people—not necessarily the films' directors. See, for example, *Special Circumstances* (Marianne Teleki, US, 2006), *A Promise to the Dead: The Exile Journey of Ariel Dorfman* (Peter Raymont, US, 2007), *Khanimambo Mozambique (Gracias Mozambique)* (Constance Latourte, France, 2009), and *Copihue Rojo* (Amaya Clunes Gutiérrez, Chile, 2010).

100. Claudia Bossay, "A Family's History/A Country's History: The Films of Ariel and Rodrigo Dorfman," *Jewish Film & New Media* 2, no. 1 (2014): 64–88; Gonzalo Barroso Peña, "El exilio chileno durante la dictadura de Pinochet a través del cine documental," *Textures* 27 (2023), accessed July 23, 2024, https://publications-prairial.fr/textures/index.php?id=448; Elizabeth Ramírez-Soto, "Traveling Memories: Women's Reminiscences of Displaced Childhood in Chilean Postdictatorship Documentary," in *Doing Women's Film History: Reframing Cinemas, Past and Future*, ed. Christine Gledhill and Julia Knight (Urbana: University of Illinois Press, 2015), 139–50; Antonio Traverso, "Nostalgia, Memory, and Politics in Chilean Documentaries of Return," in *Dictatorships in the Hispanic Worlds: Transatlantic and Transnational Perspectives*, ed. Patricia L. Swier and Julia Riordan-Goncalves (Lanham, MD: Farleigh Dickinson University Press, 2013), 49–78; and Catalina Donoso Pinto, "Sobre algunas estrategias fílmicas para una propuesta de primera persona documental," *Comunicación y Medios* 26 (2012): 23–30.

CHAPTER 7. ARCHIVAL RETURNS AND DIGITAL FUTURES

1. Key readings on memory and postdictatorship cinema include, among many others: Ramírez-Soto, *(Un)veiling Bodies*; Ana Ros, *The Post-Dictatorship Generation in Argentina, Chile, and Uruguay: Collective Memory and Cultural Production* (New York: Palgrave, 2012); Paola Margulis, ed., *Transiciones de lo real: Transformaciones políticas, estéticas y tecnológicas en el documental de Argentina, Chile y Uruguay* (Buenos Aires: Libraria, 2020); Antonio Traverso,

"Dictatorship Memories: Working through Trauma in Chilean Post-dictatorship Documentaries," *Continuum* 24, no. 1 (2010): 179–91; and Verónica Garibotto, *Rethinking Testimonial Cinema in Postdictatorship Argentina: Beyond Memory Fatigue* (Bloomington: Indiana University Press, 2019). Beatriz Tadeo Fuica's book on Uruguayan film and video, in turn, has a strong emphasis on archives and the materiality of the moving image. See Beatriz Tadeo Fuica, *Uruguayan Cinema, 1960—2010: Text, Materiality, Archive* (Edinburgh: Tamesis, 2017), 10–18.

2. Jacques Derrida, *Archive Fever. A Freudian Impression*, trans. Eric Prenowitz (Chicago: University of Chicago Press, 1995), 1.

3. See Asli Özgen and Elif Rongen-Kaynakçi, "The Transnational Archive as a Site of Disruption, Discrepancy, and Decomposition: The Complexities of Ottoman Film Heritage," *The Moving Image* 21, nos. 1–2 (2021): 77–99; Giovanna Fossati, "For a Global Approach to Audiovisual Heritage: A Plea for North/South Exchange in Research and Practice," *NECSUS* 10, no. 2 (2021): 127–33; and Seipati Bulane-Hopa, "Repatriation: The Return of Indigenous Cultural Content," *Journal of Film Preservation* 85 (2011): 4–13.

4. Nelly Richard, "La conmemoración de los 40 años del golpe militar... y después," in *Latencias y sobresaltos de la memoria inconclusa (Chile: 1990—2015)* (Córdoba: Editorial Universitaria Villa María, 2017), 31.

5. Michael Lazzara, *Civil Obedience: Complicity and Complacency in Chile Since Pinochet* (Madison: University of Wisconsin Press, 2020), 123. On the expansion of victimhood, see also Stern, *Reckoning with Pinochet: The Memory Question in Democratic Chile, 1989–2006* (Durham, NC: Duke University Press, 2010), 131–32, and Ramírez-Soto, *(Un)veiling Bodies*, 5–6 and 152.

6. Stern, "Introduction to the Trilogy," xx.

7. For poignant testimonies about these experiences, see Rebolledo, *Memorias del desarraigo*.

8. For example, the NGO Hijas e hijos del exilio–Chile (Daughters and Sons of Exile–Chile) was founded in August 2018, after a year functioning as a closed Facebook group, originally called Chile: Hijas e hijos del exilio, víctimas directas de la dictadura (Chile: Daughters and Sons of Exile, direct victims of the dictatorship). The original Facebook name thus highlights the political claim that needed to be made: that the children of exile were also *direct* victims of the dictatorship. See María Virginia Rojas Quiroga, "Surgimiento y conformación de una comunidad," accessed July 23, 2024, chrome-extension://efaidnbmnnnibpcajpcglclefindmkaj/http://conti.derhuman.jus.gov.ar/2021/08/seminario/mesa_42/quiroga_mesa_42.pdf.

9. Ramírez-Soto, *(Un)veiling Bodies*, 5.

10. Hirsch, "Generation of Postmemory," 103–8.

11. Foster, "Archival Impulse," 3–22.

12. Stern, "Introduction to the Trilogy," xxvii.

13. Ramírez-Soto, "Traveling Memories," 143.

14. Another example is Álvaro de la Barra's *Venían a buscarme* (2016), in which the director included footage from *Queridos compañeros*, an exile fiction film completed by his uncle, Pablo de la Barra, in Venezuela in 1978. See the preface for a detailed discussion.

15. The other members of the team were Catalina Donoso Pinto, Luis Horta, Elizabeth Ramírez-Soto, Laura Senio Blair, and Constanza Vergara.

16. See chapters 2, 4, and 5 for further discussion of their work.

17. Vázquez's actual words were "Yo me desexilié en 1993" (I de-exiled in 1993). For the term *desexilio*, see Ramírez-Soto, "Traveling Memories," 439; and Benedetti, *El desexilio y otras conjeturas*, 39–42.

18. "It is possible to go into exile voluntarily and then return, yet still not fully arrive" is Naficy's sentence. Naficy, "Introduction: Framing Exile," 3.

19. Ramírez-Soto and Donoso Pinto, *Nomadías*.

20. Cineteca Universidad de Chile, "Centro de documentación," accessed July 23, 2024, http://cinetecavirtual.uchile.cl/cineteca/index.php/About/centro-de-documentacion.

21. For online platforms, see Play FicValdivia, "Colección Marilú Mallet," https://playficvaldivia.cl/coleccion-marilu-mallet/ and "Colección Valeria Sarmiento," https://playficvaldivia.cl/coleccion-valeria-sarmiento/; and Cineteca Nacional Online, "El cine de Angelina Vázquez Ribeiro," www.cclm.cl/colecciones/el-cine-de-angelina-vazquez-riveiro/. For cable TV broadcasts, see ARTV, "Material Expuesto," www.youtube.com/watch?v=lj7iFaPmaxo&list=PL96z_z7QsE2tM4ABzQU4HpZjFBYEhQP7F&ab_channel=canalartv. (All of these links were accessed July 23, 2024.) Other film series devoted to these three women exile filmmakers included the 14th Festival de Cine Chileno (2022), Festival Internacional de Cine Recobrado (2022), Muestra Valeria Sarmiento (2018), and special screenings in the cine clubs Cineclub Proyección (2018) and Cineclub Sala Sazié (2016 and 2022).

22. See also the accompanying book by Balsom, Peleg, and Haus der Kulturen der Welt, *Feminist Worldmaking and the Moving Image*.

23. Janet Ceja Alcalá, "Imperfect Archives and the Principle of Social Praxis in the History of Film Preservation in Latin America," *The Moving Image* 13, no. 1 (2013): 81.

24. Naficy, *Making of Exile Cultures*, 7–10.

25. Caroline Frick, *Saving Cinema. The Politics of Preservation* (Oxford: Oxford University Press, 2011), 13.

26. Adelheid Heftberger, "The Current Landscape of Film Archiving and How Study Programs Can Contribute," *Synoptique: An Online Journal of Film and Moving Image Studies* 6, no. 1 (2018): 58.

27. See Derek Gillman, *The Idea of Cultural Heritage*, rev. ed. (Cambridge: Cambridge University Press, 2010), 44–9; and Frick, *Saving Cinema*, 14, 159.

28. Paolo Cherchi Usai, "The Politics of Film Repatriation" (paper presented at the Seventh Orphan Film Symposium, New York, April 2010).

29. Caroline Frick, "Repatriating American Film Heritage or Heritage Hoarding? Digital Opportunities for Traditional Film Archive Policy," *Convergence: The International Journal of Research into New Media Technologies* 21, no. 1 (2014): 3.

30. Andrew Prescott, "Archives of Exile, Exile of Archives," in *What Are Archives? Cultural and Theoretical Perspectives: A Reader*, ed. Louise Craven (Aldershot, UK: Ashgate, 2008), 133.

31. Cherchi Usai, "Politics of Film Repatriation," n.p.
32. Cherchi Usai, "Politics of Film Repatriation," n.p.
33. Kristen Weld, *Paper Cadavers: The Archives of Dictatorship in Guatemala* (Durham, NC: Duke University Press, 2014), 13.
34. On the two streams, see Ancelovici and Paranaguá, "Cine chileno del exilio," 197; Pick, "Tradición y búsqueda," 103; and Pick, "Chilean Cinema: Ten Years of Exile (1973–1983)."
35. Fossati, "For a global approach to audiovisual heritage," 127–33.
36. Fossati, "For a global approach to audiovisual heritage," 129.
37. Fossati, "For a global approach to audiovisual heritage," 127.
38. Pick, "Cronología del Cine Chileno en el Exilio 1973/1983," 15–21. This filmography was elaborated by Pick with the support of Cinemateca Chilena.
39. Cineteca Nacional de Chile, *Imágenes de Chile en el mundo: Catastro del acervo audiovisual chileno en el exterior* (Santiago: Cineteca Nacional de Chile, 2008), 8.
40. Cineteca Nacional de Chile, *Imágenes de Chile en el mundo*, 8–9.
41. Archives with open online catalogs that were researched for this book include EYE Filmmuseum (EYE), British Film Institute (BFI), Arsenal Institut für Film und Videokunst (Arsenal), Deutsche Kinemathek, Berkeley Art Museum and Pacific Film Archive (BAMPFA), and Fondazione Archivio Audiovisivo del Movimento Operaio e Democratico (AAMOD).
42. A provisional list of lost or yet to be found Chilean exile films includes *Dulce patria* (Beatriz González, 1976), *Siempre seremos ucranianos* (Leutén Rojas, 1977), *Casamiento de negros* (José Echevarría, 1978), *La batalla contra el miedo* (Marcos Galo, 1979), and *La escuela* (Reinaldo Zambrano, 1980). The films that Álvaro Ramírez made in East Germany have recently been "found" in Berlin's Bundesarchiv and are now the subject of a research project undertaken by filmmaker Angelika Levi and her students. See Arsenal Institute for Film and Video, "Found Futures II: Brigada Archivología Chile/Exil DDR," accessed July 23, 2024, www.arsenal-berlin.de/en/cinema/film-screening/found-futures-ii-brigada-archivologia-chile-exil-ddr-jordanian-friendship-society-2188/.
43. Beatriz Tadeo Fuica and Julieta Keldjian, "Digital Super 8mm: Evaluating the Contribution of Digital Technologies to Film Archives in Latin America," *The Moving Image* 16, no. 2 (2016): 78.
44. Ramírez-Soto, "*Habanera*," 89. The metaphor borrows the title from Raúl Ruiz's *The Scattered Body and the World Upside Down* (1975).
45. While the central focus of this chapter is on institutional archives, it is important to remember that these are not the sole places holding rare exilic materials. Informal archives and personal collections of directors, producers, and their heirs are also sites to hunt for Chilean exile films.
46. Dan Streible, "The State of Orphan Films: Editor's Introduction," *The Moving Image* 9, no. 1 (2009): x.
47. For a detailed account of the relationship between Arsenal and Chilean cinema, see Villarroel and Mardones, *Señales contra el olvido*, 48–65, 85–117, and 149–59. See also Arsenal Institute for Film and Video, "Film Database," accessed July 23, 2024, https://films.arsenal-berlin.de/.

48. For a short history of other Chilean film archives, see Mónica Villarroel, "Cineteca Nacional de Chile: Dilemas y desafíos en tiempos digitales," *Imagofagia*, no. 22 (2020): 390–91.

49. Though not an archive properly speaking, another entity worth mentioning in this process of return is Goethe-Institut Santiago. Through the work of its Cinematheque director Isabel Mardones, Goethe-Institut has been instrumental in bringing digital files of exile films by Antonio Skármeta, Carlos Puccio, Juan Forch, and Vivienne Barry and has been a frequent collaborator of Cineteca Nacional de Chile, Cineteca de la Universidad de Chile, and MMDH in their public programs.

50. Manuel Martínez Carril, "Half a Century of Film Archives in Latin America," *Bulletin FIAF* 44 (1992): 5.

51. Maria Rita Galvão, "La situación del patrimonio fílmico en Iberoamérica," *Journal of Film Preservation* 71 (2006): 44.

52. Rielle Navitski, "Reconsidering the Archive: Digitization and Latin American Film Historiography," *Cinema Journal* 54, no. 1 (2014): 121.

53. See Bruno Cuneo's and Luis Horta's interventions in Universidad Alberto Hurtado, "Fondos documentales e investigación sobre cine chileno del exilio," November 17, 2020, YouTube video, accessed July 23, 2024, www.youtube.com/watch?v=XNOoSNqBzWk. See also Frick, *Saving Cinema*, 114–115, 153; and Navitsky, "Toward a Global Film Preservation Movement? Institutional Histories of Film Archiving in Latin America," *JCMS: Journal of Cinema and Media Studies* 60, no. 4 (2021): 188–90.

54. Ramírez-Soto, "Double Day of Valeria Sarmiento," 154–77.

55. Cuneo in Universidad Alberto Hurtado, "Fondos documentales e investigación sobre cine chileno del exilio."

56. Cuneo in Universidad Alberto Hurtado, "Fondos documentales."

57. IMEC, "Ruiz, Raoul (1941–2011)," accessed July 23, 2024, https://portail-collections.imec-archives.com/ark:/29414/a011431350998gxsoZy. These materials were also donated by Sarmiento.

58. Salinas Muñoz and Stange, *Historia del Cine Experimental*.

59. Cineteca Universidad de Chile, "Historia," www.uchile.cl/portal/extension-y-cultura/cineteca/presentacion/58993/historia; and Cineteca Virtual, Universidad de Chile, "Historia," http://cinetecavirtual.uchile.cl/cineteca/index.php/About/Index. Both were last accessed July 23, 2024. See also Salinas Muñoz and Stange, *Historia del Cine Experimental*, 87–90.

60. This thirty-year interval should not be taken as a sign that there were no archival efforts before the early 2000s. An unavoidable institution in this regard is Cinemateca Chilena, discussed in chapter 1.

61. MMDH, "Definiciones estratégicas," accessed July 23, 2024, https://mmdh.cl/museo/definiciones-estrategicas.

62. Mauro Basaure, "Museo de la Memoria en conflicto," *Anuari del conflicte social* 4 (2015): 659–85; Mauro Basaure, "Hacia una reconstrucción de los conflictos de la memoria: El caso del Museo de la Memoria y los Derechos Humanos en Chile," *MAD* 37 (2017): 113–42; and Minerva Campos Rabadán, "La propuesta audiovisual y el discurso del Museo de la Memoria y los Derechos Humanos," *Fotocinema* 20 (2020): 294.

63. Stern, "Introduction to the Trilogy," xx.
64. See MMDH, "Memorias de exilio" and "Destino Exilio," accessed July 23, 2024, https://mmdh.cl/destino-exilio.
65. *Ciclo de cine chileno sobre el exilio* ran from August to December 2014 and included twenty-nine films. In addition, *Desexilio del cine chileno: 40 años de la Cinemateca Chilena del Exilio* was co-organized with Cineteca de la Universidad de Chile as homage to the work of Chaskel's and Ancelovici's Cinemateca Chilena. This program included eleven films and ran from September to November 2014. See MMDH, "Memoria Anual" (2014), 51, accessed July 23, 2024, https://mmdh.cl/museo/gestion/memorias.
66. For a catalog of the museum's audiovisual archive up to 2015, see *Archivo Audiovisual: Colección del Museo de la Memoria y los Derechos Humanos* (Santiago: Ocho Libros/Museo de la Memoria y los Derechos Humanos, 2015).
67. Biblioteca del Congreso Nacional de Chile, "Ley 21.045," accessed July 23, 2024, www.bcn.cl/leychile/navegar?idNorma=1110097. See also Villarroel, "Cineteca Nacional de Chile," 390–91.
68. I thank Cineteca Nacional's former director, Mónica Villarroel, and its former head of documentation (now director), Marcelo Morales, for facilitating access to these agreements.
69. Villarroel, "Cineteca Nacional de Chile," 394.
70. Cinémathèque française, "Raoul Ruiz: Du 30 Mars au 30 Mai 2016," accessed July 23, 2024, www.cinematheque.fr/cycle/raoul-ruiz-315.html; and Cineteca Nacional de Chile, "¡Celebremos a Ruiz!" (film program, August 2016).
71. Floris Paalman, Giovanna Fossati, and Eef Masson, "Introduction: Activating the Archive," *The Moving Image* 21, nos. 1–2 (2021): 2.
72. See SFI, *Clownens dröm*, accessed July 23, 2024, www.filmarkivet.se/movies/clownens-drom/. For SFI's digitization practices, see Frida Bonatti and Per Legelius, "How I Learned to Stop Worrying and Love Digital Archives: Digital Archiving Practices at the Swedish Film Institute," *The Moving Image* 19, no. 1 (2019): 144–50. For Cinémathèque française's Henri, see Henri, Raoul Ruiz, accessed July 23, 2024, www.cinematheque.fr/henri/#raoul-ruiz. For Unicité and Ciné Archives, see Céline Barthonnat, "L'audiovisuel au service du Parti communiste français (1968–1976)," in *Des radios de lutte à Internet: Militantismes médiatiques et numériques*, ed. Françoise Blum (Paris: Publications de la Sorbonne, 2012), 137–51; and "Coopérative de production et de diffusion du film (CPDF) et SARL Unité cinéma télévision (Unicité), 1945–1994," 206J/1–345, Archives départementales de la Seine-Saint-Denis, accessed July 23, 2024, https://francearchives.gouv.fr/fr/findingaid/6c15d258d38409cf058d01099118daebf662b2bf.
73. For the broader Latin American scene, see Navitski, "Reconsidering the Archive," 121–28; and Juana Suárez, "New Buildings, New Pathways Toward Dynamic Archives in Latin American and the Caribbean," *The Moving Image* 21, nos. 1–2 (2021): 26–54. For studies about the online platforms of Chilean archives, see Luis Horta, "Archivos y recursos: Los medios digitales en la preservación del patrimonio fílmico chileno," in *La imagen en las sociedades mediáticas latinoamericanas: Actas de la IX Bienal Iberoamericana de Comunicación* (Santiago: Instituto de la Comunicación e Imagen, Universidad de Chile, 2013),

796–803; Mónica Villarroel, "Los desafíos del archivo online: CineChile.cl y Cinetecanacional.cl," *Secuencias* 47 (2018): 131–33; and Villarroel, "Cineteca Nacional de Chile," 387–404.

74. Cineteca Virtual, Universidad de Chile, "Cine chileno del exilio," accessed January 3, 2023, http://collectiveaccess.cinetecavirtual.uchile.cl/cineteca/index.php/Browse/objects/facet/collection_facet/id/34/view/images/key/e7ea7a9363bf62768d1a37a4a0c78efa.

75. Tadeo Fuica and Keldjian, "Digital Super 8mm," 74.

76. Villarroel, "Los desafíos del archivo online," 131. See also Cineteca Nacional de Chile, Cineteca Nacional Online, accessed July 23, 2024, www.cclm.cl/cineteca-nacional-de-chile/.

77. Villarroel, "Cineteca Nacional de Chile," 397.

78. Until the launch of Conectados con la memoria, MMDH did not have a streaming option on its website. On the physical site, nonetheless, the third floor of the museum houses its Centro de Documentación Audiovisual (CEDAV), a space with several touchscreen monitors for in-room consultation. The catalog offers a rich variety of exile titles.

79. Horta, "Archivos y recursos," 797–800.

80. Paolo Cherchi Usai et al., eds., *Film Curatorship: Archives, Museums, and the Digital Marketplace* (Vienna: SYNEMA, 2008), 195. See also Anna McCarthy, "The Fetishism of the Content Commodity and Its Secrets" (paper presented at IKKM Conference: Being With, Weimar, April 18–20, 2013).

81. Cherchi Usai et al., *Film Curatorship*, 5.

82. Cineteca Nacional de Chile, "El cine chileno en el exilio: Diez películas en línea," accessed July 23, 2024, www.cclm.cl/especial/el-cine-chileno-en-el-exilio/.

83. Jessica Gordon Burroughs, "The Pixelated Afterlife of Nicolás Guillén Landrián: Migratory Forms," *JCMS: Journal of Cinema and Media Studies* 59, no. 2 (2020): 25. Gordon-Burroughs offers a fascinating study of the digital afterlives of the Cuban National Film Archive by focusing on the work of neglected filmmaker Nicolás Guillén Landrián.

84. I borrow the idea of digital returns from Caroline Frick's scheme of "digital repatriation." See Frick, "Repatriating American Film Heritage," 2–3.

85. Frick, "Repatriating American Film Heritage," 3.

86. Antoinette Burton, "Introduction: Archive Fever, Archive Stories," in *Archive Stories: Facts, Fiction, and the Writing of History*, ed. Antoinette Burton (Durham, NC: Duke University Press, 2005), 7–9.

87. Fossati, "For a Global Approach to Audiovisual Heritage," 127.

88. I use the verb *activate* in the polysemic sense given in Paalman, Fossati, and Masson, "Introduction: Activating the Archive," 4.

89. Jane M. Gaines, "Political Mimesis," in *Collecting Visible Evidence*, ed. Jane M. Gaines and Michael Renov (Minneapolis: University of Minnesota Press, 1999), 84–102.

EPILOGUE

1. Marcos Uzal, "L'histoire, pour l'avenir," *Cahiers du cinéma* 811 (July/August 2024): 5.

2. Response by Nicole Brenez in "Quelle(s) Histoire(s)? Approches d'une discipline," *Cahiers du cinéma* 811 (July/August 2024): 19. Feminist scholars also make this argument: what is needed is not an improved history with the added names of previously absent women filmmakers, but an entirely new film history that rethinks issues like authorship, labor, and collaboration. See Isabel Seguí, "Auteurism, Machismo-Leninismo, and Other Issues: Women's Labor in Andean Oppositional Film Production," *Feminist Media Histories* 4, no. 1 (2018): 11–36.

3. Brenez, "Political Cinema Today."

4. Response by Brenez in "Quelle(s) Histoire(s)?," 19.

5. See, for example, many of the contributions in Nadia Yaqub, ed., *Gaza on Screen* (Durham, NC: Duke University Press, 2023).

6. For the political dimensions of this understanding of restoration, see Anabelle Aventurin and Léa Morin, "Non-Aligned Film Archives," *Non-Fiction 03: The Living Journal* (Article 16), accessed July 23, 2024, https://opencitylondon.com/non-fiction/issue-3-space/non-aligned-film-archives/.

Index of Filmmakers

Pages in italics refer to images

Agüero, Ignacio: *Cien niños esperando un tren* (One Hundred Children Waiting for a Train), 159
Aguiló, Macarena: *El edificio de los chilenos* (The Chilean Building), 183
Alarcón, Sebastián: *Noch nad Chili* (Night over Chile), 28, 93; *La primera página* (The First Page), 80, 92
Álvarez, Santiago: *El tigre saltó y mató, pero morirá . . . morirá* (The Tiger Leaps and Kills, but It Will Die . . . It Will Die), 55
Ancelovici, Gastón: *Die Fäuste vor der Kanone* (Fists against the Cannons), 33, 34, 50, 96, 112–13, 122; *Memories of an Everyday War*, 35
Araneda, Cecilia: *Chile: A History in Exile*, 179

Barrios, Jaime: *Desaparecidos* (Missing Persons), 56, 58–59
Benavente, David: *Re-torno* (Re-turn), 169, 194
Bichi, Daniela; Toth, Markus: *Vuelta y Vuelta*, 182

Caiozzi, Silvio: *Julio comienza en Julio*, 175; *La luna en el Espejo*, 175
Caiozzi, Silvio; Perelman, Pablo: *A la sombra del sol* (In the Shadow of the Sun), 16
Carmona, Alejandra: *En algún lugar del Cielo* (Somewhere in Heaven), 179
Castilla, Sergio: *Gentille Alouette* (The Colonel's Star), 28; *Gringuito*, 163; *La historia*, 202; *Pinochet: Fascista, asesino, traidor, agente del imperialismo* (Pinochet: Fascist, Murderer, Traitor, Agent of Imperialism), 110, *111*, 202; *Prisioneros desaparecidos* (Missing Prisoners), 42, 96, 191, 201; *Quisiera, quisiera tener un hijo* (I Wish, I Wish I Had a Son), 27, 91, 111, 202, 237n11
Castillo, Carmen: *Calle Santa Fe*, 178; *La flaca Alejandra*, 178; *El país de mi padre*, 178
Céspedes, Leonardo: *Färg mot fascismen!* (Color against Fascism!), 201, 242n9; *Jag give dej en song* (I Give You a Song), 57
Chaskel, Pedro: *Al sur del mundo* (To the South of the World), 159; *Che, hoy y siempre* (Che, Today and Always), 75;

265

Chaskel, Pedro (*continued*)
Constructor cada día, compañero (Constructor Every Day, Comrade), 75; *Una foto recorre el mundo* (A Photo Travels through the World), 75; *Los ojos como mi papá* (Eyes Like My Dad), 40, 98, 171, 198; *Por la vida* (For Life), 159; *Somos +* (We Are More), 159

Chaskel, Pedro; Ríos, Héctor: *Venceremos*, 97, 108

Colectivo Cine-Ojo: *Chile, no invoco tu nombre en vano* (Chile, I Don't Invoke Your Name in Vain), 58, 167; *Días de Octubre* (October Days), 167; *Exilio* (Exile), 167

Covacevich, Álvaro: *El diálogo de América* (The Dialogue of America), 53, 92

de la Barra, Leonardo: *Éramos una vez* (Once We Were), 183

Dorfman, Rodrigo: *Generation Exile*, 179

Fajardo, Jorge: *Jours de fer* (Steel Blues), 122; *Matan a mi mañungo* (They Kill My Manuel), 57–59

Fajardo, Jorge; González, Rodrigo; Mallet, Marilú: *Il n'y a pas d'oubli* (There Is No Forgetting), 21, 44, 67, 109, 122–26, 128, 187

Forch, Juan: *Papá te habla desde lejos* (Dad Speaks to You from Afar), 159

Forch, Juan; Börner, Michael: *Chile lebt* (Chile Lives), 27, 28

Forch, Juan; Herrmann, Jörg: *Hitler-pinochet*, 63, 64

Francia, Aldo: *Valparaíso, mi amor* (Valparaíso, My Love), 13, 92

Galo, Marcos: *Lettre du Chili* (Letter from Chile), 57

Gonçalves, Rodrigo: *Espungabera: A New Dawn*, 75; *Let the Flowers Survive*, 75; *Pintores mozambicanos* (Mozambican Painters), 75; *Rebelión ahora* (Rebellion Now), 74–75, 161

Gonçalves, Rodrigo; Nestler, Peter: *Así golpea la represión* (This Is How the Repression Hits), 74

González, Beatriz: *Dulce Patria* (Sweet Homeland), 92

González, Rodrigo: *J'explique certaines choses* (I Explain a Few Things), 122, 123

Guzmán, Patricio: *The Battle of Chile*, 4, 5, 16, 88, 90, 96, 114, 178, 216n4, 236n4, 238n38,247n3; *El botón de nácar* (The Pearl Button), 178; *Chile, Obstinate Memory*, 4, 178, 179; *La cordillera de los sueños* (The Cordillera of Dreams), 178; *En nombre de Dios* (In the Name of God), 35, 99, 100, 167; *Nostalgia de la luz* (Nostalgia for the Light), 178

Guzmán, Rafael: *Conversación en el exilio con Raúl Ampuero* (Conversation in Exile with Raúl Ampuero), 194

Hadaschik, Joachim: *Begegnungen der Freundschaft* (Encounters of Friendship), 61; *Wir werden siegen durch die Solidarität* (We Will Triumph with Solidarity), 61

Henríquez, Patricio: *Imágenes de una dictadura* (Images from a Dictatorship), 35

Heynowski, Walter; Scheumann, Gerhard: *Der Krieg der Mumien* (The War of the Mummies), 88

Hübner, Douglas: *Dentro de cada sombra crece un vuelo* (Within Every Shadow There Grows a Flight), 92

Latin American Film Project: *A los pueblos del mundo* (To the Peoples of the World), 32, 109

Lilienthal, Peter: *La Victoria*, 32, 37

Littin, Miguel: *Acta General de Chile* (General Statement on Chile), 160–63, 170; *Actas de Marusia* (Letters from Marusia), 92; *Alsino y el Cóndor* (Alsino and the Condor), 43, 196; *El chacal de Nahueltoro* (The Jackal of Nahueltoro), 13, 93, 116; *Los naúfragos* (The Shipwrecked), 194; *El recurso del método*, 196; *Sandino*, 28, 43; *La tierra prometida* (The Promised Land), 16, 44, 45, 46, 84, 93, 113–15

Lübbert, Orlando: *Aufenthalt auf Erden* (Residency on Earth), 75; *Die Fäuste vor der Kanone* (Fists against the Cannons), 33–34, 50, 96, 112–13, 122

Mallet, Marilú: *2, Rue de la mémoire* (2 Memory Street), 120; *Les Borges*, 20, 28, 65–69, 119; *Chère Amérique* (Dear America), 42, 120, 183; *Double Portrait*, 120; *Je ne sais pas* (I Don't Know), 67; *Journal inachevé* (Unfinished Diary), 22,

41, 128, 130–32, 135, 137–38, 140–41, 150, 250n53; *Lentement* (Slowly), 27–68, 122; *Les Lettres*, 22, 131, 132, 150; *À force des points*, 119; *Sur les Traces de Marguerite Yourcernar* (Searching for Marguerite Yourcenar), 120
Marker, Chris: *L'ambassade* (The Embassy), 55
Mendoza, Leo: *Lamento de una rima* (Lament of a Rime), 28

Navarro, Sergio: *Exilio y retorno* (Exile and Return), 165
Nestler, Peter: *Lördags Chile* (Chile Film), 55

Puccio, Carlos: *Aquí donde yo vivo* (Here Where I Live), 171

Racz, Juan Andrés: *Cuando despierta el pueblo* (When the People Awakens), 84
Ramírez, Álvaro: *La historia es nuestra y la hacen los pueblos* (History Is Ours and It Is Made by the People), 109
Realización colectiva: *Recado de Chile* (Message from Chile), 35, 48, 51, 57, 96, 107
Rojas, Leutén: *Canadian Experience*, 40; *Compañeros: From the Strings of My Guitar*, 191; *I Remember Too*, 39
Rojas, Leutén; Gutiérrez, Leopoldo: *Nicaragua: The Dream of Sandino*, 76
Rossi, Antonia: *El eco de las canciones* (The Echo of Songs), 182
Ruiz, Raúl: *A TV Dante (Cantos IX–XIV)*, 164; *Cofralandes*, 164; *De grands événements et des gens ordinaires* (Of Great Events and Ordinary People), 128; *Derrière le mur* (Behind the Wall), 36; *Les Destins de Manoel* (Manoel's Destinies), 38; *Diálogo de exiliados* (Dialogues of Exiles), 38, 41, 88–90, 115–18, 121, 123, 238n42; *La expropiación* (The Expropriation), 37, 235n4; *The Expulsion of the Moors*, 38; *The Golden Boat*, 36, 38; *Images de débats* (Debates), 46; *Mémoire des apparences* (Life is a Dream), 28; *Mensch verstreut und Welt verkehrt/Utopía* (The Scattered Body and the World Upside Down/Utopia), 37–38; *Le retour d'un amateur de bibliothèques* (The Return of a Library Lover), 160–61, 164, 170; *Las soledades* (The Solitudes), 164; *Sotelo*, 40; *La telenovela errante* (The Wandering Soap Opera), 36, 164; *Tres tristes tigres* (Three Sad Tigers), 13, 37, 236n5; *Les trois couronnes du matelot* (Three Crowns of the Sailor), 38; *La Ville des pirates* (City of Pirates), 38

Sapiaín, Claudio: *Canto libre* (Free Song), 57; *Eran unos que venían de Chile* (They Were Some Who Came from Chile), 170–73; *Sången lever generaler!* (The Song Doesn't Die, Generals!), 56, 92, 201; *Una vez más mi país* (Once Again My Country), 173
Sarmiento, Valeria: *Amelia Lopes O'Neill*, 120; *La femme au foyer* (The Housewife), 41, 120–22, 183; *Gens de toutes parts ... gens de nulle part* (People from Nowhere ... People from Everywhere), 121; *El hombre cuando es hombre* (A Man When He is a Man), 28, 121; *J'ai rencontré l'arbre à pain*, 190; *Le mal du pays* (Nostalgia), 40–41; *Notre mariage* (Our Wedding), 28, 44, 121; *El planeta de los niños* (The Planet of Children), 121; *Rosa la China*, 120
Skármeta, Antonio: *Ardiente Paciencia* (Burning Patience), 147; *Wenn wir zusammen lebten ...* (If We Lived Together ...), 22, 130, 131, 142–47, 149, 250n49
Soto, Helvio: *Caliche sangriento* (Bloody Nitrate), 13, 92; *Il pleut sur Santiago* (It's Raining on Santiago), 27, 42–43; *La triple muerte del tercer personaje* (The Triple Death of the Third Character), 28

Tirado, Wolfgang; Reiter, Jacqueline: *Guambianos*, 28, 76; *Nicaragua, Development Under Fire*, 78
Tirado, Wolfgang; Reiter, Jacqueline; Alcalay, Mike; Luna, Amina; Ortiz, Oscar; Álvarez, Roberto: *Nicaragua, la otra invasión* (Nicaragua, the Other Invasion), 77–78
Tirado, Wolfgang; Reiter, Jacqueline; Burgos, Roberto: *Gracias a Dios y a la Revolución* (Thank God and the Revolution), 77

Vázquez, Angelina: *Apuntes nicaragüenses* (Sketches on Nicaragua), 21, 72, 73, 76,

Vázquez, Angelina (*continued*)
120, 206; *Así nace un desaparecido* (This Is How a Disappeared Is Born), 120; *Dos años en Finlandia* (Two Years in Finland), 73, 120; *Fragmentos de un diario inacabado* (Fragments from an Unfinished Diary), 22, 27, 72, 73, 130, 131, 133, 135, 136, 140, 142, 150, 160, 161, 163, 170; *Gracias a la vida (o la pequeña historia de una mujer maltratada)* (Thanks to Life), 47, 69, 72–73, 120; *Presencia lejana* (Distant Presence), 72, 120

Vera, Luis: *Åkersberga—Chillan tur och retur*, 201; *Consuelo: En illusion* (Consuelo), 165; *Hechos consumados* (Children of Fate), 165

Winter, Horst: *Gladys Marín*, 61

Zurita, Diego: *Los descendientes* (The Descendants), 182

General Index

activism, 9, 15, 58
agitational films, 21, 110, 112, 126, 167, 208
Aguilar, Gonzalo, 249n34
Alarcón, Sebastián, 29; 33, 44–45, 80, 92, 93, 101, 175, 176, 195
Aldunate, Isabel, 140–42
allegory, 6, 73, 116
Allende, Salvador, 2, 12–14, 27, 53, 59, 85, 87, 88, 98, 105–106, 121, 122, 129, 137, 144
alternative film and video, 166–69
Altman, Rick, 57
Álvarez, Carlos, 110
Álvarez, Santiago, 55, 96, 110
Análisis (magazine), 156, 162, 168
Ancelovici, Gastón, 33, 34, 35, 47–50, 52, 96, 97–98, 107–107, 112, 126, 163, 167. *See also* Cinemateca Chilena
anti-colonialism, 11, 13, 74
anti-fascism, 9, 60–63, 74, 90–91, 98
Araujo, Ana María, 15, 124
archives, 1, 3, 11, 17, 19, 22, 23, 31, 48, 49, 107, 179–202, 207; Archivo Ruiz-Sarmiento, 184, 192–93, 199; Cineteca Nacional de Chile, 49, 183–84, 189–91, 195–96, 198–202; Cineteca Universidad de Chile, 131, 160, 184; Fédération internationale des archives du film (FIAF), 50, 195–96, 200; Institut Mémoires de l'édition contemporaine (Institute for Contemporary Publishing Archives), 193; international, 50, 97, 189–90, 194, 197, 199, 201; online, 197–99; Pacific Film Archive (PFA), 4
Arsenal-Institut für Film und Videokunst (Arsenal Institute for Film and Video Art), 33, 82, 191
Asociación de Profesionales y Técnicos del Cine (Association of Film Professionals and Technicians) (APTA), 72
avant-garde the, 159
Aylwin, Patricio, 157
Azevedo, Gilberto, 37

Bakhtin, Mikhail, 248n23, 249n44
Balmes, José, 105
Barrios, Jaime, 35, 56, 58, 93
Barry, Vivienne, 29, 260n49
Baudrillard, Jean, 37
Baytelman, Shlomit, 101
Beeston, Alix, 150
Benedetti, Mario, 154
Bergala, Alain, 44

Bergin, Cathy, 8
Berlant, Lauren, 220n45
Bishop, Karen Elizabeth, 30, 217n12
Boisier, Cecilia, 147, 250n49
Bolzoni, Francesco, 88–89
Boym, Svetlana, 170, 176
Bravo, Sergio, 99, 100–101
Brenez, Nicole, 11, 205, 206
Bruzzi, Stella, 134, 137
Bueno, Carmen, 16, 114
Burke, Francesca, 8
Burton, Julianne, 95, 113, 114

Cáceres, Yenny, 37, 89
Cahiers du Cinéma (magazine), 38, 114, 205
Caiozzi, Silvio, 173, 175
Campo, Javier, 222n62, 222n67, 243n17
Campos Pérez, Marcy, 242n11
Casa de las Américas, 106
Castilla, Sergio, 3, 29, 32–33, 46, 110–11, 126, 163, 175, 202, 236n11, 241n90
Castillo, Carmen, 178
Castillo, Patricia, 254n73
Castro, Fidel, 53
Castro, Hernán, 35, 99, 100–101, 167
Castro, Oscar, 146–48
Catelli, Nora, 143, 149
Catholic Agency for Overseas Development (CAFOD), 77
Centro de Cine Experimental, 13, 193
Chaskel, Pedro, 3, 35, 47–50, 52, 73–76 passim, 84, 90, 96, 97, 107–108, 159, 193. *See also* Cinemateca Chilena
Cherchi Usai, Paolo, 186–87
Chilean exile cinema: 1, 6, 16–19, 27, 29, 31, 206–207; affect in, 102; bonds within, 51–52; centrifugal force of, 33, 34; as process, 29; routes of, 32–35; 51–52
Chilefilms, 3, 14, 85, 86, 113, 195
cine-clubs, 45, 49, 166, 191; Cineclub Vrijheidsfilms, 45
cine-geography, 20, 30–31, 52, 55, 74, 75, 79, 82, 206
cinema. *See* Chilean exile cinema
cinéma engagé, 13
Cinemateca Chilena, 20, 31, 47–52, 84, 97–98, 106–107, 112, 242n11. *See also* Ancelovici, Gastón; Chaskel, Pedro
circulation, 1, 4, 7, 12, 20, 29, 31, 43–47, 49, 51, 55, 79, 81, 98, 100, 155, 166–67, 172, 190, 203, 208–209
Clifford, James, 223n7

Cold War, the, 1, 6, 9, 12, 16, 21, 44, 59, 74, 81, 97
Colectivo Cine-Ojo, 167
Collette, Jean-Yves, 249n35
comedy, 142
Communist Party: Chilean, 11, 14, 60–61, 91, 155, 162, 197; French, 37, 197; USSR, 91
confession, 140–42, 249n44
Contreras, Miria, 106
Cooper, Karen, 45
coproductions, 7, 29, 41–42, 44, 83, 95, 96, 101, 173, 186, 191
Correa, Ricardo, 101
Cortínez, Verónica, 33, 87
coup: in Argentina, 15; in Bolivia, 15; in Brazil, 15; in Chile, 87–88, 91, 93–99 passim, 107, 111, 112–14, 122, 141, 150, 160, 168, 181–83, 185, 202, 214n4; in Uruguay, 15
Cozarinsky, Edgardo, 37
Cuevas, Raúl, 35

Daney, Serge, 38, 44
Dávila, René, 16
de la Barra, Leonardo, 32, 39, 146
Demers, Pierre, 66
democracy, 83, 101, 154–55, 157–58, 161, 163–68, 173–77, 181–82, 193
Derrida, Jacques, 180
Deutsche Film-Aktiengesellschaft (DEFA), 29, 61–64, 159
diary film, 20, 22, 119, 128, 130, 131, 134, 145–49, 154
diaspora, 5, 9, 17, 20, 22, 51, 88, 119, 154, 158, 179, 182
Didi-Huberman, Georges, 243n22
dislocation, 36–39, 124
distribution, 20, 29, 31, 39–40, 42, 43–49, 65–66, 68–69, 79, 83, 88, 93, 95, 100, 158, 190; alternative, 159, 167–68, 191, 253n59; bootlegging, 4, 46, 172; Development Education Center (DEC), 45; informal, 45–46, 101, 167–68; Les amis de la Cinémathèque Chilienne, 49; problems of, 101; regional, 44–45; Third World: Tricontinental Film Center, 45; Third World Newsreel (TWN), 45; Workers' Film Association, 45. *See also* circulation
Djagalov, Rossen, 56, 59, 74, 76, 91–92, 224n18, 235n80
documentary film, 39, 56, 65, 129, 134, 137, 209; anti-fascist, 98; and archival

General Index | 271

images, 208; feminist, 28; and fiction, 132, 166; performative, 137, 139, 148; of return, 154; social, 68, 137; and solidarity, 59, 61, 78; "visitor film," 61
Donoso, José, 93,165
Donoso Pinto, Catalina, 119
Durán, José, 113, 114
Ďurovičová, Nataša, 2

Echeverría, José, 33
Eco, Umberto, 149
Edelstam, Harald, 3
Elton, Federico, 3, 216n6
embassies, 2, 5, 9, 31–33, 187
Encuentro de Cineastas Latinoamericanos en Solidaridad con el Pueblo y los Cineastas de Chile (Encounter of Latin American Filmmakers), 47, 82, 83, 96
Engelbert, Manfred, 87
Eshun, Kodwo, 20
exhibition, 1, 4, 20–21, 29, 31, 49, 66, 79, 195, 199, 203; alternative, 45. *See also* cine-clubs; film festivals; museums
exile, 5–6; and archives, 180–203; and the arts, 15–16; Chilean, 15; and de-exile, 154; internal, 51; and return, 5, 153–54; temporality of, 94; and transnational film history, 207–208. *See also* diaspora; dislocation

Fajardo, Jorge, 29, 124, 125
Feldman, Seth, 138
feminist film, 20, 21, 28, 119–22, 126, 131, 134, 150, 205, 208
film festivals, 44, 80–102, 108; affective domain of, 81; Berlin Film Festival, 82; Cannes Film Festival, 44, 82, 93; in Caracas, 21, 81, 83–86, 93; Festival Franco Chileno de Video Arte, 159; Festival Internacional de Documentales de Santiago (Santiago International Documentary Film Festival) (FIDOCS), 4, 178; Festival of the New Latin American Cinema, 35, 94; in Havana, 83, 94–97, 127; International Film Festival Rotterdam, 44, 82, 236n5; Leipzig Film Festival, 4, 21, 48, 81, 83, 91, 92, 97–99, 102, 167; Locarno Film Festival, 36, 44, 82; Moscow Film Festival, 21, 92, 165; Oberhausen Short Film Festival, 80, 92; Pesaro Film Festival, 4, 21, 44, 81, 83, 86–90, 93, 95, 115, 117, 118, 127, 238n42; Portuguese Cinema Festival, 66; San Sebastián Film Festival, 21, 44, 81, 83, 99–100, 101–102, 167; Soviet; 90–94; Tashkent, 21, 44, 91–92, 95; and Third World Filmmakers Meetings, 83–84; Valdivia International Film Festival, 183, 184; Viña del Mar International Film Festival, 22, 83, 84, 94, 96, 101–102, 155, 164, 173–77, 184
film history, 7, 8, 28, 176, 200, 205, 207, 209; Chilean, 18, 185; and exile, 207–208; feminist, 150; forgotten, 209; global, 18; Italian, 87; national, 185, 186, 207; transnational, 7, 8, 185, 188, 207
Forch, Juan, 29, 159
Fossati, Giovanna, 188, 200
Frente de Libertação de Moçambique (Mozambican Liberation Front), 74
Frente Patriótico Manuel Rodríguez (Manuel Rodríguez Patriotic Front), 162
Frente Sandinista de Liberación Nacional (Sandinista National Liberation Front), 28, 73, 75–79, 98
Frick, Caroline, 186, 262n84
friendship, 21, 31, 37, 38, 61, 71, 73, 81
Fundación de Ayuda Social de las Iglesias Cristianas (FASIC), 156, 166, 251n13

Gabriel, Teshome, 115, 239n53
Gaines, Jane M., 202
Galván, Moreno, 105, 106
García Espinosa, Julio, 4, 90
García Márquez, Gabriel: *La aventura de Miguel Littin clandestino en Chile* (Clandestine in Chile), 96, 162–63
geopolitics, 20, 55, 59, 78, 97
Gerasimov Institute of Cinematography, 33
Getino, Octavio, 110–12
Godard, Jean-Luc, 116
Gonçalves, Rodrigo, 29, 51, 74–76, 92, 160, 161, 198
González, Beatriz, 158–59
González, Rodrigo, 246n81
González-Celis, Alejandra, 254n73
Gould, Deborah B., 220n45
Gray, Ros, 20
Grossman, Victor, 97
Gutiérrez Alea, Tomás, 4
Guzmán, Patricio, 3, 4, 16, 32, 82, 85, 89, 90, 92, 94, 100, 127–28, 163, 178, 209, 214n4, 216n6, 238n38, 247n3

Harnecker, Marta, 4
Henríquez, Patricio, 163
Heynowski, Walter, 55, 74, 101

home, 120, 122, 128, 136, 153
homecoming, 5, 22, 83, 150, 156–63, 170; archival, 199; and exile, 153, 207; impossibility of, 158; institutional, 83, 173, 175; narratives of, 20, 164–66, 177; permanent, 163–64; temporary, 160–63. *See also* exile: and return
Hübner, Douglas, 159

Indseth, Lilian, 3, 32
Institut national de l'audiovisuel (National Audiovisual Institute) (INA), 37–38, 41–42, 46, 132, 190, 194, 196
Instituto Cubano del Arte Industria Cinematográficos (ICAIC), 3, 35, 40, 42, 43, 48, 75, 91, 94, 95, 96, 191, 196, 198, 235n80
Instituto Nacional do Cinema in Mozambique, 29
Instituto Nicaragüense de Cine (Nicaraguan Film Institute) (INCINE), 43, 96, 235n80
International Organization for Migration (IOM), 32
internationalism, 11, 21, 51, 61, 62, 75, 78, 79, 98, 105, 206
Ivens, Joris, 56, 74

Jeong, Seung-hoon, 217n16

Karmen, Roman, 56, 74
Keldjian, Julieta, 198
Kelley, Robin D. G., 219n34
Kocking, Leonardo, 101, 173–74

labor, 21, 40, 72, 123, 125; migration, 65, 67, 68; movement, 97, 112
Latin American Film Project, 57, 81
Lazzara, Michael, 181
Lebow, Alisa, 130, 146
Levi, Carlo, 105
Lilienthal, Peter, 38, 147
Littin, Miguel, 14, 21, 29, 33, 43, 82, 84–86, 90, 92–96 passim, 108, 112, 116, 118, 126, 160–62, 164, 174, 176, 198, 209
Lobato, Ramon, 46
López, Ana M., 7
Lübbert, Orlando, 39, 93, 100, 126, 163, 175, 198

Maasri, Zeina, 8
Macchiavelo, Carla, 106
Mahler, Anne Garland, 12

Maison de la Culture du Havre, La, 37
Mallet, Marilú, 21, 22, 29, 41, 66, 67, 68, 119, 125, 126, 128–40, 142, 149–50, 163, 174, 183–84, 247n9, 247n11, 249n31
manifestos, 14, 80; Chilean Resistance-Cinema Front, 80; and Littin, Miguel, 85, 86, 113, 115, 118, 237n21
Mardones, Isabel, 80
marginality, 39, 40, 73
Marker, Chris, 74, 216n5
melodrama, 120–21
memory, 6, 93, 98, 113–15, 118, 153, 170–72, 177, 179–85, 194, 195; collective, 59, 130, 178
Mendoza, Leo, 33
Menz, Bernardo, 3
Mestman, Mariano, 84, 222n62
Mikkonen, Anita, 73, 133, 135
Mistral, Gabriela, 225n24
Mora, Luis, 33, 39
Moreiras, Alberto, 38, 62
Moreno Galván, José María, 105, 106
Mouesca, Jacqueline, 17, 242n17
Movimiento de Izquierda Revolucionaria Party (MIR), 14, 32, 69, 90, 133, 155, 238n42
Müller, Jorge, 16
museums, 11, 14, 17, 23, 29, 31, 179–81, 184–86, 190, 192, 195, 199–200, 207; Museo de la Memoria y los Derechos Humanos (MMDH), 181–82, 184, 192, 194, 198, 200; Museo de la Solidaridad Salvador Allende (Museum of Solidarity Salvador Allende), 106; Museo Internacional de la Resistencia Salvador Allende (International Museum of Resistance Salvador Allende), 106

Naficy, Hamid, 6, 19, 40, 65, 73, 124–25, 153, 164, 177, 184, 214n13, 222n65, 226n49
national cinema, 18, 99, 189
National Film Board of Canada (NFB), 29, 35, 42, 55, 65–69, 76, 78, 109, 119, 122, 125, 129, 131, 132, 137, 138, 143, 187, 197
neorealism, 13, 87
Neruda, Pablo, 53, 147
Nestler, Peter, 74
New Chilean Cinema, 13, 92
New Latin American Cinema (NLAC), 13, 14, 18, 21, 36, 48, 84, 87, 91, 94, 95, 149; festivals of, 13, 35, 91, 173, 174

nostalgia, 69, 119, 163, 170–71, 176, 177; counter-, 154

Olave, Daniel, 176
Oñate, Rody, 155, 156
Operación Verdad (Operation Truth), 105

Paranaguá, Paulo Antonio, 48, 95, 100, 101
Pedrosa, Mário, 105
Perelman, Pablo, 70, 71, 131–34, 150, 161
performativity, 139, 141, 143, 145
Pick, Zuzana M., 18–19, 29, 48, 56, 67, 77, 83, 88, 95, 108, 115, 118, 125, 128, 131, 150, 176, 184, 189
Pinochet, Augusto, 2, 27, 64, 98, 110, 157, 162, 172, 177
Pinto, Iván, 249n46
Puccio, Carlos, 163

Quilapayún (band), 53, 97

Racz, Juan Andrés, 32, 46, 84, 163
Ramírez, Álvaro, 259n49
Ramírez-Soto, Elizabeth, 35, 41, 42, 119, 121, 128, 132, 150, 158, 164, 182, 190, 215n19, 226n45, 247n11, 248n17, 250n53
Ramos, Érica, 101
Ranvaud, Don, 87
Reiter, Jackie, 28, 67
repatriation, 11, 19, 75, 180–81, 185–87, 195; archival, 209; film, 19, 23, 185. *See also* return
resistance, 8, 18, 20, 47, 57, 70, 77, 80, 86–90, 93, 102, 106–30, 133, 140, 155, 162, 166–68, 178, 208; cinema of, 8, 17, 21, 50, 81, 83, 86, 94, 102, 107–109, 114, 115, 118, 119, 126, 186, 206, 208; and exile, 108; feminist, 119–22; and memory, 59; strategies of, 116
return: archival, 22, 185, 188, 199, 200, 207, 209; fictions of, 164–66; history of, 155–58; impossibility of, 155; permanent, 163–64; temporary, 160
revolution: democratic, 12; exporting, 12; Nicaraguan, 21, 55, 75–79; Sandinista, 73, 77–80, 96, 98
Reyes, Jaime, 35, 167
Richard, Nelly, 112, 159, 252n25
Robles, Fedora, 35
Rojas, Leutén, 18, 40, 76, 163, 226n47
Rojo, Grínor, 222n64
Rubbo, Michael, 76, 128–29, 136–40

Ruiz, Raúl, 20, 21, 35–40, 42, 72, 82, 86–90, 115–19, 132, 160, 163–64, 192, 196, 209, 226n41, 238n42, 242n17; *Das kleine Fernsehspiel* (The Little Television Play), 42; *Poetics of Cinema*, 38; *South*, 42

Said, Edward, 149
Salas, Pablo, 35, 159
Salazkina, Masha, 7, 8, 91, 92
Santiago, Hugo, 37
Santoni, Alessandro, 59
Sapiaín, Claudio, 90, 92, 170
Sarmiento, Valeria, 21–22, 37, 40–42, 86, 90, 119–22, 126, 128–29, 132, 150, 163–64, 174, 183–84, 192; *Das kleine Fernsehspiel* (The Little Television Play), 42; *South*, 42
Scheumann, Gerhard, 55, 74
Schumann, Peter, 176, 242n17
Shohat, Ella, 2
Silva, Alexsandro de Sousa e, 253n41
Siskind, Mariano, 36
Skármeta, Antonio, 32, 37, 131, 143–49, 163; *La insurrección*, 147; *No pasó nada*, 147; *La Victoria*, 32, 37
socialism, 2, 12–14, 37, 59, 75, 76, 118, 182
solidarity, 7–9, 55; affect of, 11; events, 53, 167; as genre, 11, 20, 55–59, 61, 74, 206; geopolitics of, 59–65; global, 75, 208; lived, 21, 69–74, 119; and political subjectivity, 9, 11–12, 20, 55, 62, 63, 74; practices of, 9, 11, 29, 52, 59, 67, 207
Solomon, Stefan, 150
Soto, Helvio, 30
Spanish Civil War, 11, 56, 69, 91, 105
Stam, Robert, 2
studios: Deutsche Film-Aktiengesellschaft (DEFA), 29, 61–64, 159; Mosfilm, 29, 45, 195
subjectivity, 22; collective, 122, 142–49; in diary film, 129–38, 143, 149; exilic, 126, 129–31, 146; and performance, 140, 142; and resistance, 94
superproductions, 42–43, 75
Svenska Filminstitutet (SFI), 29, 191, 197, 201, 202

Tadeo Fuica, Beatriz, 198
Tadros, Jean-Pierre, 66
Teleanálisis (television program), 157, 168, 172
television, 2, 27, 29, 35, 41–46, 68, 83, 102, 159, 160, 173, 181, 184, 209; archives,

television (*continued*)
22, 190, 194; British Broadcasting Corporation (BBC), 194; Channel Four, 41–42; commissions, 41–42; CUNY TV, 46; *Das kleine Fernsehspiel* (The Little Television Play), 42; public, 112; public access, 29, 45–46; Radio Televisión Española (RTVE), 43, 161; Radio-televisione italiana (RAI), 194; Yleisradio (YLE), 41, 69; Zweites Deutsches Fernsehen (ZDF), 32, 41, 42, 194, 225n37
Tercer Año, Equipo, 4
Third Cinema, 18, 77, 93, 110, 115, 149
Third Worldism, 6, 12, 89
Tirado, Wolfgang, 76
Toubiana, Serge, 38, 114
Trabucco, Sergio, 158, 173, 174, 176
transnational cinema, 6–7, 9–12, 19, 206–207; and exile, 20
transnationalism, 2, 6–7, 12, 41, 43, 207; and exile, 188; and solidarity, 12
Triviño, Jorge, 101
Trnka, Jamie H., 62, 63

Ulloa, Yessica, 100
Unidad Popular (Popular Unity Coalition) (UP), 2, 13–15, 18, 21, 48, 59, 74, 85–86, 88–89, 94, 97–98, 105, 106, 109, 112, 118, 121–24
United Nations (UN), 56, 58
United Nations Educational, Scientific, and Cultural Organization (UNESCO), 40
United Nations High Commissioner for Refugees (UNHCR), 32
universities, 2, 4, 14, 66, 160

Valdés, Cristián, 33, 92, 93
Vásquez, Ana, 15, 124
Vázquez, Angelina, 21, 29, 41, 47, 51, 55, 69–73, 78, 119, 120, 126, 130–36, 142, 149–50, 160–61, 183–84, 198, 206
Vera, Luis, 165
video: alternative, 22, 65, 67, 100, 158–60, 166–69, 178
Villarroel, Mónica, 80
Von Gennep, Arnold, 246n85

Weld, Kristen, 188
world cinema, 2, 6–8, 19–20, 23, 82, 180, 189, 191, 200, 203, 206–207, 217n16; and archives, 188; history, 2, 20, 23, 184, 188, 207
Wright, Thomas, 155, 156

Ziewer, Christian, 147

Founded in 1893,
UNIVERSITY OF CALIFORNIA PRESS
publishes bold, progressive books and journals
on topics in the arts, humanities, social sciences,
and natural sciences—with a focus on social
justice issues—that inspire thought and action
among readers worldwide.

The UC PRESS FOUNDATION
raises funds to uphold the press's vital role
as an independent, nonprofit publisher, and
receives philanthropic support from a wide
range of individuals and institutions—and from
committed readers like you. To learn more, visit
ucpress.edu/supportus.